BETWEEN NATIONAL AND ACADEMIC AGENDAS

Ethnic Policies and 'National Disciplines'
at the University of Latvia, 1919–1940

PER BOLIN

Södertörns högskola

Södertörns högskola
SE-141 89 Huddinge

www.sh.se/publications

Cover Image, taken from
Latvijas Universitāte Illūstrācijās, p. 10. Gulbis, Riga, 1929.
Cover: Jonathan Robson
Layout: Jonathan Robson and Per Lindblom

Printed by E-print, Stockholm 2012

Södertörn Studies in History 13
ISSN 1653-2147

Södertörn Academic Studies 51
ISSN 1650-6162

ISBN 978-91-86069-52-0

Contents

Foreword 5

1. Nationalising Academia 9

2. From Imperial to National Universities
The University System in the Russian Empire 1800–1919 45

3. Creating a 'Castle of Light'
The Forming of the University of Latvia during the First Republic 57

4. Language Matters
the Question of Tuition Language 117

5. "Foreign Elements"
Demarcation and Conflict between Latvian and Jewish Students
at the University of Latvia, 1919–1940 129

6. Making an Impression
the Official University Journal 173

7. Developing 'National Disciplines'
Archaeology, Folklore, History, Latvian Linguistics and Literature,
1919–1934 183

8. The University under Dictatorship
Changes in National Policies and the Academics
under the Ulmanis Regime, 1934–1940 259

9. Conclusions 295

Appendix 311
References 317
Literature 327

Foreword

> ... only he is called upon and should attempt to write the history of a nation who belongs to the makers of that history – who belongs to that particular nation.
>
> *Kārlis Ulmanis, President of Latvia, Inaugural address to the First Conference of Baltic Historians, Riga, 15 August 1937*

I have not followed Kārlis Ulmanis' advice. During the last decade I have tried to understand and contribute to modern Latvian history, in spite of my being Swedish. I have done this in the belief that all scholarship benefits from the constant exchange of ideas and interpretations between 'insiders' and 'outsiders', between historians belonging to different nations and different scholarly traditions.

In this endeavour I would not have made much progress without the vital co-operation of two Latvian colleagues and friends, Vita Zelče and Aldis Pūtelis. Vita has for more than a decade given me advice, insights, and, what now amounts to, a minor library on Latvian history. She has scrutinized all my previous writings on Latvian issues, and somehow on this occasion too found the time to read the entire first version of this manuscript. Over the years Vita has saved me from making innumerable blunders. In addition to all of this she has very generously given me access to, and the use of, her collection of photographs concerning the University of Latvia and its academics. I am immensely grateful to her.

Aldis Pūtelis, for an equal amount of time, has enlightened me with his knowledge of Latvian folklore. Early in our acquaintance he showed me the famous folklore collection of Krišjānis Barons in the Latvian Academy of Science, still kept in the original custom-built cupboard – an unforgettable experience. Aldis has continued to give me sound advice over the years, and also provided me with vital contacts among Latvian folklore researchers. For all this I remain deeply indebted.

Other colleagues were also of great help. In Latvia, historian Aivars Stranga has on several occasions found the time to give me advice and direction. Among my colleagues here at Södertörn University, I am especially indebted to ethnologist Mats Lindqvist and political scientist Fredrika Björklund. In the late 1990s we were part of a large research project, *Nations and Unions*, led by Mats, focusing on the reconstruction of national identity in Latvia. Many of the ideas in the present book originate from the work in this project, and over the years I have benefited enormously from discussions with the two of them. In Fredrika I also had a travelling companion; together we tried to understand the complexities of Latvian history and culture, besides exploring Riga's café repertoire.

Early versions of most chapters have been discussed at the Advanced History Seminar and the CBEES Advanced Seminar at Södertörn University. Comments from the participants advanced my work a great deal. Anu-Mai Kõll, Director of CBEES, has been very supportive of my work. The first version of the manuscript for this book was reviewed in great detail by historians David Gaunt and Lars Ekdahl, who suggested many improvements for the text. David has also commented on many earlier versions with his usual intellectual sharpness. For this I am beholden to him. My colleague at CBEES, Anna Storm, also gave me some sound advice for improving the final chapter. Many thanks!

This book would have been impossible to write without the support of my teachers in the Latvian language: Anette Reinsch-Campbell, Lilita Zaļkalns and Juris Rozītis. *Liels paldies!* I would also like to extend my sincere thanks to the librarians and archivists who have given me such excellent support. In Stockholm, invaluable assistance was provided by Dace Lagerborg and Michał Bron from Södertörn University library. In Riga, archivist Gunta Minde at the State Historical Archive (LVVA) has been incredibly helpful in my archival searches. To the many librarians at Misiņa Bibliotēka in Riga, I would also like to extend my gratitude for patiently supplying me with reading material over the years. Thanks indeed Patrick Hort, who has done a tremendous job of reading through the entire manuscript and transforming my sometimes less than elegant sentences into proper English.

Two of the chapters have appeared in print previously, although in much shorter versions. An earlier version of chapter 2 was published in the anthology *Re-inventing the Nation. Multidisciplinary Perspectives on the Construction of Latvian National Identity*, edited by Mats Lindqvist. In addition to that an early version of chapter 5 has previously been published in Latvian, in the historical journal *Latvijas Arhīvi*, under the title "'Svešie elementi'. Latvijas Universitātes latviešu un ebreju studentu demarkācija un konflikts (1919–1940)". The present versions have been considerably extended and – hopefully – improved.

The Foundation for Baltic and East European Studies (*Östersjöstiftelsen*) generously provided the financial means for this study, for which I am naturally very appreciative.

Last, but certainly not least, I am beholden to Christina, who for several years now has patiently listened to my incessant ravings about obscure Latvian academics. She, herself a historian, has also given me a lot of sound advice. She may be rather peeved when she reads that I have not taken it all: In the end I decided not to have a separate chapter on methodology. I hope she is able to forgive me.

CHAPTER 1

Nationalising Academia

> If we are not a nation, it is because we have no Colleges, no University, to create and cherish our intellectual life. With a National University, we shall make ourselves a nation.
>
> T. C. Edwards, Principal of University College, Aberystwyth, Wales, 1896.

In October 1920 the government-appointed organisation committee, set up to create the new Latvian university in Riga, met to discuss the pressing need to recruit a professor of medicine. However, the discussion soon got out of hand. The Faculty of Medicine's candidate was not an ethnic Latvian, but a Baltic German. This was rather controversial. The Latvian playwright, Jānis Rainis, a member of the committee, questioned whether a man noted for his hostility towards 'our people' should have an appointment at the University of Latvia, an institution that in his opinion should be infused with the spirit of national culture. Rainis's view was supported primarily by non-academic members representing various Latvian organisations, but also by some of the academics. The professor of Baltic linguistics, Jānis Endzelīns, argued in favour of approval, claiming that scientific competence alone should constitute the ground for academic appointments, not ethnicity. Much to the chagrin of the dean of the Faculty of Medicine, Roberts Krimbergs, an ethnic Latvian who stressed in vain the faculty's acute need for the appointee, the candidate did not receive enough votes in the committee and was consequently not appointed. Krimbergs and the Faculty of Medicine had to swallow this defeat, though not without protests.

* * *

This book deals with the complex national issues raised when a new university was formed in one of the successor states of the disintegrated Russian Empire: Latvia. The situation was remarkable in several respects. A previously subordinated ethnic majority, the Latvians, now obtained political power and could use the resources of the state to further their national project. One of these high priority projects was the creation of a national university teaching in Latvian, a language which the previously hegemonic minority, the Baltic Germans, had regarded as a peasant vernacular wholly unfit for cultural or academic purposes. At the same time, the new state of Latvia emerging in 1919 was actually a multi-ethnic parliamentary democracy containing several ethnic minorities with full citizenship rights. What tensions ensued when the majority group tended to use the state to further its national agenda? How would this be reconciled with academic practice, as indicated by the position taken by Jānis Endzelīns in the meeting described above, that appointments at a university should be decided by scholarly and scientific competence alone, irrespective of ethnicity?

Obviously, Jānis Rainis and Jānis Endzelīns had very different opinions about what should actually constitute a 'national' university. Was it to be an institution where the academics belonging to the titular nation should work in the 'cultural spirit' of the people, or an institution that would be a national symbol primarily on account of academic excellence? Or, as Roberts Krimbergs argued, should it be an institution that gives priority to the education of well-qualified doctors for Latvian hospitals?

While this book does concern the creation of a university, it is definitely *not* a standard university history. Such histories often depict 'success stories': how universities are founded and subsequently developed. The aim of this study is to explore the *national* angle, the tensions involved in forming a university as a national project in a multi-ethnic society during a very brief period in time. Before proceeding, we should therefore consider the complicated relationships between nations, intellectuals, and academia.

* * *

A recurrent theme in recent theoretical approaches to nationalism and national identity has been the important role of intellectuals in the construction of a nation's image and boundaries. This is actually a notion that unites scholars from both the 'modernist' and the 'perennialist' camps, the two perspectives that in recent decades have divided much of the research on nations. Among the 'modernists', Miroslav Hroch and Eric Hobsbawm have stressed the importance of intellectuals and local administrators in the emergence of 'new' nations in Eastern Europe. Schoolteachers, journalists, folklorists and historians codified vernaculars into 'national' languages, collected and systemised 'national' folklore, and traced the previously obscure past of the perceived nation. Local administrators and schoolteachers seized on the language question, pressing for an increased use of the 'national' as opposed to some other administrative imperial language.

According to Hroch, the gradual break-up of hierarchical, nobility-dominated orders in the early nineteenth century and the increasing official use of German within the Habsburg Empire led intellectuals belonging to other ethnic groups, like the Czechs, to feel acutely disadvantaged. The fervour, in this particular case, for developing the Czech language and having it used in printing, education and administration must be seen in the light of the perceived undue and unjust primacy of German-speakers, not merely as a spread of Romanticism. In this way, the goals and objectives of the 'nation' could be furthered while substantially reducing the competition for jobs and positions from intellectuals belonging to other nations or ethnic groups.[1]

Perhaps less easy to place in the 'modernist' camp, Benedict Anderson has developed a complex theory on the origins of nations that, at least partly, highlights the importance of intellectuals. Especially when analysing the 'last wave' of postcolonial nationalism, Anderson stresses the efforts of nationalist intellectuals in the colonial empires to codify certain vernaculars into 'print languages' for the purpose of education and administration. This, he claims, served as a crucial vehicle in the construction of new post-colonial nations. Anderson has also pointed to the pivotal role of native-born administrators educated by the colonial authorities. These intellectuals were given access to the national histories of their respective colonial power, providing them with 'blueprints' for their own national liberation. For Anderson, too, a crucial element in the forging of new nations was the acute sense among intellectuals of an ethnic group that they were collectively disadvantaged compared to the administrators of European origin. They could even feel subordinated to other native administrators belonging to an ethnic group more favoured by the colonial authorities. Moreover, the spatial pattern of the careers of the educated indigenous administrators, or, in Anderson's own terms, the 'journeys' of these bureaucratic 'pilgrims', essentially mapped and defined the territory of their projected nation.[2]

For a 'modernist' like Ernest Gellner, it was perhaps not the intellectuals as such who produced the nations: rather, it was the needs of industrial society in terms of literacy and rationality. Intellectuals were, nevertheless, important carriers of this modernization process.[3] Liah Greenfeld, on the other hand, clearly gives a pivotal role to the university-educated *Bildungsbürgertum* in the development of German conceptions of the nation during the nineteenth

---

[1] Hroch, Miroslav (1985): *Social Preconditions of National Revival in Europe. A Comparative Analysis of the Social Composition of Patriotic Groups among the Smaller European Nations*; Hroch, Miroslav (2004): "From ethnic group toward the modern nation: the Czech case", pp. 104–107; Hobsbawm, Eric J (1992): *Nations and Nationalism*, especially 'Introduction' and chapter 2.
[2] Anderson, Benedict (1991): *Imagined Communities. Reflections on the Origin and Spread of Nationalism*, especially chapter 7.
[3] Gellner, Ernest (1983): *Nations and Nationalism*, chapter 3.

century.[4] More recently, Michael Kennedy and Ronald Grigor Suny have contributed to the theoretical discussion by defining the role of the intellectuals as *articulators* of the nation.[5]

Among the 'perennialists' or 'ethnosymbolists' there has been a similar interest in the intellectuals who codify and express myth-symbol complexes and common conceptions of the past – 'mythomoteurs' according to Anthony Smith.[6] Smith argues that in modern times intellectuals have played a crucial role in rediscovering and reinterpreting symbols and myths connected to the ethnic past, thereby creating the foundations for modern nations.[7] The fundamental disagreement between a 'modernist' like Gellner and an 'ethno-symbolist' like Smith really concerns the weight, importance and presumed authenticity of the cultural traces of pre-modern times for the formation of nations. While Smith sees these cultural artefacts as essential lifelines in historical time, an authentic and defined cultural repertoire, Gellner views them as contemporary constructions, selected pieces of a multi-faceted, open-ended cultural heritage assembled and adapted to the needs of modern nationalist movements.[8]

Summing up, it seems clear that the important role of university-trained intellectuals in the construction of nations has been elaborated within several theoretical approaches to the formation of nations. However, while disagreeing on some fundamental issues, many of these studies have provided a clearer picture of intellectuals as either inventors, codifiers, re-interpreters or articulators of the nation. What have been considerably less explored are the connections between these intellectuals in general, their positions within the academic field and their roles in the formal institutions of universities.

This phenomenon, the nationalisation of academia, is the main focus of the present study. As a background there are three distinct European processes: first, the decline of Latin as the predominant and trans-national academic language, and its replacement by state-supported vernaculars at the universities; second, the substantial expansion of state-financed university systems in Europe during the 19th century, and third, the ongoing process of nationalising state structures in Western and Northern Europe during this century. Taken together, these processes occasioned an increasingly strong connection between nation and academia.

---

[4] Greenfeld, Liah (1992): *Nationalism. Five Roads to Modernity*, chapter 4.
[5] Kennedy, Michael D & Suny, Ronald Grigor (2001): "Introduction".
[6] Smith, Anthony D (1986): *The Ethnic Origin of Nations*, pp. 13–16.
[7] Smith, Anthony D (1991): *National Identity*, pp. 91–98; Smith, Anthony D (1995): *Nations and Nationalism in a Global Era*, pp. 65–81; Smith, Anthony D (1999): *Myths and Memories of the Nation*, pp. 9–13; Guibernau, Montserrat & Hutchinson, John (2004): "History and National Destiny", p. 1.
[8] For a recent critique of the 'ethnosymbolist' position, see Özkirimli, Umut (2003): "The nation as an artichoke? A critique of ethnosymbolist interpretations of nationalism", pp. 346–348.

However, these tendencies were probably more obvious in some academic disciplines than in others. Scholarly research has suggested that some particular disciplines within the humanities contributed spiritually to the shaping of nations during the 19th century, especially history, folklore, archaeology, literary studies and linguistics. Following the Herderian Romanticist tradition, folklore and ethnography emerged as academic disciplines with the overriding aim of documenting and preserving the allegedly 'genuine' folk culture, which was perceived as being rapidly eroded by the forces of modernisation. Folk tales, folksongs, folk dress and traditional implements all told a tale of the perceived ancient national past. At the same time, these folk cultures were seen as clearly distinct from each other, so that folklorists drew cultural boundaries between nations. The cultural artefacts which differed from those of other nations were deemed particularly 'genuine'. Folklorists and the public institutions of museums thus contributed to the forming of an official national culture that had to be documented and salvaged before its expected erosion by the forces of modernisation.[9]

While folklorists and ethnographers were essential in the nation-building process in many established European states, their activities were far more contentious in the ethnically mixed territories of the Habsburg and Romanov Empires. Especially in the Habsburg lands, the ethnographic codification of culture and of peasant vernaculars was not a clear-cut process: cultural expressions and language dialects had to be connected to one of several competing national projects. Ethnographers studying popular peasant cultures therefore also made important, but often coincidental, contributions to the nationalisation of these cultural expressions: they were understood and mediated in the context of *one* specific nation rather than others.[10]

The status of folklore in the national project seems to have been especially important when the intellectuals involved in these projects could not adduce the existence of proto-national state structures in the past. Some of the new European states emerging after World War I therefore continued to place great symbolic and emotional value on their reconstructed cultural heritage, funding extensive folklore archives and building open-air museums devoted to the 'national' peasant culture.[11] This was certainly the case in Finland, Latvia and

---

[9] Leerssen, Joep (2006): "Nationalism and the cultivation of culture", p. 570. For Nordic examples, see the anthology *Folklore och nationsbyggande i Norden*, (1980); Löfgren, Orvar (1989): "The Nationalization of Culture", pp. 5–22.
[10] Gellner, Ernest (1998): *Language and Solitude. Wittgenstein, Malinowski and the Habsburg Dilemma*, pp. 130–132.
[11] Alver, Brynjulf (1980): "Nasjonalisme og identitet. Folklore og nasjonal udvikling", pp. 5–14. For the Latvian case, see Bula, Dace (2000): *Dziedātājtauta. Folklora un nacionālā ideoloģija*.

Ireland, where mythical folklore heroes like Väinämöinen, Lāčplēsis and Cuchulaine were turned into pervasive national symbols.

In a similar manner, the codification of peasant dialects into acknowledged languages was a crucial concern in many national movements. While some European languages were standardised relatively early on through the dynamics of 'print capitalism', some demotic languages were instead constructed through the conscientious efforts of nationalist intellectuals. These languages were standardized in an elaborate process of eliminating differences in grammar, spelling and vocabulary between the different demotic dialects, establishing a 'correct' version of the language through the production of authorized grammars and dictionaries.[12]

In Central and Eastern Europe in the late 19th century, the main established print languages were German, Russian, Polish and Hungarian, primarily used in education and administration.[13] When Latin was abandoned for academic purposes, these established languages and connected literatures became an important part of the university curricula, making a national imprint on academia. In the Russian university system, for instance, the introduction of professorships in the Russian language and literature became an important part of the nationalisation process.[14] However, for those involved in the codification of peasant vernaculars like Latvian and Lithuanian, it became a crucial matter to have them acknowledged as proper languages, utilised for printing purposes and also preferably in education and public administration. It was also a major concern to have these languages acknowledged within academia, with posts at universities for the scholarly study of their grammar and literature.

Such aspirations were underpinned by some developments in 19th century academia, especially within the increasingly prestigious discipline of philology.[15] The 'discovery' of Sanskrit, and the conjecture that it constituted the origin of all Indo-European languages, had two paradoxical effects. On the one hand, it united philologists in various parts of Europe in the common scholarly task of explaining

---

[12] Kamusella, Tomasz (2001): "Language as an instrument of nationalism in Central Europe", p. 240; Kamusella, Tomasz (2009): *The Politics of Language and Nationalism in Modern Central Europe*, p. 10. For the concept 'print capitalism' and its influence on the standardization of languages, see Anderson (1991).

[13] The Czechs are something of a special case, according to Peter Sugar the only 'bourgeois' national project in this part of Europe. As such, the Czechs were relatively successful in promoting their nation in competition with primarily the ethnic Germans within the Habsburg Empire. See Sugar, Peter (1994): "Nationalism in Eastern Europe", pp. 172–173. A variant of Czech had actually been used as an administrative language from the 14th century; it virtually disappeared as a print language in the 18th century but underwent a 'resurrection' in the 19th century. See Kamusella (2001), pp. 236–237; Kamusella (2009), pp. 99–108.

[14] Byford, Andy (2007): *Literary Scholarship in Late Imperial Russia. Rituals of Academic Institutionalisation*, pp. 26–39.

[15] Hutchinson, John (2004): "Myth against myth: the nation as ethnic overlay", p. 111.

language developments. On the other hand, the very image of a 'family' of separate Indo-European languages depicted in neat classifications underpinned the notion of a world 'naturally' divided into nations. For some philologists, like the Russian Buslaev, this scholarly pursuit should go beyond the study of grammar and reach the 'soul of the nation'.[16] Philology in this manner developed both a national and a transnational dimension.

The scholarly investigations of the Indo-European languages also gave some hitherto marginal languages greatly increased prestige and legitimacy. The prime example here is no doubt that of Lithuanian, promoted by German philologists as an archaic Indo-European language of great purity. These findings were eagerly grasped by Lithuanian nationalist intellectuals in the late 19th century, and seen as a decisive proof of their nation's antiquity and high cultural standing.[17] Academic findings thus became part of a nationalist repertoire.

Moreover, explorations into folklore and language had a spatial dimension: they strengthened the connections between the perceived national culture and a specific territory. First, it was a matter of not just investigating and codifying folklore and language *per se*, but also of defining the territory where these cultural phenomena predominated. Second, applying a more historical dimension, it could show where this culture had predominated previously. This process of defining national space – the territory that either had belonged or *should* belong to the nation – surely lends substantial force and resilience to nationalist movements.[18] Folklorists and linguists clearly supplied nationalist intellectuals with these kinds of cultural material related to a specific territory and its historical past.

Another of the 'national' subjects, archaeology, emerged as an academic discipline in the early 19th century, primarily in Britain, France and Spain. The main reason was the need for curators to manage museums of antiquities, primarily of Roman and Greek origin. This was part of a general tendency among Western European powers in the late 18th and early 19th century, seeking legitimacy and prestige in the retrieving and displaying of remnants of these supposedly superior civilisations. As a part of the Romantic movement in the early 19th century, however, archaeology became increasingly geared towards the

---

[16] Byford (2007), p. 28.
[17] Spires, Scott (1999): "Lithuanian linguistic nationalism and the cult of antiquity", pp. 485–495. Naturally, this does not mean that the findings of academic philology contributed much to the mobilisation of Lithuanian peasants for the national cause – here the Imperial Russian pressure for conversion to Orthodoxy and the prohibition of printing in the Latin alphabet were more material reasons for a popular national resistance. See Valantiejus, Algis (2002): "Early Lithuanian nationalism: sources of legitimate meanings in an environment of shifting boundaries", pp. 318–322.
[18] Penrose, Jan (2002): "Nations, states and homelands: territory and territoriality in nationalist thought", pp. 284–285.

recreation of the nation's past. Danish archaeologists, for instance, played an important role in the development of the discipline when intellectuals of what was then a comparatively insignificant state chose to explore its supposedly heroic Viking past.[19]

Outside Europe, colonial powers frequently excavated and 'restored' impressive monuments in order to increase the legitimacy of colonial rule. At the same time, the very same monuments could be invested with very different meanings by the budding national movements in the colonies. Benedict Anderson has shown how the 'restoration' of the temple complexes of Angkor, Cambodia, by the French, and Borubudor on Java by the Dutch colonial administration, were later given radically different meanings by Khmer and Indonesian nationalists, showing instead the mighty achievements of their supposed ancestors.[20]

In Mexico, liberated from colonial Spain in the early 19th century, archaeology and museums became a paramount concern. While the symbol of the Catholic 'Our Lady of Guadalupe' was stressed by the creole elite as a rallying point for all 'Mexicans' during the struggle for independence, a century later a new national identity, focusing on Mexicans as *mestizos,* instead made deliberate use of the remnants of the pre-Hispanic native empires. These impressive monuments and artefacts excavated by archaeologists in the early 20th century were used by the political elite to weld together a new conception of Mexican identity. However, while the nationalist archaeologists strove to add the cultural artefacts of the native high cultures to a common Mexican repertoire of symbols, they simultaneously expected that contemporary Indian communities should abandon their native languages in favour of Spanish in order to be fully assimilated in the Mexican nation.[21]

After the German and Italian unifications, archaeology increasingly became more national and ethnic. Prehistoric archaeology was now supposed to explore the cradle of the nation, preferably harking back to some supposed 'Golden Age'. The concept of 'culture' became central in archaeological research, and the links between these material cultures and ethnicity were increasingly taken for granted.[22] Archaeological scholarship in this way helped to project the existing or aspiring nations backwards in time.[23] Ancient hill forts, burial sites and monuments were seen as the remnants of the nation's glorious past, and government

---

[19] Trigger, Bruce G (1993): *Arkeologins idéhistoria*, pp. 95–97; Díaz-Andreu, Margarita (2001): "Guest editor's introduction: Nationalism and archaeology", pp. 430–434.
[20] Anderson (1991), pp. 178–184.
[21] Brading, D A (2001): "Monuments and nationalism in modern Mexico", pp. 522–530.
[22] Díaz-Andreu, (2001), p. 436.
[23] Hillerdal, Charlotta (2010): *People in Between. Ethnicity and Material Identity – a New Approach to Deconstructed Concepts*, pp. 15–16; 75–78; 158.

funds for excavations became readily available. At the same time, archaeology provided the nationalist intellectuals with a repertoire of powerful symbols. Through their claims of authenticity, important finds could underpin notions of the nation's presumed antiquity and rootedness in its specific territory.[24]

At the same time, archaeological research and findings could be used in several different ways. An interesting example can be found in early Irish archaeology. The first generation of Irish archaeologists were primarily Protestants, and their contribution to the 19th century Celtic Revival was motivated by the perceived need to overcome the contemporary religious split by focusing on a common Celtic heritage. Early medieval buildings, such as round towers and Romanesque churches, and finds like the celebrated Tara brooch, were transformed into symbols expressing a common Irish past. To some extent these symbols could also be subsumed into an Imperial British context, for instance with Queen Victoria wearing jewellery modelled on ancient Celtic designs. However, the primarily Catholic national movement could easily appropriate these symbols and integrate them in their specific repertoire. Catholic university colleges started to include archaeology among the subjects taught in the 1870s. In this way, Irish archaeology became increasingly connected to the nationalist discourse of the Irish Catholic middle classes.[25] The archaeological findings from Celtic times could obviously be integrated in markedly different nationalist and imperial contexts.

Consequently, within late 19th and early 20th century archaeology there was clearly a strong tendency to provide the ongoing ethnographical studies with an ancient past: material objects defining certain cultures were interpreted in terms of ethnicity and early nationhood. The political uses of archaeology increased markedly in the late 19th century, in particular after 1920 when many politicians in the post-Versailles states became interested in the search for proto-national roots.[26] Many archaeologists in these newly emerged states were soon involved in government-funded excavations aiming to prove the historical depth of the titular nation in the state territory.[27]

History, naturally, developed in a similar way to archaeology. The role of history as an academic discipline in the construction of nation states has been acknowledged for some time, but has attracted considerably increased attention

---

[24] Smith, Anthony D (2001): "Authenticity, antiquity and archaeology", pp. 442–447. Smith, however, does not consider the option that archaeological finds naturally also could challenge such nationalist notions, not merely confirm them.
[25] Hutchinson, John (2001): "Archaeology and the Irish rediscovery of the Celtic past", pp. 505–515.
[26] Díaz-Andreu (2001), pp. 437–438.
[27] See further below, chapter 7.

during the past decade.²⁸ There has recently been strong interest among historians, especially in the discipline's role in the forming of national master narratives.²⁹ A major tendency has been the deconstruction of these master narratives, displaying and analysing the elements of the storylines. Hayden White's *Metahistory,* as well as rhetoric and narratology within literary studies, have been the main theoretical inspirations.³⁰

Typically, the national histories written from the 19th century onwards emphasised the 'people' rather than realms or dynastic monarchs, inventing a shared tradition while at the same time providing a pantheon of national heroes and also, naturally, its collection of villains and traitors. These histories projected the past of the nation backwards in time, and also contained a teleological element in supposing that the nation's liberation or separate state was the 'natural' goal of historical development.³¹ Conceptions of the past in nationalist rhetoric most often adhered to the following triadic structure: a glorious past, followed by a degraded present, and finally a future of national redemption.³²

In some stateless nations especially, historians emerged as 'founding fathers of the nation': this was certainly the case with Palacký for the Czechs, Hrushevsky for the Ruthenians/Ukrainians and Iorga for the Romanians.³³ At the same time, some historical works inspired budding national movements in spite of the authors' own political leanings. The works of the Irish historian Standish James O'Grady, for instance, inspired the 19th century Celtic Revival in Ireland even though O'Grady himself was primarily a British Unionist.³⁴

However, some tensions in the narratives were not resolved. The constructors of these new master narratives often had to suppress evidence of previous cleavages in the supposedly homogeneous nation. In *ancien régime* societies, categories of social class were sometimes ethnified, with nobilities claiming a different origin to that of the common people. French noblemen could point to

---

²⁸ Pearson, Raymond (1999): "History and historians in the service of nation-building", passim.
²⁹ See especially the recent anthology *Nationalizing the Past. Historians as Nation Builders in Modern Europe* (2010), edited by Stefan Berger and Chris Lorenz.
³⁰ See, for instance, Eckel, Jan (2010): "Narrativizations of the Past: The Theoretical Debate and the Example of the Weimar Republic", pp. 26–36; Leerssen, Joep (2010): "Setting the Scene for National History", pp. 71–73.
³¹ See Leerssen (2010), pp. 74–75; Baár, Monika (2010): "Heretics into National Heroes: Jules Michelet's Joan of Arc and František Palacký's John Hus", pp. 128–148.
³² Levinger, Matthew & Lytle, Paula Franklin (2001): "Myth and mobilisation: the triadic structure of nationalist rhetoric", 177–187.
³³ Hutchinson (2004), p. 112.
³⁴ Caball, Marc (2010): "History and Politics: Interpretations of Early Modern Conquest and Reformation in Victorian Ireland", pp. 150–156. The Catholic Alexander Martin Sullivan wrote a history of Ireland closer to the themes of the national movement, portraying Ireland as a morally superior nation oppressed by the English. Ibid., pp. 161–166. Note, however, that neither of them was a strictly academic historian; O'Grady had studied Law, while Sullivan was primarily a journalist and politician.

Frankish ancestors while claiming that the peasants stemmed from the Gauls; Spanish *hidalgos* referred to their supposedly Visigoth forefathers. Most typical, perhaps, is the myth of a separate 'Sarmatian' origin for the Polish *szlachta*. Constructing national narratives therefore often meant actively forgetting and suppressing such previous divisions. According to the famous dictum of the French philosopher Ernest Renan, the nation is equally a matter of selective remembrance and selective forgetting.[35]

In Finland, academia became increasingly torn between the 'fennomans' and the 'svekomans', each developing their own historical master narrative.[36] Another type of tension can be seen in national histories of empires. Historians of especially the Russian, French and British empires during the 19th century tended to weld together the dominant ethno-national group with the boundlessness of expanding empires, creating a certain fluidity between national and imperial identities. The dominant nations – Russians, Frenchmen and Britons – were given a kind of messianic role in creating the empires, while in the process becoming less defined as nations.[37]

The construction of national historical narratives was an established part of academic work in the late 19th century in many of the established states of Western Europe. Within the multinational territories of Central and Eastern Europe, however, these matters were considerably more contested. Alternative master narratives emerged, tied to the different aspiring nations, often written by historians unable to find posts at the Imperial universities. The Czech historian František Palacký, for instance, clearly irritated his fellow German historians by publishing a history of Bohemia in the Czech language – parallel to his edition in German. These alternative historical narratives, focusing on the 'smaller nations', gained a very central position in the post-imperial setting after Versailles. In the emerging states of Estonia and Latvia historians belonging to these titular nations formed new master narratives in opposition to similar endeavours among Baltic German historians.[38]

In the 1920s a division emerged within European scholarship. Historians in France and Belgium, marked by the blatant nationalisation of historical scholarship during the war, moved towards a transnational understanding of

---

[35] Renan, Ernest [1882]: "Qu'est-ce qu'une nation?" Cited in Anderson (1991), p. 6.
[36] Engman, Max (1994): "National Conceptions of History in Finland", pp. 52–53.
[37] Mycock, Andrew & Loskoutova, Marina (2010): "Nation, State and Empire: The Historiography of 'High Imperialism' in the British and Russian Empires", pp. 233–258; Colley, Linda (1994): *Britons. Forging the Nation 1707–1837*, pp. 364–375.
[38] Baár (2010), p 133; Hackmann, Jörg (2010): "Narrating the Building of a Small Nation: Divergence and Convergence in the Historiography of Estonian 'National Awakening', 1868–2005", pp. 170–182. See also below, chapter 7.

history.[39] In Northern and Western Europe, many scholars began to question the traditional national historical narratives. At the same time, the construction of new national master narratives became a priority in the post-imperial states of Central and Eastern Europe. Here, the ties between nation and academia remained strong.

Nations and universities

As we have seen, in the past two decades, archaeologists, ethnologists, linguists and historians have written a number of studies on the articulation, codification and narration of the nation within their respective fields. While no doubt of great value, these studies have primarily been inward-looking, focusing on the development of the specific discipline's scholarly production. Only rarely have they dealt with the question of how and to what extent these academic disciplines could codify such national imaginings within the institutional structures of universities.

In fact, the connections between nations and universities are riddled with paradoxes. During the 19th century, science and scholarship seem to have become more national *and* at the same time more international in character. Particularly within the natural sciences, cooperation between scientists from different states increased markedly during the century leading up to World War I, forming a conception of a common 'learned republic' transcending national and state boundaries. Scientific results and progress, it was maintained, had nothing to do with the scientist's nationality. These international tendencies seem to have been strongest in certain university faculties, primarily within medicine and the natural sciences. However, a similar open exchange of ideas was also common within the humanities. Here, scholars preoccupied with matters concerning national culture exchanged views with colleagues in other parts of Europe, forming what Dutch cultural historian Joep Leerssen has called 'a common philological template'.[40] Proponents of different national projects actually supported and assisted each other across state boundaries. Towards the end of the 19th century, international congresses and commissions had been established in virtually all academic disciplines.[41] By 1900 the modern European

---

[39] Schöttler, Peter (2004): "French and German Historians' Networks: The Case of the Early Annales", pp. 123–125.
[40] Leerssen (2006), pp. 567–568.
[41] Metzler, Gabriele (2010): "Deutschland in den internationalen Wissenschaftsbeziehungen, 1900–1930", pp. 55–59.

universities had developed into a paradoxical combination of cosmopolitanism and nation-statehood.[42]

In more general terms, the expansion, specialisation and professionalisation of academia during the 19th century tended to create a common set of notions and practices on scientific and scholarly methods and standards, and also on the system of academic recruitment and promotion – to use a Bourdieuian term, a commonly shared academic *habitus*.[43] According to these shared conceptions, appointments and promotions within academia should be based solely on verified qualifications, not on class, kinship ties, ecclesiastical influence, economic position or political patronage.[44] Also, universities should ideally be completely autonomous and thus removed from the power struggles of the political arena. While this was naturally never completely possible, the emerging academic *habitus* concerning recruitment and promotion based on merit did become a major characteristic of most European university systems, albeit with some national variations.[45]

At the same time, however, there was a tendency towards a more national meaning of some of the newly established academic institutions. In the German system of higher education, the creation of Berlin University in 1810 spearheaded a movement towards autonomous universities where the emerging professoriate claimed to be designated interpreters of the nation rather than educators of clergymen or civil servants.[46] In this politically much divided territory, before German unification in 1871, the university network provided a cultural system or specific semiotic space, materially supporting the develop-

---

[42] Stichweh, Rudolf (2004): "From the *Peregrinatio Academica* to Contemporary International Student Flows: National Culture and Functional Differentiation as Emergent Causes", p. 349.
[43] It should be pointed out, though, that Bourdieu's main point in his seminal work *Homo academicus* is that societal elites manage to circumvent the meritocratic principles within academia by using their cultural capital and special career paths; Bourdieu (1996), in particular chapters 2–4. The main concern here, however, is the establishment of commonly shared notions of verifiable academic merits as the base for recruitment and promotion within European university systems, and how these notions came into conflict with nationalist concerns. Bourdieu does not deal with the problem of transnational processes; he largely seems to take the national extension of the academic field as a given. See Wagner, Peter (2004): "Varieties of Interpretations of Modernity: On National Traditions in Sociology and the Other Social Sciences", p. 37.
[44] On the professionalisation of academia during the 19th century, see Torstendahl, Rolf (1996): "The transformation of professional education in the nineteenth century", pp. 115–123.
[45] It has to be recognised that the power of the established professoriate over recruitment meant that 'objective' merits were not enough to secure a successful academic career. Contacts and networking remained essential. In the German university system before 1914, for instance, Jews, Social Democrats and Pacifists had far less chance of academic promotion. See Paletschek, Sylvia (2010): "Was heist 'Weltgeltung deutscher Wissenschaft?' Modernisierungsleistungen und -defizite der Universitäten im Kaiserreich", pp. 38–39.
[46] Delanty, Gerard (2001): *Challenging Knowledge. The University in the Knowledge Society*, pp. 33–37.

ment of a common German national identity. University professors, and the educated *Bildungsbürger*, were among the main proponents of German nationalism and unification.[47]

The expansion of the European university system during the 19th century also meant that many of the nationally inclined intellectuals were now able to find academic positions in their respective countries. In this era of 'official' nationalism, leading scholars and scientists were also increasingly given a symbolic stature: they were cast in the role of 'heroes of the nation', embodying what was seen as the excellent qualities of the nation to which they belonged. Somewhat paradoxically, the international stature of the academic 'hero' would tend to increase national prestige. Furthermore, universities were now increasingly situated within defined national academic systems, distinctly separated from those of other states. Each university system formed what could be seen as a separate semiotic space, teaching and publishing research primarily in the state language.[48] Knowledge became situated in a national context.

In a wider European perspective, the specific connections between nation and university differed considerably. In the established state structures of Western and Northern Europe, universities tended to provide what R. D. Anderson has called 'national elites' for the growing state bureaucracy. While not overtly nationalist in character, British university education still centred on English history, the creation of the British Empire, and the glories of the British parliamentary tradition.[49] In this manner, universities were permeated by a state-centred nationalist ideology. The same seems to have applied in Denmark and Sweden. In France, on the other hand, the emergence of a modern university system imbued with a national ethos seems to have been occasioned by the general movement towards national regeneration after the traumatic defeat by Prussia in 1870–1871.[50]

Still, in some of the composite states of Western and Northern Europe, 'new' nations emerged during the 19th century, striving for the creation of separate national universities, for example the Welsh, the Irish, and Norwegians. As the quote at the beginning of this chapter indicates, the university movement in Wales saw the establishment of a national university as vital for the recognition of the Welsh nation.[51]

In Ireland, a majority of Irishmen perceived Trinity College, Dublin, as being far too strongly tied to England and the Anglican Church instead of serving as a

---

[47] Greenfeld (1992), pp. 358–371.
[48] See Sörlin, Sverker (1996): "Science and National Mobilisation in Sweden", pp. 31–40.
[49] Anderson, R. D. (1996): "The Formation of National Elites: The British Case", pp. 115–119.
[50] Weisz, George (1983): *The Emergence of Modern Universities in France, 1863–1914*, pp. 87–88; 369–371.
[51] Anderson, R. D (1996), pp. 119–120.

university catering to Irish national needs. The Catholic Church hierarchy, it seems, deeply distrusted the Protestantism and rationalism of Trinity College, instead advising aspiring Irish Catholic elites to abstain from university education. At the same time, intellectuals within the Gaelic League criticised the narrow definition of Irish as Catholic, instead promoting the Irish language as a means for the nation to distance itself from English political and cultural supremacy. The revival of the Irish language, however, never obtained substantial popular support. In 1908, finally, a compromise was found: Trinity College was retained, and a National University with separate colleges in Dublin, Cork and Galway was created. While formally non-denominational, these colleges were clearly favoured by Catholic students. At the same time, Queen's College, Belfast, became a separate university with strong connections to the Ulster Protestants.[52] The Irish universities were consequently separated along denominational and, increasingly, national lines. The colleges of the National University became very important in the forming of the Free State's educated Irish Catholic elite in the 1920s.

In Norway, the founding of a new university in Kristiania/Oslo in 1813, the final year of the Danish composite state, was initially an important symbol for Norwegian national self-sufficiency. When forced into a union with Sweden the following year, the first generation of Kristiania's university professors emerged as important actors on the Norwegian political scene. Towards the end of the century, however, the ties between the university academics and the growing national movement seem to have become perceptibly weaker. When the scholarly research on the Norwegian language and history did not match the conceptions of the national movement, the university academics disappointed the nationalists by predominantly siding with scholarship.[53]

In Central and Eastern Europe, the connections between nation and university varied markedly. In the Habsburg Empire, the virtual monopoly of Latin and German as the languages of academic instruction was gradually dismantled by a series of compromises with aspiring nations within the realm. Latin was retained longer in the Hungarian part of the empire, while German predominated at other universities; the Vienna and Prague Universities, for instance, replaced Latin by German as the language of instruction in 1784, while Budapest University retained the use of Latin until 1844.[54] Later, the *Ausgleich* of

---
[52] Robinson-Hammerstein, Helga (1996): "The Irish Nation and University Education in the Nineteenth Century", pp. 155–163.
[53] Langholm, Sivert (1996): "The New Nationalism and the New Universities – The Case of Norway in the Early 19th Century", pp. 139–150.
[54] Kamusella (2009), pp. 104; 124; 130; 375. At the final partition of Poland-Lithuania in 1805, Kracow University became part of the Habsburg territory and had to shift its language of instruction from Polish to German.

1867 naturally secured the status of Hungarian as the predominant language of instruction in that part of the Empire, but the Poles and the Czechs also managed to gain recognition for universities using their respective languages. The universities of Krakow and Lwów/Lvív were transformed from German to Polish-speaking universities in 1867, and the Charles University in Prague was divided into separate German and Czech-speaking universities in 1882 after a long struggle over the use of the Czech language in higher education. For both the Poles and the Czechs, these universities became important nodes of the nationalist movement, forming the national elites that later dominated the independent states emerging after World War I.[55] The election of philosopher Tamáš Masaryk as the first president of the Czechoslovak republic is the most evident example.

Some of the other Habsburg nations were not quite as successful, especially those in the Hungarian part of the empire. The Romanians, for instance, only managed to establish some theological seminars catering to their denominational churches.[56] Still, intellectuals belonging to some of these subjected nations could sometimes find space to manoeuvre within the institutions of Habsburg universities. Consider, for instance, the appointment of the Ruthenian/Ukrainian nationalists Iakiv Holovatsky, professor of the Ruthenian language and literature, and Mykhailo Hrushevs'kyi, professor of Ukrainian history, at the 'Polish' university of Lwów/Lvív. Ruthenian and Ukrainian identities among the tiny Galician strata of intellectuals were actually encouraged by the Vienna government as a way of restraining Russian influence in this region. Just before World War I, the Ruthenians/Ukrainians were promised a separate university in Lwów/Lvív.[57]

After the war, several of the Habsburg universities were re-nationalised in their respective successor states. The Krakow and Lwów universities had been Polish-speaking even before the war and the new Polish state could now take over the management of and Polonise the previously Russian-speaking Warsaw University. As a part of the general assimilation policy directed at Slavic-speaking minorities, the chairs in Ukrainian language and history at Lwów University were abolished. In a similar process of nationalising a former Habsburg university, the new Czechoslovakian state took control of the previously Hungarian-speaking university in Pozsony/Bratislava and change the

---

[55] Havránek, Jan (1996): "The Czech, Slovak and Polish Intellectuals in the Habsburg Monarchy between the State and the Nations", pp. 132–136; Gellner (1998), p. 125.

[56] Pálfy, Zoltán (2003): *National Controversy in the Transylvanian Academe: The Cluj/-Kolozsvár University, 1900–1950*, p. 62.

[57] See Snyder, Timothy (2003): *The Reconstruction of Nations. Poland, Ukraine, Lithuania, Belarus, 1569–1999*, pp. 128–129; Himka, John-Paul (1999): "The Construction of Nationality in Galician Rus: Icarian Flights in Almost All Directions", pp. 127–128, 131, 135, 137.

language of instruction. The German-speaking university in Czernowitz was similarly transformed into the Romanian state university of Cernăuți

Historian Zoltán Pálfy has studied in great detail how the Hungarian university of Kolozsvár, previously catering primarily to the educated Hungarian middle class in Transylvania, was re-formed as the Rumanian university of Cluj.[58] Before 1914 Transylvania was characterised by an ethnic composition that reflected social class. The ethnic Romanians constituted a narrow majority, most of them living in rural areas and belonging to the peasant class. They were clearly underrepresented at Koloszvár University before 1914; in the academic year 1912/13 they constituted only twelve per cent of the student body. Most of the young Romanian men in higher education sought a place in the priesthood, and studied at theological seminars catering to their respective Churches. Hungarian students dominated the university, while Jews and ethnic Germans constituted sizeable minorities, thirteen and five per cent respectively.[59]

When Romania took control of Transylvania after the World War I practically all of the Hungarian academic staff and students left the region. For a while they established their university in 'exile' in Budapest. However, the university library, as well as other academic equipment, had to be left behind. Kolozsvár University was immediately Romanianised, changing its name to Cluj. Romanian was introduced as the only permissible language of instruction, and the only remaining Hungarian element was a chair in Hungarian literature. A new set of professors and lecturers was hastily put together, primarily academics from Bucharest in the old Kingdom of Romania and ethnic Romanian professors previously employed at various Habsburg universities. This evidently caused some friction. The 'Habsburg' academics wanted the new university to be modelled on Western academia, particularly the German university system. Most of all, they did not want Cluj University to become a satellite of Bucharest. Their colleagues from Bucharest, however, preferred to impose the model of their mother university and apparently did not approve of 'regionalist' tendencies.[60]

The ethnic composition of the students also changed dramatically. Ethnic Romanians now predominated, and only a handful of Hungarian students were initially enrolled. By 1926/27, students belonging to the ethnic minorities in Transylvania constituted thirty per cent of those enrolled at Cluj University:

---
[58] Pálfy (2003).
[59] Pálfy (2003), table 6, p. 72; table 11, p. 89; table 18, p. 112. Ethnic Germans are here synonymous with those having German as their 'mother tongue'; Jews are defined by religion.
[60] Pálfy (2003), pp. 127–135; 161; 203. Pálfy, however, does not explore in detail the tensions between the Romanian 'Habsburg' academics and their 'Old Kingdom' colleagues. The latter were also more influenced by the state-centred French university system – most of the Romanian students at universities abroad before 1914 had studied in France. See Karady, Victor (2004): "Student Mobility and Western Universities: Patterns of Unequal Exchange in the European Academic Market, 1880–1939", p. 372.

Hungarians 17.5 per cent, Jews seven per cent, and Germans 4.7 per cent. Since the Romanian government did not acknowledge academic diplomas from universities in Hungary proper, the ethnic Hungarians in Transylvania who were not prepared to go into exile increasingly chose to study at Cluj rather than at Budapest University.[61] In both Romania and Hungary, however, universities were gradually turned into major institutions for nationalising culture. Especially in the multi-lingual borderlands of the Habsburg successor states, imposing the culture and history of the titular nation became a primary concern.

This naturally made it difficult for ethnic minorities to retain any cultural autonomy regarding language and educational matters. The Romanian government strongly opposed the implementation of specific minority rights, and resisted international pressure to devise such legal frameworks.[62] In the 1930s the situation for the ethnic minorities deteriorated markedly. A severe Romanianisation campaign had a deep impact on all levels of Romanian society from 1934 onwards. At the universities, 'numerus Vallachicus' measures were introduced, whereby the ethnic Romanians were to constitute eighty per cent of the student body: the same proportion as in the general population. These measures were a blow for the Hungarian, Jewish and German middle classes, traditionally much disposed to enter higher education. As the Romanian political system became more and more authoritarian towards the end of the 1930s, members of these minorities were increasingly seen as 'aliens'. University education and posts in public administration were increasingly perceived as being reserved for the 'autochthonous race', i.e. the ethnic Romanians.[63]

The nationalisation of Kolozsvár/Cluj University entailed a complete shift from Hungarian to Romanian in terms of language, academic staff, and students. Further nationalisation campaigns during the 1930s severely reduced the educational and career options of the ethnic minorities, while simultaneously enhancing the prospects for members of the titular nation, the Romanians. There was also a shift in scholarly priorities. Apart from a general turn towards Romanian language, history and culture, the historians at Cluj University were also given the specific task of establishing Romania's historical right to Transylvania.[64]

---

[61] Pálfy (2003), pp. 146–147; table 25, p. 179. Compared to prewar times, Hungarians and Hungarian-speaking Jews seem to have been the groups most negatively affected by Romanianisation.
[62] Pálfy (2003), p. 126. Romania thus circumvented the minority protection clauses in the 1919 Versailles Treaty. See Riga, Liliana & Kennedy, James (2009): "Tolerant majorities, loyal minorities and 'ethnic reversals': constructing minority rights at Versailles 1919", p. 461–464.
[63] Pálfy (2003), pp. 166–171; 188–189.
[64] Pálfy (2003), p. 133.

Compared to the situation in the Habsburg Empire and its successor states, developments in the Russian Empire were very different. In the 18th century the main academic languages were French, German and Latin, but during the course of the following century the Russian university system became increasingly monolithic and oriented towards Russian-ness in terms of language and culture. As will be described in more detail in the following chapter, the essentially Polish universities of Vilnius/Wilna and Warsaw were closed in 1831–1832, and only Warsaw University was later allowed to reopen as a Russian-speaking institution. The German-speaking academic institutions in the Baltic Provinces – Dorpat University and Riga Polytechnical Institute – were forced in 1889 to switch to instruction in Russian.[65]

By 1900, therefore, the Tsarist university system uniformly used Russian as the language of instruction. At the same time, aspiring young men from subordinated nations, such as Estonians, Latvians and Lithuanians, were to some extent assisted by the Imperial government in furthering their academic careers in Russia proper. In the same way as in the Habsburg case, the Imperial government often tried to balance the influence of the more powerful national groups – Baltic Germans, Poles – by giving some support to the subordinate nations. However, individuals from these demotic nations – like Estonians, Latvians and Lithuanians – had to make their academic careers in an Imperial and Russian-speaking context. Moreover, in most cases these careers and intellectual activity had to take place in Russia proper, outside the imagined national territory.[66]

This also meant that the successor states emerging after the fall of the Romanov Empire often had to form national universities virtually from scratch. In Latvia and Lithuania, particularly, there was precious little in terms of previous academic structure. While many of the Habsburg successor states could use the experience, equipment and staff of established universities from prewar times, this was not the case in Riga or Kaunas. When the new states of Latvia and Lithuania were formed in 1918–20, they did not possess any universities from the Imperial period. As will be shown in more detail later, when the Latvian government established the new *Latvijas Universitāte* in Riga, it only had access to some academics and buildings belonging to the previous Riga Polytechnical

---

[65] French in fact served as a sociolect uniting the Russian, Baltic German and Polish imperial elites during the 18th century, while German was seen as most suitable for philosophical and metaphysical studies. Polish was used as a language of instruction at Vilnius/Wilno University only for a very short period, between 1816 and 1825. See Kamusella (2009), pp. 369–370; 375–376.

[66] It was quite common in the 19th century for nationalist intellectuals and academics to pursue their careers outside their home territories. See Leerssen (2006), p. 565; Valantiejus (2002), pp. 327–328.

Institute. Similarly, Lithuanian initiatives to reopen the old Vilnius University, a rather symbolic act since this institution had been closed since 1832, were thwarted by the Polish occupation of the Vilnius region. Instead, the Lithuanian government had to create an entirely new university in Kaunas, an institution later named after the national symbol Vytautas the Great.

This meant that the creation of new, national universities had to be a very rapid, dramatic process in these countries. The nationalisation of academia in the Habsburg successor states and, naturally, even more so in the Western and Northern parts of Europe, took place over a comparatively long period. In the suddenly emerging Baltic States, there was by comparison an extremely rapid transformation from an imperial to a national context. Academic staff had to be hastily recruited, curricula formed and students enrolled within a completely new organisational framework. Investigating the creation of a national university in one of these countries is therefore likely to yield a clearer view of the dilemmas involved in the nationalisation of academia.[67]

The aim of this book is to investigate the conflicts and compromises involved when the agenda of nationalist politicians and intellectuals was put into practice at the University of Latvia in Riga. On the one hand, a reasonable assumption seems to be that the nationalist politicians and intellectuals in this successor state exerted strong pressure to ensure the creation of higher education that would match the nationalist agenda and materialise and codify the movement's notions and imaginings of the Latvian nation. On the other hand, the university was also bound by another, more international kind of agenda: the academic insistence on acknowledged scholarly practice, and the priority of academic excellence in all matters of recruitment and promotion. This, what I will henceforth call the 'double agenda' undoubtedly occasioned conflicts and compromises among the academic and political agents forming the new university. These matters had to be negotiated in several arenas, most importantly in the ruling bodies of the university and the Ministry of Education.

At the same time, it is reasonable to assume that the conceptions of the 'nation' and the 'national' were neither uniform nor monolithic. These notions could undoubtedly be defined in a number of different ways among the various members of the political and intellectual elite.[68] For those involved in the forming of the University of Latvia, the conception of a 'national' university

---

[67] See Grüttner, Michael, Hachtmann, Rüdiger, Jarausch, Konrad H, John, Jürgen, & Middel, Matthias (2010): "Wissenschaftskulturen zwischen Diktatur und Demokratie. Vorüberlegungen zu einer kritischen Universitätsgeschichte des 20. Jahrhunderts", p. 15, on the importance of studying the effects of sudden and dramatic political changes on academic institutions and practices.

[68] See Kornprobst, Markus (2005): "Episteme, nation-builders and national identity: the reconstruction of Irishness", pp. 408–417.

could presumably have had several different meanings. For some, the emphasis would be on the university as a centre of academic excellence, a source of national pride in a wider European context of higher education. The quality of research and the promotion of prominent scholars and scientists as 'heroes of the nation' would be a primary concern. For others, the prime focus would instead be on a university using the national language, in this case Latvian, never before used in academic circumstances. Finally, the conception of a 'national' university could also be invested with a more narrowly *ethnic* meaning: a university where ethnic Latvian students were given instruction by ethnic Latvian academics.

These different meanings on what constituted a 'national' university were the cause a series of conflicts and compromises among the members of the organisation committee set up to form the new University of Latvia. Indeed, the conflicts and different understandings of the actual meaning of the 'national' university were particularly outspoken and visible during the formative first years of the new university's existence. A closer look at the recruitment and language policies during this initial period is therefore an important part of the study.

There is also a special reason for studying the formation of the university rather than the educational system at lower levels. I would argue that the dilemmas concerning the meaning of 'national' education were probably much more pertinent on the university level. On the lower levels of the educational system the ethnic minorities in Latvia were granted the right to establish their own publicly-funded school systems and use their own languages for teaching.[69] This was far less desirable or easily accomplished at the university level. Moreover, the creation of a new and essentially Latvian university carried far greater symbolic weight as the fulfilment of long-nurtured nationalist dreams. It was also seen as an intellectual achievement that would obliterate their previous subordinate position and include the Latvians among the highly cultured nations of Europe.

There is also a special theoretical point in choosing Latvia as the prime object for this investigation. We have here a case where an emerging post-imperial state was based primarily on a majority ethnic group that had previously been politically and culturally disadvantaged. In the part of the Russian Empire that in 1918–1919 devolved into independent Latvia, the primary role in terms of political, economic and cultural power had previously been played by Baltic Germans and, to a minor extent, Russians. Forming a new university using what had previously been seen as an uncultured peasant vernacular as the academic language of instruction is therefore likely to have produced an arena of conflict

---

[69] Smith, David J (2010): "Inter-war Multiculturalism Revisited: Cultural Autonomy in 1920s Latvia", pp. 33–38.

involving intellectuals belonging to the majority nation on one side, and academics belonging to previously dominant ethnic groups on the other.

The Latvian academics and politicians forming the new university in 1919 did so in what must be seen as a virtually post-colonial situation, with the previously hegemonic ethnic group still residing in the country.[70] This particular situation – where the previously hegemonic ethnic group is turned into a minority, while the formerly subordinated majority assumes political power – has recently been theorised as 'ethnic reversal'. Typical of these cases is that the previously hegemonic group faces a limited number of options, none of which seems particularly palatable: assimilation, exodus, confrontation or, at best, the defence of at least some measure of cultural autonomy. At the same time, members of this group are seldom viewed in a positive light by politicians belonging to the state-bearing majority, especially during the early, sensitive and precarious stages of nation-building.[71] In the Latvian context, it is quite probable that the Baltic German elite continued to play the part of an 'internal negative Other' in the forming of a Latvian national identity during the 1920s.[72]

In more Bourdieuian terms, this means that the previously very important cultural capital of the educated Baltic Germans lost most of its value, in fact risked becoming a negative asset. While the academic field is always an area of contest between different factions in their attempts to classify and define good scholarship and science, this situation became considerably more complicated when the established practices connected with the academic agenda were challenged by the demands from the different national agendas.[73]

---

[70] The Baltic German nobility dominated the provinces of Estland, Livland and Kurland all through the 19th century, viewing themselves in clearly colonial terms. Keeping themselves aloof from the peasants speaking Estonian or Latvian vernaculars, they remained separate in terms of rank, *Stand*, language, culture and ethnicity. See Whelan, Heidi W (1999): *Adapting to Modernity. Family, Caste and Capitalism among the Baltic German Nobility*, pp. 25–29.

[71] Riga & Kennedy (2009), pp. 464–465. However, Riga and Kennedy base their analysis on the Versailles Minority Treaties in 1919, where Latvia and Estonia were *not* included – yet they are probably the most clear-cut cases of 'ethnic reversals' among the successor states. Instead, they focus primarily on the Polish Jewry, who no doubt constituted a vulnerable minority in the nationalising Poland, but hardly an example of 'ethnic reversal'. See ibid., pp. 470–474.

[72] Pille Petersoo makes this point regarding Estonia, but the Latvian situation was surely very similar. See Petersoo, Pille (2007): "Reconsidering otherness: constructing Estonian identity", p. 124.

[73] Bourdieu, Pierre (1996): *Homo academicus*, in particular chapters 1 and 2. Bourdieu, however, is primarily interested in the contradictions between an academic legitimacy based on inherited symbolic capital and connected to social power, and a legitimacy based on internal practices of the academic field. Being situated in an established French nation-state, he does not really consider the complexities occasioned by the mobilisation of national agendas.

'Nationalising states' and minority rights

A special problem in the post-imperial successor states has to do with the attempts to combine the nationalist agenda with democratic principles, citizenship and minority rights.[74] Latvia contained sizeable ethnic minorities: primarily Baltic Germans, Jews, and Russians, comprising altogether around 25 per cent of the population. According to common democratic principles, people belonging to these minorities should have equal rights as citizens to receive education and academic posts at the universities. The question is: could this be accomplished at universities where the nationalist agenda of the majority ethnic group demanded the priority of the titular nation?

Rogers Brubaker's concept 'nationalising states' seems to be relevant here. Brubaker's main concern is the post-communist states emerging in the 1990s, but his analytical framework is clearly also applicable to the Baltic states in the 1920s. Brubaker identifies three elements in nationalising states: First, states that are ethnically heterogeneous but still try to adapt to the nation-state model, giving preference to the language and culture of the majority nation. The political representatives of this 'core nation' claim a special 'ownership' of the state, which according to their agenda should serve the interests of the core nation rather than those of citizens in general. Second, the presence of ethnic groups seeking cultural and/or political autonomy, seeking special rights as 'national minorities' and resisting assimilation with the majority nation. According to Brubaker, these national minorities should be seen, not as groups defined by ethnic demography, but rather as diverse and competing political stances taken by the groups' representatives. Third, the existence of 'external homelands' with the potential to serve as alternative national projects for these minorities.[75]

According to Brubaker, nationalising states' policies as regards the minorities can be either 'assimilationist' or 'dissimilationist': aiming to include the minorities in the core nation, or keeping them distinctly separate. In his case study of Poland during the interwar period, Brubaker shows that the Polish nationalising policies aimed to Polonise the Slavic-speaking minorities of Ukrainians and Belarusians, while the assimilation of the German and Jewish minorities was generally regarded as unlikely or undesired.[76]

The concept 'nationalising state' seems to be particularly apt for the analysis of the Baltic and Central European successor states experiencing 'ethnic reversals',

---

[74] Cattaruzza, Marina (2010): "'Last stop expulsion' – The minority question and forced migration in East-Central Europe: 1918–49", p. 114.
[75] Brubaker, Rogers (1996a): "Nationalising states in the old 'New Europe' and the new", pp. 411–437; Brubaker, Rogers (1996b): *Nationalism reframed. Nationhood and the national question in the New Europe,* pp. 4–6; 55–69; 83–84.
[76] Brubaker (1996b), pp. 86–93.

where previously subordinated majority groups suddenly became state-bearing nations after 1918. Here, the nationalising process was decidedly more rapid and dramatic than most previous cases of nation-building during the 19th century.[77] In a theoretical sense, the use of the concept 'nationalising state' could be seen as an extension of Miroslav Hroch's classic A-B-C stages of national mobilisation, where the nationalising state using its resources to promote the language and culture of the majority ethnic group could be seen as a stage D.[78]

Brubaker's notion of 'nationalising states' mainly concerns the triadic relationship between these three elements, or rather relational fields: the nationalising states, national minorities, and external homelands. He does not, however, discuss the democratic dilemmas inherent in the nationalising states, with the 'core nation' claiming a special 'ownership' of the state. Such dilemmas are very relevant for the present study. How could the political agenda of the 'core nation' be reconciled with the citizen rights of the minorities?[79]

Analysing Latvia in the 1920s and 1930s therefore entails an investigation of the relationship between the titular nation and the ethnic minorities, in this case in particular to what extent academic work and higher education were accessible for individuals belonging to the minorities. At the same time, it must be recognised that the nationalising process among the majority nation could be many-sided and sometimes even contradictory. There was probably no general consensus on what actually constituted a 'real' nation-state, or the best means of achieving it, even among the members of the majority nation.[80]

Analysing Latvia as a 'nationalising state' also entails a closer look at the problem of ethnic categorisation. On these matters I am primarily influenced by constructivist theory, and view ethnicity as a social process involving interaction and communication between people who perceive themselves as different from others, and that ethnicity means establishing a set of boundary markers that define and clarify this perceived difference. These boundaries are, however, malleable and negotiable, allowing for changes in the composition of the ethnic group and the adoption of new ethnic identities depending on the particular historical situation.[81]

The Western borderlands of the Russian Empire were definitely multi-ethnic, but with some ethnic groups certainly more dominant than others. In the Baltic

---

[77] I therefore disagree with Taras Kuzio, who in his critique of Brubaker sees no material difference between these two processes. Kuzio, Taras (2001): "'Nationalising states' or nation-building? A critical review of the theoretical literature and empirical evidence", p. 139.
[78] Hroch (1985).
[79] For an overview of models for handling such dilemmas, see Smooha, Sammy (2002): "Types of democracy and modes of conflict management in ethnically divided societies", passim.
[80] See Brubaker (1996b), pp. 65–66.
[81] Eriksen, Thomas Hylland (1998): *Etnicitet och nationalism*, pp. 9–56.

Provinces of Estland, Livland and Kurland, Baltic Germans had for centuries constituted the land-owning elite and the great majority of the town burghers. During pre-modern times, Estonians and Latvians were predominantly peasant serfs, but later also workers and tradesmen in towns and cities. By the early twentieth century there was a small segment of Latvian urban bourgeoisie and intellectuals. Towards the Eastern border there was an established population of Russians, some of them Old Believers. Jews became an important part of the townspeople during the nineteenth century, especially in Riga and the Kurland towns. German and Russian were official languages and used in printing and education, while Latvian and Estonian dialects were commonly used in everyday communication. Many people were bi- or even trilingual.

Religious affiliation, which served as a distinct boundary marker towards Jews and Orthodox Russians, did not separate Protestant Latvians from Baltic Germans. This probably made the ethnic divide between the latter groups somewhat easier to negotiate. At the same time, the Baltic Germans were generally keen to maintain their political and economic superiority, and carefully maintained the ethnic boundary to the 'uncultured' Latvians and Estonians. The Baltic German elite seems to have had little inclination to Germanize the entire population.[82] On the contrary, in a pre-modern society the elite probably gained certain advantages from having the essential class structure reinforced and buttressed by ethnic divides.

Naturally, during modernisation this mixed ethnic setting led to situations where ethnic identities became blurred and malleable. As is often the case, assimilating to the most prestigious ethnic group was seen as a rational strategy. During the latter part of the nineteenth century, some aspiring Latvians therefore attempted to cross the ethnic divide and assume a Baltic German identity through education and acculturation, seeing Germanization as the only viable road to social advancement. They were, however, disparaged as renegades by the Latvians involved in the growing national movement, while at the same time seen only as *Halbdeutsche* by most Baltic Germans.

Especially among the Baltic German *literati*, the notion of their supposed cultural superiority was an important vehicle in their struggle for societal influence, in competition with both the landed nobility and the 'rustic' non-Germans. Even the lower-class ethnic Germans, the *Kleindeutsche*, were keen to demarcate against Latvians and Estonians.[83] Crossing ethnic barriers was therefore a very difficult and complex issue, in principle only possible through education and acculturation.

---

[82] von Schrenk, Erich (1933): *Baltische Kirchengeschichte der Neuzeit*, pp. 104–108.
[83] Whelan (1999), pp. 30–33.

At the same time, Baltic German society was itself sharply divided by estate or *Stand*. The nobility strenuously defended their feudal seigneurial rights, demarcating against ethnic German burghers and *literati*. The nobles from the three provinces could not even agree to form a common Diet. While some accommodation occurred between the nobility and the *literati* from the 1870s onwards, the common Baltic German ethnic identity remained relatively weak until the early twentieth century.

In Lithuania, though, ethnic Poles and Lithuanians were united by their common religion, Catholicism. Moreover, over the centuries of joint Commonwealth with Poland the Lithuanian landed elites had become Polonised, while Lithuanian dialects were increasingly seen as merely peasant vernaculars. The predominance of Polish culture, with Polish as the only print language besides Latin and Russian, certainly served as an incitement for many with an ethnic Lithuanian background to assume a Polish identity. The Imperial ban on printing Lithuanian in the Latin alphabet, imposed in 1864 and only lifted in 1904, seriously impeded the development of a standardized Lithuanian print language, which also made it more difficult for nationalist activists to envisage the Lithuanians as an ethnic group defined primarily by language.

In fact, the standardization of the Lithuanian language was a strongly contested issue. Becoming a proper print language in the nineteenth century, the Lithuanian nationalists disagreed about which of the existing dialects should form the base for the standard. Eventually the dialect of Suvalkai in the South-West was chosen, probably because the main group of nationalists originated from this area. As a consequence, standard Lithuanian became markedly different from the standard Latvian based on the Riga dialect, thereby reinforcing the demarcation between the developing Lithuanian and Latvian nations.[84]

The fluidity and malleability of ethnic boundaries naturally makes ethnic categorisation very problematic. Imperial censuses before 1897 therefore preferably used denomination rather than nationality as the main form of categorisation. Sorting the population in religious terms, as Orthodox, Catholics, Lutherans, Jews and Muslims, was naturally easier than trying to define 'nationality' among a multilingual and highly mixed population. However, sometimes the Imperial authorities were forced by special circumstances to categorise people in terms of ethnicity. For instance, when punitive regulations were imposed on the 'Poles' after the failed 1863 rebellion, the local authorities implementing these laws had to define what a 'Pole' actually was. Who was to be included in this

---

[84] Kamusella (2009), pp. 186–187. Apart from this imposed language difference, the main boundary marker between the related Latvian and Lithuanian nations was the denominational one, Lutherans versus Catholics, and also the administrative division between the German-dominated Baltic Provinces and the Polish/Russian-dominated Kovno/Kaunas and Wilno/Vilnius gubernias.

category: Catholics generally, or merely Catholic gentry, or Catholic landowners belonging to a specific territory, and perhaps also individuals of 'Polish' descent having converted to Orthodoxy?[85]

During the second half of the nineteenth century, Imperial policy on the national question in the Western borderlands contained a number of paradoxes. Prom-oting the conversion of Lutheran and Catholic peasants to Orthodoxy was one strategy to 'Russify' the population and secure its loyalty to the Tsar. At the same time, Imperial rule had to rely on the local elites, Baltic German and Polish, for effective local government. The Baltic German nobility, therefore, could to some extent counteract the conversion of Latvian and Estonian peasants by arguing that, as Lutherans, they would wield a less effective rule over an Orthodox peasantry. The great majority of Latvians in the Baltic Provinces, at least partly for these reasons, remained Lutheran, belonging therefore to the same religious category as the Baltic Germans.

There were, however, no serious attempts among the Baltic Germans to Germanize the majority populations of Latvians and Estonians. Only after the extensive peasant upheavals in 1904–1905 did some noble-sponsored ethnic-national German associations emerge with the vision of transforming the Baltic provinces in a national direction. By then the development of national move-ments among the Estonians and Latvians had made such plans completely futile.[86] Instead, the aftermath of the upheavals led to a clearer demarcation along strictly ethnic lines, separating Baltic Germans from Latvians and Estonians. Local politics and voluntary associations, for instance, were primarily organised on the basis of ethnicity.

Ethnic categorisation remained a crucial element in the Latvian state that emerged in 1918. In the process previously described as 'ethnic reversal', the titular nation, the Latvian *tauta*, was demarcated from the ethnic minorities, the several *tautības* of Baltic Germans, Russians and Jews. This self-perception, less pervasive in Imperial times, became of paramount importance during the First Republic.[87] A decisive tension between ethnicity and citizenship remained: those belonging to the minorities were Latvian citizens, but were definitely not part of the Latvian *tauta*.

At the same time, the definition of the Latvian nation was not entirely clear-cut. The new state included the region of Latgale, which had previously been part of Vitebsk province in Russia proper. Its population was highly mixed, consisting of ethnic Russians, Jews, Poles and Latgallians – Latvians who spoke a

---

[85] Staliūnas, Darius (2000): "'The Pole' in the Policy of the Russian Government: Semantics and Praxis in the Mid-Nineteenth Century", pp. 45–67.
[86] Whelan (1999), pp. 34–35; 311–312.
[87] See Plakans, Andrejs (2010): "Celebrating Origins: Reflections on Latvia's Ninetieth Birth-day", pp. 16–17.

markedly different dialect from standard Latvian and who were predominantly Catholic. One object of the 'nationalising state' would therefore be to homogenise the majority ethnic group, creating a more unified Latvian *tauta*.

Problems and questions

The implementation of a nationalising agenda at the University of Latvia seems to have met with two forms of constraint: first, the uncertainties and different interpretations of what actually constituted a 'national' university, and second, ethnic categorisation and democratic notions of minority and citizen rights.

The present study will therefore focus on four problem areas: first, problems concerning the recruitment of academics to the new university. Here, it is to be expected that a more narrow 'ethnic' agenda, insisting that the university should be staffed with academics belonging to the titular nation, could not easily be reconciled with a primarily 'academic' agenda emphasising the importance of scholarly and scientific excellence. Should a mediocre academic belonging to the titular nation be preferred over a clearly more merited academic from one of the minorities? What were the attitudes towards academics belonging to the previously hegemonic group, the Baltic Germans?

Studying actual cases of recruitment is a good way of unveiling conflicts connected to different meanings and visions of the 'national' university, since these cases concerning specific individuals necessitated an open discussion where proponents of different views had to speak up.[88] The arenas where these conflicts and compromises were staged and negotiated were primarily the organisation committee, given the task of establishing the University of Latvia in the initial years, and its successor, the university council. Did the leading academics within these influential bodies form opposing groups, each advocating its conception of the 'national' university? Is it possible to discern a predominant view concerning these matters? Did this situation change in any material way during the formative period of the 1920s?

Second, problems concerning the composition of the student body at the new university. Again, according to the 'ethnic' agenda, this is a case of expectations that the university should primarily serve as an academic institution for aspiring youths from the titular nation, and provide that nation with a stratum of educated administrators, professionals and intellectuals. At the same time, *Latvijas Universitāte* was created in a multi-ethnic state containing several ethnic minorities. Baltic Germans had previously constituted an educated elite. To what extent could and would youths from this ethnic group enrol at the new Latvian

---

[88] See Bolin Hort, Per (2003b): "The Latvian Nation and the Intellectuals. The Forming of Latvia's University during the First Republic", passim.

university? Moreover, as was the case in several of the Romanov and Habsburg successor states, Jewish youths were often eager to take part in higher education. To what extent were these students welcomed to enrol at *Latvijas Universitāte*?

Here, the academics forming the new university faced a dilemma: to what extent should they adhere to a narrowly 'ethnic' agenda and favour the enrolment of Latvian students over those belonging to the minorities – while at the same time adhering to notions of enrolment based on merit, the fair and equal treatment of all applicants, and the general principles in a parliamentary democracy of equal treatment of all citizens? How was this dilemma negotiated and resolved?

Third, problems concerning the recruitment of academic staff and the codification of academically accepted knowledge in the disciplines that were closest to 'national' matters, such as archaeology, history, folklore, literary studies and linguistics. Concerning these key disciplines, nationalist circles undoubtedly exerted pressure so that the academics would present and codify what was seen as the true and relevant knowledge of the nation's past, culture, and language. It is to be expected that in these sensitive areas, tolerance of opposing views, especially those emerging from academics belonging to the previously hegemonic minority groups, was far less than in other academic disciplines. Also, these matters probably resonated much more strongly on the political level, involving leading politicians in the funding and encouraging of 'desirable' academic findings regarding vital elements of the nation's past and cultural heritage.

At the same time, it should be recognised that the trained and experienced Latvian academics congregating in Riga in the early 1920s had all developed their careers in another university system, primarily that of Tsarist Russia. To what extent were they ready to support and give academic credence and legitimacy to the notions of Latvian culture and history that prevailed among the nationalist activists and politicians? On these matters, therefore, one would expect a considerable degree of tension between different interpretations of culture and history. Even among the ethnic Latvian academics there was probably a good deal of disagreement about the actual form of national narratives under construction. In more Foucauldian terms, it is perhaps possible to see this as a tension between several different *épistémès* or 'knowledge regimes' within the academic sphere: the previously hegemonic Imperial Russian knowledge regime, Baltic German conceptions of history and culture, the Latvian nationalist master narratives, and finally the transnational academic knowledge regime with its insistence on evidence, scholarly method and logical deduction.[89] When, and to what extent, is it possible to discern a 'national turn' or the construction of national master narratives among the Latvian academics

---

[89] For Foucault's term *épistémè*, see Foucault, Michel (1972): *Vetandets arkeologi*, pp. 213–214.

in the humanities? To what extent did the scholars at the University of Latvia form a common *epistemic community* connected to a national master narrative?[90]

Fourth, problems concerning the shift in the negotiations between these knowledge regimes, the academic and 'ethnic' agendas, when Latvia shifted from parliamentary democracy to dictatorship in the mid-1930s. Kārlis Ulmanis, leader of the Farmers' Union, dispensed with parliamentary rule and instigated a general Latvianization policy. How did the new authoritarian setting and its increasingly national prerogatives influence the 'double agendas' at the university? Is it possible to detect a decisive shift during this period towards a predominantly 'ethnic' meaning of the national university, as in the Romanian case described by Pálfy? Or did the University of Latvia remain relatively autonomous, with considerable room for concerns tied to the academic agenda?

* * *

Apart from Pálfy's dissertation and subsequent work on the Kolozsvár/Cluj University, comparatively little has been written on the subject of nationalising academia. His case was also relatively straightforward, with national academia and university models already existing in the Kingdom of Romania. In the Latvian context, there are some valuable university histories written after 1990 (those produced in Soviet times are not very useful, since their accounts of conditions during Latvia's First Republic are heavily influenced by the contemporary political agenda). However, the modern histories of the University of Latvia are mainly concerned with the university's general development and do not address the specific problems involved in the nationalisation of academia that concern us here.[91] More attention has been paid to the struggles over higher education in the newly established Soviet Union, and

---

[90] For the concept 'epistemic community', see Haas, Peter M (1992): "Introduction: epistemic communities and international policy coordination", pp. 1–35. Haas defines an 'epistemic community' as "a network of professionals with recognized expertise and competence in a certain domain and an authoritative claim to policy-relevant knowledge within that domain". Ibid., p. 3.
[91] See *Latvijas Universitāte 75 (1994)*; *Latvijas Valsts universitātes vēsture 1940–1990* (1999). The latest contribution, *Latvijas Universitāte 90 gados. Dzīve.* (2009), is especially valuable for its imaginative use and reproduction of source material. See also Jānis Stradiņš's work on the Academy of Sciences and Latvian academics; Stradiņš, Jānis (1998): *Latvijas Zinātņu akadēmija: izcelsme, vēsture, pārvērtības*. For Lithuania, see Šenavičiene, Ieva & Šenavičiene, Antanas (2002a): "Universiteto organizavimo pradžia Aukštieji (vakariniai) kursai", and Šenavičiene, Ieva & Šenavičiene, Antanas (2002b): "Vytauto Didžiojo universiteto struktūra 1922–1950 metais: geneze, raidos, metmenys".

also the subsequent Sovietization of Baltic and Eastern European academia after World War II.[92]

Audronė Janužytė's doctoral thesis on Lithuanian historians as nation-state builders and founders of the Vilnius/Kaunas University in 1919 is nevertheless in some respects of great relevance to the present study. Still, Janužytė is primarily interested in these historians' *ideas* about Lithuanian nationhood and the establishing of a Lithuanian university, not the problems and complications associated with the actual creation of a national university in a multi-ethnic society. Her theoretical approach is also somewhat questionable. Probably in an attempt to demonstrate the 'modernity' of this generation of Lithuanian historians, she is keen to show that some of them had views of nations and nationalism that resemble those of present-day scholars, in particular Anthony D Smith. However, the value of these observations is perhaps somewhat questionable. Smith's definition of what constitutes a nation is actually very close to common self-conceptions among nationalist activists: hence it is hardly surprising that one can find some similarities.[93]

Janužytė certainly contributes some interesting material on the foundation of the Lithuanian university in Kaunas, formally inaugurated in 1922. However, she is primarily interested in the role of the academic historians in this process, which makes it difficult to understand the more general problems connected with the recruitment of academic staff and students to this new institution. One further problem with Janužytė's approach is that she does not clearly distinguish between academically trained historians and national activists writing on Lithuanian history primarily as a means to raise national consciousness.

Using a comparative perspective

While this study focuses specifically on the formation of the University of Latvia in Riga, some efforts have been made to present comparisons with similar processes elsewhere. Of particular interest here are comparisons with

---

[92] See David-Fox, Michael (1997): *Revolution of the Mind. Higher Learning among the Bolsheviks, 1918–1929; Latvijas Universitātes Vēstures un filozofijas fakultātes vēsture padomju laikā. Personības, struktūras, idejas, 1944–1991* (2010) Keruss, Jānis, Lipša, Ineta, Runce, Inese & Zellis, Kaspars (ed.). For a more general analysis, see Connelly, John (2000): *Captive University. The Sovietization of East German, Czech, and Polish Higher Education, 1945–1956.*
[93] Janužytė, Audronė (2005): *Historians as nation state-builders: The Formation of the Lithuanian University 1904–1922*, pp. 44–46; 88–89. For a short version of Smith's position, see Smith, Anthony D (1989): "The origins of nations", p. 342. After defining the nation as "a named community of history and culture, possessing a unified territory, economy, mass education system and common legal rights", Smith continues: "I take this definition from the ideals and blueprints of generations of nationalists and their followers". This means, naturally, that Smith's definition of nation rests on the self-conceptions of nationalist activists.

the creation of the Lithuanian university in Kaunas, another 'national' university that had to be established from scratch in a newly created post-imperial state. As a part of the comparative approach, the book will focus on differences and similarities in terms of strategies, conflicts and compromises connected to the specific circumstances of forming a 'national' university in a newly established multi-ethnic state. The Estonian university at Tartu is also of definite interest here, although the Estonians could to some extent build on an existing academic structure: Dorpat/Ju'rev University.

As mentioned earlier, the states of Latvia, Estonia and Lithuania were similar in that they were all dominated by titular nations based on previously under-privileged peasant populations. However, some important differences should also be taken into account: first, Lithuania abandoned democracy much earlier than Latvia and Estonia – in 1926 compared to 1934. What effects did this have? Second, there is a difference regarding 'ethnic reversal'. In Latvia the previously dominant ethnic group – the Baltic Germans – continued to a large extent to live in Latvia after 1918. Although a rather small minority compared to the ethnic Latvian population, they still wielded much influence and did not readily surrender their cultural supremacy. In Lithuania, on the other hand, the previously dominant ethnic group – the Poles – remained in the country to a lesser extent as influential transmitters of culture. Also, defining the ethnic boundaries between speakers of Lithuanian and Polish was more difficult, since the Lithuanian nobility had been Polonised for centuries. Moreover, foreign relations between Lithuania and Poland remained very strained in the interwar period after the latter's annexation of Vilnius district in 1920. How did these differences in the relations between the titular nations and the previously hegemonic ethnic groups affect the shaping of university politics?

The comparisons with the other Baltic states will, however, be limited in this study. They will primarily be used to indicate ways in which the policies and practices developed at the University of Latvia differed from those of other universities in the region. For the same reason, some even more limited comparisons will be made with the situation at Polish, Romanian and Czech universities.

Sources and method

The main material for this study is the archival records of *Latvijas Universitāte*, primarily the minute books of the organisation committee between 1919 and 1922, the minutes of the university council from 1922 onwards, and the records of the Faculty of Philology and Philosophy. I have also used various records on the recruitment of academics, the organisation of the various disciplines, language use in teaching, and statistics on students and lecturers, especially those containing ethnic categorisations. Records of the Ministry of Education, *Izglītības Ministrijas*, have also been used, primarily correspondence and investigations on matters concerning the university. These records are all kept at the Latvian State Historical Archive in Riga. These archival records have been supplemented with some published works on the establishment of the university, and the printed histories of *Latvijas Universitāte* produced during the First Republic.

I have focused in particular on two periods: first, the founding years between 1919 and 1924. I presume that these were the most dramatic years; a period when most of the academics were recruited, the disciplines organised, curricula devised and teaching begun. A great many strategic decisions on recruitment of academic staff and the reception of students were taken during these initial and very formative years. As a part of these strategic decisions, discussions about the actual meaning of a 'national university' took place in the organisation committee and the university council. Details of the recruitment process, especially the problems involved in retrieving Latvian academics from the Soviet Union, can be found in the correspondence included in the university staff records. To some extent, the published memoirs of some of the academics have been used to fill in the picture.

When investigating the tensions between different 'knowledge regimes' in the humanities, I have made extensive use of the faculty meeting minutes. Focusing especially on recruitment matters, I have paid special attention to the discussions on the appointments of academics belonging either to the titular nation, the ethnic minorities, or holding foreign citizenship.

I have also analysed the scholarly output of these academics, trying to establish to what extent and at what point in time national master narratives were constructed. I have primarily analysed the books and articles of the Latvian academics in what I will henceforth call the 'national disciplines': archaeology, history, folklore, and Latvian linguistics. I have also used biographical data on the academics in order to make an analysis in terms of generations. Here, I have primarily distinguished between the academics who were fully established within the Imperial Russian system, those who managed to get academic posts through the creation of the University of Latvia, and finally the new generation who received their basic training at this institution during the 1920s. Besides focusing on these disciplines within the humanities, I have analysed the contents of the university's own journal, *Latvijas Universitātes Raksti (LUR)* in order to discover what image the university wanted to project towards the wider academic community and to what extent a national agenda is discernible in this material.

Concerning the conflicts between Latvian, Russian and Jewish students in the early 1920s, I have made special use of the archive material connected with the committee investigating these instances. The prime material is to be found in the university records, but some documents in the Ministry of Education archive have also been used.

The second period studied more intensely concerns the Ulmanis dictatorship, 1934 to 1940. The specific question here is to what extent academic work and priorities changed under authoritarian rule. The university council and faculty meeting minutes during this period are, however, much less rewarding than those of the preceding period: any opposition towards the new regime and its policies could obviously not be voiced openly at such meetings. However, staff records have been used to investigate changes in recruitment policy, and the records of the Historical Institute at least give some insights into the construction and priorities of this institution. University histories and articles by academics in popular journals also identify the members of the university staff who cooperated most closely with the Ulmanis regime during this period.

Using what Ricœur has called 'the hermeneutics of suspicion', I have carried out a close reading of these records, trying to find traces of conflicts and compromises when this group of disparate Latvian academics and politicians set about creating the new university. In particular I have looked for the possible different meanings of a 'national' university that can be detected in these discussions, and also signs of conflicts over ethnic matters, especially the recruitment of non-Latvian academics and the enrolment of students from other ethnic groups than the titular nation.

Disposition

The sequence of the empirical chapters is as follows: first I will provide a general overview of the Imperial Russian academic system and the transition towards national universities in the Baltic successor states. In chapter 3, the main focus is on the recruitment of academics to the newly established *Latvijas Universitāte*, and especially the dilemmas facing the university leadership when it proved hard to find properly qualified ethnic Latvian academics. Chapter 4 contains a deeper analysis of the problems connected with the choice of tuition language, while chapter 5 concerns the dilemmas encountered by the university leadership when it transpired that a considerable proportion of the students enrolled in the early 1920s were Jews, not ethnic Latvians. In chapter 6 the official journal of the new university is scrutinised, while the development of the 'national disciplines' in the humanities is examined in chapter 7. Chapter 8 deals with the changes at the university, in terms of curricula and academic staff, occasioned by the authoritarian regime that took power in May 1934, and in chapter 9 I try to draw some overall conclusions. In order to help the reader to distinguish between all the perhaps unfamiliar academics at *Latvijas Universitāte*, a list of some basic biographical information can be found in the Appendix.

CHAPTER 2

From Imperial to National Universities
The University System in the Russian Empire
1800–1919

Before focusing on the formation of the University of Latvia, it is necessary to take a brief look at the universities of the Russian Empire. From a European perspective the Russian university system is relatively young, developing primarily during the eighteenth and nineteenth centuries. In fact, of the Russian-speaking universities, only Moscow University was founded before 1800. Thus, the Imperial Russian universities were relatively new institutions and situated on the very edge of the European system. By 1818, seven universities were in operation: St Petersburg, Moscow, Kazan, Kharkov, Wilna/Vilnius, Warsaw and Dorpat.[1] The first four used Russian as the language of instruction. Polish was used at Wilna/Vilnius University until 1825, when it was replaced by instruction in Russian. Warsaw University fared similarly in the early 1830s. German remained the language of instruction at Dorpat University during the greater part of the nineteenth century.[2] In 1828, the previously Swedish university of Åbo/Turku was moved to Helsinki and turned into an Imperial university, primarily using Swedish as the language of instruction.[3] Six years later, a new university in Kiev was founded, but granted less autonomy than the other Russian universities – probably because a substantial number of the Kiev professors were Poles.[4] In the modernisation effort that followed the humiliating

---

[1] Meyer, Klaus (1987): "Die Universität im Russischen Reich in der ersten Hälfte des 19. Jahrhunderts", pp. 37–43.
[2] Kamusella, Tomasz (2009): *The Politics of Language and Nationalism in Modern Central Europe,* p. 381. Actually, Latin was the official language of instruction when the Wilna/Vilna University reopened in 1803. Polish gradually took over, but in 1825 Russian became the official language when Polish political organisations were detected among the students. See also Krapauskas, Virgil (2000): *Nationalism and Historiography: The Case of Nineteenth-Century Lithuanian Historicism,* p. 66.
[3] Leikola, Anto (1996): "In Service of the Truth or of the Emperor. Some reflections on the loyalties of the University of Finland", p. 125.
[4] Remy, Johannes (2000): *Higher Education and National Identity. Polish Student Activism in Russia 1832–1863,* p. 61. However, the charters of the other Imperial universities were amended to resemble Kiev's only two years later – surely a sign of a more autocratic rule during Tsar Nicholas.

experience of the Crimean War, the expansion of the Russian university system continued with Odessa (1865), Tomsk (1878) and Saratov (1909).[5]

The universities of Wilna/Vilnius and Dorpat had by far the largest numbers of students. Wilna/Vilnius, which primarily provided higher education for the Polish-Lithuanian nobility, actually had more than half of the Empire's total studentship by 1809. The more provincial universities of Kharkov, Kazan, Tomsk and Saratov attracted very small student bodies, and also had considerable problems in finding adequate academic staff. Recruited German professors found the language barriers problematic: they could seldom lecture in Russian, while the students knew very little German and Latin.[6] In order to lessen the dependence on foreign academics, the University Charter of 1835 introduced new professorial chairs in Russian and Slavic languages and literature.[7]

The universities were primarily designed to supply trained officials for the Imperial bureaucracy. At the same time, they were career-welding institutions of the local elites, primarily the nobility. However, during the nineteenth century they were also seen as possible breeding-grounds of nationalist sentiment and discontent. The Polish students especially were regarded as potentially disloyal troublemakers. After the failed Polish rebellion in 1830–1931, the Imperial government closed the Polish-dominated universities of Wilna/Vilnius and Warsaw. Instead, a Russian-speaking university in Kiev was founded in 1834 with the express aim of countering Polish cultural influence in the Western provinces.[8] During the rest of the nineteenth century, the re-opening of a Polish-speaking university was rendered impossible by persistent government suspicions. Warsaw University was eventually reopened, but only as a Russian-speaking institution. As such, its academic standard markedly deteriorated.[9]

Neither does the government seem to have appreciated the presence of Polish students at the Russian universities, since they were suspected of spreading liberal and nationalist ideas. Limits were therefore imposed on the number of Polish students at Russian universities, and the main government policy was to direct Polish youths to the university in Kiev. The Polish elite was to be Russified by exposure to higher education in Russian.[10] For this reason, the symbolically

---

[5] Byford, Andy (2007): *Literary Scholarship in Late Imperial Russia. Rituals of Academic Institutionalisation*, pp. 14–16.
[6] Krapauskas (2000), pp. 47–48.
[7] Byford (2007), p. 16.
[8] Remy (2000), p. 72. In order to strengthen the Russian character of Kiev University, some of the Polish academics were dismissed in 1837–1939. See ibid., p. 85.
[9] Porter, Brian (2000): *When Nationalism Began to Hate. Imagining Modern Politics in Nineteenth-Century Poland*, pp. 80–81.
[10] Remy (2000), pp. 74–75; Porter (2000), pp. 85–86. It is very difficult to establish the proportion of Poles at Russian universities, since the very definition of 'Pole' is problematic. Statistics were generally based on religion and estate, not nationality. According to Remy's

important Wilna/Vilnius University remained closed until the fall of the Romanov Empire.[11]

The Polish nation in the eighteenth and early nineteenth centuries was primarily defined by class and literary culture, not ethnicity. The nobility of the Commonwealth saw themselves as 'Poles', whether their basic ethnicity was Polish, Lithuanian or Ruthenian/Ukrainian. Not until the mid-nineteenth century did the conception of 'Poles' also begin to include Polish-speaking peasants, accompanied by a more general Polonisation of non-noble Lithuanians and Ruthenians. Only by the time of the 1863 rebellion, fuelled by the need to gain wider popular support, did the Poles start to envisage a federal Commonwealth constituted by the separate nations of Poles, Lithuanians and Ruthenians/Ukrainians.[12]

In fact, the general anti-Polish policies of the Imperial government after 1863 seem to have included a tendency to limit the Polish cultural predominance over adjacent peasant-dominated nations, such as the Lithuanians and the Ruthenians. As a result, these national projects, often led initially by the clergy, distanced themselves from Polish culture and became more firmly tied to the Imperial context. Towards the end of the nineteenth century a major part of the Lithuanian students were educated at Moscow University, some of them on scholarships created specifically for ethnic Lithuanians.[13]

Loyalty to the Tsar was, however, a predominant characteristic of Helsinki University, officially renamed the Alexander University. Here, there were strong links between the university professors, the state administration of the Grand Duchy of Finland, and the Lutheran clergy. The university catered primarily to the educational needs of the state bureaucracy, and students were organised in 'nations' in accordance with their regional origin within the Grand Duchy. From within this relatively loyalist and conservative framework, however, moderate forms of cultural nationalism could emerge, exemplified by the writing of Finnish history and the collection of Finnish folklore.[14] Enrolling only aspiring

---

calculations for the year 1836, however, it seems that Poles predominated at Kiev University, while constituting a relatively small group at the Moscow and St Petersburg Universities. See Remy (2000), pp. 77–80.

[11] Staliūnas, Darius (2000a): *Visuomene be universiteto?*, pp. 188–198; Janužytė, Audronė (2005): *Historians as nation state-builders: The Formation of the Lithuanian University 1904–1922*, pp. 249–50.

[12] Walicki, Andrzej (1999): "Intellectual Elites and the Vicissitudes of 'Imagined Nation' in Poland", pp. 259–273. The momentary 'openness' of the Polish nation even included the Warsaw Jews who supported the 1863 rebellion – they were defined as 'Poles of Mosaic persuasion', notwithstanding the uprising's the general Catholic character. Ibid., p. 274.

[13] For the Ruthenian case, see Himka, John-Paul (1999): "The Construction of Nationality in Galician Rus': Icarian Flights in Almost All Directions", pp. 113–124.

[14] Kolbe, Laura (1996): "Rural or urban?", pp. 52–54. A problem here, however, was the parallel existence of Swedish and Finnish as educational and administrative languages,

male youths from the various regions of Finland, and instilling in them a strong sense of belonging to both their specific region of origin and to Finland, Alexander University certainly helped to promote a Finnish national identity – in spite of its inherent loyalism and conservatism.

Apart from the University of Helsinki, the only university outside Russia proper possessing a considerable autonomy was Dorpat, present-day Tartu in Estonia. Originally founded by the Swedish government in the seventeenth century, it had been re-opened in 1802 as a German-speaking institution, catering primarily to the needs of the Baltic German elite. The teaching staff was until the early 1890s primarily composed of Baltic Germans and professors born in the German lands.[15] Dorpat, therefore, was actually part of the German network of universities, as well as part of the Imperial Russian university system.

Between 1855 and 1880, Dorpat University enjoyed a period of relative autonomy. The previously mandatory use of Russian student uniforms was discontinued, and student corporations flourished. The university was especially popular among the Livland and Estland Baltic German nobility, while their Kurland peers tended to prefer universities in the German states.[16] While the student corporations were primarily organisations of the Baltic German elite, students belonging to the Estonian and Latvian groups could also form separate organisations, important focal nodes for the small groups of nationalist intellectuals.[17]

Although Dorpat University remained open and continued to function until World War I, preconditions changed materially in the early 1890s when its professors and lecturers were forced to abandon German and use only Russian as the language of instruction and administration.

The russification process, 1855–1914: 'Nationalising' or 'Homogenising' the Empire?

While this process is generally seen as 'Russification', one should perhaps not view it simply as a matter of language and culture, or more specifically as the replacement of one administrative language with another. During the first century under the Romanovs, the most clearly perceived difference between the

and conflicts over whether the Grand Duchy contained two nations or one nation using two languages.

[15] Tankler, Hain (1996): "Dorpat, a German-speaking International University in the Russian Empire", pp. 97–98.

[16] Whelan, Heide W (1999), *Adapting to Modernity. Family, Caste and Capitalism among the Baltic German Nobility*, pp. 190–191.

[17] von Taube, Arved & von Rimscha, Hans (1968): "Die deutschbaltischen Korporationen", pp. 20–21; Joonson, Arnold & Ney, Gottlieb (1968): "Die estnischen Korporationen", pp. 35–36; Komsars, Andrijs (1968), "Die lettische Korporationen", pp. 49–50.

Baltic provinces and Russia proper was not language, but religion. The Lutheranism of Estland, Livland, and Kurland was certainly more provocative than the local use of German. The same could be said, perhaps even more strongly, about Catholicism in the former Polish-Lithuanian part of the Empire.[18] Religious belonging formed the most important mind-set and mode of categorisation. Indeed, categorisation by religious denomination remained the most important sorting mechanism in the imperial censuses throughout the Romanov era. Religious categories were no doubt perceived as far more stable and unequivocal than more changeable and debatable categories such as ancestry or language use.

However, a strong connection also existed between 'Russian-ness' and religious Orthodoxy. Practically by definition, Russians could not be Catholics, Lutherans, or Jews. Inclusion in a Russian nation therefore presupposed conversion to Orthodoxy. In the nineteenth century the Imperial centre actually made some attempts to induce Lutherans and Catholics to embrace the Orthodox faith, buttressing these initiatives by making 're-conversion' illegal. However, the clergy naturally resisted a full-scale conversion policy, but so did Baltic German and Polish elites, who could quite plausibly argue that their political control over the potentially rebellious Estonian, Latvian, Lithuanian, and Belarusian peasants would be much weaker if the landlords did not have the same religious affiliation and Church organisation as the peasants and farm-workers. Political stability was for a long time far more important to the Imperial centre than spreading the use of the Russian language.

At the same time, the Imperial government to some extent tried to balance the power of the local elites by promoting issues brought forward by Latvians, Estonians and Lithuanians. Towards the end of the nineteenth century these tendencies had become far stronger. The failed Polish uprising in 1863 led to an Imperial policy of suppressing Catholics, but at the same time aimed at separating the Lithuanians from the Poles, who in the mind of the authorities remained the main foe of Imperial rule. Government officials, for instance, tried to impose the use of Lithuanian rather than Polish in church services and Catholic seminaries.[19] Many Latvian and also some Lithuanian intellectuals of the first wave of nationalism therefore saw Imperial power and even limited Russification as a step towards increased autonomy for their own budding nation. For them, the main 'enemy' was the local Baltic German and Polish elites.

---

[18] On imperial Russian notions of a combined Catholic/Polish identity, see Weeks, Theodore R (1996): *Nation and State in Late Imperial Russia. Nationalism and Russification on the Western Frontier, 1863–1914*, pp. 54–59.
[19] Weeks, Theodore R (2000): "Official Russia and the Lithuanians, 1863–1905", p. 73–76. However, these attempts largely failed. The Catholic Church remained firmly Polonised.

This was particularly true for the first Latvian national intellectuals. Barred from careers in the Baltic provinces, they often had to find employment in Russia proper. One of them, Krišjānis Valdemārs, even attempted to found Latvian colonies inside Russia in order to develop a sense of Latvian autonomy outside the range of Baltic German influence. However, this issue split the Latvian national intellectuals: some advocated an alliance with the Slavophiles and Imperial circles, others adhered more to a German or Herderian concept of the nation.[20]

From the mid-nineteenth century, the pressure from important administrative circles in St Petersburg to 'Russify' the empire increased markedly.[21] Still, it is questionable whether Russian nationalism should be seen as the prime reason for this process. Even though a nationalist press had gradually emerged and clamoured for the mandatory use of the Russian language on all educational and administrative levels in the Western part of the Empire, the government did not hesitate to shackle nationalist journalists if they felt a need to do so. Also, as we have seen, it is doubtful whether the Russifying measures really were designed to include the populations in the Baltic and North Western provinces in an imagined Russian nation. It is probably more accurate to see the Russification process as part of a slow consolidation and administrative centralisation of the unwieldy Romanov Empire.[22]

The prime movers behind the Russification process were therefore to be found in administrative circles in St Petersburg. Their main goal was not to promote Russian nationalism as such, but rather to standardise the Imperial administration in terms of language, law, and local government. The overriding objective was the preservation of the state against the destructive forces of nationalism and liberalism.

These moves, however, questioned the local supremacy and status of the ethnic elites in the Empire's Western peripheries. In the Baltic provinces, the process of Russification led to serious conflicts with the Baltic German nobility, who had for centuries possessed a virtual local monopoly in the provincial law courts and administrative bodies. Indeed, it is quite possible that high-ranking Russian officials saw the complete Russification of all administrative bodies as a way to extend the number of posts and the range of their bureaucratic careers. In

---

[20] Apals, Gints (2008): "Izvēles iespējas latviešu kultūrpolitiskajai orientācijai 19. gadsimta kontekstā", pp. 67–73. Sentiments among the Estonian intellectuals were very similar. See Raun, Toivo U (2003): "Nineteenth and early twentieth-century Estonian nationalism revisited", p. 135.

[21] The standard text on the Russification of the Baltic territory is still Thaden, Edward C (ed.): *Russification in the Baltic Provinces and Finland, 1855–1914*. Thaden and his co-authors manage to surmount language barriers and provide a truly comparative analysis of the Russification process in the different Western regions of the Empire.

[22] Thaden, Edward C (1981): "The Russian Government", pp.15–53; Weeks (1996), pp. 5–18.

Benedict Anderson's terms, the Russification process can be seen as an extension of the possibilities for Russian administrative 'pilgrims' to gain official positions in the relatively affluent Western provinces. The Baltic German nobility's local monopoly would be broken, and Russian officials could be employed on all levels of administration.[23] At the same time, this opened up positions at lower levels of the administrative apparatus for aspiring young Latvians and Estonians, which in turn enhanced the social base of the budding national movements.[24]

The second important arena of the Russification process was the educational system. A government *ukaz* had already made the teaching of Russian mandatory in the entire elementary school system in the 1850s, but it had not been generally implemented in the Baltic provinces. The official Manasein inquiry in 1882–1983 highlighted the failure in these provinces to transmit a firm knowledge of the Russian language, history and culture to the local population. On the elementary school level, the introduction of Russian as the predominant language of instruction was more successful in the Baltic provinces than in the Lithuanian-speaking areas. In Kovno/Kaunas province, the attempts to Russify the Lithuanians by these measures largely failed: many Catholic parents fearing Orthodox indoctrination of their offspring simply did not send them to school.[25]

Manasein also recommended that Russian should replace German as the teaching language at Dorpat University and at all teachers' seminaries.[26] By Russifying the educational structure from the top down, Russian would in time completely dominate lower levels as well. Making Russian the mandatory language of instruction at the University of Dorpat naturally aroused fierce resistance among German-speaking academics, and also among the local German elite as a whole. Many Dorpat professors had scanty knowledge of Russian and would not have been in a position to pursue their teaching if Russian was made the mandatory language of instruction. Manasein, however, clearly saw the Dorpat professors as an important local elite promoting a sense of German separateness, and also as a group that, in his opinion, had excessively strong cultural links with Imperial Germany.[27] In Benedict Anderson's terminology, the 'pilgrimages' of these academics no doubt comprised the universities of the German-speaking parts of Europe, but hardly those in Moscow

---

[23] The access of German nobles to imperial posts in St Petersburg and elsewhere was, however, not impeded. Imperial careers had already for a long time demanded fluency in Russian. In the 'Polish' territory in the Western provinces, such an exclusion of the Polish elite occurred mainly after the failed 1863 rebellion. See Weeks (1996), pp. 54–59.
[24] Raun (2003), pp. 139–140.
[25] In Kovno province in the late 19th century, only 6 per cent of the children attended schools. Weeks (2000), p. 79.
[26] Thaden (1981), p. 58.
[27] Thaden (1981), p. 59.

or Kiev. The efforts of the Dorpat professors to retain the use of German, and to keep their statutes unaltered was therefore unsuccessful.[28]

In 1889, Dorpat University was forced to use Russian as the sole language of instruction. It was officially renamed Jur'ev University in 1893, and integrated in the Imperial Russian university system.[29] After this imposed Russification, almost half of the ethnic German professors moved to Germany. The proportion of ethnic German professors at Dorpat/Jur'ev consequently decreased from 87 per cent in 1889 to seventeen per cent in 1910.[30] Russian student uniforms were reintroduced, and the proportion of Baltic Germans among the students fell from 82 per cent in 1880 to sixteen per cent in 1910.[31] The essentially German university of Dorpat had in effect been transformed into the Russian university of Jur'ev, catering to the educational needs of the Romanov Empire.[32]

The era of 'Russification' between the mid-1880s and 1905 must be seen in retrospect as a rather futile attempt to squeeze a vast, multi-national, and badly organised empire into a national costume of Russian design. After the Polish rebellion in the 1830s, the Imperial centre became considerably less inclined to allow the elites in the Western borderlands a free hand in local administration. Guided by what was perceived as the negative Polish example, the Imperial officials increasingly geared policies towards centralisation and the mandatory use of Russian in administration and the educational system.

However, these attempts to 'nationalise' the Empire antagonised the hitherto loyal national elites along the Western borders: Finns, Baltic Germans, and Imperial supporters among the Poles. The Baltic German and Finnish elites in particular, who had constituted a very important part of the Imperial bureaucracy and armed forces, were incensed and alienated by this heavy-handed national policy.[33] The Baltic German nobility, who in the early nineteenth century had made a point of their unswerving loyalty to the Tsar, now gradually became disenchanted with Imperial service. They became more entrenched in their home provinces, and a smaller proportion of them aimed for careers within the range of the Empire.[34] Within the academic world,

---

[28] *Baltische Monatsschrift*, 1902, no 4, contained a lengthy article on this issue. Possibly, the Baltic German *literati* had not completely given up hope of re-establishing German as the language of instruction at Dorpat. After the turbulences in 1905, demands to have local control of the instructional language in education were indeed brought forward by the political parties founded by the Baltic German elite. See *Baltische Monatsschrift*, 1905, no 11.
[29] Garleff, Michael (1987): "Die Universität Dorpat im 19. Jahrhundert", p. 148.
[30] *History of Tartu University, 1632–1982* (1985), table 1, p. 137.
[31] Whelan (1999), pp. 226–227; 266. By 1910, Russian-speaking students from interior Russia constituted the majority of the students.
[32] Tankler (1996), pp. 97–98.
[33] See Henriksson, Anders (1983): *The Tsar's Loyal Germans. The Riga German Community: Social Change and the Nationality Question*.
[34] Whelan (1999), pp. 156, 228–229.

Russification and the abolition of university autonomy turned many previously loyal and conservative Baltic German academics into supporters of wide-ranging reforms.[35]

Russification of higher education in the Baltic provinces may also have clarified the links between 'nation' and prevailing educational pyramids for intellectuals stemming from the predominantly peasant populations of Estonians, Latvians, and Lithuanians. With the sudden breakdown of the Russian Empire in 1917, the formation of universities using 'national' languages became a most pressing issue in the new states emerging from the previous Baltic and North Western provinces.

From Dorpat/Jur'ev to Tartu University

The new Estonian government undoubtedly had a material advantage when establishing Tartu University. Here, the national aims for higher education could be materialised by taking over a pre-existing university structure. What had previously been the German University of Dorpat and the Russian University of Jur'ev was now transformed into an Estonian state university. Its previous role as an educator of imperial officials was now replaced by a firm tie to the Estonian state and its need for university-trained specialists.

However, even if the new Tartu University could build on previous academic structures, the transition was not an easy matter. Most of the academic staff had been evacuated to Voronezh during the war, and a short-lived German *Landesuniversität* had been created in Dorpat in 1918. When the new Estonian government came into power in 1919, it had to cope with the absence of most of the old academic staff. The number of ethnic Estonian academics had risen after 1900, especially in Medicine, but they were still far too few to replace the Russians and Baltic Germans who had left.[36] Recognising this, the organisers decided to invite specialists from Germany, Russia, and Finland in order to make the university operational. Finnish academics in particular were wanted, partly no doubt because of their close ethnic affinity, but also because Finns would find it much easier to start lecturing in the Estonian language. Finnish scholars and scientists, such as the historian Arno Rafael Cedergren, the archaeologist Aarne Michael Tallgren, the ethnographer Ilmari Manninen, and the geographer Johannes Gabriel Granö, made considerable contributions to the academic setting of Tartu in the early 1920s.[37]

---

[35] Hagen, Manfred (1987): "Hochschulunruhen und Regierungspolitik im russischen Reich vor 1914", pp. 57–61.
[36] For a perhaps over-optimistic account of Estonian academics before the war, see Martinson, Karl (1990): "1900–1914: A Turning-Point in Estonian Science", pp. 365–384.
[37] *History of Tartu University, 1632–1982* (1985), pp. 171–172; 185–187.

Still, when Tartu University reopened in the autumn of 1919, the teaching staff was clearly dominated by academics with Baltic German backgrounds. Only a third of the professors, and half of the entire teaching staff, consisted of ethnic Estonians in 1920.[38] Tartu University was therefore forced to rely on academic staff who found it difficult to lecture in Estonian. In fact, more than half of the lectures during the first term were conducted in Russian.[39] Having been the only academic language at the Imperial universities for the last twenty-five years, Russian continued to some extent to be used as the language of instruction during the 1920s. Only very gradually did Estonian academics, and the Estonian language, take over at Tartu University.

'Restoring' Vilnius University

The oldest university in the area, Vilnius University founded in 1579, was closed by the Imperial government in 1832 on the grounds that it was seen as a stronghold of the Polish nationalist opposition. While previously a university dominated by Jesuits and teaching in Latin, by the end of the eighteenth century Polish had become the language of instruction. In the turmoil at the end of World War I, 'restoring' Vilnius University became a crucial symbolic question for both Polish and Lithuanian nationalists.[40] The prospects for a Lithuanian university in Vilnius were, however, hardly ideal. The previous Imperial ban on printing in Lithuanian using the Latin alphabet, the poorly developed school system and the decidedly lower levels of literacy compared to the emerging states of Latvia and Estonia, made some nationalists question the feasibility of founding a Lithuanian university. Others, such as the historian and politician Petras Klimas, vigorously advocated the 'restoration' of a Lithuanian Vilnius University as a crucial national undertaking. Only within a national institution of higher education, he claimed, was it possible to develop a strong and nationally minded elite.[41]

After the Polish annexation of Vilnius and the surrounding region in 1919, Vilnius/Wilna University was reopened as a Polish institution, the Stefan Bathory University. The Lithuanian university had to be located in the new capital, Kaunas, and was opened in 1922. The delay was at least partly due to

---

[38] Siilivask, Karl (1987): "Über die Rolle der Universität Tartu bei der Entwicklung der inländschen und internationalen Wissenschaft", p. 121, table 2.

[39] *History of Tartu University, 1632–1982* (1985), p. 173. Even though a majority of professors were ethnically Baltic Germans, they were used to lecturing in Russian. Russian was also the only language that could be understood by every student.

[40] Janužytė (2005), pp. 150–186. The Imperial Academy of Medicine and Surgery was allowed to function until 1842, and the Theological Academy until 1844. See also Reklaitis, Povilas (1987): "Die Vierhundert-Jahr-Feier der Universität Wilna/Vilnius in den Jahren 1978 und 1979", pp. 369–373.

[41] Janužytė (2005), p. 155.

dissension in the Lithuanian Constituent Assembly on the nature of the new university. The Christian Democrats wanted a Catholic university with an emphasis on the humanities, while Social Democrats, Social-Populists and the Union of Farmers wanted a secular university geared more towards the natural sciences.[42]

According to Janužytė, the university organisers were initially relatively open about the recruitment of academics and the language of instruction. Since there was a decided lack of qualified Lithuanian academics, it was deemed necessary to recruit professors from foreign universities in order to reach an acceptable standard of education. This meant that the language of instruction could not be Lithuanian only; Russian and Polish should also be allowed. Since the Lithuanian language had never been used before in academic contexts, not even everybody among the ethnic Lithuanian professors would be able to lecture in it. The use of several languages of instruction was also considered necessary because of the very small number of scholarly and scientific works printed in Lithuanian.[43]

---

[42] Ibid, pp. 213–220.
[43] Janužytė (2005), pp. 166–167; 178–179. The provisional University Statute of 1919 ruled that lectures should be delivered in Lithuanian or other (unspecified) languages.

CHAPTER 3

Creating a 'Castle of Light'
The Forming of the University of Latvia during the First Republic

"Scientiae et Patriae"
Motto of Latvijas Universitāte

In the aftermath of World War I, the new Latvian state emerged as a result of the simultaneous implosion of the Romanov and German empires. The former hegemonic group, the Baltic Germans, was almost completely replaced by politicians and intellectuals stemming from the majority nation, the Latvians, in a process of 'ethnic reversal'. Not surprisingly, this had radical implications for academia. The crucial matter of creating a Latvian 'national' university may be seen as a way of structuring this new nation in both symbolical and practical terms. This academic institution provided an arena for fulfilling the cultural imperatives of rewriting the nation's past history and recreating its folklore culture. Moreover, tuition at this university would now be conducted in Latvian, a language which had hitherto been seen as a simple peasant vernacular, completely unfit for the purpose of academia or still more abstract reasoning. In these various ways the new university would ensure the cultural independence of the new autonomous Latvia, making obsolete the earlier predominance of the Baltic German and Imperial Russian cultural spheres.

The academics who eventually assembled at *Latvijas Universitāte* should therefore be seen as important formative agents, structuring the new forms of national 'imaginings'. At the same time, it should be recognised that those in charge of the formation of the new university had to handle a number of problems and dilemmas. One of the major problems will be the focus of this chapter: the recruitment of a sufficient number of well-qualified academics, preferably fluent in Latvian, in order to make the university operational. The difficulties were no doubt manifold. Since ethnic Latvians had traditionally been a subordinated peasant population, the strata of trained academics among them was very thin. Also, the existing group of academics with a Latvian background had primarily made their university careers within the Imperial Russian system, using Russian as the language of instruction and in most cases posted at universities in Russia proper. Their academic work had therefore been done within an Imperial Russian 'knowledge regime' or epistemic community, based on the academic experiences at these universities. To what extent would the established ethnic Latvian academics be able to embrace and adapt to a national 'knowledge regime' at the projected university in Riga? Would they be at all motivated to join the unknown and unproven *Latvijas Universitāte*?

On the matter of ethnicity, the organisers of the new university in Riga certainly faced a serious dilemma. While Latvian academics were presumably relatively scarce, there was probably no lack of well-qualified Baltic Germans, the previously hegemonic group. To what extent would they be welcome among the staff of *Latvijas Universitāte*? Here, it seems, the national aspirations connected to the university would conflict in some way with what I will call an 'academic agenda': the university's task of providing higher education based on solid scholarly and scientific research. European academia adhered to a specific 'knowledge regime': a set of notions of scientific quality and scholarly excellence, and also notions of constituting an international community based on reason and enlightenment. These notions would presumably exist uneasily alongside narrow and over-emphasised national aims.

The main problem addressed in this chapter concerns precisely this uneasy combination of national and academic aims in the creation of the new university in Latvia. How could these aims be combined: promoting the nation while at the same time achieving academic excellence? What kind of conflict on these matters arose during the formative period of *Latvijas Universitāte*? Did these dilemmas divide the Latvian academics, some advocating a university promoting excellence and a more ethnically diverse staff, others preferring a more 'ethnic' university recruiting predominantly Latvian academics?

Finally, while the majority national group strove to fit an essentially multi-ethnic society into the excessively tight costume of a nation-state, the rights of the minorities could not be totally neglected. The new democratic regime had to handle hostile reactions from the former elite groups, but also more reasonable demands for cultural autonomy put forward by liberal representatives of the ethnic minorities.[1] Did this have any effect on recruitment policies at *Latvijas Universitāte*?

---

[1] For liberal conceptions of cultural autonomy in Latvia and Estonia during the 1920s, see Hiden, John (2004): "Paul Schiemann on Reconciling 'Nation' and 'State'", pp. 9–21; Smith, David (2004): "The 'Russian Question' Yesterday and Today. Mikhail Kurchinskii and the Lessons of the Inter-War Period", pp. 24–44.

Creating a national university: links with the past

In Latvia, it must be said, the situation at the end of the war was somewhat different from that in Estonia and Lithuania. Latvia's territory, established in 1920, did not house any former Imperial university. Traditionally, Latvian students had received their higher education at the German-speaking Dorpat University, or at the Russian-speaking universities of St Petersburg and Moscow. However, in Riga the Baltic German commercial and political elite had founded a local institution of higher education, *Baltisches Polytechnikum*, in 1862, catering primarily to the needs of commerce and engineering.[2] The educational language here was initially German, and the teaching staff consisted primarily of academics from German states, Austria, and Switzerland.[3] The *Polytechnikum* should, together with Dorpat University, really be seen as an eastern outpost of the wide-ranging German-speaking academic world. Within this world, which comprised the universities of Dorpat, Königsberg, and Vienna in the East, as well as Basel in the South and the Rhineland universities in the West, academics could move freely during their training and careers, largely irrespective of state boundaries. Riga's *Polytechnikum* was simply a new dot on the map of German-speaking academics.

As the name *Baltisches Polytechnikum* implies, the students targeted for recruitment were primarily young men from the German-speaking middle class of the Baltic provinces of Estland, Livland and Kurland. A closer look, however, reveals that almost half of the students appear to have been of Jewish or Polish extraction. In both cases, the main reason for this can be found in the discriminatory Imperial legislation directed at Jewish and Polish youths, restricting their enrolment at universities within the 'Russian' part of the Empire.[4]

The pressure for Russification from imperial quarters towards the end of the nineteenth century eventually forced the Riga Polytechnical Institute, as it was now called, to use only Russian as the language of instruction from 1896 onwards.[5] The imposed requirement to teach in Russian meant that many of the Institute's primarily German-speaking academics preferred to move to other institutions within the German cultural sphere. However, with tuition in Russian, and its degrees now valid when applying for posts within the Imperial bureaucracy, an increasing part of the studentship now also became Russian.

---

[2] Redlich, Clara (1987): "Das Rigaer Polytechnikum 1862–1918", pp. 241–262.
[3] *Latvija 19. gadsimtā. Vēstures apceres* (2000), pp. 291–292, 319.
[4] Stradiņš, Jānis (1994): "Akadēmiskā izglītība Baltijā un Latvijas Universitātes priekšvēsture", pp. 30–31; Jēkabsons, Ēriks (2005): "Poļu studenti Rīgas Politehniskajā institūtā (19. gs. II puse – 1915. gads", pp. 57–60. For the same reasons, a substantial number of Polish academics found employment at RPI. See also *Latvija 19. gadsimtā. Vēstures apceres* (2000), pp. 320–30; and *20. gadsimta Latvijas vēsture I.. Latvija no gadsimta sākuma līdz neatkarības pasludināšanai 1900–1918* (2000), pp. 301–302.
[5] Redlich (1987), p. 251.

The Riga Polytechnical Institute was, to a great extent, removed from the German academic world and integrated in a new Imperial Russian setting.

The presence of ethnic Latvians at the Polytechnical Institute was, however, rather slight. Most Latvians were farmers and farm-workers, and their children had access to a very basic elementary education after the mid-nineteenth century. While not actually barred from higher education, enrolment at the Polytechnical Institute still required German-speaking (after 1896: Russian-speaking) secondary schooling, which most Latvians lacked. Only with the emergence of a Latvian middle class, and a more affluent stratum of farmers, was there an economic and societal basis for a larger group of Latvian students. The actual proportion of Latvian students at the Polytechnical Institute, which is hard to establish due to the problem of ethnic categorisation, does not seem to have exceeded five per cent. Only after the 1905 revolution did the proportion of Latvian students rise perceptibly.[6]

Similarly, the teaching staff included very few ethnic Latvians. Moreover, those who were able to make academic careers in this German sphere did so not as Latvians, but as Baltic Germans. In order to cross the social divide, these Latvians were also required to cross the ethnic boundary, Germanize their names, and become part of a wider German cultural sphere. One of them, the economist Karl August Lieventhal, son of a Latvian organist and poet and director of the *Polytechnicum* between 1886 and 1891, obviously changed his family name from the Latvian Līventāls as part of this transition process.[7] Another excellent example is probably the most renowned of the 'Latvian' academics at the Institute, Pauls Valdens/Paul Walden, an eminent chemistry professor. Educated at Leipzig, Odessa, and St Petersburg, Valdens/Walden actually managed to bridge the German and Russian academic systems. Although originally a son of a Latvian farmer, he became a leading member of the Baltic German scientific community in Riga. In this environment, his ethnic Latvian 'roots' appear to have meant very little to him.[8] Both Līventāls and Valdens became fully integrated in the Riga Baltic German community.

---

[6] Stradiņš (1994), p. 31; *Latvija 19. gadsimtā. Vēstures apceres*, pp. 320–330.
[7] Johansons, Andrejs (1987): "Die Lettländische Universität in Riga 1919–1940", pp. 255–256; *Latviešu literatūras vēsture. 1. sējums. No rakstītā vārda sākumiem līdz 1918. gadam* (1998), p. 104. During the last phase of the Institute, as "Baltische Technische Hochschule" during the German occupation of 1917, German was of course reinstated as the language of instruction. However, Latvian was not completely disregarded. One post in the Latvian Language and Literature was created within the 'Commercial' department of the Hochschule. Evidently the Latvian language was seen as essential when trading with Latvians! See *Latvijas Universitāte 1919–1929*, (1929), p. 18.
[8] Stradiņš (1994), pp. 25–28; *Latvija 19. gadsimtā. Vēstures apceres*, pp. 328–329. The case of Pauls Valdens is explored more fully below.

As is well known among historians of the nationalist movement, the right of Latvians to remain Latvian even when educated was one of the prime aims of the first generation of nationalist intellectuals. The Germanization of successful Latvians was seen as a grave threat to the emerging Latvian nation. If this process was not impeded, the ethnic label "Latvian" would remain virtually synonymous with "peasant" – as indeed it was among many Baltic German landowners. The first generation of university trained nationalists, such as Krišjānis Barons, Atis Kronvalds, Kaspars Biezbārdis, Juris Alunāns, and Krišjānis Valdemārs, therefore self-consciously – and to the Baltic Germans certainly provocatively – presented themselves as *both* Latvians and intellectuals.[9]

Ironically, though, most of this first generation of Latvian nationalist intellectuals had to reside outside the Baltic provinces due to the persecution of the Baltic German nobility in Livland and Kurland. Valdemārs and Barons formed a circle of 'exiles' in St Petersburg and Moscow, where they developed Latvian political and cultural issues within the framework of a Russian setting.[10] Similarly, Latvian students organised 'ethnic' societies and corporations at Dorpat/Jur'ev and St Petersburg.[11] These Latvian societies became a very important vehicle for the forming of a 'national' consciousness among students in 'exile'.

Nevertheless, with very few exceptions, Latvians who graduated from universities before World War I did so in an Imperial Russian context.[12] Traditionally, the main goal for aspiring Latvian students was the old Swedish/German/Russian university of Dorpat/Jur'ev. Mapping the existence of Latvian university-trained professionals in the early twentieth century, Fricis Mīlenbahs found that almost half of them – 46 per cent – had received their education at Dorpat/Jur'ev, at that time a Russian-speaking university. 27 per cent had received their training in Riga, while another 27 per cent had been educated at a university in Russia proper, primarily in St Petersburg or Moscow. Mīlenbahs' investigation also showed that more than half, or 55 per cent, of the university-trained Latvians stayed in Russia rather than return to the Baltic provinces.[13]

---

[9] Biezbārdis, Kaspars (1865): *Der Sprach- und Bildungskampf in der Baltischen Provinzen Russlands*; Kronwald, Otto [Kronvalds, Atis] (1872): *Nationale Bestrebungen*.
[10] Šalda, Vitālijs (2000): "Jaunlatvieši Maskavā", pp. 53–68.
[11] See Stradiņš (1994), pp. 33–34 on Latvian student corporations at St Petersburg and Moscow.
[12] The most important exception is perhaps Kārlis Ulmanis, leader of the Farmers' Union and later the authoritarian ruler of Latvia between 1934 and 1940, who was educated in Germany and the USA.
[13] Mīlenbahs, Fricis (1908): *Latvieši un latvietes Krievijas augstskolās*, p. 133. The calculation is based on the number of ethnic Latvians who had received university training within the Russian empire and were still alive in 1905. Interestingly, Mīlenbahs only calculated with Latvians born in Kurzeme and Vidzeme – at that time the present Latvian province of Latgale was a part of the Russian *gubernija* of Vitebsk, and appears not to have qualified as a part of his projected 'Latvia'. The omission of 'Latgale' from the investigation naturally means that

Reasons for not returning could be either that educated Latvians felt discriminated against by the German elite in the Baltic Provinces, or that Imperial Russia could offer a much wider range of employment and positions than was the case in the home province. One of the future professors at *Latvijas Universitāte*, folklorist Pēteris Šmits, wrote in his unpublished autobiography that enrolling as a young student at Moscow University felt like liberation compared to the constricted feeling he had experienced in his German-dominated Riga gymnasium. Šmits eventually became a professor of Chinese in Vladivostok, and returned to Riga only in 1920.[14]

This perceptible drain of Latvian intellectuals, and also a more general fear of cultural Germanization or Russification, spurred the Latvian nationalists to envisage the creation of higher education in Latvian. Especially for Atis Kronvalds, who was employed at the teacher-training seminary in Dorpat/Jur'ev in the 1860s and 1870s, the matter of Latvian as an *educational* language was a crucial issue. While the use of Latvian in the lower school system was, naturally, their most immediate concern, Kronvalds also saw the establishment of higher education in Latvian as the only way for Latvian culture to match German or Russian culture in the future. Kronvalds argued strenuously against German claims of cultural superiority, and advocated an extension of the use of Latvian in the educational system.[15]

Indeed, the role of the Latvian language in education was a crucial issue for the first generation of Latvian nationalists. They believed there was a great need for 'educated men' who remained firmly Latvian.[16] A key group in this process was, naturally, the Latvian elementary schoolteachers. Besides moulding the coming generation, they were the interpreters and transmitters of notions on the history and culture of the province. For the national intellectuals, it was vital that these

---

Mīlenbahs somewhat underestimated the number of academically trained ethnic Latvians in Imperial Russia. Unfortunately, Mīlenbahs did not record the number of Latvian professionals who had received their training outside the Empire. However, investigating the cohort of Estonians receiving higher education between 1800 and 1918, Ela Martis has found that 93 per cent of them had studied at universities within the Russian Empire. The figure for Latvians is probably very similar. See Martis, Ela (1985): "The Role of Tartu University in the National Movement", p. 322.

[14] Pēteris Šmits's unpublished autobiography, pp. 24–26, cited in Pakalns, Guntis (2011, forthcoming): "Pēteris Šmits". I am very grateful to Guntis Pakalns for sharing with me his as yet unpublished article on Šmits.

[15] Kronvald, Otto (1872), see in particular chapters 1–3.

[16] See professor K. Kundziņš's historical overview, *Latvijas Universitāte 1919–1929*, (1929), p. 6. The gender dimension in this issue is more than obvious. There are no indications that the nationalists felt that the Latvian nation needed educated *women*. Writing in 1940, the historian of education Ansis Kurmis maintained that it was the work of the nationalist schoolteachers – obviously *men* – to open the eyes of the quiet country *boys* to the tragic situation of the Latvian nation. Kurmis, Ansis (1940): "Baltijas skolotāju seminārā nozīme latviešu garīgās kultūras celšanā un suverēnas Latvijas tapšanā", p. 16.

schoolteachers could in fact become the first strata of intellectual professionals among the Latvians who could actually remain ethnic Latvians. Consequently, the pedagogical seminaries created in the nineteenth century became a contested field between German claims of cultural superiority and hegemony and the desire from some Latvian students to retain their ethnic identity.

It must be said, though, that most of the powerful German nobility in the Baltic provinces were evidently suspicious of popular education. They obviously saw little need for Latvian peasants to receive any formal education, apart from basic literacy and some religious instruction. Proposals for educational reforms were therefore not very well received by the noble-dominated *Landtag*, and the existing rudimentary school system remained seriously under-funded.[17]

Among those Germans seriously involved in the question of popular education, the main strategy appears to have involved the transformation of intelligent young Latvian schoolteachers into admirers and proponents of the allegedly superior German culture.[18] The pedagogical seminary created by the Kurland *Ritterschaft* at Irlava in 1841 in fact seems to have had a firmly 'German' character, and the Latvian students in most cases Germanized their names and joined the group the nationalists derogatorily called *kārkluvācieši* – 'Osier Germans'.[19] Also the seminary founded in Valmiera/Valka in 1839 was much influenced by German culture, even though it was directed by a Latvian – Jānis Cimze.[20] Although Cimze contributed substantially to the Latvian folklore-inspired choral-singing movement in the late nineteenth century, he apparently continued to doubt whether Latvians would be able to form a real nation comparable to those in Western and Northern Europe. "A nation", he wrote, "is like a tree in flower. The Latvians are merely roots in the ground".[21] These opinions clearly made Cimze less popular among the nationalist intellectuals.

After the mid-nineteenth century, however, a gradual distancing from German influence is perceptible. In 1869, Kronvalds organised a conference of schoolteachers in the 'Latvian' part of Livland, a meeting that for the first time conducted its discussions in Latvian.[22] National sentiments also began to gain

---

[17] *Latvija 19. gadsimtā. Vēstures apceres* (2000), pp. 262–285.
[18] The alternative strategy, filling schoolteacher positions with ethnic Germans, was hardly feasible, considering the requisite number of teachers who had command of Latvian and the low level of salaries.
[19] Kurmis (1940), pp. 10–11. The term probably refers to the very pliable and bendable nature of this plant compared with the more 'masculine' notions connected with the oak, an important tree in Latvian folklore.
[20] Kurmis (1940), pp. 11–12.
[21] Kurmis (1940), p. 12. Cimze published a collection of choir melodies, *Dziesmu rota*, which contained Latvian folksongs adapted to German musical conventions, but also some German folk-melodies. Consequently, Latvian nationalist intellectuals tended to question Cimze's work. See Vīksna, Māra (1996): "The History of the Collection of Folklore in Latvia", pp. 86–87.
[22] Tomāss, E (1940): "Semināra vēsture. Semināra dibināšana, darbība, likvidācija", p. 27.

ground in the teacher-training seminaries. In Dorpat, Kronvalds instigated evening classes for Latvian students, and in Riga a new seminary was founded which distanced itself more than its predecessors from the Baltic German cultural hegemony. This seminary was devised to supply Russian-speaking villages with teachers, and attracted only students from Latvian, Estonian, and Russian families.[23] Gradually, a more 'national' group of Latvian schoolteachers emerged, forming the main body of the growing national movement, and busying themselves organising choral societies, local libraries, and other kinds of local voluntary association. They also constituted the main readership for, as well as the main contributors to, the first independent Latvian press.[24]

Consequently, this group of Latvian schoolteachers was viewed with some suspicion by the Baltic German elite, ever mindful of the distinction of rank. According to the Latvian historian Alfrēds Altements, before 1850 teachers were sometimes required by contract to have only clothes sewn in the same cloth as the peasants, and were also forbidden to wear boots.[25] Obviously, the purpose was to keep their social status on the same level as the peasants. After the 1905 revolution, Latvian schoolteachers were to a great extent singled out as 'ringleaders' and punished. According to Kurmis, at least thirteen former pupils of the Riga seminary were executed, and many more were sentenced to hard labour or brutal forms of corporal punishment.[26]

The possibilities for Latvian elementary schoolteachers to further national demands within the school system were, however, severely curtailed during the period of Russification between the 1880s and 1905. The official requirement that the entire school system should be conducted in Russian was naturally a blow also to the aspirations of cultural hegemony among the Baltic German elite. For Latvian schoolteachers, however, this requirement also made it very difficult to promote and develop the Latvian language and culture. A further result was that the level of popular education decreased markedly, particularly because many Baltic German nobles withdrew their patronage from local schools when these became 'Russified'.[27]

---

[23] Kurmis (1940), pp. 12–13. Of the 1,017 teachers trained at the seminary in Riga, 75 per cent were Latvians, 11 per cent Estonians, and 13 per cent Russians. The absence of ethnic Germans is explained by the fact that Russian and Latvian were the only languages of instruction. See Tomāss (1940), pp. 29–30.
[24] Kurmis (1940), pp. 16–17; Altements, Alfrēds (1939a): "Studijas nacionālās atmodas vēsturē", pp. 48–50. Bear in mind, however, that both Kurmis and Altements wrote in a strongly nationalist manner.
[25] Altements (1939a), p. 49.
[26] Kurmis (1940), pp. 22–23.
[27] *20. gadsimta Latvijas vēsture I. Latvija no gadsimta sākuma līdz neatkarības pasludināšanai 1900–1918* (2000), pp. 287–291.

For many in the first generation of Latvian academics, the pedagogic seminary had constituted an inroad to a further career in higher education. Many of them were sons of farmers, and the most obvious goal for these intellectually aspiring boys was to become a village schoolteacher. Moreover, those who took this route and experienced the political struggle about language matters on the school level, and ensuing conflicts with Baltic German landlords and pastors, may also have tended to become more nationalist in their outlook.

Consider, for instance, the career of the linguist Juris Plāķis. A farmer's son from Talsi in Kurzeme, Plāķis attended the primarily Russian-speaking 'Baltic' teacher-training seminary that had been removed from Riga to Kuldīga. After graduation he worked as an elementary schoolteacher for ten years, but having taken part in the 1905 rebellion he was forced to resettle in Siberia. There he studied linguistics at the university at Irkutsk and later Kazan, before returning to the newly established Latvian republic in 1920. Back in Riga he was appointed to the staff of the new university, at that time officially *Latvijas Augstskola*, and also participated in several political commissions on language and education.[28] As will be developed in more detail later, Plāķis eventually became one of the leading proponents of a more narrowly 'ethnic' meaning of the university.

A second connection between Latvians and academia was the Latvian Society in Riga, *Rīgas Latviešu Biedrība*, which formed a 'scientific' committee already in the late 1860s. The purpose of this committee was to support the collection and exhibition of Latvian culture and artefacts. One of the important instigators was Fricis Brīvzemnieks, a nationalist Latvian living in Moscow, who in 1869 called for an extensive collection of Latvian ethnographic material.[29] The Riga Latvian Society duly organised an ethnographic exposition at the 1896 Archaeology Congress in Riga, which seems to have made an impression on German and Russian scholars. The society also supported various projects aimed at developing and standardizing the Latvian language. A special orthographic commission, including several established academic linguists such as Jānis Endzelīns and Pēteris Šmits, was formed in 1908. Attempts to form a history department within the 'scientific' committee largely failed, however, due to the lack of academically trained Latvian historians.[30]

---

[28] *Latvijas Universitāte 1919–1929*, (1929), pp. 177–178; Kļaviņa, Sarma (2010): "LU profesora Jura Plāķa dzīves un ciešanu ceļi, 1869–1942", pp. 18–40.
[29] Stradiņš, Jānis (1998): *Latvijas Zinātņu akadēmija: izcelsme, vēsture, pārvērtības*, pp. 59–61. It should be noted, however, that the field of ethnography was also of interest to Baltic German and Russian scholars, who primarily saw the Latvians as a more 'primitive' people soon to be included in the 'superior' German or Russian nations. See Strods, Heinrihs (1990): "Die Erforschung der traditionellen Kultur des lettischen Volkes in der zweiten Hälfte des XIX. und den Beginn des XX. Jahrhunderts", pp. 327–332.
[30] Stradiņš (1998), pp. 66–69.

After the turn of the century, the Latvian Society also joined the struggle to expand the use of Latvian in the education system. During World War I, Dr Ā. Butuls organised a special 'committee of higher education' within the Latvian Society with the aim of founding a new university, using Latvian as the language of instruction. Naturally, what made this development possible was the fact that by 1917, Imperial-Russian authority in the Baltic provinces had been substantially undermined.[31] Latvian nationalist aspirations that could not previously have been expressed without risking deportation suddenly appeared on the political agenda.

In 1917 a 'Committee for a Latvian University' was formed in northern 'Latvia', primarily by academics previously attached to Moscow University, for instance Pauls Dāle and Kārlis Straubergs, and also the future Minister of Education, Kārlis Kasparsons. A congress of Latvian schoolteachers at Dorpat/Tartu in the summer accepted the committee's programme and mobilised the best-known Latvian academics at nearby Dorpat/Jur'ev University, J. Lautenbachs, E. Felsbergs, J. Osis, and E. Pauķulis, to support these ideas.[32]

For the Latvian state that emerged out of the turmoil of 1918/19, the matter of higher education swiftly became a priority. Using the facilities and premises of the Riga Polytechnical Institute (RPI), *Latvijas Augstskola* was founded in 1919. However, several parties have claimed the honour of being the actual founder of this establishment. Baltic Germans naturally pointed to the previous tradition of the Polytechnical Institute. The university's main building was actually constructed by the Riga Baltic German elite for the Polytechnical Institute. To complicate matters even more, the temporary Latvian Bolshevik government under Pēteris Stučka founded a *Latvijas Augstskola* in Riga in February 1919 before retreating into the Soviet Union. During the Soviet era after 1945, the Communist party therefore did not miss the opportunity to claim that Pēteris Stučka had actually founded *Latvijas Universitāte*, and in Soviet times it was officially named after him.[33]

Finally, the independent Latvian state formed in 1918/19 and again in 1991 naturally claimed to be the university's sole and legitimate founder. The official founding date of *Latvijas Universitāte* (albeit as an *augstskola*) is therefore 28 September 1919. However, a closer look reveals that the planning committee of the new university was in fact composed of distinctively different bodies of academics. Some had previously belonged to the institution founded by the

---

[31] *Latvijas Universitāte 1919–1929*, (1929), p. 13.
[32] Dāle, Pauls (1921): *Vēsturisks pārskats par Latvijas Augstskolas nodibināšanu un viņas darbību pirmā (1919/20.) mācības gadā*, p. 5.
[33] *Pētera Stučkas Latvijas Valsts universitātei 50 gadi* (1969), p. 5. There was a similar incident in Vilnius in 1919, when the Bolsheviks, in temporary control of the city, proclaimed a 'Common Labour University' as the successor to Vilnius University. See Januzytė, p. 184–186.

Stučka regime in the spring of 1919, for instance the physicist Gulbis, the mathematician Lejnieks, the bacteriologist Kirhenšteins, and the agronomist Lejiņš. Others had been prime activists in the Valmiera-based Committee for a Latvian university, among them in particular Dāle and Straubergs.[34]

The main body of academics in the summer of 1919 was, however, made up of at least sixty professors and lecturers from the old Riga Polytechnical Institute (RPI) who had already returned to Riga from Moscow during the Stučka regime. Here, Pauls Valdens/Paul Walden as the director of the evacuated RPI played an important role in bringing many of its Baltic German academics back to Riga. Valdens acted as principal during the spring of 1919, and professors from the RPI also served as deans in all five technical and science faculties.[35] At the same time, ethnic Latvian academics established at Russian universities were expected to flock to Riga.

In conclusion, the first generation of teaching staff at *Latvijas Augstskola*, the official name, was therefore a blend of these three rather diverse groups of academics. Some specific dilemmas immediately arose: how would the Latvian academics returning to Riga from Russian universities cooperate with the Baltic Germans connected to the previous RPI? How would the emerging provisional Latvian government handle the national and ethnic issues when forming the new university?

Making things work: national and academic concerns

The organisation committee for the new university was formed in the summer of 1919, and consisted initially of representatives from three groups: academics belonging to the previous Riga Polytechnical Institute (RPI), delegates from key governmental ministries, and finally representatives of some Latvian professional organisations. At the inaugural meeting in August, six Baltic German academics represented the faculties: von Stryk, Jacobi, Fischer, Buchholz, von Denffer and von Hedenström. Another Baltic German, Alfred Sommer, participated at the meeting as an expert on Medicine. The new university – in contrast to the old RPI – was to have a Faculty of Medicine. Sommer had in fact attempted to start medical training in Riga already in the spring of 1919.[36]

The ministries represented on the committee were the Treasury, Trade and Industry, Communication, and Agriculture. The conveners belonged to the Ministry of Education: the minister Kārlis Kasparsons and the former principal of RPI, the ethnic Latvian Pauls Valdens. The Latvian professional organisations

---

[34] Dāle (1921), p. 13.
[35] Stradiņš (1994), pp. 32, 37.
[36] Vīksna, Arnis (2011): *Latvijas Universitātes Medicīnas fakultāte 1919–1950*, pp. 21–23.

invited were those connected to the fields of engineering, law, education and agronomy. Sub-committees for each faculty were swiftly put together to plan the further recruitment of academic staff.[37]

Very soon, however, ethnic Latvians replaced Baltic German academics as provisional deans of some of the projected faculties: Jānis Bergs, representative of the Latvian agronomists, replaced the original committee member Buchholz. Bergs had strong ties to the Latvian Farmers' Cooperatives, and had previously been the director of one of their experimental farms.[38] Similarly, the Latvian architect Eižens Laube was chosen rather than the Baltic German von Stryk, and Alfred Sommer was replaced by the Latvian Eduards Zariņš as the organiser of the projected Medical Faculty.[39]

In the Faculty of Law and Economics, the Baltic German lawyer August Loeber was appointed dean instead of the RPI academic Alfred von Hedenström. This seems to have been a matter of proficiency in Latvian, but perhaps also of perceived political loyalty. Loeber had close links with the Latvian provisional government, and was appointed senator in 1918.[40] Consequently, while seven Baltic Germans represented academia at the inaugural meeting of the organisation committee, only four were appointed as provisional deans for the first academic year: August Loeber, Law and Economics, Paul von Denffer, Mechanics, Waldemar Fischer, Chemistry, and Edgar Jacobi, Engineering.[41]

The very composition of the organisation committee, comprising prominent Baltic German academics, representatives of the ministries of the provisional Latvian government and Latvian professional organisations, probably created a basic uncertainty regarding the principles on which the construction of the new faculties would rest. Should academic merit have priority in recruitment matters rather than the government's political concerns or the Latvian organisations' national aims? Moreover, the voting procedure on appointments required a two-thirds majority, which meant that a sizeable minority in the committee could block any controversial candidate. In addition, all academic appointments had to be approved on the political level at the Ministry of Education.

---

[37] LVVA. Latvijas Universitātes fonds, 7427/6/1. Organisation Committee Minutes, 1919/08/08; 1919/08/12. Originally, the committee's name was "Committee for the Reorganisation of the Former Riga Polytechnical Institute".
[38] *Latvijas Universitāte 1919–1929* (1929), pp. 277–279.
[39] Zariņš was actually a pharmacologist, and was replaced as dean a year later by the newly-arrived Roberts Krimbergs. *Latvijas Universitāte divdesmit gados 1919–1939* (1939), I, p. 589.
[40] LVVA. Latvijas Universitātes fonds, 7427/13/985. Staff records. According to the official history published in 1929, Loeber lectured in Latvian from the very beginning. *Latvijas Universitāte 1919–1929* (1929), p. 558.
[41] LVVA. Latvijas Universitātes fonds, 7427/6/1, Organisation Committee Minutes, 1919/09/02; 1919/08/12; 1919/08/19, 1919/08/28. Dean Laube actually supported the appointment of von Stryk to a post in architecture, but the latter's inability to lecture in Latvian was held against him. Ibid., 1919/09/26; 1919/10/03.

3. CREATING A 'CASTLE OF LIGHT'

A key figure on the organisation committee was the young psychologist Pauls Dāle, who, in the absence of Kasparsons and Valdens, acted as chairman and representative of the Ministry of Education at the committee's third meeting in August.[42] Educated at Moscow University and an active force within the local Latvian Society, he appears to have sketched the outlines of a future Latvian university as early as 1916.[43] Dāle returned to the Baltic provinces during the war and took part in the first attempts to organise higher education in the Latvian language in Valmiera in 1917. After taking part in the War of Liberation in the summer of 1919, he assumed a dual role as elected *docents* at the new *augstskola*, while at the same time acting as chairman of the organisation committee and the chief official of the department of higher education at the Ministry of Education.[44] Dāle also authored the first historical account of the new university's initial years, thus providing a founding narrative for later official histories.[45]

As chairman of the organisation committee, Dāle's main responsibility was to make the new *augstskola* operational in a very short time. However, the practical problems soon proved to be substantial. As mentioned previously, the Estonians were able to take over the premises and equipment of the old University of Dorpat/Jur'ev and transform it into the Estonian University of Tartu, besides retaining a substantial number of the experienced Baltic German academic staff. For the new Latvian government, on the other hand, the material situation was much less straightforward. While it could command the resources of the Riga Polytechnical Institute, these seem to have consisted primarily of its buildings. Much of the laboratory equipment and most of the library had followed the Institute's wartime evacuation to Moscow.[46] Moreover, most of the academics of the old RPI who had returned to Riga could only lecture in German and Russian, the established university languages – not in Latvian.

At the same time, the new provisional Latvian government was determined that a national university should be established in Riga, and also that it should primarily use Latvian as the language of instruction. During the university's initial years, however, there were still some uncertainties about which the language of instruction should be. The constitution of the 'early' *Latvijas Augstskola* in the spring of 1919 actually specifies both Latvian and Russian as languages of tuition.[47] The organisation committee that took over in the summer

---

[42] LVVA. Latvijas Universitātes fonds, 7427/6/1, Organisation Committee Minutes, 1919/08/19.
[43] Šilde, Ādolfs (1976): *Latvijas vēsture, 1914–1940*, p. 50.
[44] LVVA. Latvijas Universitātes fonds, 7427/13/342. Staff records.
[45] Dāle (1921).
[46] LVVA. Izglītības ministrijas fonds, 1632/2/604. Rīgas Politehniskā institūta pieņemšanas komisija. Minutes 1920/09/21, 1920/07/28; Dāle (1921), p. 17.
[47] Resolution on *Latvijas Augstskola*, Spring 1919, §. 14. In Dāle (1921), p. 12. See also Stradiņš (1994), pp. 36–37.

of 1919 clearly had to navigate between the historical legacy of Russian as the prime academic language and nationalist demands for the promotion of Latvian. As will be shown more fully later, it seems that opinions within the organisation committee differed as regards the extent to which Latvian's 'monopoly' within the university should be taken. During this formative period, a persistent conflict on language matters is clearly discernable.

The language issue was tied to the dilemma of the university's dual aims: to provide academic excellence in education and research, and to participate in the structuring of the new Latvian nation-state. That the new university was designed to fulfil a national agenda is unquestionable. For many of the nationalist activists this was a means of materialising Atis Kronvalds' dream: to create an institution of higher education that uses the Latvian language. At the inauguration ceremony on 28 September 1919 this was expressed symbolically in the choral version of the nationalist poem *Gaismas pils*, 'Castle of Light', which prophesies that the 'spiritual riches' of the Latvian people will one day be manifest after the long period of foreign bondage.[48] The express aim of the new university was to gather a 'national treasure of knowledge' on matters concerning the native land, its history, geography, language, and spiritual culture.[49] Deliberately avoiding the use of the previously dominant academic languages, Russian and German, the festive speeches were held in Latvian and French.[50]

However, even the inaugural speeches contain a difference that is significant for the situation in Latvia during the First Republic: the Minister of Educations Kasparsons talked mainly about Latvia as *zeme*, land or territory, while Prime Minister Ulmanis spoke primarily about the Latvian *tauta*, people or nation.[51] Kasparsons used a wider, more inclusive definition of 'nation' as citizens living in the territory, while Ulmanis chose a more narrowly ethnic definition.

These conflicting notions of Latvian-ness, the ethnic on the one hand and the territorial based on citizenship on the other, remained problematic throughout the First Republic. While the ethnic minorities were granted cultural rights, including their separate school systems, their right to influence the agenda and structure of *Latvijas Universitāte* was questioned. When, for instance, representatives from the Jewish cultural community approached the organisation committee in 1920, asking that the new university would initiate research on 'Jewish questions' in law and the humanities, the committee found this completely unmotivated and unnecessary. Moreover, the committee concluded, if such considerations were taken into account, other ethnic minorities could

---

[48] LVVA. Latvijas Universitātes fonds, 7427/6/20. Augstskolas atklāšanas materiāli.
[49] *Latvijas Universitāte 1919–1929* (1929), p. 6.
[50] LVVA. Latvijas Universitātes fonds, 7427/6/1, Organisation Committee Minutes, 1919/09/19.
[51] The speeches are recorded in Dāle (1921), pp. 33–37.

make similar demands, which was clearly not desirable.[52] The essential Latvianness of the new university was not a matter for negotiation or compromise.

Naturally, besides fulfilling a national agenda, the new university was required to serve the needs of the new Latvian state by educating a new stratum of Latvian-speaking scientists, scholars, administrators, and professionals. In order to do this, however, academics would have to be found who could staff the new faculties and make the whole structure operational. These academics also had to be qualified to fulfill the university's second aim: to provide education and to carry out research of a very high standard. Here, the explicit ambition was to place the University of Latvia among the best academic institutions in the world.[53]

The question remains, however, whether these two aims were entirely compatible. When *Latvijas Augstskola* in its 'new' form started to operate in the autumn of 1919, the organisers soon ran into serious difficulties. The recruitment of both students and teaching staff proved to be unexpectedly complicated. The requirement that all classes were to be held in Latvian was somewhat problematical in a context where all public secondary schools had hitherto used Russian or, in some instances, German as the educational language. Even if some ethnic Latvians had indeed received a high school education, it had been in a language other than Latvian. To some extent, this problem was alleviated by the fact that some Latvian private secondary schools had been set up after 1900, so that by 1919 the pool of students able to pursue academic studies in Latvian was somewhat larger than previously.[54] Still, the great majority of prospective students did not belong to this pool.

Also, it should be remembered that ethnic Latvians constituted around 75 per cent of the population in the newly established territory. Thus, ethnic Baltic Germans, Russians, Jews, and Poles, in many cases assumed to have very limited knowledge of Latvian, made up a sizeable minority. How were talented students from the minority groups to be handled by the university if their skills in Latvian were insufficient for them to benefit from tuition in that language? Were supportive measures for these students considered, for instance language courses in Latvian? More ominously: was there a hidden agenda that the university should be ethnically exclusive, devised for Latvian students only?

Yet another problem was the conspicuous lack of academic textbooks in the Latvian language, clearly a very difficult situation for any new, ambitious university. Finally, a perhaps even more serious problem was the relative scarcity of

---

[52] LVVA. Latvijas Universitātes fonds, 7427/6/1, Organisation Committee Minutes, 1920/12/22. It was deemed sufficient that linguistics included the semitic languages.
[53] *Latvijas Universitāte 1919–1929* (1929), pp. 30–31.
[54] *Latvijas Universitāte 1919–1929* (1929), p. 12.

qualified professors and lecturers who could actually teach in Latvian. The organisation committee realized as early as August 1919 that the lack of teaching staff would be a serious setback during the first term.[55] As indicated earlier, the general lack of Latvian academics should be attributed in the first place to the prevailing structures of ethnicity and class in the Baltic provinces. Moreover, practically all Latvians who had received higher academic degrees had done so at either Russian or German universities and all those who had managed to pursue an academic career had lived for a long period outside the newly established Latvian territory. Most of them were to be found at Russian universities and the Soviet authorities prevented many of them from returning to Latvia before the Peace Treaty was signed in the summer of 1920.

A further problem was that some of these academic 'exiles' apparently no longer perceived themselves primarily as ethnic Latvians. In many cases, receiving a thorough Russian or German education led to a crossing of ethnic demarcations and the assumption of another national identity – or, alternatively, a 'supra-national' Imperial identity. Finally, academic considerations may well have induced some scholars and scientists of Latvian extraction to refrain from returning to Riga. Even if they still perceived themselves as Latvians, it is rather unlikely that the prospect of joining a small, Latvian-speaking university was more palatable to them than having access to a much wider range of Russian or German universities. They obviously had a choice between having a virtual monopoly in a smaller place that excluded competing 'non-nationals' without the required proficiency in Latvian, and continuing as academic 'pilgrims' in a considerably wider context, Russian or German. It should be remembered that notions about 'sons of the nation' ready to return and use the newly won independence are a vital part of all nationalist imaginings – and not necessarily true.

For most of the Latvian academics who had succeeded in establishing themselves at other universities, the wider career prospects and broader academic discourse within the Russian and German systems seem to have had decided advantages. Two things would have been likely to promote the return of Latvian academics to the new university in Riga: the collapse of academic prospects in their country of residence, and a deeply-felt nationalist conviction about the necessity of participating in the creation of the first Latvian university.

The question is: how strong were nationalist inclinations among the established ethnic Latvian academics? In this context it should perhaps be pointed out that the previous links between the Latvian nationalist movement and academia were generally not very well developed. In spite of a university training, very few of the figureheads of the nationalist movement in the late nineteenth century were actually active in higher education. Folklorist Krišjānis

---

[55] LVVA. Latvijas Universitātes fonds, 7427/6/1, Organisation Committee Minutes, 1919/08/28.

Barons was primarily employed as a private tutor at a manor outside Moscow – it was in this capacity that he organised the legendary collection of Latvian folksongs. He was never active within academic folklore studies. Similarly, Krišjānis Valdemārs worked primarily as an independent writer and on Imperial commissions, not within academia. Atis Kronvalds was, as we have seen, something of an exception, being involved in a teachers' training seminary, but this was a branch of academia that is closely tied to popular education. Within the *Jaunā strāva*, the more radical or Social Democrat wing of the national movement, the most prominent members were journalists, writers, and schoolteachers, not established academics.[56] For the most part, the intellectuals of the Latvian nationalist movement clearly did not hold posts at universities.

There were, however, some interesting exceptions. One of them, from the first generation of Latvian nationalists, was Jēkabs Velme, a lecturer in German at Moscow University and a member of the circle of 'exiles' around Krišjānis Valdemārs. Velme actually succeeded Valdemārs as the leading organiser of Latvian intellectuals in Moscow, publishing the important periodical *Austrums* from 1885 onwards. He was also the founder and first chairman of the Moscow Latvian Society. However, Velme remained in Moscow until 1923, when he returned to Riga at the age of sixty-eight to assume a post as lecturer in German at the university.[57]

Another member of Valdemārs's circle in Moscow who joined the teaching staff at *Latvijas Augstskola* was the historian Jānis Krīgers-Krodznieks, who at the age of seventy was elected *privātdocents* in 1921.[58] In honour of their long struggle for Latvian causes, Krodznieks and Velme were, together with another representative of the 'older' generation, the linguist and literary historian Jēkabs Lautenbahs, elected as honorary doctors by their faculty in 1924. Some bonds, albeit not particularly strong, therefore existed between the first generation of nationalist intellectuals and the academic staff being assembled in Riga.[59]

Among the more radical *jaunstrāvnieki*, a few had started an academic career before 1914 and joined the University of Latvia in the formative years. Among the most important of these was Teodors Zeiferts, a former school inspector who became lecturer in the Latvian language in 1920 and also the editor of the official

---

[56] See Zelče, Vita (2000): "Jaunstrāvnieki", pp. 60–80.
[57] LVVA. Latvijas Universitātes fonds, 7427/13/1876. Jēkabs Velme's staff records; *Latvijas Universitāte 1919–1929* (1929), pp. 219–220.
[58] LVVA. Latvijas Universitātes fonds, 7427/13/877. Staff records. The position of *privātdocents* entailed a relatively small teaching assignment, usually four hours a week. It was by no means a full-time occupation.
[59] On Velme, Krodznieks and Lautenbahs, see also chapter 7 below.

journal of the Ministry of Education.[60] Zeiferts wrote primarily on Latvian literature. Another important radical nationalist pedagogue was Aleksandrs Dauge, who was called to Riga in 1920 as *docents* in Education. Perhaps more importantly, Dauge also held office as Minister of Education during the formative years 1921–1922.[61] In this office he replaced another member of the *jaunstrāvnieki* group, Kārlis Kasparsons, who had served at the Ministry of Education between1918 and 1920.[62]

The political context in the early years of the Latvian Republic was very complicated. Beside the two major parties, the Social Democrats and the Farmers' Union, a number of smaller parties emerged: left-wing parties, ethnic parties connected to various ethnic minorities, and regional parties from the easternmost province, Latgale.[63] During the period of the Constitutional Assembly, 1920–1922, fluctuating political alliances led to frequent Cabinet reshuffling and this tendency continued during the first elected *Saeima*. On the whole, though, it was the Social Democrats and their allies who had the most important political role in the early 1920s. This also meant that academics connected to the *jaunstrāvnieki* group often headed the Ministry of Education during some of the first, very formative years of *Latvijas Universitāte*.

Recruitment matters: finding suitable academics

One of the main problems facing the organisation committee in 1919 was how to bring 'home' established Latvian academics from various parts of the Russian Empire. No efforts were to be spared. All prominent academics employed at Russian universities received telegrams telling them that they had been elected professors at the new national university in Riga, and exhorting them to return to their 'fatherland'. Among those addressed were the philosopher Jēkabs Osis, the linguist Jānis Endzelīns, the art historian Ernsts Felsbergs, the historian of literature Jēkabs Lautenbahs, the Egyptologist Francis Balodis, the linguist and China expert Pēteris Šmits, and the professor of medicine Roberts Krimbergs.[64]

---

[60] Zelče (2000), p. 68; *Latvijas Universitāte 1919–1929* (1929), pp. 226–227. For a description of the *jaunstrāvnieki* intellectuals connected to the paper *Dienas Lapa*, see *Latvija 19. gadsimtā. Vēstures apceres* (2000), p. 415–421, 474–489.
[61] Zelče (2000), p.63; *Latvijas Universitāte 1919–1929* (1929), p. 199.
[62] Zelče (2000), p. 64. However, linguist Juris Plāķis, belonging to the nationalist Right, also served as Minister of Education during a short period between Kasparsons and Dauge. See LVVA. Latvijas Universitātes fonds, 7427/13/1329. Staff records.
[63] Zelče, Vita (2008a): "Latvijas satversmes sapulces vēlēšanu kampaņa 1920. gada marts-aprīlis", pp. 92–121.
[64] LVVA. Latvijas Universitātes fonds, 7427/6/1, Organisation Committee Minutes, 1919/09/02; Dāle (1921), p. 22. The situation seems to have been similar in Estonia, where some outstanding Estonian scholars at Russian universities were repatriated in the early

Due to the persistent turmoil in Russia, however, these messages did not all reach their destination. To facilitate matters, the Foreign Ministry was instructed to provide papers and material assistance for those Latvian academics who desired to leave Russia.[65] Pauls Dāle, in his very important dual role as a member of the organisation committee and director of the department of higher education at the Ministry of Education, moved to get financial assistance for these selected Latvian professors to travel through Russia.[66] He even tried to make the Estonian government place a railway carriage at the disposal of professor Lautenbahs in Tartu so that he could move his scholarly library to Riga.[67]

However, convincing established academics of Latvian extraction that they should return 'home' does not appear to have been straightforward. To their disappointment, the organisers of the new university in Riga found that some of the approached academics at Russian universities were rather sceptical about the whole project. Disbelief in the new Latvian state's ability to provide adequate funding, and the serious lack of academic textbooks in the Latvian language, seem to have been major concerns among these sceptics.[68] For others, the removal to Riga was beset by practical difficulties, especially if it involved the transportation of scholarly collections and libraries, and, hopefully not least, the academics' own families.

Francis Balodis, for instance, a renowned archaeologist and Egyptologist, was a professor at the University of Saratov by the Volga when summoned to Riga by the organisation committee.[69] According to his autobiography, Balodis actually received the summons considerably later, and was given the choice by the *cheka* of either remaining in Soviet Russia in his capacity as professor or leaving within twenty-four hours without his scholarly collection, and also without his wife. Under these circumstances, Balodis maintains that he chose to remain in the Soviet Union as professor and vice-principal until 1924, when he finally

---

1920s. See Rothmets, Helen (2011): "The repatriation of Estonians from Soviet Russia in 1920–1923: a test of Estonian citizenship and immigration policy", p. 180.

[65] LVVA. Izglītības ministrijas fonds, 1632/2/633. Sarakste ar Latvijas Augstskolu par mācības spēku pieņemšanu darbā. Letter from the Organisation Committee to Latvia's chargé d'affaires, Moscow, 1920/12/08.

[66] LVVA. Izglītības ministrijas fonds, 1632/2/608. Sarakste par mācību spēku pieņemšanu augstskolā, par vēstures-filoloģijas fakultātes pārdēvēšanu. Letter from Pauls Dāle, IM section for higher education, to the Minister of Education, 1919/12/13, asking for 100,000 Roubles to enable three Latvian professors to return to Latvia.

[67] LVVA. Izglītības ministrijas fonds, 1632/2/608. Sarakste par mācību spēku pieņemšanu augstskolā, par vēstures-filoloģijas fakultātes pārdēvēšanu. Letter from Pauls Dāle, Ministry of Education, to the Ministry of Foreign Affairs, 1919/08/30.

[68] *Latvijas Universitāte 1919–1929* (1929), p.15.

[69] LVVA. Latvijas Universitātes fonds, 7427/13/123. Staff records

managed to obtain permission to participate in an archaeology conference in Vienna together with his wife. Their true destination, however, was Riga.[70]

However, the case of Francis Balodis may have been slightly more complicated than he chose to express in his memoirs. He moved as a student to Moscow University in 1906, and was clearly very well received. "In spite of the fact that I always emphasised my Latvian nationality", he wrote in his memoirs, "no doors were ever closed to me in Russia, up to the point when I was summoned to take up the post in Riga".[71] Balodis was in fact able to make a distinguished career in the Imperial Russian academic system. At Saratov he had an influential position within the faculty, and also occupied a new archaeological niche in excavating the ancient cities of the Golden Horde on the Volga. He states that he did not resolve to try to move to Riga until 1922, when contact had been established with vice-principal Razums at the University of Latvia. Apparently, for a long time he found it quite rewarding to continue his academic work in Russia. The University of Saratov continued to operate without any major interference from the Bolshevik government until 1923, when matters changed drastically. Balodis's faculty was transformed into a teachers' training college, and his academic work was subjected to political censorship. Only then, it seems, was Balodis convinced that serious scholarly work at Saratov had become impossible.[72]

In a nationalist narrative it would, of course, be entirely natural for Latvian academics to strive to return to the 'fatherland'. It should be borne in mind, however, that many of these academics had previously seen the entire Romanov Empire as the territory for their careers. Consider, for instance, the case of the medical men Mārtiņš Zīle and Jānis Ruberts. Both of them were educated at Dorpat/Jur'ev University, and later made their careers in present-day Ukraine. Both of them also married Baltic German women, and worked in a completely Russian-speaking environment. Zīle worked as a doctor and academic in Crimea and Odessa for twenty-seven years before returning to Latvia in 1922; Ruberts was occupied in a similar manner in Kiev for eighteen years. While the nationalist feelings of Zīle and Ruberts should perhaps not be entirely disregarded, it still seems reasonable to assume that it was primarily the political chaos in Ukraine and the strictures of Bolshevik rule that made them eager to travel to Riga in 1922.[73] In his autobiographical writings, linguist and national conservative Juris Plāķis described Zīle and Ruberts as 'supra-national' due to their choice of wives and their many years in the Ukraine.[74]

---

[70] Balodis, Francis (1941): *Våld och frihet. En lettisk universitetsprofessors minnen*, pp. 121–123. In the spring of 1924 Balodis had been transferred to a post at Moscow University.
[71] Balodis (1941), p. 50.
[72] Balodis (1941), pp. 95–108.
[73] LVVA. Latvijas Universitātes fonds, 7427/13/1504 and 7427/13/2010. Staff records.
[74] Kļaviņa (2010), p. 45.

Some of the targeted Latvian professors, such as Francis Balodis, were either prevented from leaving their Russian universities or unwilling to do so. Then there was the philosopher Jēkabs Osis, who died from typhus as an evacuee in southern Russia before he could reach Latvia. Still, by the end of 1920 most of the targeted academics appear to have come to Riga. Lautenbahs, Felsbergs, Endzelīns, Šmits, and Krimbergs all duly arrived to form a prestigious body of professors at the University of Latvia.[75] They were joined by some Latvian academics whose arrival in Riga was perhaps not fully anticipated by the organisers. One of these rather unexpected acquisitions was the eminent economist Kārlis Balodis who had served as a professor in Berlin since 1905. Apparently, Balodis was not one of the 'targeted' academics but nevertheless received a very warm welcome from the organising committee.[76] He was actually given the honour of making one of the inaugural speeches when the *augstskola* was officially declared open in September 1919.[77] Several of these high-ranking Latvian academics were immediately added to the organising committee, among them Endzelīns, Felsbergs, Krimbergs and Balodis. This clearly enhanced the committee's academic authority.

However, the fact that a number of ethnic Latvian academics converged on Riga in 1919–1920 does not constitute conclusive evidence that the organisation committee's recruitment policies were entirely successful. The first recruitment effort was confined to very distinguished academic names, so it is difficult to tell how many of the younger generation of Latvian academics with a more modest stature remained, willingly or not, within the Soviet Russian university system. The records of *Latvijas Universitāte* mainly mention the academics who actually managed to come to Riga, but there are some indications that several of those who were 'targeted' later had great difficulty in leaving Soviet Russia.[78] This seems to have been the case for several Latvian academics in southern Russia and the Ukraine.[79] Others, apparently, were not convinced that their academic life would be better in Latvia. Pauls Dāle, in his official account of the founding year, admitted that in many cases the attempts to convince Latvian academics to return from Russia had been fruitless.[80] A combination of a Latvian national

---

[75] LVVA. Latvijas Universitātes fonds, 7427/13. Staff records; Dāle (1921), p. 56.
[76] LVVA. Latvijas Universitātes fonds, 7427/6/1, Organisation Committee Minutes, 1919/09/09.
[77] Andersons (1987), p. 256.
[78] See, for instance, LVVA. Latvijas Universitātes fonds, 7427/6/1, Organisation Committee Minutes, 1920/09/22; 1920/12/08; 1921/03/16; 1921/07/01; 1921/08/31.
[79] LVVA. Latvijas Universitātes fonds, 7427/13/1504, Copy of letters from principal Felsbergs to the Latvian Foreign Secretary, 1921/02/26; 1921/11/14; 1922/05/03; 1922/06/02. The deans of the faculties wanted more effort to be made to secure the return of Latvian academics from the Ukraine. LVVA. Latvijas Universitātes fonds, 7427/6/1, Organisation Committee Minutes, 1921/02/23.
[80] Dāle (1921), p. 55.

appeal, the turmoil caused by the Russian Civil War, and the uncertainties connected with the first years of Soviet rule, however, probably made possible the recruitment of at least a considerable number of Latvian academics from Russian universities.[81]

The official histories of the University of Latvia have naturally emphasised the 'successful' recruitment of established Latvian academics such as Felsbergs, Endzelīns, and Krimbergs; these histories in fact being themselves significant contributions to the nationalist project embedded in the creation of *Latvijas Universitāte* Therefore, these 'stories' tend to omit some phenomena and persons who do not fit the general picture. One person often conspicuously absent in the official histories is the eminent professor of Chemistry Pauls Valdens/Paul Walden, who had been employed at the Riga Polytechnical Institute between 1885 and 1919.[82] A Latvian by birth, Valdens had made a distinguished career in the Imperial Russian university system and become firmly integrated in Baltic German society. As shown previously, he returned to Riga together with many other academics of the former RPI, and assumed the office of Principal at the *Augstskola* founded during the Bolshevik regime. University records show that Valdens also took a very active part in the initial meetings of the organisation committee, and was actually elected chairman with a huge majority in September 1919.[83] It seems fairly clear that Valdens was designated as the prime candidate for the office as Principal of the new university. He was also the major link between the Baltic German academics of the former Riga Polytechnical Institute (RPI) and the Latvian provisional government.

Shortly after his election as committee chairman, however, Valdens went to Germany for research purposes, and, to the obvious chagrin of his committee colleagues, did not reappear as promised. Naturally eager not to lose one of the prime figureheads of the new national university, Dāle sent a number of missives exhorting Valdens to return and reassume his position in Riga. Valdens promised several times to return, but for various reasons the homeward journey was always

---

[81] *Latvijas Universitāte 1919–1929* (1929), p. 22. The 'disorder' in Soviet Russia was probably the main reason why a number of German and Russian professors and lecturers employed at the Polytechnical Institute, now evacuated to Moscow, applied for posts at the new university in Riga. See LVVA. Latvijas Universitātes fonds, 7427/6/171, Sarakste ar iestādēm un organizācijām par lietpratēju norādīšanu dažādās zinātnes nozarēs..., for permission for such teaching staff to re-enter Latvia.

[82] The eminent Latvian historian of science Jānis Stradiņš has written on some aspects of the Valdens case, but he has not really explored the 'national' angle that is my main concern here. See Stradiņš (1994), pp. 39–40.

[83] LVVA. Latvijas Universitātes fonds, 7427/6/1, Organisation Committee Minutes, 1919/09/16. Valdens received a massive 16 votes, the other candidates Paegle and Dāle received 4 and 1 respectively.

postponed. Finally, he wrote to the committee informing them that he had been persuaded to accept a permanent chair at Rostock University, Germany.[84]

Within the organisation committee, Valdens's prevarications gave rise to some dissension. The economist Kārlis Balodis maintained that every effort should be made to secure Valdens's return. Other members, however, described him as 'uncommitted' and argued that people with more heart and enthusiasm were needed to develop the new Latvian university. Valdens was formally removed as chairman of the organisation committee in November 1919 and replaced by psychologist Pauls Dāle.[85] Still, Valdens's professorship in Chemistry was left vacant, and efforts to persuade him to return to Riga continued during the following year.

Valdens replied to these missives in June 1920. In a letter in German to the Ministry of Education, he declared that in principle he was willing to return to Riga, but only on condition that his scientific, juridical, and material conditions were not in any way impaired. He demanded conditions similar to those he presently enjoyed in Rostock as director of a Chemical Institute at a 500-year-old university. In addition, he demanded the right to pick his own scientific collaborators and to lecture in the language of his own choice, i.e. in German. The national cause appears to have been of very little consequence to him. In his letter, Valdens openly declared that in the interests of science he had for decades held himself aloof from all kinds of 'national and political chauvinism'.[86]

In his reply, Dāle appears to have bent over backwards in order to secure Valdens's return; and yet, in the end the latter chose to remain at Rostock permanently.[87] For the University of Latvia, the loss of Valdens was naturally a severe blow. He was one of the very few ethnic Latvians who had a solid reputation in the international scientific community, and would no doubt have been an excellent figurehead for the new university.[88] Valdens would have fitted

---

[84] LVVA. Latvijas Universitātes fonds, 7427/6/1, Organisation Committee Minutes, 1919/09/23; 1919/11/12.
[85] LVVA. Latvijas Universitātes fonds, 7427/6/1, Organisation Committee Minutes, 1919/11/12; 1919/11/26.
[86] LVVA. Latvijas Universitātes fonds, 7427/13/1826. Personal file. Letter from Valdens to the Ministry of Education, 1920/06/30. On Valdens's scepticism towards the national aims of *Latvijas Augstskola*, see also Stradiņš, Jānis (1982): *Etīdes par Latvijas zinātņu pagātni*, p. 234.
[87] LVVA. Latvijas Universitātes fonds, 7427/13/1826. Personal file. Letter from Dāle to Valdens, 1920/07/20; Valdens to the Ministry of Education, 1920/09/04; 1921/02/24. When Valdens's last letter had been read to the committee in March 1921, the efforts to persuade him to return finally ceased. Latvijas Universitātes fonds, 7427/6/1, Organisation Committee Minutes, 1921/03/09.
[88] Naturally, the matter of Valdens's ethnicity is not clear-cut. Indisputably from a Latvian family, Valdens nevertheless seems to have adapted fully to a German- and Russian-speaking academic world. In 1920 he preferred to use German in his correspondence with Latvian academics and politicians, and the loyalty he professed in his letters was directed primarily

admirably in the role of an academic 'hero of the nation', and his 'defection' was certainly a great setback for the organisers.[89] However, the Valdens case also clearly shows that not every academic was interested in complying with the university's national agenda. During the political turbulence in the spring and summer of 1919, Valdens appears to have been rather cool on national matters, expressing instead a strictly professional academic outlook.[90] For Valdens, apparently, material conditions, resources for scientific work, and participating in a first-class academic community were more important than helping to materialise the old dream of the Latvian nationalists: to create a university in Latvian territory using the Latvian language.

While Valdens was evidently solicited with much fervour in spite of his deep affinity with German academic circles, others with reasonable Latvian credentials seem to have been disregarded as too 'foreign'. Two out of the four passably 'Latvian' professors in Tartu, Arvids Thomsons and Jānis Sanders, were, judging from the official correspondence, not among those called to professorships in Riga. In the eyes of the organisation committee they apparently had become too Germanized, too Russified or too 'supra-national' in order to be strategic targets for recruitment.[91] Ethnic demarcation and definition were not an altogether easy process in the Imperial Russian academic world.

The number of ethnic Latvians recruited, however, did not correspond very well to the new university's actual needs. As mentioned previously, many of the established academics at Russian universities, or evacuated from Dorpat/Jur'ev to Russia proper, were prevented by the Soviet authorities from returning to Latvia until the summer of 1920. This was the case, for instance, with Endzelīns, Krimbergs, Felsbergs, Plāķis, and Aleksandrs Dauge.[92]

In some faculties, the difficulties in finding Latvian-speaking academic staff were greater and more chronic than in others. These problems seem to have been particularly substantial in the faculties of Mechanics, Chemistry, Medicine,

---

towards his *alma mater*, which he called 'Rigasche Hochschule', not to the new Latvian state or the new university.

[89] In the autumn of 1920 there was a row in the Organisation Committee over whether Valdens should be officially recognized as the first principal of the *augstskola*. While some members wanted the committee to above all consider the matter's academic aspects, the majority decided that Valdens had never been formally elected, and therefore Felsbergs should be recognized as the first principal. This, naturally, also served to obliterate Valdens from the official history of *Latvijas Universitāte*. Latvijas Universitātes fonds, 7427/6/1, Organisation Committee Minutes, 1920/09/24.

[90] Stradiņš (1994), pp. 39–40.

[91] *History of Tartu University, 1632–1982* (1985), p 138.

[92] LVVA. Latvijas Universitātes fonds, 7427/6/1, Organisation Committee Minutes, 1920/01/28; 1920/02/11. The University actually despatched vice-principal Razums to the Soviet-Latvian peace negotiations to press for the release of Latvian academics and educational material (presumably equipment belonging to the old RPI). Ibid., 1920/04/14.

and Law and Economics. The lack of qualified Latvian-speaking academics made it virtually impossible to give the Latvian language the desired complete monopoly at the new university.

This dilemma was apparent right from the start. The organisation committee had decided in September 1919 that Latvian should be the language of instruction but that Russian or German could be used "when this was necessary".[93] But what constituted a necessity? A particular dilemma was posed by the predominantly Baltic German academics connected to the former RPI. Here, the organisation committee had access to a set of established professors and lecturers, some of them with a considerable international reputation. Unfortunately, many of them could teach only in Russian and German. In this concrete and delicate situation, should the organisation committee appoint the undoubtedly most qualified but non-Latvian-speaking academics from the RPI, or should they select younger and less qualified Latvians?

This predicament certainly occasioned some turbulence and dissension within the committee. Agronomist Paulis Lejiņš suggested in September 1919 that, in order to secure its national aims, the *augstskola* should primarily select young, competent candidates who could speak Latvian. This, he maintained, had already been done in his own Faculty of Agronomy,[94] which was more consistent than the other faculties in severing links with the previous RPI. Only two of the established Baltic German academics were offered positions, and this faculty became the new university's most ethnic Latvian one. The composition of its academics had evidently been worked out in close cooperation with the provisional government's Ministry of Agriculture, where Lejiņš had played a key role before being appointed *docents* at the new *augstskola*.[95] As shown above, the provisional dean, Jānis Bergs, was closely connected to the Latvian farmers' cooperatives. The political influence of the ministry and the farmers' associations was exceptionally strong when it came to forming the Faculty of Agronomy.

Paulis Lejiņš therefore proposed that the same principles should apply when selecting staff for the other faculties. Younger and less academically merited

---

[93] LVVA. Latvijas Universitātes fonds, 7427/6/1, Organisation Committee Minutes, 1919/09/04.

[94] Indeed, inquiries from the old Baltic German professor of agronomy, von Knierim, who established this discipline during the RPI period, regarding the possibility of regaining his position in Riga, appear to have been duly ignored. See LVVA. Izglītības ministrijas fonds, 1632/2/633. Sarakste ar Latvijas Augstskolu par mācības spēku pieņemšanu darbā. Letter from von Knierim to the Education Minister, 1919/09/27. On von Knierim's work at the RPI, see Morjānova, Irīna (2004): "Materiāli Rīgas politehniskā institūta vēsturē (1901–1907)", pp. 62–64.

[95] *Latvijas Universitāte divdesmit gados, 1919–1939* (1939) I, p. 433. The two RPI professors in the Faculty of Agronomy, Arnold Buschmann and Eugen Ostwald, both in all probability Baltic Germans, apparently kept a low profile in the faculty and never served as dean or a delegate to the university council.

Latvian-speakers should be given preference over more qualified candidates who could not teach in Latvian. The committee majority backed Lejiņš's proposal initially and only approved candidates whom they knew for certain were Latvian-speakers.[96]

This elicited a vigorous counter reaction from the predominantly non-Latvian staff in the Faculty of Mechanics. The dean, the Baltic German professor Paul von Denffer from the former RPI, threatened to resign immediately if the faculty was not allowed to select candidates according to their scientific merits.[97] In the face of this resistance, the committee back-pedalled. Chairman Pauls Dāle described the incident as a 'misunderstanding', and maintained that the faculty naturally had the final say in electing academic candidates. Paul von Denffer was unanimously asked to remain as dean.[98]

This incident shows that the more overtly nationalizing programme of the organisation committee, promoted most forcefully by Lejiņš, Paegle and Dāle, could not be implemented in full, due at least partly to the strong resistance from established academics connected with the previous RPI. Naturally, the new university needed to establish a scientific and scholarly reputation, which would certainly have suffered if this struggle over 'ethnic' preference became protracted and generally known. In more Bourdieuian terms, the organisation committee could not easily – or openly – disregard the prevailing norms and practices of academe.

Just a few weeks after the exchanges between von Denffer and the committee, there was a renewed discussion about whether to condone lectures in the German language. The Faculty of Architecture wanted to elect von Stryk, an established academic from the previous RPI who was clearly incapable of lecturing in Latvian. The committee member from the Latvian Society, Spricis Paegle, argued strongly against the election of staff that was not proficient in Latvian and the committee majority postponed the appointment, deciding that every effort should be made to find Latvian-speaking academics. The appoint-

---

[96] LVVA. Latvijas Universitātes fonds, 7427/6/1, Organisation Committee Minutes, 1919/09/16.

[97] LVVA. Izglītības ministrijas fonds, 1632/2/608. Sarakste par mācību spēku pieņemšanu augstskolā, par vēstures-filoloģijas fakultātes pārdēvēšanu. Letter from von Denffer to the Vice-Principal, 1919/09/17; Latvijas Universitātes fonds, 7427/6/1, Organisation Committee Minutes, 1919/09/19. Naturally, von Denffer may have been prompted to take this stand due to ethnic and colleagual ties, and not solely to considerations of scientific standards. He was born in Jelgava, was a Latvian citizen and had been professor at the former Riga Polytechnical Institute for twenty years before joining *Latvijas Augstskola* in 1919. Latvijas Universitātes fonds, 7427/13/372, Staff records.

[98] LVVA. Latvijas Universitātes fonds, 7427/6/1, Organisation Committee Minutes, 1919/09/19. The matter appears to have been very sensitive. At the same committee meeting, the information that possibly only one of the faculty candidates in Law and Economics could lecture in Latvian was received in silence.

ment was then rejected at a subsequent meeting.⁹⁹ It is quite possible that the prolonged and somewhat unexpected absence of Pauls Valdens, the main link between the Baltic German academics of the RPI and the provisional government, considerably weakened the bargaining clout of von Denffer and the other Baltic German deans.

Paulis Lejiņš and Spricis Paegle continued to press the language issue on several occasions during the autumn of 1919.¹⁰⁰ Eventually the organisation committee adopted the policy that former staff from the RPI should be employed if there was a definite need for their particular qualifications. Otherwise, Latvian-speakers should be given preference. Former staff of the RPI who opposed the Latvians' national strivings should also be disregarded. Loyalty to the newly emerging state was obviously seen as crucial – perhaps not surprisingly, since at that time several hostile armed forces were still on Latvian soil. Only by spring 1920 did the provisional Latvian government actually have full control over its territory.¹⁰¹

However, this sceptical attitude to Baltic German academics and the emphasis on proficiency in Latvian created considerable obstacles in the recruitment process, and contributed to a severe shortage of staff in some faculties. The situation was particularly difficult in the Faculty of Medicine, and this evoked some critical responses from the Latvian community. On 24 August 1919 the Latvian newspaper *Brīvā Zeme* criticized the organisation committee for dragging its feet in employing the Baltic German professor of anatomy Alfred Sommer, who had by then reputedly obtained a post at Tartu University instead. The paper voiced the opinion that an overzealous application of the language requirement would make it very hard to find good academics for the new university.¹⁰² Sommer had, as mentioned above, actually taken part in the first meetings of the organisation committee, but had left for Tartu when he was not immediately offered a position in the Faculty of Medicine.¹⁰³

---

⁹⁹ LVVA. Latvijas Universitātes fonds, 7427/6/1, Organisation Committee Minutes, 1919/09/26; 1919/10/03.

¹⁰⁰ LVVA. Latvijas Universitātes fonds, 7427/6/1, Organisation Committee Minutes, 1919/12/10; 1919/12/19.

¹⁰¹ Dāle (1921), p. 25. In the autumn of 1919 the provisional Latvian government was still threatened by a remaining German army under von der Golz and the nominally 'White Russian' troops of Bermont in Kurzeme, while the Bolsheviks controlled a large part of Latgale in the east.

¹⁰² LVVA. Izglītības ministrijas fonds, 1632/2/608. Sarakste par mācību spēku pieņemšanu augstskolā, par vēstures-filoloģijas fakultātes pārdēvēšanu. Paper clippings, added to the letter from professor Sommer applying for a post in Riga. *Brīvā Zeme* was the main paper of the Farmers' Union, the party behind Prime Minister Kārlis Ulmanis, and this article may have mirrored a political conflict between Ulmanis and Kasparsons, Minister of Education, on this issue.

¹⁰³ LVVA. Latvijas Universitātes fonds, 7427/6/1, Organisation Committee Minutes, 1919/08/08; 1919/08/19. Professor Zariņš admitted in November that the delay of Sommer's

Even the section of higher education of the Latvian Association of Riga, one of the prime movers behind university education in the Latvian language, appears to have worried about the organisation committee's recruitment policy. In 1919 they wrote to the Ministry of Education, expressing concern that recruitment to the natural sciences would be seriously hampered if well-qualified academics of other nationalities were not accepted.[104]

There were also some reactions from students when the lack of merited academic staff in some vital subjects became apparent. In 1920, the law students in the Faculty of Law and Economics appealed to the principal to recruit professors of law from some of the Russian universities – otherwise, they argued, the quality of tuition in this discipline would suffer seriously. This demand was furthered to the organisation committee, where it appears to have had, at most, a lukewarm reception.[105]

Troublesome relations: the Faculty of Law and Economics

Relations between the Faculty of Law and Economics and the organisation committee appear to have been rather strained in the early years. Not only was the requirement to teach in Latvian very hard to meet for many of the academic staff; it also emerged that one of the faculty's most prominent academics soon found himself under a political cloud. Professor Kārlis Balodis had received a very warm welcome from colleagues in the organisation committee when he returned to Riga from Berlin just in time for the inauguration ceremony. An economist with a solid international reputation, Balodis was no doubt expected to be an important figurehead of the new university. The organisation committee duly appointed him vice-principal. However, in January 1920 a government decision barred him from this position. It transpired that Balodis was in fact a German citizen and was unwilling to adopt Latvian citizenship for fear of losing some of his material assets in Germany. The Latvian government, therefore, seems to have viewed him with

---

appointment was the first debacle leading to the sorry state of the Faculty of Medicine. Ibid., 1919/11/19. Arnis Vīksna, in his recent monograph on the Faculty of Medicine in Riga, prefers to see Sommer's departure to Tartu as a rational choice: the material conditions for starting academic training in medicine were far better than in Riga. Vīksna, A (2011), p. 25. Sommer remained as professor of anatomy at Tartu University until 1929. See Tankler, Hain & Rämmer, Algo (2004): *Tartu University and Latvia, with an Emphasis on Relations in the 1920s and 1930s*, p. 102.

[104] LVVA. Izglītības ministrijas fonds, 1632/2/608. Sarakste par mācību spēku pieņemšanu augstskolā, par vēstures-filoloģijas fakultātes pārdēvēšanu. Letter, 1919/09/05.

[105] LVVA. Izglītības ministrijas fonds, 1632/2/632. Sarakste ar Latvijas Augstskolu par mācības spēku ievēlēšanu. Request from law students to the Organistaion Committee, 1920/06/07.

some suspicion: his loyalty was questioned and his Latvian ethnicity was, in their eyes, clearly not enough.[106]

However, a general meeting of students strongly protested against the Cabinet's treatment of Balodis, declaring it to be an example of undue political interference and a serious infringement on academic liberties.[107] The Balodis affair was undoubtedly embarrassing for the organisation committee. A prospective figurehead of the national university could not possibly at the same time be a German citizen. Probably feeling that his credibility had diminished, Balodis immediately resigned as dean and the relations between his faculty and the organisation committee were obviously strained.[108]

These tensions spilled over to the sensitive matter of recruitment. On several occasions, representatives of the Faculty of Law and Economics argued for the need to recruit 'foreign' academics, especially in Law where there was a great need for qualified lecturers, and to give academic competence clear priority.[109] The organisation committee, however, was not keen to recruit Russian specialists in Law. Paulis Lejiņš, in particular, repeatedly questioned initiatives to persuade Russian academics to come to Riga. Very few such recruitments actually materialised in the initial years, primarily because the organisation committee, even when grudgingly convinced of the necessity, was only prepared to offer Russian academics two-year contracts. Such very limited tenure appears to have been rather unpopular among the Russians, since their reception by Soviet-Russian universities after the period in question would no doubt be rather uncertain.[110]

A year later, in 1921, a new controversy arose between the Faculty of Law and Economics and the organisation committee. The faculty had elected the jurist Pauls Mincs as professor. Mincs had studied Law at Dorpat/Jur'ev and Moscow Universities, and had been teaching at the new university in Riga since 1919.[111] However, Mincs was not an ethnic Latvian; he belonged to the Jewish *tautība*,

---

[106] LVVA. Latvijas Universitātes fonds, 7427/6/1, Organisation Committee Minutes, 1920/01/07; 1920/01/21. Indeed, Balodis appears to have had political ambitions in both Latvia and Germany. When he found himself blocked from influencing economic policy in Latvia, he for a while played with the idea of finding a position in Weimar Germany instead. See Balabkins, Nikolajs and Šneps, Manfrēds (1993): *Kad Latvijā būs labklājības valsts. Tautsaimnieks Kārlis Balodis*, pp. 149–150. In 1922, Balodis still defined his citizenship as 'German'. LVVA. Latvijas Universitātes fonds, 7427/13/128. Staff records.
[107] LVVA. Izglītības ministrijas fonds, 1632/2/632. Sarakste ar Latvijas Augstskolu par mācības spēku ievēlēšanu. Missive from a general meeting of students, 1920/02/15.
[108] LVVA. Latvijas Universitātes fonds, 7427/6/1, Organisation Committee Minutes, 1920/02/18.
[109] See, for instance, LVVA. Latvijas Universitātes fonds, 7427/6/1, Organisation Committee Minutes, 1920/06/02; 1920/09/24.
[110] LVVA. Latvijas Universitātes fonds, 7427/6/1, Organisation Committee Minutes, 1920/06/02.
[111] LVVA. Latvijas Universitātes fonds, 7427/13/1162. Staff records.

and was also politically active in one of the Jewish political parties.[112] This prompted some discussion within the organisation committee. Lejiņš, Dāle and Maldons held that Mincs, although described as a 'very capable person', was far too occupied with politics to simultaneously hold a chair at the university.

Felsbergs, who was also deeply involved in politics, clearly found this hypocritical. Several prominent academics at the university were active in the provisional parliament. Jānis Čakste, one of the leading politicians in the Latvian struggle for independence and the Republic's first president, had actually been elected professor in the Faculty of Law and Economics. Moreover, Kārlis Puriņš, dean of the same faculty between October 1919 and March 1920, served as Minister of Finance for a short period in 1920.[113] There were many ties and interconnections between the Latvian academics at the *augstskola* and the government ministries.

On the matter of Pauls Mincs, dean Birkhāns, speaking on behalf the faculty, warmly recommended his election. Obviously a sensitive matter, the decision was postponed, allowing Dāle and Felsbergs to interrogate Mincs about the extent of his political obligations. Finding the interview satisfactory, the committee later decided to appoint Mincs, but on one condition: his lectures were to be held in Latvian. Even so, it should be noted that four members voted against the appointment.[114] Pauls Mincs, together with Mečislavs Centneršvērs in Chemistry and Naum Lebedinski in Zoology, was one of the very few Jewish professors appointed at the University of Latvia during the First Republic.[115]

The case of Centneršvērs is especially interesting in that it illustrates the problems connected with ethnic categorisation. Born in Warsaw and educated at Leipzig and St Petersburg, Centneršvērs worked in the Riga Polytechnical Institute (RPI) from 1898. Due to the imperial ban on state employment of Jews,

---

[112] Mincs belonged to the National Democratic Party, which consisted primarily of educated middle-class Jews. See Mendelsohn, Ezra (1987): *The Jews of East Central Europe between the World Wars*, p. 248.

[113] *Latvijas Universitāte divdesmit gados, 1919–1939* (1939) I, p. 749; II, p. 534.

[114] LVVA. Latvijas Universitātes fonds, 7427/6/1, Organisation Committee Minutes, 1921/02/16; 1921/02/23. It should perhaps also be noted that the Organisation Committee had, without discussion, one month previously voted solidly against the appointment of the Jewish jurist Max Lazarson/Makss Lazarsons. Ibid., 1921/01/19. Lazarson later became a leader of a leftist Zionist party in the *Saeima*. See Garleff, Michael (2005): "Die baltischen Staaten und die Juden 1918–1940", p. 103.

[115] Centneršvērs belonged to the former RPI staff that was taken over in 1919. The appointment of Lebedinski appears to have been smooth: 24 'ayes', 2 against and 2 abstaining. LVVA. Latvijas Universitātes fonds, 7427/6/1, Organisation Committee Minutes, 1921/10/12. The absence of openly anti-Semitic or anti-Jewish comments in the minutes makes it more difficult to argue that Jewish academics especially were systematically discriminated. Consider, for instance, the committee's refusal in 1921 to appoint J. Goldšteins as *privāt-docents* in physics. Should this be seen as an instance of discrimination? See ibid., 1921/10/26. For a more thorough discussion of discrimination against Jewish academics, see chapter 5.

he was dismissed in 1902 but reinstated as docent in 1908. He was one of the evacuees when the RPI was removed to Moscow in 1915, returned to Riga in 1918 and was appointed professor of chemistry at *Latvijas Augstskola* in September 1919. He exchanged his Polish citizenship for Latvian in 1922 but in university questionnaires consistently stated that his *tautība* was Polish and his religion Jewish. At the same time he was married to a Baltic German woman, and corresponded with university officials in German. In spite of these ambiguities, the university administrators recorded his *tautība* as 'Jewish'.[116]

Returning to the Faculty of Law and Economics, it seems that its attitude to the appointment of academics of Baltic German extraction was comparatively open. In 1921, for instance, the dean, Ernests Birkhāns, strenuously tried to convince the organisation committee to accept the faculty's appointment of Friedrich Treu, son of a Baltic German RPI professor, as *docents*. Perhaps not surprisingly, the principal, Ernsts Felsbergs, along with Lejiņš and Paegle, argued against this, proposing instead that an ethnic Latvian candidate should be appointed. To Birkhāns's obvious disappointment, the election of Treu was not condoned by the organisation committee.[117]

Like the technical and science faculties, the Faculty of Law and Economics had strong personal ties with the former RPI. In the summer of 1920, the ethnic composition of its teaching staff was categorised as follows: nine Germans, four Latvians, one Jew and one Englishman.[118]

Most of the Baltic Germans had previously worked at the RPI. This group of experienced academics included, among others, Benedikt Frese, professor in Roman law, with an impressive academic record from Russian universities, Friedrich Hänsell, a statistician and economic historian, and Alfred von Hedenström, who lectured mainly on the geography of commerce and on modern history. Frese and von Hedenström were in their early fifties when they were appointed, Hänsell a few years younger. They all contributed considerable academic expertise, but Frese and Hänsell especially seem to have had difficulties lecturing in Latvian.[119]

---

[116] LVVA. Latvijas Universitātes fonds, 7427/13/311. Personal file. The case of Naum Lebedinski is also difficult to interpret. A Swiss citizen but born in Odessa, he was appointed professor of zoology in 1921. In his first employment file he noted his religion as 'Mosaic', the following year he left that particular section blank, and yet a year later he denoted himself 'evangelical-Lutheran'. It remains unclear whether Lebedinski actually converted, or simply found it easier to denote himself a Lutheran. LVVA. Latvijas Universitātes fonds, 7427/13/984. Staff records.

[117] LVVA. Latvijas Universitātes fonds, 7427/6/1, Organisation Committee Minutes, 1921/03/16; 1921/03/22.

[118] LVVA. Latvijas Universitātes fonds, 7427/6/37a. Pārskats par Latvijas augstskolas, vēlāk Universitātes, nodibināšanu un viņas darbību. Overview of the ethnic composition of the teaching staff in the faculties, 1920/06/26.

[119] LVVA. Latvijas Universitātes fonds, 7427/13/504; 7427/13/624; 7427/13/633. Staff records.

As we have seen, von Hedenström was one of the original members of the organisation committee, but the office of dean was immediately handed to Latvian colleagues. The dean in charge from spring 1920, Ernests Birkhāns, was an ethnic Latvian who also had strong ties with the former RPI. He studied there and was later sent abroad on a government scholarship to study trade and commerce at Leipzig University and other institutions in Western Europe. He returned and lectured at the RPI from 1900, was an exile in Moscow and the Caucasus during the war and joined the newly formed *Latvijas Augstskola* in 1920 at the age of forty-eight.[120]

Together with economist Kārlis Balodis, Birkhāns belonged to a 'middle' generation of well-qualified academics, trained at both German and Imperial Russian institutions, but he was also an old colleague of several of the Baltic German academics in the faculty. While certainly not averse to the general national agenda of *Latvijas Augstskola*, both Birkhāns and Balodis seem to have given priority to the faculty's pragmatic need to recruit competent academics in Law and Commerce. Especially in Law, Birkhāns and Balodis several times suggested the election of ethnic Russian academics in order to manage the teaching assignments. The number of students enrolled at the faculty rose swiftly, from 174 in the autumn of 1919 to 556 the following year.[121] The urgent need for teaching staff led, as we have seen, to some confrontations with the organisation committee.

Eventually, the persistent lack of ethnic Latvian academics qualified in Law convinced the committee that it was necessary to appoint trained specialists belonging to other nationalities – but only for limited periods, not full tenure. This ensured that during the initial years, the 'middle' generation of professors in this discipline, apart from the previously mentioned Pauls Mincs, were primarily of Russian, Polish or Baltic German extraction.[122] This group included the ethnic Russian Vladimir Bukovski, appointed in September 1921, and the ethnic Pole Vjačeslav Gribovski, first appointed in October 1920. Bukovski was an experienced judge and had served in courts in Jelgava and Riga for almost twenty years before his appointment. He had also been a member of the Latvian commission for the codification of a new civil law. Gribovski, on the other hand, was a very experienced academic, having previously been professor at various

---

[120] *Latvijas Universitāte divdesmit gados, 1919–1939* (1939), II, p. 523.
[121] *Latvijas Universitāte divdesmit gados, 1919–1939* (1939), I, pp. 735–736.
[122] The only ethnic Latvian professor in law during the formative years was in fact the state president Jānis Čakste, but his many political duties meant that he only taught courses in international law during the academic year 1920–1921. See *Latvijas Universitāte divdesmit gados, 1919–1939* (1939), I, pp. 747–749; II, pp. 524–535; Stradiņš, Jānis (1999): "Jānis Čakste un demokrātijas ideju iedibināšana Latvijā", p. 9.

Russian universities for eleven years. Both were in their early fifties when appointed by the organisation committee.[123]

The Latvians in the Law Department during these initial years belonged to a 'younger', less influential generation: Kārlis Dišlers and Pēteris Lejiņš were in their early forties when appointed *docenti* at *Latvijas Augstskola* in 1920.[124]

Summing up, the situation in the faculty did not correspond very well with the expectations of a national agenda. The ties with the former Baltic German Riga Polytechnical Institute (RPI) were strong, and academics from that institution clearly dominated the faculty in the initial years. Moreover, the most prominent of the Latvian academics, economist Kārlis Balodis, did not meet national expectations either: he refused to relinquish his German citizenship, and was henceforth barred from academic office. Faced with a lack of qualified Latvian academics, the faculty leadership struggled to reconcile the national policies of the organisation committee with the faculty's commitment to teach a rapidly increasing number of students.

Worse trouble: the Faculty of Medicine

The sharpest and most persistent conflict over the recruitment of non-Latvian academics seems to have arisen between the Faculty of Medicine and the organisation committee. Here, the lack of qualified staff seems to have been most serious while the courses were over-filled with medical students. In the autumn of 1919, more than three hundred students enrolled in the Faculty of Medicine, making it the second largest at the new *augstskola*.[125] Professor Eduards Zariņš, a pharmacologist who on Alfred Sommer's departure for Tartu was put in charge of developing the Faculty of Medicine, repeatedly complained that it was impossible to run the faculty without adequately trained staff.[126] Apparently, at

---

[123] LVVA. Latvijas Universitātes fonds, 7427/13/570; 7427/13/283. Staff records.
[124] *Latvijas Universitāte divdesmit gados, 1919–1939* (1939), II, pp. 526, 531. This group also included the judge Aleksandrs Būmanis, appointed as part-time *docents* in October 1921. LVVA. Latvijas Universitātes fonds, 7427/13/287. Staff records.
[125] According to Vīksna, 334 students had registered for studies in medicine in early October 1919. However, the resumption of warfare in Latvia during the autumn meant that teaching in the Faculty of Medicine was much reduced until February 1920. Vīksna, A (2011), p. 31. According to the *augstskola's* own statistics, 85 students were registered in the Faculty of Medicine in December 1919. LVVA. Latvijas Universitātes fonds, 7427/6/54, Gadu statistiskās ziņas par studentu un mācības spēku sastāvu.
[126] LVVA. Latvijas Universitātes fonds, 7427/6/1, Organisation Committee Minutes, 1919/09/12; 1919/09/23; 1919/11/19. Sommer seems to have preferred a position at Tartu University, and was appointed professor of anatomy there already on 25 August 1919. Vīksna, A (2011), p. 25.

that point Zariņš had only four medical doctors at his disposal as lecturers.[127] Some Latvian academics at Russian universities had been summoned to Riga but those who favoured this option had great difficulties in leaving the Soviet Union.

As an emergency measure, the organisation committee accepted the election of the Swedish anatomist and physical anthropologist Gaston Backman, although the salary he demanded was considered far too high.[128] Within the committee, Paulis Lejiņš and several others opposed Backman's appointment, arguing that all professors at the *augstskola* should receive the same salary. This time, however, Lejiņš was forced to back-peddle and acknowledge the great value of recruiting established foreign academics for the new university.[129]

Things did not improve much during the following spring. In April 1920 Zariņš declared to the committee that there was a need for at least one qualified professor of surgery, and nominated the Baltic German Otto Hohlbeck as the faculty's candidate. Lejiņš was again critical, asserting that this was contrary to the previous decision of giving priority to Latvian as the language of instruction. Dāle and bacteriologist Augusts Kirhenšteins from the Faculty of Agronomy argued that it was far more constructive to send Latvian doctors abroad to get the necessary specialist training, Dāle adding that this was also the Ministry of Education's belief.[130]

When Hohlbeck was turned down in a formal election a few months later, Zariņš reacted with great disappointment and announced his resignation as dean. The split vote in the committee indicates that there were strong differences of opinion. One of the other deans expressed his surprise at the organisation committee's lack of confidence in the Faculty of Medicine's judgement, and their insensitivity to the desperate staffing conditions in that faculty.[131] When shortly afterwards a professorship in surgery was announced for open application, the committee bypassed several well-merited foreign academics and appointed the Latvian surgeon Jēkabs Alksnis as *docents*.[132]

---

[127] LVVA. Latvijas Universitātes fonds, 7427/6/47, Medicīnas fakultātes darbības pārskats, 1919. g – 1938. g. All of them, except Zariņš, were members of the Society of Latvian Physicians. See Vīksna, A (2011), p. 26.
[128] LVVA. Latvijas Universitātes fonds, 7427/6/1, Organisation Committee Minutes, 1919/09/30; 7427/13/114, Staff records.
[129] LVVA. Latvijas Universitātes fonds, 7427/6/1, Organisation Committee Minutes, 1919/12/19; 1920/01/07.
[130] LVVA. Latvijas Universitātes fonds, 7427/6/1, Organisation Committee Minutes, 1920/04/14.
[131] LVVA. Latvijas Universitātes fonds, 7427/6/1, Organisation Committee Minutes, 1920/06/30.
[132] Vīksna, A (2011), p. 34. Alksnis was an experienced surgeon who had run a private clinic in Liepāja before the war. He had very good connections with Latvian political circles, having served as a medical officer and war clinic surgeon during the War of Liberation. He immediately became a member of the Organisation Committee. *Latvijas Universitāte divdesmit gados, 1919–1939* (1939), II, pp. 401–402.

3. CREATING A 'CASTLE OF LIGHT'

The arrival of the long-awaited professor Roberts Krimbergs from Kharkov in September 1920 was naturally a great relief, but understaffing remained a chronic problem. A new batch of students had enrolled, 241 in the Faculty of Medicine alone.[133] Apart from Krimbergs, practically all lecturing during the first two years was delivered by only three professors: the Latvians Paukulis in pathology and Zariņš in pharmacology, and the Swedish anatomist Gaston Backman in most other subjects.[134]

Krimbergs, the new dean, soon complained bitterly about the persistent lack of teaching staff in the Faculty of Medicine, which, he maintained, made it impossible to organise tuition at a reasonably scientific level.[135] When the organisation committee made an effort to find more staff, it seems to have had its fair share of bad luck. One of the eagerly expected Latvian medical professors, Kundziņš, could not be persuaded to leave Tartu since the Estonian government refused to let him bring his voluminous scientific collection of anatomical samples.[136] Of three professors recruited later, one died before arrival, and another decided after a brief and apparently discouraging visit to Riga to remain in his native Poland.[137]

The third recruit, the eminent Baltic German professor Karl Dehio, however, caused some more serious friction between the Faculty of Medicine, the organisation committee, and the government. In October 1920 the appointment of Dehio was proposed by Krimbergs and the Faculty of Medicine, and the organisation committee duly elected him professor by a clear majority.[138] However, the following week the Latvian government refused to condone Dehio's appointment, and made no secret of the fact that the reasons were entirely political.[139] Dehio had served as principal at the briefly existing German

---

[133] LVVA. Latvijas Universitātes fonds, 7427/6/54, Gadu statistiskās ziņas par studentu un mācības spēku sastāvu.
[134] LVVA. Latvijas Universitātes fonds, 7427/6/37a. Pārskats par Latvijas augstskolas, vēlāk Universitātes, nodibināšanu un viņas darbību. Overview of the teaching staff in the faculties, 1919/20; *Latvijas Universitātes piecgadu darbības pārskats 1919–1924* (1925), p. 178.
[135] LVVA. Izglītības ministrijas fonds, 1632/2/633. Sarakste ar Latvijas Augstskolu par mācības spēku pieņemšanu darbā. Letter from Krimbergs to the Ministry of Education, complaining that the Faculty of Medicine under the present circumstances could not meet scientific standards.
[136] LVVA. Latvijas Universitātes fonds, 7427/6/1, Organisation Committee Minutes, 1919/09/23; 1919/11/19; 1920/02/04.
[137] LVVA. Latvijas Universitātes fonds, 7427/6/1, Organisation Committee Minutes, 1920/09/08. The organising committee accepted that the Faculty of Medicine could recruit Polish staff on one-year contracts, but these efforts seem to have been fruitless.
[138] LVVA. Latvijas Universitātes fonds, 7427/6/1, Organisation Committee Minutes, 1920/10/13.
[139] LVVA. Latvijas Universitātes fonds, 7427/6/1, Organisation Committee Minutes, 1920/10/20.

university of Dorpat in 1918–1919, and was probably therefore seen as being far too close to supposedly 'disloyal' Baltic German political circles.[140]

Krimbergs found the situation untenable: he claimed that the faculty needed three specialists in internal medicine, now they had none. Even Spricis Paegle, the non-academic member from the Latvian Society who usually advocated a preference for Latvian-speakers in all recruitment matters, found the government's refusal to endorse the organisation committee's election deeply insulting. The committee defiantly resolved to adhere to its previous decision to appoint Dehio, and that the Ministry should be approached in order to explain the difficult circumstances in the Faculty of Medicine.[141]

In the week that followed, the Dehio affair took an entirely new turn. The Minister of Education, the national conservative linguist Juris Plāķis who had replaced the more liberal Kasparsons, had announced that he would only reconsider Dehio's appointment if the latter was re-elected by an overwhelming majority of the organisation committee.[142] Krimbergs claimed that the talks with the minister had improved the prospect of having Dehio accepted. The commission's discussions, however, soon showed that Krimbergs had been far too optimistic. While some of the members, among them the newly arrived professor of linguistics, Jānis Endzelīns, were quite prepared to consider scientific competence only and rely on the Faculty of Medicine's opinion, it emerged that many of the other members now clearly opposed Dehio's appointment. One of the latter was the celebrated playwright Jānis Rainis, who for the first time exercised his right to attend the committee in his capacity as an elected Honorary Fellow. Rainis spoke strongly against Dehio, claiming that he was much too involved in Baltic German politics and also a known enemy of 'smaller nations'. For Rainis, appointing someone like Dehio to a university that should, as he put it, embody the spirit of the Latvian nation, was simply unthinkable.

Others, especially the committee members representing the Latvian organisations, sided with Rainis, declaring that Dehio was in fact an enemy of the Latvian people and his eventual election would be an insult to the *augstskola* and to Latvian society in general. When the matter was finally put to the vote, instead of the clear majority needed to appoint Dehio, there was a narrow majority against.[143] Evidently, the political resistance to Dehio's

---

[140] *Latvijas Universitātes piecgadu darbības pārskats 1919.–1924.* (1925), pp. 179–180; Seesemann, Heinrich (1987): "350 Jahre Universität Dorpat", p. 362.
[141] LVVA. Latvijas Universitātes fonds, 7427/6/1, Organisation Committee Minutes, 1920/10/20.
[142] Juris Plāķis was actually a *docents* in linguistics at the *augstskola*, and a previous member of the Organisation Committee. LVVA. Latvijas Universitātes fonds, 7427/13/1329. Staff records. Politically he was a national conservative. On Plāķis, see chapter 5 and 7.
[143] LVVA. Latvijas Universitātes fonds, 7427/6/1, Organisation Committee Minutes, 1920/10/27. The vote was 13 for Dehio, 14 against, and 2 abstaining.

appointment had grown considerably within the organisation committee, making his election impossible.

Frustrated by the seemingly endless shortage of staff, the Faculty of Medicine immediately filed a formal protest. Since two of the faculty's appointments had been overruled by the organisation committee, the faculty declared that it could no longer to take responsibility for the situation. The complaint had a rather cool reception: Dāle maintained that he could not see any constructive potential in such negative actions.[144] Instead of subsiding, however, the conflict between the Faculty of Medicine and the organising committee seems to have deepened. Krimbergs now reopened the case of Otto Hohlbeck, whose appointment the committee had previously turned down. The Faculty of Medicine moved to re-appoint Hohlbeck, Krimbergs again nominating him for formal election by the organisation committee. Hohlbeck failed to get the required two-thirds majority, and was consequently turned down once more. The linguist Endzelīns, who had evidently supported Hohlbeck, deplored that in his opinion the committee's academic members, the deans, had been far too silent in the discussion about Hohlbeck. Instead, the meeting had been dominated by the politically appointed non-academic members. Arguments on issues such as scientific competence and under-staffing, Endzelīns claimed, had not been sufficiently voiced.[145]

Reacting angrily to the second rejection of Hohlbeck, Krimbergs and the Faculty of Medicine launched an open attack on the organisation committee. At a committee meeting, Krimbergs claimed that the refusal to appoint Hohlbeck had not been based on consideration of his scientific merits: it therefore had nothing to do with science or academic standards. This attack undoubtedly drew embarrassing attention to the dilemma of reconciling academic and national prerogatives. The art historian Ernsts Felsbergs, who chaired the meeting in Dāle's absence, declared that he found Krimbergs's allegations insulting and would immediately resign his chairmanship if the committee did not give him its full support. Krimbergs in turn would not be moved, claiming that he had the entire Faculty of Medicine behind him on this issue.

The meeting developed into a ferocious argument. Krimbergs insisted that the Faculty of Medicine alone was competent to judge Hohlbeck's scientific record, and the committee's repeated refusals to appoint candidates selected by the faculty simply could not be tolerated. In this matter he received some support from the linguist Endzelīns, who again criticised the other deans for not speaking out in support of the 'academic' side of the discussion. Felsbergs, on the

---

[144] LVVA. Latvijas Universitātes fonds, 7427/6/390, LU Medicīnas fakultātes sēžu protokoli, 1920/12/06; 7427/6/1, Organisation Committee Minutes, 1920/11/03.
[145] LVVA. Latvijas Universitātes fonds, 7427/6/1, Organisation Committee Minutes, 1920/11/17; 1920/11/24.

other hand, could not publicly admit that the committee's appointments were not based on a serious evaluation of scientific records – that would surely have eroded the committee's academic credibility as well as the new *augstskola's* reputation. Lejiņš reiterated his position that 'foreign' academics should only be recruited if they were truly 'eminent' – which he evidently thought Hohlbeck was not. In this matter, Lejiņš was supported by some of the committee's non-academic members.

After some calls for calm and moderation, the committee voted that Krimbergs's statements did not actually constitute an insult and should be seen instead as expressions of 'groundless suspicions'. The committee voted solidly in favour of this interpretation: fourteen for, two against, and seven abstaining, which presumably means that Krimbergs and Zariņš from the Faculty of Medicine were the only ones who actively voted against. Evidently, it was simply out of the question to openly admit that appointments of professors were subject to political vetting. Lejiņš, who had advocated a more sharply formulated statement directed at Krimbergs, left the meeting shortly afterwards.[146]

After this, Krimbergs again rallied the Faculty of Medicine behind him. The Faculty Board fully supported his stand and maintained that they alone were competent to judge the scientific qualifications of appointees.[147] The discontent within the faculty was further fuelled by the difficulties experienced in selecting assistants: the organisation committee would only accept assistants who could teach in Latvian. Lejiņš declared that this was essential: otherwise, he claimed, the academic chairs at the university would in future be taken over by 'foreigners'.[148]

This conflict appears to have been notably acrimonious and the discussion in the organisation committee continued. The linguist Endzelīns, perhaps the most active proponent of recruitment based primarily on academic merit, was obviously not convinced that the vetoing of some of the Baltic German medical specialists was reasonable. He publicly voiced his opinion that the appointment of Dehio, for instance, had been blocked purely due to the candidate's Baltic German ethnicity. Felsbergs and Dāle argued strongly against this interpretation. They both maintained that it was Dehio's 'politics' which made him unsuitable,

---

[146] LVVA. Latvijas Universitātes fonds, 7427/6/1, Organisation Committee Minutes, 1920/12/01. Besides arguing against Krimbergs, Lejiņš had accused the committee secretary, Broedermans, for making partial formulations in previous protocols. When the committee supported Broedermans against these charges, Lejiņš left the room.

[147] LVVA. Latvijas Universitātes fonds, 7427/6/390, Medical Faculty Board Minutes, 1920/12/06.

[148] LVVA. Latvijas Universitātes fonds, 7427/6/1, Organisation Committee Minutes, 1921/03/02. The term used was 'sveštautības spēks'. See also ibid., 1921/03/16, where Krimbergs managed to gain acceptance for an assistant in pathological anatomy *for one year* after averring that no-one else was to be found, and that the person in question had a 'sufficient' command of Latvian.

not his ethnicity; this was described as a 'misunderstanding'. Endzelīns remained unimpressed, claiming that there was no evidence that Dehio was in fact hostile to the Latvian nation.[149] The matter was naturally very sensitive. Apart from purely academic considerations, basic democratic principles ruled out open discrimination of citizens belonging to the 'minorities'.

The Faculty of Medicine's resentment at these failed appointments did not fade away. Almost twenty years later, when Krimbergs and Prīmanis wrote an official historical overview of the faculty, they could not refrain from recounting some details of the Hohlbeck and Dehio affairs.[150] These critical passages stand out in an official 'story' whose main narrative was a recapitulation of the successful establishment of the University of Latvia.

It should be added, however, that the organisation committee appears to have been much more favourably disposed to another Baltic German specialist in internal medicine, Mazing – although even Endzelīns found his demand for a *twenty*-year grace period before having to teach in Latvian clearly unacceptable. Mazing was nevertheless appointed, but never took up his post in Riga.[151] Not until 1922 was the problem of recruiting a competent professor in internal medicine apparently resolved when the ethnic Latvian Mārtiņš Zīle, previously professor in Odessa, managed to reach Riga.[152]

In conclusion, the conflict over the recruitment of 'foreign' academics apparently came to a head in the Faculty of Medicine because this faculty had the most explosive combination of preconditions: a severe shortage of staff, a very large admission of students, and, probably, a set of academics who were above all scientists and pragmatists and not prepared to give priority to nationalist concerns that would lower the quality of teaching. The professors of Medicine, including those whose Latvian ethnicity cannot be questioned, clearly gave priority to pragmatic and professional considerations. As has been shown above, the Faculty of Medicine seems to have been far more ready to recruit 'foreign' academics than many members of the organisation committee. Professor Krimbergs at one point even tried to make use of Latvia's Berlin

---

[149] LVVA. Latvijas Universitātes fonds, 7427/6/1, Organisation Committee Minutes, 1920/12/15. Felsbergs added, probably with little foundation, that 'many' specialists in internal medicine were able to lecture in Latvian. Krimbergs hardly found this very helpful.
[150] *Latvijas Universitāte divdesmit gados, 1919–1939* (1939), I, pp. 590–592.
[151] LVVA. Latvijas Universitātes fonds, 7427/6/1, Organisation Committee Minutes, 1920/12/15; 1920/12/22; 1921/02/02. The committee also voted in favour of calling the ethnic Russian professor Maksimov from St Petersburg University. Ibid., 1921/04/13. Like Mazing, however, Maksimov never joined the University of Latvia.
[152] LVVA. Latvijas Universitātes fonds, 7427/13/2010. Staff records; 7427/6/1, Organisation Committee Minutes, 1922/04/22. Zīle later became principal of the University of Latvia for the period 1927–28.

embassy in an attempt to attract medical specialists from Germany, a line of action that no other faculty used.[153]

Another reason why this conflict came to the fore in the Faculty of Medicine may have been precisely because the leading professors, Krimbergs and Zariņš, were ethnic Latvians. In some of the technical and natural science faculties there was also a lack of properly trained scientists, but here the staff was to a far greater extent dominated by Baltic Germans from the former RPI. Running the risk of being seen as disloyal 'foreigners', these academics probably did not find it prudent to challenge the organisation committee's authority in the same direct manner as Krimbergs and Zariņš.

In the committee, as we have seen, there appears to have been a decided resistance to the recruitment of ethnic Baltic Germans and Jews, with especially Lejiņš and the non-academic members insisting that 'native' candidates should be preferred. Since appointments required a two-thirds majority in the committee, it was fairly easy for the 'nationalist' side to block the election of academics from the ethnic minorities.[154] In spite of the fact that most of the qualified medical professors in the area belonged to the Baltic German *tautība*, only one of these was actually appointed professor at the University of Latvia – and he eventually chose to decline the invitation. By summer 1923, all four medical departments were directed by ethnic Latvian professors: Krimbergs, Paukulis, Ruberts and Zīle. Only one Baltic German, Roman Adelheim, was part of the teaching staff, and there were certainly no Jews. The professors included three foreign citizens: two Swiss and one Swede.[155] In contrast, at the re-organised Tartu University in Estonia, twelve of the first recruited professors of medicine were either ethnic Germans or German-speaking Jews.[156]

As we have seen, the result was severe understaffing and difficulties in complying with scientific standards.[157] Not just the staff, but also the medical students, voiced their discontent with the situation several times.[158] In the

---

[153] LVVA. Latvijas Universitātes fonds, 7427/6/1, Organisation Committee Minutes, 1920/11/17. Without apparent success, it must be added.
[154] Endzelīns and Broedermans spoke openly out about this situation, finding the committee's voting regulations far too rigorous. LVVA. Latvijas Universitātes fonds, 7427/6/1, Organisation Committee Minutes, 1920/11/24. The University Constitution from 1923 changed this, allowing for a simple majority in the university council when appointing professors. See *Latvijas Universitātes Satversme*, 1923/03/28, §§ 58–59.
[155] Vīksna, A (2011), pp. 41–42; *Latvijas Universitāte divdesmit gados, 1919–1939* (1939), I, pp. 617–618.
[156] *History of Tartu University, 1632–1982* (1985), p. 197. Already during the autumn term of 1919 the Faculty of Medicine at Tartu was staffed with five professors.
[157] According to Dāle, the Swedish anatomist Backman had complained to him that lectures in the Faculty of Medicine were held by practising doctors, not trained academics. LVVA. Latvijas Universitātes fonds, 7427/6/1, Organisation Committee Minutes, 1920/12/15.
[158] LVVA. Izglītības ministrijas fonds, 1632/2/633. Sarakste ar Latvijas Augstskolu par mācības spēku pieņemšanu darbā. Letter of complaints from medicine students to the Ministry of Edu-

organisation committee, however, the 'nationalist' members were much keener to retrieve ethnic Latvian academics from Soviet Russia, or to send Latvian doctors abroad to receive the required specialist training. Naturally, this policy was supported by Latvian physicians who were eager to be given such opportunities.[159] The group organising the Faculty of Medicine in 1919 had very strong links to the Latvian Society of Physicians, and several of them remained on the teaching staff even though they had not received any advanced academic training in medicine. In this way, the professional strategies of Latvian medical doctors became intertwined with ethnic policy at the new university.

On the political level, it seems that the Latvian government was much more prepared to provide extra money to recruit Latvian medical academics from the Soviet Union than to facilitate the recruitment of non-Latvians.[160] However, when these well-merited Latvian academics managed to reach Riga, they proved to be more interested in safeguarding academic standards than in pursuing narrow ethnic policies. Krimbergs, as well as his colleagues Ruberts and Zīle, adopted a position closer to academic and pragmatic concerns in their dealing with the university leadership.

The organisation committee: national, academic and pragmatic concerns

As we have seen, the organisation committee's propensity to favour the recruitment of ethnic Latvians and Latvian-speakers developed at times into a clear conflict between members who were more 'academic' and pragmatic on the one hand and more 'nationalist' on the other. On the 'nationalist' side it is possible to distinguish Pauls Dāle, the members from the Ministry of Education and the Latvian Society, and, perhaps most clearly, the agronomist and first vice-principal Pauls Lejiņš.

Like Dāle, Lejiņš belonged to a younger generation of academics, being appointed *docents* in 1919 at the age of thirty-six.[161] He represented the Faculty of Agronomy, one of the most 'Latvian' faculties in terms of teaching staff and

---

cation, 1920/09/10; LVVA. Latvijas Universitātes fonds, 7427/6/1, Organisation Committee Minutes, 1920/11/24.
[159] LVVA. Izglītības ministrijas fonds, 1632/2/633. Sarakste ar Latvijas Augstskolu par mācības spēku pieņemšanu darbā. Letter from med. Dr Alksnis to the ministry 1920/09/02, complaining that money was wasted on recruitment attempts directed at Polish academics instead of relying on Latvian professionals.
[160] In 1922 the government provided 50,000 Roubles in order to bring 'home' the medical professors Ruberts and Zīle from Kiev and Odessa respectively. LVVA. Izglītības ministrijas fonds, 1632/2/612, Sarakste ar Latvijas Universitāti par mācību spēkiem, mācību darbu, budžetu u. c., 1921. g. – 1922.g. Letter from Ministry of Finance to the Ministry of Education, 1922/09/12.
[161] *Latvijas Universitāte divdesmit gados, 1919–1939* (1939), I, p.234. Lejiņš was an agronomist specialized in cattle breeding.

language of instruction.[162] As we have seen, there is some evidence that established Baltic German agronomists were not invited to join this faculty – younger Latvians were deliberately selected instead.

One of the most forceful committee members advocating the 'Latvianization' of the *augstskola*, Paulis Lejiņš seems to have pursued these principles relentlessly during his period as vice-principal. When academics belonging to an ethnic minority were put forward by the faculties, Lejiņš frequently questioned the faculty's choice and insisted that 'native' candidates should be given preference. He appears to have been quite content to advocate the selection of Latvians who had not the requisite academic qualifications: this should be remedied, he argued, by arranging for them to study abroad.[163] Such a long-term strategy, however, certainly did not satisfy deans who urgently needed qualified academic staff to manage the teaching assignments.

Lejiņš's nationalist prerogatives, perhaps also his quarrelsome style, appear to have involved him in conflicts with several other committee members. In the aftermath of the sensitive Hohlbeck and Dehio affairs, Lejiņš wrote to Dāle, complaining that professor Zariņš from the Faculty of Medicine had called him 'German-hater' and 'chauvinist'. Feeling the need to explain his position, Lejiņš declared that he was in no way hostile to Latvian citizens belonging to other 'nationalities' if they had supported the Latvian government during the recent War of Liberation, or at least had remained neutral and were now loyal "in thought and deed". However, he nevertheless felt it reasonable that all government institutions, including the newly started university, should contain a representative proportion of ethnic Latvians. That meant that at least 75 per cent of the academic staff should belong to the majority nation. Moreover, the university must, he argued, echoing the opinion of Jānis Rainis, be infused with a Latvian spirit.[164]

---

[162] Already in the spring of 1920, 80 per cent of the teaching in agronomy was done in Latvian. Together with Philology and Philosophy, this made them the most 'Latvian' of the faculties. See *Latvijas Universitāte divdesmit gados, 1919–1939* (1939), I, p. 29.

[163] Apart from the above instances when Lejiņš advocated the sending abroad of Latvian doctors rather that appointing ethnic German academics, see also LVVA. Izglītības ministrijas fonds, 1632/2/632. Sarakste ar Latvijas Augstskolu par mācības spēku ievēlēšanu. Letter from P. Lejiņš to Dāle, 1920.07.01, where he in a similar manner suggested that the young Latvian philologist Arnolds Spekke should be sent abroad to improve his research record rather than the committee appointing the 'foreign' professor Schischmarewa. In this matter, however, Lejiņš was unsuccessful. Schischmarewa was finally elected (but in fact never took up the post). LVVA. Latvijas Universitātes fonds, 7427/6/1, Organisation Committee Minutes, 1920/09/24.

[164] LVVA. Izglītības ministrijas fonds, 1632/2/632. Sarakste ar Latvijas Augstskolu par mācības spēku ievēlēšanu. Letter from P. Lejiņš to the Ministry of Education, 1920/07/01; 1920/12/08; P. Lejiņš, "Personigā lietā", n.d.

This document shows that Lejiņš 'national' stance went further than merely promoting the use of Latvian as the academic language in every faculty. His agenda was clearly more ethnic, with its insistence on the great majority of staff being ethnic Latvians. However, it is interesting that in the organisation committee's discussions, Lejiņš and other members on the 'national' wing always framed their arguments in terms of language proficiency, not ethnicity. Openly advocating an ethnic principle in recruitment was clearly not an option because that would be incompatible with established academic norms and practices. To some extent, therefore, the requirement that recruited academics should be proficient in the Latvian language seems to have served as a cloak for what was really a selection based on ethnicity.

For Lejiņš, therefore, the national university project seems to have stood for the appointment of ethnic Latvian academics, and the organisation of higher education in accordance with the Latvian national spirit. Considerations of academic excellence, and the pragmatic need of qualified lecturers, seem to have been a secondary concern. As we have seen, Lejiņš consistently questioned practically all proposed appointments of non-Latvians. Apart from the previously described conflict with the dean of the Faculty of Medicine, Lejiņš had recurrent bouts with the deans of other faculties where the use of non-Latvian academics was perceived as a necessity. This was especially the case in the technical faculties, the natural sciences, architecture, and law and economics.

Sometimes his stubborn opposition must have exasperated the deans. In 1921, for instance, he demanded that two German-speaking assistants in architecture whose appointments had not been formally condoned should not receive any salary until the summer – in spite of the fact that they had taught classes during the spring term. Naturally, the dean of Architecture found this completely unreasonable.[165]

Indeed, the appointment of assistants was often contested in the committee. While even some of its more 'national' members could recognise the need to recruit some 'foreign' academics in fields where ethnic Latvians could not be found, an entirely different stance was taken on junior positions in the faculties. Here, the 'nationalist' line was that assistants and sub-assistants should only be appointed if they had command of Latvian. Apparently, this was a strategy to ensure that the next academic generation would be solidly Latvian.

The principle of only appointing Latvian-speaking assistants certainly caused some conflicts within the committee. On several occasions the Faculty of Medicine and the Faculty of Architecture, for instance, proposed the appointment of

---

[165] LVVA. Latvijas Universitātes fonds, 7427/6/1, Organisation Committee Minutes, 1921/04/06; 1921/04/13. No vote was taken on this proposition, which means that Lejiņš did not have any support on the matter in the committee.

assistants whose proficiency in Latvian was questioned by the organisation committee. The deans often argued that the proposed assistant possessed special skills that the faculty urgently needed. The outcome of such appointments varied considerably; the dean making the proposal often used his academic prestige to back his candidate. On the matter of sub-assistants, however, Paegle managed to get a majority vote for the general principle that, in order to be appointed, they must be knowledgeable in Latvian.[166]

However, Paulis Lejiņš' influence in the organisation committee appears to have already become somewhat weaker in the autumn of 1920. On 1 September Ernsts Felsbergs was elected the first acting principal and Lejiņš, who had fulfilled these duties during the first year resigned as vice-principal in November. By that time, some very influential ethnic Latvian professors had returned from Russian 'exile' and joined the organisation committee, thus changing its composition.

One of these 'returnees' was the distinguished professor of linguistics, Jānis Endzelīns. While his 'national' inclinations cannot be doubted, he nevertheless stood out as the main proponent of a recruitment policy based primarily on academic merit rather than ethnic categorisation. He consistently argued for the need of competence and academic excellence in the selection of candidates.[167] Being one of the most acclaimed academics at the new *augstskola*, Endzelīns's opinions on these matters naturally carried great weight.[168] Lejiņš's academic record was far more modest; he was not appointed professor until 1932.[169]

It is also conceivable that many of the newly-arrived Latvian academics had a different kind of national agenda and invested a different meaning in the new university. Many of them belonged to a 'middle' generation of academics who had pursued their careers within the Imperial university system and had wide networks bridging ethnic and national boundaries. For some of them, most notably Jānis Endzelīns, the national project seems to have been more about developing good 'national' scholarship and science and enhancing the

---

[166] LVVA. Latvijas Universitātes fonds, 7427/6/1, Organisation Committee Minutes, 1922/06/30. Exceptions from this rule could only be granted by the committee. The few applications brought forward were rejected. See, for instance, ibid., 1922/10/22.

[167] In other instances, Endzelīns took a thoroughly nationalist stand. In June 1920, for instance, he criticised the temporary Parliament for dallying in their border negotiations with Estonia, demanding that the committee make a forceful statement on this issue. See LVVA. Latvijas Universitātes fonds, 7427/6/1, Organisation Committee Minutes, 1920/06/29.

[168] The wide recognition of Endzelīns's academic standing is seen, for instance, in his clear election to the post as editor of the publication committee of the new *augstskola*. LVVA. Latvijas Universitātes fonds, 7427/6/1, Organisation Committee Minutes, 1920/12/22. See also below, chapter 6. Endzelīns's important role as professor of linguistics and as the first dean of the Faculty of Philology and Philosophy will be analysed in chapter 7.

[169] *Latvijas Universitāte divdesmit gados, 1919–1939* (1939), I, p. 234.

academic standard of *Latvijas Universitāte* than barring colleagues from non-Latvian backgrounds.

Moreover, many of the prestigious 'newcomers' in the early 1920s belonged to the Faculty of Philology and Philosophy, whose weight in internal university politics was therefore much increased. This is shown, for instance, in the election of the art historian and classical scholar Ernsts Felsbergs as the first principal. Many of this faculty's academics were soon heavily involved in *their* version of the national project: the codification of the Latvian language, culture, and history. These new circumstances appear to have greatly reduced the influence of Paulis Lejiņš and the Faculty of Agronomy. After his resignation as vice-principal, Lejiņš seems to have become relatively marginalised in university politics. He was not elected to the newly established university council in 1922, and did not hold any other posts at university level in the rest of the 1920s.[170]

The members of the organisation committee clearly invested different meanings in the new university. The deans of the Faculty of Medicine appear to have been most pragmatic, advocating the appointment of Baltic German specialists, condoning the continued use of German as tuition language, and also continuing to use German textbooks because they were the best alternative available. For them, the main priority was to create a national university that would provide the medical students with up-to-date scientific knowledge – and thereby provide Latvian hospitals with good doctors. Dean Roberts Krimbergs was also well acquainted with German medical academia, having received scientific training at the universities of Heidelberg and Berlin.[171]

Academic priorities were voiced most frequently by the deans of the technical faculties, the natural sciences and law and economics. These faculties had stronger ties with the previous Baltic German dominated RPI, and were led by deans with ample experience of the Russian and German university systems. As professional scientists they were primarily bound to the established academic conception that recruitment should be based on academic merit, and they were also more pragmatic about the choice of teaching language. As the

---

[170] LVVA. Latvijas Universitātes fonds, 7427/13/1000, Staff records. Lejiņš's last initiative in the Organisation Committee is perhaps typical: he questioned a collection in favour of suffering academics in the Soviet Union, claiming that collections should instead be made in favour of suffering Latvians in Latvia. Ibid., 7427/6/1, Organisation Committee Minutes, 1922/04/22. Lejiņš instead went into politics, being an elected *Saeima* delegate for the Social Democrats between 1922 and 1934. See Šilde (1976), pp. 708–716. In the 1930s he was dean of the Faculty of Agronomy for four years. *Latvijas Universitāte divdesmit gados, 1919–1939*. (1939), I, p. 235. During the first Soviet occupation in 1940–1941, Lejiņš, served for a short while as Minister of Education. After World War II Paulis Lejiņš re-emerged as the first president of the LPSR Academy of Sciences. See Stradiņš (1998), pp. 137–139; Stradiņš, Jānis (2004): "Totalitāro okupācijas režīmu represijas pret Latvijas zinātni un akadēmiskajām aprindām", p. 138.

[171] *Latvijas Universitāte divdesmit gados, 1919–1939* (1939), II, p. 416.

aforementioned incident with von Denffer highlights, they also disliked matters concerning candidates' ethnicity interfering with the process of staff selection. These faculties were clearly dominated by Baltic Germans in the early years. Latvian academics were usually in a minority in these faculties and generally also belonged to a younger generation.

Some of the Latvian scholars in the organisation committee also defended fundamental academic notions. Especially the Latvian linguist Jānis Endzelīns repeatedly questioned the committee's refusal to endorse the appointment of some merited Baltic German or Russian candidates. Endzelīns seems to have championed the ideals of academic excellence; probably because of his unquestionable Latvian credentials he was able to advocate this view from a stronger position than most of the other deans. For Endzelīns, evidently, the meaning of a national university was strongly connected with its reputation as an institution of high academic standards.

The organisation committee's 'national' wing, on the other hand, for the most part consisted of members of Latvian associations, primarily Spricis Paegle, the chairman, Pauls Dāle, and the representatives of the Faculty of Agronomy, particularly Paulis Lejiņš. Paegle evidently saw it as his mission to promote the Latvian-ness of the new university and thereby materialise the hopes and dreams of the nationalist movement. Dāle, in his mediating role between the *augstskola* and the provisional government, was probably under political pressure to curtail the influence of Baltic German academics and promote the appointment of Latvians. Lejiņš was certainly the most outspoken of the members of the 'national' wing, clearly advocating a more 'ethnic' selection of Latvian candidates over more academically qualified Baltic Germans. This was certainly a reflection of the 'ethnic reversal' in terms of political power that was taking place in Latvia at the end of World War I.

At the same time, Lejiņš's own discipline of agronomy may have been something of a special case. Predominantly a nation of farmers, young Latvians seeking higher education had tended to choose agronomy. Specialists in dairy production and other agriculturally based industries were also in great demand from Latvian farmers' cooperatives; associations that in a sense served as prototypes and training-schools for Latvian political organisations.[172] Kārlis Ulmanis, leader of the Farmers' Union, was himself an agronomist specialising in dairy production. There were, consequently, strong bonds between the farmers' cooperatives, emerging Latvian political organisations, agrarian specialists and the discipline of agronomy. There were probably strong political reasons

---

[172] Johan Eellend has developed this argument for the Estonian case. See Eellend, Johan (2007): *Cultivating the rural citizen. Modernity, agrarianism and citizenship in late Tsarist Estonia*, especially chapter 11.

why this particular academic discipline could not be allowed to be dominated by Baltic German academics.

However, the conflict between pragmatic, academic and 'national' aims does not necessarily mean that the only dividing line lay between the 'Latvian' faculties and those more dominated by Baltic German academics. In his memoirs, the historian Arnolds Spekke describes the main conflict in the university's early years as the one between the Faculty of Philology and Philosophy on the one hand and the Faculty of Agronomy on the other – actually the two faculties with the most predominantly 'Latvian' teaching staffs.[173] Spekke describes this conflict mainly in terms of politics, Left versus Right, not nationality or academic standards. We should therefore bear in mind that academic conflicts are often very complex. However, Spekke did not experience these conflicts first hand, and his account may also be influenced by hindsight.[174]

From organisation committee to university council

The original organisation committee was replaced by the new university council in September 1922. The statutes were changed in three important respects: first, the voting procedure on academic appointments was amended to require just a simple majority.[175] As shown above, the voting procedure in the organisation committee had stipulated a two-thirds majority for academic appointments, making it relatively easy for the more 'nationalist' members to block the election of non-Latvian academics.

The provision about a qualified majority had in fact been questioned for some time by the committee's academic members. In March 1922, deans of several faculties moved that the committee's voting rules on appointments should be amended to require a simple majority. The main reason was probably the frustration many of the deans had experienced when the faculties' candidates had been blocked by a committee minority. An immediate problem, however, was that the organisation committee had been unable to select a new vice-principal for student and educational matters. In spite of several attempts, none of the candidates managed to get the necessary two-thirds majority. However, the committee's non-academic members refused to alter the voting

---

[173] LVVA. Latvijas Universitātes fonds, 7427/6/37a. Pārskats par Latvijas augstskolas, vēlāk Universitātes, nodibināšanu un viņas darbību. Overview of the teaching staff, 1919/1920
[174] Spekke, Arnolds (2000): *Atmiņu brīži*, p. 92. Spekke belonged to the younger generation of Latvian academics and did not personally participate in the internal *augstskola* debates during the founding years.
[175] See *Latvijas Universitātes Satversme* (1923), §§ 58–59.

arrangements.¹⁷⁶ This rather impractical and embarrassing situation persisted until the committee was replaced by the university council.

Another important change was that the external, non-academic members of the Latvian professional organisations were no longer included. As a result, the member from the Riga Latvian Society, Spricis Paegle, one of the most forceful promoters of a national perspective in the previous committee, no longer had a seat. This probably meant that the Council's 'national' wing was decidedly less able to block appointments on ethnic grounds. Moreover, there was less direct political involvement in university matters since the governmental ministries were not represented either. The new university council consisted entirely of academics holding positions at *Latvijas Universitāte*.

The university's new constitution also ruled that deans of faculties and members of the university council must be Latvian-speakers and Latvian citizens.¹⁷⁷ This meant that those among the established Baltic German professors who could not meet the language requirement were henceforth barred from these positions. Finally, with the establishment of a fully independent and autonomous university, academic appointments no longer had to be approved by the government. As shown above, the government had previously intervened in a few instances and refused to accept the election of Baltic German academics. All such matters would henceforth be decided by the university council – with the important exception of academics who were not Latvian citizens. Their appointment still had to be approved by government.

In addition to these amendments to the statutes, it must be noted that the 'national' wing's most vociferous academic, Paulis Lejiņš, was not re-elected. Taken together, these changes implied that recruitment policy would henceforth be less influenced by ethnic considerations. On the other hand, by 1922 the most pressing recruitment issues had been solved, and the new university had a teaching staff of reasonable academic standard in most of its faculties.

The university council soon implemented some changes in recruitment policy. While permanent positions were rarely offered to academics who were not Latvian citizens, it seems to have become easier for the faculties to obtain approval for the appointment of foreign academics for limited periods. When there was an obvious lack of ethnic Latvian specialists in some fields, foreigners might be acceptable, usually for between two and five years.

This was a conscious strategy to attain high academic standards in some fields while at the same time allowing a younger generation of Latvian academics to mature and eventually take over. On these matters, the university council was somewhat more pragmatic about the appointment of foreign academics than its

---

[176] LVVA. Latvijas Universitātes fonds, 7427/6/1, Organisation Committee Minutes, 1922/03/15.
[177] *Latvijas Universitātes Satversme* (1923), § 5.

predecessor. In the Faculty of Law and Economics, for example, an ethnic Russian professor in civil law, Vasilij Sinaiski, was immediately appointed when the university council replaced the organisation committee.[178] Similarly, an open application for the hitherto vacant professorship in surgery was advertised in a number of foreign medical journals, and some eminent Russian surgeons were also encouraged to apply.[179]

Academic leadership also underwent a perceptible change in generational and ethnic terms. In some faculties, the 'younger' generation of academics took over already in the early 1920s. This seems to have been the case in the Faculty of Law and Economics, where, as mentioned earlier, the first deans, Kārlis Balodis and Ernests Birkhāns, had had some heated exchanges with the organisation committee over the recruitment of non-Latvian academics. From the autumn term of 1922 onwards, this faculty was led by two representatives of a 'younger' generation, Kārlis Dišlers and Jānis Kārkliņš, two *docenti* who actually alternated as deans for the rest of the First Republic.[180] Henceforth, the 'middle' generation, Kārlis Balodis and Ernests Birkhāns, as well as established but 'foreign' professors such as Pauls Mincs, Benedikts Frēze and Vladimirs Bukovskis, were not appointed to any of the faculty's leading positions.

In the technical and science faculties, academic leadership gradually passed from the Baltic German professors from the previous Riga Polytechnical Institute to their younger ethnic Latvian colleagues. In Engineering, for instance, the first dean, professor Edgar Jacoby, was replaced by Edmunds Ziemelis in 1922.[181] Similarly, the following year the Faculty of Mechanics' forceful dean, Paul von Denffer, resigned and was replaced by his younger Latvian colleague, Emils Āboliņš.[182]

By 1923 all the deans of Baltic German extraction had been replaced by ethnic Latvians.[183] The Baltic German professors from the previous RPI were allowed to remain at the university until retirement, but after 1923 they played a very minor role in the academic leadership. This probably meant that they

---

[178] LVVA. Latvijas Universitātes fonds, 7427/6/1, University Council Minutes, 1922/10/22; 7427/13/1569, Staff records. In the same manner, the Soviet citizen Aleksandr Kruglevski was appointed *privātdocents* in criminal law in November 1924 – initially for a three-year period, but he eventually obtained permanent tenure. Ibid., 7427/13/174. Staff records.

[179] In the end, though, two of the internal Latvian candidates were appointed. Vīksna, A (2011), pp. 41–42; 51.

[180] Dišlers was forty-two in 1920, Kārkliņš forty-three. Both formed their academic careers during the 1920s. They alternated as dean until 1938, when Kārkliņš could not assume this office since he was elected vice-principal. *Latvijas Universitāte divdesmit gados, 1919–1939*. I, (1939), pp. 736–740; II, pp. 526–528.

[181] *Latvijas Universitāte divdesmit gados, 1919–1939* (1939), I, p. 339.

[182] *Latvijas Universitāte divdesmit gados, 1919–1939* (1939), I, p. 553.

[183] LVVA. Latvijas Universitātes fonds, 7427/6/1, University Council Minutes, 1923/04/25; 1923/05/02.

also were much less able to secure career paths for promising students from the Baltic German community.

According to Pierre Bourdieu, control over career possibilities for younger academics is one of the main ways in which prestigious professors exercise power.[184] This power was now taken over by ethnic Latvian academics. A younger generation of ethnic Latvian academics was fostered in every faculty in the 1920s and 1930s, gradually replacing the 'older' and 'middle' generations of non-Latvians. The preference for young male Latvian-speakers when filling junior academic positions, like assistants and sub-assistants, ensured that in time the university staff would become more and more 'nationalised'.

However, this process was fairly protracted, depending primarily on the death or retirement of Baltic German academics in the technical and science faculties. Among the 'older' RPI professors of chemistry, for instance, Glasenapp died in 1923, Fischer in 1934, and Blacher in 1939, while Centneršvērs retired in 1930.[185] With this general phasing out of the Baltic Germans, as well as an increasing number of teaching staff, the proportion of academics categorised as belonging to the Latvian *tautība* rapidly increased from sixty per cent in 1920 to 76 per cent in 1922/23, 81 per cent in 1930/31 and 89 per cent in 1938/39.[186]

However, when it came to recruiting foreign academics, nationality seems to have been more important than merit. There was a clear preference for Finns, Swedes, Norwegians, Austrians and Swiss – academics from small and supposedly friendly nations – rather than Germans and Russians. These academics, however, never had a sizeable effect on the ethnic composition of the teaching staff. In 1922 they totalled ten persons, less than three per cent of the academic staff. This was actually the highest number and proportion that academics from these small countries ever had at *Latvijas Universitāte* during the First Republic. In the 1930s their proportion of the academic staff was little more than one per cent.[187]

Some Swiss and Swedish academics joined the Faculty of Medicine, a few more were appointed in the Faculty of Philology and Philosophy. The recruitment of Finns and Austrians appears to have failed almost completely. In spite of this predominant policy of recruitment in terms of nationality, the main group of 'non-Latvian' academics remained those categorized as 'Germans', i.e.

---

[184] Bourdieu, Pierre (1996): *Homo academicus*, see, in particular, chapter 4.
[185] *Latvijas Universitāte divdesmit gados, 1919–1939* (1939), I, p. 390. Similarly, in the Faculty of Mechanics the 'old' RPI professor Richard Henning died in 1922 and Reinhold Feldweg in 1931, while Paul von Denffer and Gustav Taube remained as emeritus professors until 1939. Ibid., p. 555.
[186] LVVA. Latvijas Universitātes fonds, 7427/6/37a. Pārskats par Latvijas augstskolas, vēlāk Universitātes, nodibināšanu un viņas darbību. Overview of the teaching staff in the faculties, 1919/20.; *Latvijas Universitāte divdesmit gados, 1919–1939* (1939), I, p. 30.
[187] *Latvijas Universitāte divdesmit gados, 1919–1939* (1939), I, p. 30.

primarily Baltic German citizens of Latvia, who constituted about 60 per cent of the 'non-Latvian' academics.[188]

A German Response: the Herder Institute

Latvia's educational system after 1919 was partitioned along ethnic lines. Each recognised *tautība* could exercise considerable autonomy under the auspices of the state, organising schools primarily with their own language of instruction.[189] This was part of a more general policy of 'cultural autonomy' for the minorities, a key issue especially for the Baltic German community.[190] However, as we have seen, on university level Latvian was proclaimed as the official language. Certainly as a response to the explicitly Latvian profile of the new university, the Baltic German minority founded the Herder Institute in Riga in 1921. This institution was devised to promote German culture, organise public lectures, and provide academic courses in the German language. For the remaining Baltic German population in Riga, the preservation of their German culture and heritage was clearly a paramount concern.[191]

In the early 1920s the status of the Institute was a contested issue, since the Latvian government was unwilling to allow the minorities the right to form their own institutions of higher education.[192] An important force behind a formal recognition of the Herder Institute was the Board of German Education at the Ministry of Education, which in fact constituted a pressure group for the extension of education in the German language. When in 1927 the German party coalition in the *Saeima* could act from a position of strength, the Herder Institute was formally recognised by the Latvian state.[193]

However, this victory appears to have been rather hollow. In spite of the formal recognition, the Herder Institute never received any government funding

---

[188] *Latvijas Universitāte divdesmit gados, 1919–1939* (1939), I, p. 30. There were only two really long-term recruitments of Swiss academics: Nussberger and Schneider in the Faculty of Philology and Philosophy. The Swedes stayed only for limited periods, and the recruited Finn Tiander left under a cloud after only a brief period at *Latvijas Universitāte*. See below, chapter 7. Schneider left in 1928, apparently because the faculty did not approve of his involvement in Freudian psychoanalysis. See ibid., p. 176.
[189] On the German school system in Latvia, see "Vācu izglītība Latvijā" (1930), pp. 587–595.
[190] Cerūzis, Raimonds (2002): "Vācu minoritāšu faktors Vidus- un Austrumeiropā starpkaru periodā: vispārējais un īpašais", pp. 95–103.
[191] See Björklund, Fredrika (2003): "The Rhetoric of the Nation. Baltic Germans in the First Latvian Democracy", pp. 75–114.
[192] LVVA. Izglītības ministrijas fonds, 1632/2/699. Herdera Institūta lieta. Letter from the Government Office to the Ministry of Education, 1924/01/03.
[193] LVVA. Izglītības ministrijas fonds, 1632/2/699. Herdera Institūta lieta. Letter from the Herder Society to the Prime Minister, 1927/07/05. The new constitution of the Herder Institute.

and its degrees were not valid for posts in Latvia.[194] The vision of creating a German-speaking university in Riga, parallel to the University of Latvia, could therefore not be fully realised. In a longer perspective, the organisers of the Herder Institute had to look beyond the Latvian context to find sufficient support for its existence. Only by being integrated into the university structure of the *German* state, and receiving direct subsidies from German Ministries, could the Herder Institute function as an institution of higher education.[195]

In general terms, the response of the Baltic German minority to the "national" universities of Tartu and Latvia was to organise separate institutions using German as the educational language. In Tartu, the "Dorpater Deutsche Hochschulhilfe", organised by the ethnic German professors and lecturers at Tartu university, was meant to serve as a first step for Baltic German students before completing their academic studies at universities in Germany proper.[196] Similarly, the Herder Institute in Riga relied on a predominantly Baltic German lecturers, while organising an extensive scheme of visiting scholars from Germany.[197] Some of them, like the Scandinavianist Johannes Paul from Greifswald, could stay in Riga with a two-year tenure thanks to additional funding by the German Ministry of Culture.[198]

There were also more specific attempts to preserve German Baltic scholarship under the changed national and political circumstances. In 1929 an *Institut für wissenschaftliche Heimatsforschung* was established in Tartu, mapping what must be seen as an increasingly imaginary *Baltische Heimat* in terms of history, German place-names, 'racial' characteristics and other topics.[199] The relationship between the separate German-speaking institutions and the universities of Tartu and Latvia quite naturally remained tense.[200]

These 'national' visions and attempted implementations in the sphere of higher education had several important effects. First, students taking part in the German alternative institutions were kept separate from their Latvian peers, receiving an understanding of the Baltic territories and the Baltic past that was

---

[194] von Hehn, Jürgen (1987): "Deutsche Hochschulaktivitäten in Riga und Dorpat zwischen den beiden Weltkriegen", pp. 266–67.
[195] von Hehn (1987), p. 268.
[196] von Hehn (1987), pp. 269–70.
[197] The permanent teaching staff at the Herder Institute in 1927 comprised 31 Germans, 1 Latvian, 1 Russian, and 1 Jew. LVVA. Izglītības ministrijas fonds, 1632/2/699. Herdera Institūta lieta.
[198] Paul had written an extensive biography on Gustavus Adolphus, and later became a proponent of the Nazi Party at Greifswald University. See Nase, Marco (2009): *Johannes Paul und das Schwedische Institut der Universität Greifswald*, in particular pp. 37–39.
[199] von Hehn (1987), pp. 270–271.
[200] In 1934, for instance, the theologians of Tartu and Riga boycotted a conference in Königsberg on the grounds that theologians from the Herder Institute had been invited. See Tankler & Rämmer (2004), pp. 217–218.

mediated through the prism of German culture. Second, using Anderson's terminology, their academic and professional 'pilgrimages' became restricted to the universities and the bureaucratic structures of the German state. Previously, the young males from the Baltic German elite had been able to make their career 'journeys' and *Bildungsreisen* in both the Russian and the German imperial systems. The education of young Baltic German noblemen in the nineteenth century included visits to the most prominent German universities, like Halle, Göttingen, Berlin and Heidelberg, but also to the Moscow and Dorpat Universities.[201] After World War I, many of them left for Germany in order to obtain something more than basic academic courses, and to seek career opportunities where these qualifications were held to be valid. Consequently, the ties between these Baltic German 'pilgrims' and the German state gradually tightened.

The picture should not be simplified unduly. While initially very few in numbers, towards the end of the 1920s many young persons descending from Baltic German families in Latvia chose to enrol at the Latvian-speaking university. Statistics on higher education show that students of ethnic German background constituted about five per cent of the student body of the University of Latvia in the late 1920s and early 1930s, which was slightly more than their share of the population as a whole.[202] According to an investigation in 1928, the Baltic German students were rather evenly spread over the university's faculties.[203]

In terms of numbers, this also meant that a majority of the young Baltic German students in Riga was at the university, not the Herder Institute.[204] Consequently, it seems reasonable to deduce that some kind of split occurred in the young generation of the German ethnic group. While some increasingly took part in German educational structures and career futures, others remained in Latvia and managed to get a university education primarily in the Latvian language, and consequently received qualifications valid in a Latvian context. In this manner, the 'Latvia-oriented' Baltic German students could be

---

[201] On the *Bildungsreisen* of the Baltic German elite, see von Campenhausen, Axel (2006): "Orellen und die Familie von Campenhausen. Aus der Geschichte einer livländische Familie", p. 92, and Whelan (1999), pp. 190–197. According to Whelan, the Kurland noble families preferred to send their sons to Germany, while Dorpat was more popular among the Livland and Estland nobility.

[202] LVVA. Latvijas Universitātes fonds, 7427/6/37a. Pārskats par Latvijas augstskolas, vēlāk Universitātes, nodibināšanu un viņas darbību. Report from the Vice-Principal to the Ministry of Education on the nationality of the students at the University of Latvia, 1920/03/31. *Valsts statistikas gada grāmatas*, 1920–1934.

[203] LVVA. Latvijas Universitātes fonds, 7427/6/37a. Pārskats par Latvijas augstskolas, vēlāk Universitātes, nodibināšanu un viņas darbību. Number of students, Spring term 1928. 342 out of 7,196 students were listed as 'German'.

[204] LVVA. Izglītības ministrijas fonds, 1632/2/699. Herdera Institūta lieta. Admittedly, the exact number of 'real' students at the Herder Institute is difficult to calculate, since part of its income derived from attracting a paying audience to public lectures. Many Baltic German students probably took courses at both institutions.

more secure in attempts to enhance their family prestige in their homeland and pursue their careers there.

Tartu and Kaunas – some comparative aspects

Applying a broader comparative perspective, it seems that 'national' considerations and prerogatives had greater weight in Riga than at Tartu University in Estonia. The proportion of ethnic Latvians in the teaching staff in Riga in 1920, slightly more than sixty per cent, was somewhat higher than the corresponding figure for Estonian academics at Tartu, around fifty per cent.[205] This may be an indication of a more forceful 'national' policy of recruitment in Latvia. As we have seen, there are also some indications of a more strongly felt resistance to recruiting German and Baltic German academics in the Latvian organisation committee compared to the Estonian. It should be remembered, though, that Tartu University had the advantage of an existing university structure, and moreover had the option of recruiting Finnish scholars to key positions when no qualified Estonians could be found. This was a strategic option that the organisers of the University of Latvia never had. The more marked presence of 'foreign' academics in Tartu can to some extent be explained by the recruitment of Finnish scholars.

At both universities, however, there appears to have been a determined policy to promote younger Estonian and Latvian academics and give them high positions in the academic system even if they did not yet have a doctoral degree. Promising students from the majority ethnic groups were also awarded scholarships to enable them to pursue an academic career. During the formative years of the University of Latvia, there was clearly a predominant policy that assistants and sub-assistants must be able to teach in Latvian, and should also preferably belong to the Latvian *tautība*.[206] In this way, a younger generation of Estonian and Latvian academics was prepared to gradually replace the older and established Baltic German professors.[207] For students belonging to the national minorities, however, the prospects were probably far less promising.[208]

---

[205] Siilivask (1987), p. 121, table 2.
[206] See, for instance, LVVA. Latvijas Universitātes fonds, 7427/6/1, Organisation Committee Minutes, 1921/03/16, where this is described as a general policy.
[207] *History of Tartu University, 1632–1982* (1985), pp. 174–176
[208] As shown previously, only a couple of staff belonged to the Jewish minority at the University of Latvia during the entire First Republic. The most prominent was Pauls Mincs in Law. Mincs was formally appointed in September 1919, when there was a tremendous need for lecturers in Law. See *Latvijas Universitāte divdesmit gados, 1919–1939* (1939) I, p.30; ibid., II, pp. 531–532; LVVA. Latvijas Universitātes fonds, 7427/13/1162. Staff records. In spite of the large number of Jewish students enrolled at the university during the 1920s and 1930s, none of them were evidently allowed to pursue an academic career – at least not in Latvia.

3. CREATING A 'CASTLE OF LIGHT'

In Lithuania, the government planned to gain academic credence by 're-opening' Vilnius University, originally founded in the sixteenth century. These hopes were dashed by Poland's annexation of Vilnius district in 1920, and the Lithuanian university opened instead in the new capital, Kaunas, in 1922. There are some indications that the recruitment of academic staff was more open than in Latvia. Historian Augustinas Voldemaras, one of the university's leading organisers, appears to have favoured the recruitment of 'foreign' professors in order to attain a high academic standard. This also meant that languages of instruction other than Lithuanian had to be tolerated. Only in a longer perspective, perhaps thirty to fifty years, Voldemaras maintained, could the new university be purely Lithuanian.[209]

Voldemaras's position resembles that of the linguist Jānis Endzelīns in Riga, giving preference to academic quality. However, it is not altogether clear to what extent Voldemaras's view predominated in Kaunas. The university council decided in March 1922 that foreign professors would only be appointed for a limited period, and should be supplied with Lithuanian-speaking assistants. Lithuanian citizens belonging to an ethnic minority and unfamiliar with the Lithuanian language were only hired on condition that at least after a fixed period they would lecture in Lithuanian.[210]

Finally, it should be noted that the international dimension of recruitment patterns and academic exchange differed markedly between the newly established Baltic states. Estonia looked especially to Finnish academia when recruiting foreign professors in the humanities, but in the natural sciences Germany was the most common goal for study trips. The organisers of the University of Latvia shunned the recruitment of ethnic German academics, preferring to appoint Swedes and Swiss even if they could only lecture in German. In Lithuania, on the other hand, academic contacts with Germany were of great importance. Most of the Lithuanian academics who received doctorates abroad during the interwar period did so at German universities. Due to the unresolved conflict over Vilnius, closer contacts with Polish academia were impossible.[211]

Conclusions

The creation of a new university in Riga was an important undertaking for the new Latvian state that emerged in 1919, for both practical and symbolic reasons. It contained three sets of expectations: first, to provide Latvia with a new segment

---
[209] Janužytė (2005), pp. 238–239.
[210] Janužytė (2005), pp. 239–240.
[211] Janužytė (2005), pp. 253; 262.

of Latvian academics, professionals, and administrators; second, to promote Latvian as an academic language used in higher education; and third, to reformulate, rewrite, and re-research vital aspects of the nation's past and culture. This chapter has investigated problems concerning the first two of these issues.

A special organisation committee was formed in the summer of 1919 with the task of forming the new university. It was originally composed of four groups: academics connected to the previous Riga Polytechnical Institute (RPI), primarily Baltic Germans; young Latvian academics who had managed to return to Riga during World War I; representatives of the ministries of the provisional government; and, finally, delegates from Latvian professional and cultural societies. Later, the committee included a group of prominent Latvian scholars and scientists, many of whom arrived after the peace treaty with the Soviet Union in 1920. The organisers of the new university obviously targeted a number of established scholars who were also ethnic Latvians, asking them to accept professorships at Riga. In this way, a handful of prominent academics was assembled, primarily within the fields of linguistics, literature, folklore, and medicine.

An important figure during the initial formative moment was the ethnic Latvian Pauls Valdens: professor of chemistry, Principal of the RPI and at the same time a representative of the Ministry of Education. He served as an important link between the predominantly Baltic German academics and the provisional government. However, after a very short time Valdens left Riga and eventually accepted a professorship in Germany. This meant that the Baltic German academics from the RPI lost some of their influence on the strategic recruitment processes that took place between 1919 and 1922. The basic dilemma for the organisers of the new university concerned the criteria for academic appointments: should academic merit have priority, should special consideration be paid to proficiency in the Latvian language, or should ethnic Latvians be preferred over more merited scholars and scientists belonging to the ethnic minorities?

Here, the organisation committee was split, its members adopting one of four positions on the recruitment question. According to one position, academic merit should be the primary selection criterion: a position closely associated with the established norms of European academia. The prominent Baltic German academics often took this position, together with the most renowned Latvian scholars – especially the acclaimed linguist Jānis Endzelīns. A second position emphasised the pragmatic need of qualified lecturers to meet the teaching assignments: again, many of the Baltic German academics argued along these lines, but the main proponents were Latvian colleagues in medicine, law, and economics, faculties with a rapidly growing number of students but, at the same time, a persistent scarcity of qualified lecturers who could teach in Latvian.

A third position on recruitment emphasised the language criterion: academic appointments should be reserved for those who could lecture in Latvian. The main supporters of this position were the less established Latvian academics in the organisation committee, but perhaps even more so the representatives of the Latvian professional and cultural societies. The fourth position, favouring ethnic Latvians over more qualified non-Latvians, was – interestingly enough – seldom taken openly, even if it seems certain that at least some of the committee's members preferred a selection based on ethnicity. However, since such a stance would in fact be discriminatory, it was seldom advocated openly during the committee meetings. Those favouring an ethnic selection, primarily agronomist Paulis Lejiņš, most often propagated instead for a strict adherence to the language criterion. This line was also taken by some of the members from the Latvian professional societies.

These four positions were in turn substantially linked to four different meanings of what constituted a national university: was it to be an institution of academic excellence, positioning the nation in a European cultural context, an institution providing the new state with well-qualified medical doctors, lawyers, and civil servants, a university enhancing Latvian to the position of an academic language, or a university where ethnic Latvian academics taught primarily ethnic Latvian students?

In the initial years, the situation regarding recruitment seems to have been in a flux, with the proponents of the alternatives constantly discussing which criterion should have preference. While Valdens' departure clearly weakened the influence of the Baltic German academics and the faction advocating the primacy of merit, the arrival of prominent Latvians from Russian and to some extent German universities appears to have reinforced the 'excellence' position. However, due to the organisation committee's composition and voting procedures, the group of more nationally inclined academics could combine with the members belonging to the ministries and the Latvian professional organisations to dominate the recruitment procedure during the university's initial formative period. The language criterion became paramount: academics who were not able to lecture in Latvian were appointed only when no reasonably merited Latvian-speakers could be found.

This policy, however, was not applied without friction. The organisation committee's unwillingness to recruit academics from other ethnic backgrounds meant that the quality of teaching in some faculties seems to have suffered due to a pervasive lack of qualified staff. Several of the committee members were reluctant to accept the recruitment of German and Baltic German academics, no doubt because these had formed the academic and cultural elite in the previously existing Baltic provinces of Russia. Appointments of Jewish and Russian academics were also rare. Here the 'national' agenda and its imperatives apparently conflicted with academic notions of quality, and, quite clearly, a more pragmatic need to organise high quality education for the rapidly growing number of students.

In this manner, recruitment policy and appointments became an area of conflict within the organisation committee. The representatives of three faculties in particular raised these issues within the committee. The dean of the Faculty of Mechanics advocated a more open recruitment policy, allowing Baltic Germans or non-Latvian citizens to be elected primarily on the basis of their scientific merits. In this endeavour he seems to have been at least partially successful. In the Faculty of Law and Economics the deans repeatedly suggested the appointment of Russian specialists in Law in order to meet the teaching assignments, but were consistently defeated by the committee.

The Faculty of Medicine was at one point even more clearly at loggerheads with the committee. The ethnic Latvian professors of medicine had to cope with severe understaffing and high student enrolment, but the organisation committee was unwilling to allow the appointment of Baltic German or Jewish professors. On this point, however, the committee appears to have come under pressure from several quarters. There was pressure from students demanding a wider recruitment of staff in order to bring the courses up to the required scientific standard, as well as some press criticism that over-restrictive recruitment policies had made the new *augstskola* less operational.

Within the organisation committee, it is clear that a major force behind the 'national' policy during the first year was the agronomist Paulis Lejiņš, the first vice-principal, Pauls Dāle, the chairman, and the engineer Spricis Paegle, the non-academic member from the Latvian Society. The celebrated Latvian nationalist playwright and poet Jānis Rainis intervened forcefully at least once, arguing strongly against the election of a Baltic German academic. While the restrictive recruitment policies were always framed in terms of proficiency in Latvian, the designated language of tuition, at least in the case of Paulis Lejiņš it seems clear that his agenda was really of an ethnic nature, promoting the appointment of ethnic Latvians. However, a selection based on ethnicity could not be advocated openly, since it would have run counter to established notions of recruitment based on merit and proper qualifications that was an essential part of the acknowledged academic field.

Pragmatic and scientific considerations on recruitment matters were primarily voiced by deans of the technical faculties, most of them Baltic Germans, and also from deans of the faculties of the natural sciences, law and economics, and medicine. Not surprisingly, it was primarily within these academic fields that it was hardest to find properly qualified Latvian scientists and scholars.

Another important advocate of the academic agenda was the professor of linguistics, Jānis Endzelīns, who after his return to Riga in June 1920 questioned the restrictive 'national' prerogatives in recruitment cases on several occasions. The opposition of Endzelīns, and of Latvian professors of medicine Zariņš and Krimbergs, was naturally more difficult for Lejiņš and Dāle to handle than the previous opposition from the Baltic German academics connected to the old Riga Polytechnical Institute. However, since all appointments required a two-thirds majority in the committee, the 'national' wing could block the election of foreign academics and those belonging to the minorities relatively easily, especially if their loyalty to the new Latvian state seemed questionable.

Endzelīns proved to be something of a problem as an academic figurehead or even 'hero of the nation'. While his academic credentials and national allegiance could not be questioned, his insistence on appointments based primarily on scientific and scholarly merit certainly caused some friction with the organisation committee's 'national' wing. This problem of failed expectations was even greater with two of the other projected academic national heroes: Pauls Valdens and Kārlis Balodis. Neither of them filled their designated role. Valdens eventually decided to pursue his academic career in Germany rather than in Latvia, expressing his disinclination to support the 'national' aims of the *augstskola*. Balodis could not reasonably fill the role of an academic 'hero' of the nation since he refused to give up his German citizenship.

The lack of reasonably merited Latvian-speaking academics in many disciplines meant that the expectations connected to the national agenda could not be met in full. The recruitment of some 'foreign' academics was unavoidable, but at the same time seen as a transitional phase, maintaining scholarly and scientific standards until such time as a younger generation of ethnic Latvian academics had developed and matured. Junior academic positions were reserved for Latvian-speakers, and grants and scholarships seem to have been consistently awarded to young Latvian male academics. Talented students from the ethnic minorities, as well as talented female students, were given considerably less chance to pursue academic careers.

In a similar manner, there was an evident conflict between the 'national' insistence on Latvian as the only language of instruction, and the 'academic' need for good scholarship and high scientific standards. The perceptible lack of Latvian-speaking academics in some disciplines, especially within mechanics, chemistry, medicine, natural sciences, and law, made it virtually impossible to organise academic studies in Latvian only. Here, evidently, in the first three years there were protracted negotiations and compromises. These language issues will be examined more closely in the next chapter.

Responding to the 'Latvian' character of the university, the Baltic Germans in Latvia attempted to create a separate, German-speaking university in Riga. These plans, however, never fully materialised. To some extent the Herder Institute managed to fulfill a role as an independent institution of higher education for a part of the German population, but its degrees were never valid in Latvia. In 'national' terms, the effect was naturally that the project of a Latvian national university was contrasted with a German counterpart. In the same way as ethnically based schools, political parties and organisations, this served to demarcate and emphasise boundaries between the different 'nationalities' within the Latvian state during the First Republic.

Summing up, it has to be said that the role of the University of Latvia in the national project was not straightforward. On the contrary, during the first formative years it was fraught with inconsistencies, conflicts, and compromises. The organisers and the academic leadership found it hard to implement a nationalist agenda in full when a sizeable part of the teaching staff could not lecture in Latvian. Naturally, even among the Latvian academics there was never a complete consensus on the realization of the 'national' project at the university. While some of them, here labelled the 'national' wing, wanted recruitment policies to be guided by a deliberate selection of either ethnic Latvian or Latvian-speaking candidates, others envisaged a 'national' university where the appointment of some established Baltic German or foreign academics was necessary in order to reach high scholarly and scientific standards. Consequently, a more consistent 'nationalist' recruitment to the new university was to some extent counteracted by academics emphasising the values of scholarly quality, the importance of international recognition, and also the pragmatic need of specialists in certain fields. The University of Latvia could and did serve as a symbolic figurehead for the nation, but its exact meaning and character were evidently a bone of contention between different notions of the actual meaning of this 'national' university. Selective and restrictive 'national' principles simply could not co-exist smoothly with the notions of merits and qualifications that predominated in the established academic field, and a notion of minority rights in a democratic society. While Latvia during the First Republic certainly should be seen as a nationalising state in Brubaker's sense, some of the nationalising policies evidently encountered limitations.

CHAPTER 4

Language Matters
the Question of Tuition Language

The question of tuition language was a complicated issue during the formative years of *Latvijas Augstskola*. For the more 'nationalist' members of the organisation committee, Latvian as the only academic language of instruction was a symbolic issue of paramount importance. At the same time, the need for academic expertise in certain areas frequently prompted the faculties to propose the appointment of scholars and scientists who did not command Latvian. Moreover, since during Imperial times many citizens belonging to the ethnic minorities had primarily attended Russian-speaking schools, proficiency in Latvian among students from these groups varied considerably. Consequently, the problem was twofold: to what extent were teaching staff able and willing to deliver lectures in Latvian – and to what extent were students able to take part in tuition in that language?

When planning for the first term of *Latvijas Augstskola* in September 1919, the organisation committee decided that the language of instruction had to be Latvian. Only under 'necessary circumstances' could lectures in Russian and German be allowed.[1] But what exactly constituted 'necessary circumstances'? This question remained a matter of contention in the first formative years.

Non-Latvian speakers among the academic staff

A specific problem concerned the academics who had previously belonged to the Riga Polytechnical Institute (RPI). Many of them were in ethnic terms Baltic Germans, Russians, Poles or Jews, and their ability to lecture in Latvian was generally limited. At the same time, in order to establish itself as a recognised university, the new *augstskola* certainly needed these experienced and well-respected academics, especially in the fields of natural science and technology. When appointed to *Latvijas Augstskola*, the professors of the old RPI were therefore promised that they could continue lecturing in German and Russian for an indefinite period. For the rest of the teaching staff, however, no such assurances were given. This remained a contested issue during the first few years.

---

[1] LVVA. Latvijas Universitātes fonds, 7427/6/1, Organisation Committee Minutes, 1919/09/04.

Besides the organisation committee, the Ministry of Education had strong views on the ability and willingness of academics from non-Latvian backgrounds to teach in the 'official' language. The Ministry's representative on the committee, the chairman Pauls Dāle, repeatedly emphasised the need to adopt Latvian as the predominant tuition language. In 1920, for instance, he demanded to know how many among the teaching staff in each faculty currently belonged to other 'nationalities', and how many of them were really able to teach in Latvian. He also wanted to know how many of the students in each faculty were unable to understand lectures in the 'official' language.[2] Armed with this information, Dāle later wrote to the vice-principal demanding an explanation as to why all the lectures in the Faculty of Mechanics were delivered in Russian, when the survey showed that only seventeen students at that faculty did not have an acceptable proficiency in Latvian.[3]

Paul von Denffer, the Baltic German dean of the Faculty of Mechanics, admitted that some among the teaching staff actually had problems lecturing in Latvian, especially those from the former RPI. He also emphasised that most of the students preferred to be taught in Russian. Moreover, he argued that Latvian still lacked many specialised technical terms, making it less suitable for tuition in Mechanics.[4] There seems to have been an obvious conflict between von Denffer and Dāle on these matters. At the organisation committee meeting that was held during this correspondence, von Denffer announced his intention of recruiting a foreign professor; Dāle rejoined by demanding a full account of all foreigners employed by each faculty.[5]

Clearly, the issue of teaching language was very sensitive. All the deans of the technical faculties were Baltic Germans from the former RPI Latvian academics were also infrequent in some of the other faculties, for instance the Faculty of Law and Economics. In his autobiographical notes, the linguist and conservative nationalist Juris Plāķis, who joined the organisation committee in 1920, states that the Latvian members met separately before the committee meetings in order to discuss tactics. One of the vital issues, it seems, was to keep all the faculties

---

[2] LVVA. Latvijas Universitātes fonds, 7427/6/37a. Pārskats par Latvijas augstskolas, vēlāk Universitātes, nodibināšanu un viņas darbību. Letters from Dāle, Ministry of Education, 1920/02/16, 1920/03/09.

[3] LVVA. Latvijas Universitātes fonds, 7427/6/37a. Pārskats par Latvijas augstskolas, vēlāk Universitātes, nodibināšanu un viņas darbību. Letter from Dāle, Ministry of Education, to von Denffer, 1920/04/12.

[4] LVVA. Latvijas Universitātes fonds, 7427/6/37a. Pārskats par Latvijas augstskolas, vēlāk Universitātes, nodibināšanu un viņas darbību. Letter from von Denffer to the Vice-Principal, 1920/04/15.

[5] LVVA. Latvijas Universitātes fonds, 7427/6/1, Organisation Committee Minutes, 1920/04/14. As shown in the previous chapter, von Denffer had as dean and committee member argued forcefully for the faculties' right to select academic staff on scientific and scholarly merit only.

together in one university, rather than having the technical faculties organise a separate academic institution. The Latvians on the committee obviously considered that a separate technical university would be completely dominated by the Baltic German academics and Latvian would never become the predominant teaching language.[6]

A closer look at actual language use in the various faculties suggests that Russian was the most important language of instruction after Latvian, even among the Baltic German academics. In chemistry, for instance, only one of the six Baltic German lecturers actually lectured in German in 1919/20 – the others preferred to use Russian, probably due to the causes indicated by von Denffer above.[7] The only exception was the Faculty of Medicine, where German, not Russian, was used.[8]

The lack of ability or willingness among some of the teaching staff to lecture in Latvian continued to cause concern. An overview of the language situation at the *augstskola* in 1921 shows that the position of Latvian as tuition language was indeed weakest in the Faculty of Mechanics, where only 29 per cent of the lectures were held in that language, followed by the Faculties of Law and Economics (38 per cent), Engineering (43 per cent), Chemistry (45 per cent), and Medicine (52 per cent).[9]

During the initial years, a series of compromises evidently had to be worked out between the political demands of implementing Latvian as the language of instruction, the need to fill vacancies in the faculties, especially within medicine, law and the technical subjects and, finally, the academic requirements of recruitment based on scholarly and scientific merit. An overview of the teaching staff in spring 1920 indicates that ethnic Latvians constituted at least sixty per cent of the total staff. However, some faculties were clearly dominated by academics whose ascribed 'nationality' was non-Latvian. This applied especially to Mechanics, where the teaching staff according to the ethnic categorisation comprised nine Germans, one Pole, one Russian, and three Latvians, and the Faculty of Law and Economics, with nine Germans, one Jew, one Englishman, and four Latvians. In terms of citizenship, however, an overwhelming majority of the professors and lecturers were Latvians: 137 out of 153 academic staff.[10]

---

[6] Kļaviņa, Sarma (2010): "LU profesora Jura Plāķa dzīves un ciešanu ceļi (1869–1942)", pp. 44–45.
[7] LVVA. Latvijas Universitātes fonds, 7427/6/37a. Pārskats par Latvijas augstskolas, vēlāk Universitātes, nodibināšanu un viņas darbību.
[8] LVVA. Latvijas Universitātes fonds, 7427/6/54, Gadu statistiskās ziņas par studentu un mācības spēku sastāvu.
[9] LVVA. Latvijas Universitātes fonds, 7427/6/54, Gadu statistiskās ziņas par studentu un mācības spēku sastāvu.
[10] LVVA. Latvijas Universitātes fonds, 7427/6/37a. Pārskats par Latvijas augstskolas, vēlāk Universitātes, nodibināšanu un viņas darbību. Overview of the teaching staff in the faculties, 1919/20. Both these faculties had strong bonds with previous departments at the Riga

In the early 1920s a praxis developed on the appointment of non-Latvian academics: many professors were given a five-year grace period before being required to teach in Latvian. For *docenti*, this period was usually set to three years; during this specified period they were permitted to lecture in Russian or German.[11] For academics in more junior positions the conditions were less accommodating, the committee frequently making the point that assistants and sub-assistants had to be fluent in Latvian in order to be appointed.

This emerging praxis seems to have served as a compromise between the need to recruit experienced 'foreign' academics and the national prerogative of fostering a younger generation of Latvian academics who would in time and after proper training become predominant at *Latvijas Universitāte*.

The praxis described above was not implemented in full: some appointments were made without any mention of language requirements. Also, as we have seen above, the problem remained that students in some faculties preferred to have lectures in Russian and German. In 1922 the principal, Ernsts Felsbergs, instigated a new survey of all faculties to see to what extent languages other than Latvian were still being used in teaching. The result showed that Russian was extensively used in some of the technical faculties, especially chemistry and mechanics, and also in mathematics and natural science. Felsbergs forwarded these findings to the Ministry of Education, making it clear that he saw the present regulations on tuition language primarily as a political, not an academic, question.[12]

Perhaps in an attempt to stave off more political interference, the deans who had conducted the survey submitted a proposal to the organisation committee, requesting confirmation of the right of the previous RPI professors to continue to lecture in the language of their choice (there were now thirteen such professors). Also, foreign professors above the age of fifty-five should not be required to lecture in Latvian. The same rule should apply to foreign lecturers in modern languages.[13]

The deans' proposal led to a long discussion in the committee. After two months it finally agreed to confirm the right of the former RPI professors appointed in 1919 to continue lecturing in Russian and German if they wished. However, they ruled that this group actually comprised eleven professors, not

Polytechnical Institute. The most 'Latvian' faculties in terms of teaching staff were Agronomy and Philology and Philosophy.

[11] LVVA. Latvijas Universitātes fonds, 7427/6/268. Sarakste ar fakultātēm, profesoriem par mācību pasniegšanu valsts valodā.

[12] LVVA. Latvijas Universitātes fonds, 7427/6/268. Sarakste ar fakultātēm, profesoriem par mācību pasniegšanu valsts valodā. Letters from Deans of Faculties, 1922/02/18, 1922/03/01, 1922/03/03, 1922/03/06; Letter from Principal Ernsts Felsbergs to the Minister of Education, 1922/03/21.

[13] LVVA. Latvijas Universitātes fonds, 7427/6/1, Organisation Committee Minutes, 1922/03/15. The proposal also included a number of exemptions and extensions for individual academics.

thirteen. The committee further decided that non-Latvian professors above the age of fifty-five should *not* be free to lecture in the language of their choice. Instead, each case would be considered individually by the future university council. The committee also turned down the deans' proposal that foreign lecturers in modern languages should be exempt from the requirement to lecture in Latvian; they would have the five-year grace period.

Instead, the previous praxis was confirmed as a uniform principle: professors who were not Latvian citizens should be given five years' grace before they were required to lecture in the Latvian language. For elected *docenti*, the grace period was shorter, only three years.[14] Jānis Endzelīns, judging the matter from a linguistic perspective, had previously questioned the committee's line, making the observation that three years' study would hardly suffice to enable academics to teach in a new language.[15] There are no indications that the committee was prepared to listen to linguistic arguments; the three-year limit for elected foreign *docenti* was confirmed.[16]

Apparently, the deans tried to gain recognition for general principles on the language question that were more 'liberal' than those which the committee found acceptable. The deans were no doubt guided by pragmatic concerns about finding qualified academics to meet the teaching assignments, and perhaps also a greater understanding of the difficulties among the older set of professors to manage the shift to Latvian. A strict application of time limits would probably mean that many established foreign academics would leave the university when their grace period expired. Moreover, the deans' initiative on the language question may have been guided by a desire to have the matter decided at university level instead of by the Ministry of Education and the *Saeima*. The committee majority, on the other hand, seems to have given priority to the overriding goal of establishing Latvian as the predominant language of tuition. It is also possible that they saw the need for established foreign academics as a passing phase: it would diminish as a younger generation of Latvian academics became more qualified.

Interestingly, in the draft of the new University Constitution signed by both Ernsts Felsbergs, the first principal, and Dāle, the chairman of the organisation committee, the only language requirement was that the holders of administrative office or university council membership had to be academics knowledgeable in

---

[14] LVVA. Latvijas Universitātes fonds, 7427/6/268. Sarakste ar fakultātēm, profesoriem par mācību pasniegšanu valsts valodā. 7427/6/1, Organisation Committee Minutes, 1922/05/31.
[15] LVVA. Latvijas Universitātes fonds, 7427/6/1, Organisation Committee Minutes, 1920/06/09.
[16] LVVA. Latvijas Universitātes fonds, 7427/6/1, Organisation Committee Minutes, 1922/05/31. The grace period was to be counted from this date, which meant that 'foreign' professors already employed were allowed to lecture in other languages until 1 July 1927.

the 'state language'. The language of instruction was actually not defined.[17] This may seem somewhat surprising, knowing Felsbergs's and Dāle's deep commitment to the establishment of a Latvian-speaking university. However, the University Constitution which the *Saeima* adopted in 1922, besides declaring that the University of Latvia was 'national' and 'autonomous', established unequivocally that the official teaching language was Latvian. Other languages could be used only with special permission from the university council.[18]

One possible explanation of the discrepancy between the draft and the final version is that Felsbergs and Dāle may have preferred to have the language question settled by the *Saeima* politicians rather than by the future university council. Since the language issue had proved so extremely difficult to resolve within the *augstskola*, causing unceasing dissent and strife between faculties and colleagues, Felsbergs and Dāle were probably quite content to have the matter finally decided at the political level. Naturally, in his double role as principal of the university and chairman of the *Saeima*'s Education Committee, Felsbergs could act as a politician on issues where he hesitated to act as principal.[19]

While a grace period for those not able to teach in Latvian was certainly a workable compromise during the following years, this was not the end of the matter. From 1925 onwards, as the established grace period expired for *docenti* there was a steady stream of applications from the faculties pleading for extensions. One of the first cases concerned the *docents* in civil litigation, Vladimir Bukovski, an ethnic Russian but a Latvian citizen since at least 1921. Bukovski had actually served in the Latvian Ministry of Justice and participated in the codification of Latvian civil law. His expertise was obviously treasured by the Faculty of Law and Economics, and his permission to continue lecturing in Russian was repeatedly extended by the university council until his death in 1937.[20]

For the professors, the grace period ended in 1927. The Faculty of Philology and Philosophy immediately applied for an extension of tenure for Walter Frost, professor of Philosophy, whose grace period was coming to an end. Frost was actually one of the very few academics at *Latvijas Universitāte* who had been recruited from Germany proper. The faculty claimed that the loss of Frost would be very deeply felt, and also maintained that he was considered a good colleague and a 'friend of Latvia'. The last phrase was evidently felt to be a necessary part of the request, considering Frost's undeniable German nationality. The

---

[17] *Latvijas Universitātes Satversme. Projekts*, (1922), pp. 1–10.
[18] Latvijas Universitātes Satversme, § 3. *Izglītības Ministrijas Mēnešraksts*, 1922:2, p. 1109.
[19] Felsbergs was a member of the *Saeima* between November 1922 and November 1925. LVVA. Latvijas Universitātes fonds, 7427/13/475. Staff records.
[20] LVVA. Latvijas Universitātes fonds, 7427/13/283. Staff records. The faculty even argued to have Bukovski's tenure extended beyond the retirement age of seventy, claiming that the faculty had no properly trained academic who could replace him.

university council duly assented to the application but emphasised that each case of this kind had to be treated individually.[21]

More applications of this sort followed. Benedikt Frese, the Baltic German professor of Roman law, was likewise granted the right to lecture in German, at least until 1932.[22] The university council seems to have been willing to grant extensions to academics strongly supported by their faculties. At the same time, it would not consider having a general rule on the language issue. A 'softer' approach might have led to a situation where non-Latvian academics would simply ignore the language requirement, while a 'tougher' approach would have meant that the university might lose some key academics who, when their grace period expired, still found it too difficult to lecture in Latvian.

Finally, there was a matter about whether Russian or German was to be the 'secondary' language of instruction. Russian was the first choice in most technical faculties, since all lecturers connected to the old Riga Polytechnical Institute had previously used that language. Most of the students from Russian and Jewish backgrounds apparently also preferred Russian. Among the younger generation of Latvian students, however, knowledge of Russian was diminishing over time, making it difficult for many of them to understand lectures in that language.

In Medicine, on the other hand, there was for some specific reasons a predominance of German. The Swedish anatomist Gaston Backman, one of the main professors in the clearly understaffed Faculty of Medicine, was not capable of lecturing in Russian. Moreover, many of the most modern medical textbooks were written in German.[23] When the committee discussed this matter, Paulis Lejiņš voiced his opinion that German should nevertheless not be used, since the *augstskola* must above all avoid coming under German cultural domination. As shown previously, Lejiņš's ethnic and in a sense 'postcolonial' version of the national project entailed separation from the Baltic Germans' previous economic, political and cultural domination. For academics like Lejiņš it was clearly

---

[21] LVVA. Latvijas Universitātes fonds, 7427/6/268. Sarakste ar fakultātēm, profesoriem par mācību pasniegšanu valsts valodā. Application 1927/01/08; Copy of Council of Deans minutes 1927/02/14; Copy of University Council minutes, 1927/02/16. Frost was born in Prussia, and had had a German academic career comprising Berlin, Königsberg, Köln and Düsseldorf. In 1922 he received tenure as professor of philosophy at the University of Latvia. LVVA. Izglītības ministrijas fonds, 1632/2/612, Sarakste ar Latvijas Universitāti par mācību spēkiem, mācību darbu, budžetu u. c., 1921.g. – 1922.g.; *Latvijas Universitāte 1919–1929* (1929), pp. 168–169.

[22] LVVA. Latvijas Universitātes fonds, 7427/13/504. Staff records.

[23] The problem of the serious lack of academic textbooks in Latvian was seldom discussed in the Organisation Committee. In 1922, however, the member from the Latvian Society, Paegle, proposed that academics at the *augstskola* should *not* be permitted to publish textbooks in foreign languages. He failed, however, to get a majority vote on this issue. LVVA. Latvijas Universitātes fonds, 7427/6/1, Organisation Committee Minutes, 1922/05/24.

impossible to accept German as an important tuition language at *Latvijas Universitāte*. Paegle, the member from the Latvian Association, expressed his dissatisfaction with the use of both German and Russian, proposing instead that English might be used as a secondary tuition language. The committee, however, was more pragmatic, deciding that German should preferably be used in Medicine if for some reason instruction in Latvian was not possible.[24]

Nevertheless, the issue continued to surface throughout the interwar period. Russian gradually lost its previous predominance but nationalist academics and students viewed the continued use of German in some faculties with suspicion. Interestingly, the Student Council proposed in 1934 that English should be given a stronger position within the university, on the grounds that this language "least threatens our cultural independence".[25] This, however, was a very premature suggestion.

Non-Latvian students and the language question

Evidently, the first generation of students at the University of Latvia had been enrolled with a prior language test. An inquiry in the spring of 1920 showed that 102 students (eight per cent) claimed they were unable to understand lectures in Latvian. Most of them belonged to the technical and science faculties. Chemistry stands out as the faculty with the greatest number of students who could not follow lectures in Latvian.[26] This situation evidently worried the organisation committee majority. On the eve of the new academic year in the autumn of 1920, concerns about the ability of students to understand lectures in Latvian prompted the committee to consider a mandatory test of language proficiency for all newly enrolled students who did not belong to the Latvian *tautība*.

Paulis Lejiņš, not surprisingly, advocated a comparatively strict examination, including listening comprehension and a note-taking test. Felsbergs and Endzelīns, however, persuaded the committee to take a 'softer' line, with just a relatively easy oral examination in the presence of faculty representatives.[27] Excluding prospective students from the minority groups who were struggling to learn Latvian would obviously be a delicate matter. However, although the test

---

[24] LVVA. Latvijas Universitātes fonds, 7427/6/1, Organisation Committee Minutes, 1920/12/08. The prime reason given was that textbooks in German were of a far better quality than those in Russian.
[25] LVVA. Latvijas Universitātes fonds, 7427/6/268. Sarakste ar fakultātēm, profesoriem par mācību pasniegšanu valsts valodā. Letter from the Student Council to the Principal, 1934/04/18.
[26] LVVA. Latvijas Universitātes fonds, 7427/6/37a. Pārskats par Latvijas augstskolas, vēlāk Universitātes, nodibināšanu un viņas darbību.
[27] LVVA. Latvijas Universitātes fonds, 7427/6/1, Organisation Committee Minutes, 1920/09/08.

was proclaimed to be 'easy', by late September only forty per cent of the minority applicants had managed to pass.²⁸

Many of the students enrolled in the autumn of 1919, without any language requirement, found it difficult to understand lectures in Latvian. In October 1920 the language of instruction again came up for debate. Students in chemistry and architecture appealed to have lectures in Russian. Here, too, Felsbergs appears to have taken a 'softer', more pragmatic line, asking the committee to show some consideration for the difficult circumstances of some of the 'foreign' students. The *augstskola*, he claimed, had a decided responsibility for the students it had allowed to enrol. Endzelīns took a firmer stance, arguing that instruction in any language other than Latvian should be allowed only if each and every student in a course demanded it. In this matter the committee majority sided with Endzelīns.²⁹

Endzelīns's position on Latvian as the language of instruction was definitely more uncompromising than his position on recruitment. As a specialist in Baltic linguistics he no doubt saw the development of Latvian into a fully accepted cultural and academic language as a main prerogative. This part of the national project would certainly be delayed if, for pragmatic reasons, students continued to be instructed in Russian or German.

The deficient command of Latvian among many of the enrolled students continued to worry. In 1921 the Council of Deans proposed that in future all new applicants must pass an exam in the Latvian language in order to be accepted. This meant, however, that ethnic Latvians would also be examined before enrolment. Endzelīns found this unreasonable, maintaining that such language tests should be reserved for non-Latvians, *cittautieši*. He was supported by Maldons, dean of the Faculty of Theology, who claimed that imposing a general and mandatory language test would be an insult to Latvian students. The member from the one of the Latvian professional organisations, Spricis Paegle, concurred with Maldons and Endzelīns.

On this matter, however, they were solidly outvoted. The committee decided that a language test would be mandatory for all new students.³⁰ The reasons are not altogether clear. Possibly, the problems with ethnic categorisation made it difficult to identify the applicants who belonged to one of the ethnic minorities. Surnames were not a clear sign: they could easily be Latvianised. However, another possible interpretation is that at least some of the deans wanted to avoid having to single out applicants belonging to the ethnic minorities. Demanding a

---

²⁸ LVVA. Latvijas Universitātes fonds, 7427/6/1, Organisation Committee Minutes, 1920/09/24. A further 30 per cent had been summoned to the test but had not turned up.
²⁹ LVVA. Latvijas Universitātes fonds, 7427/6/1, Organisation Committee Minutes, 1920/10/06.
³⁰ LVVA. Latvijas Universitātes fonds, 7427/6/1, Organisation Committee Minutes, 1921/06/01.

test of all applicants could have been part of a strategy to turn the whole matter of language tests into a dead issue.

Mechanics, chemistry and law and economics were specifically mentioned in the committee discussions as faculties where language tests were believed to be necessary. However, at the start of the 1921 autumn term there are indications that these requirements had not been met in full. It was estimated that eleven per cent of the applicants had avoided taking the language tests.[31] Repeated attempts were apparently made during the spring term to force these students to sit the Latvian exams, and again at the start of the following autumn term.[32]

Apparently, the expressed national aim of fully implementing Latvian as the predominant language of instruction meant that enrolled students were required to possess at least a basic proficiency in that language. Making language tests a condition for enrolment was seen as the obvious remedy. However, the form and severity of these tests continued to be contested. While relatively moderate tests could satisfy the educational and national aims, more difficult tests could serve as a strategic measure to exclude a large proportion of the non-Latvian applicants. If language tests give decisive advantages to native speakers, they clearly have a discriminatory function.[33] It should also be pointed out that the committee's discussions always centred on the necessity of excluding minority students who lacked the necessary proficiency in Latvian – supportive measures such as language courses do not seem to have been considered.

As will be shown in the following chapter, the insistence on stricter language tests became much stronger in 1923 following clashes between Latvian and Jewish students. By that time, morerover, the focus had shifted from the tuition language per se to the more troubling perspective of regarding some minority students as 'undesirable'.

Language use among the students clearly had a strong symbolic meaning. As will be shown in the following chapter, some of the nationalist Latvian students saw the use of Russian and Yiddish by other students as deliberate acts of provocation, and attempts were actually made to ban the use of these languages on university premises. The use of German in student politics was also contested. The Baltic German student corporations struggled in the early 1920s to gain acceptance for the use of German in the *Prezidiju Konvents*, the joint

---

[31] LVVA. Latvijas Universitātes fonds, 7427/6/1, Organisation Committee Minutes, 1921/08/27; 1921/08/31; 1921/09/07.
[32] LVVA. Latvijas Universitātes fonds, 7427/6/1, Organisation Committee Minutes, 1922/03/15; 1922/05/17.
[33] In a comparative perspective, the introduction of mandatory language examinations in Romania in 1925 seems to have had such a discriminatory effect, primarily disadvantaging ethnic Hungarians and German-speaking Jews. See Pálfy, Zoltán (2003): *National Controversy in the Transylvanian Academe: The Cluj/Kolozsvár University, 1900–1950*, pp. 157–159.

organisation for Latvian and Baltic German student corporations. The Latvian corporations, however, insisted on the exclusive use of Latvian, and by 1924 the Baltic German corporations had to drop their aspirations.[34] Latvian remained the university's only official language.

Conclusions

The 'national' insistence on Latvian as the only language of instruction could not possibly be implemented in full in the early 1920s due to the lack of qualified teaching staff who could lecture in Latvian. Especially in the natural sciences, technical subjects, medicine, and law, it appears to have been very difficult to find professors and lecturers who could meet these language requirements.

For many of these subjects, the university had to rely on the predominantly Baltic German teaching staff from the former Riga Polytechnical Institute (RPI), most of who were incapable of lecturing in Latvian. As the result of a compromise, the 'old' RPI professors were allowed to continue lecturing in Russian and German for an indefinite period. Most of the academics recruited later who belonged to one of the ethnic minorities, or were not Latvian citizens, however, were given a grace period before they were required to teach in the 'state language'.

The faculty deans took a more pragmatic view on this issue, probably because they needed to find qualified academics who could meet the teaching assignments, and also because they wanted to have the option of permanently retaining some key professors. Among the organisation committee majority, however, the nationally inspired vision of Latvian as an academic language was of paramount importance. The eventual compromise on this issue meant that professors were allowed five years before being required to lecture in Latvian, *docenti* only three. This made the shift to Latvian as the clearly predominant academic language a more gradual process.

When it came to ethnic minority students who preferred to have lectures in Russian or German, the organisation committee was far less accommodating. Here, the principle was established that a Latvian-speaking lecturer should use another language of tuition only if the entire student group demanded it. The firm establishment of Latvian as an academic language was obviously a paramount concern. Moreover, the lack of proficiency in Latvian among many first-generation students at the *augstskola* caused deep concern among the committee members, and prompted the introduction of language tests for new applicants. However, it seems clear that to some extent, these measures on language matters

---

[34] Cerūzis, Raimonds (2004): *Vācu faktors Latvijā (1918–1939). Politiskie un starpnacionālie aspekti,* pp. 187–188.

also served as a cover for more exclusionary tactics directed at the ethnic minorities. While direct discrimination of a certain group of applicants was difficult to implement in a democratic system in which minorities, at least initially, were given some access to central political institutions, selecting students on the basis of required language skills naturally seemed more 'objective'. This matter will be investigated further in the following chapter.

The university's language policies became an area of conflict between a political and nationalistic insistence on Latvian as the university's sole official language on the one hand, and the need for academic excellence and recruitment based on merit on the other. Promoting the nation through the establishment of a 'national' university was therefore not entirely straightforward. The strongly felt need to curtail Russian and German as languages of tuition had to be tempered by considerations of academic quality. Interestingly, it may well have been the case that the language issue was finally referred to the political level precisely because it had proved so difficult to handle by the academic leadership.

As we have seen, there are some indications that the language question was difficult to solve by the university itself. Two of the leading proponents of a 'national' university, the chairman of the organisation committee Pauls Dāle and the first principal, Ernsts Felsbergs, seem to have been quite content to have the principal language question settled by the *Saeima* rather than by the university council. When the University Constitution was finally adopted by the *Saeima* in 1922, it formally established the monopoly of Latvian as the sole teaching language.

It should be pointed out however that separating academia from the political system is not altogether easy. Several of the leading figures in the organisation committee and the first university council also had important political roles. Ernsts Felsbergs, the first principal, also chaired the *Saeima* Education Committee, and Pauls Dāle, apart from being the chairman of the organisation committee, led the Department of Higher Education at the Ministry of Education. Moreover, almost every Education Minister during this very formative period also held an academic post at the university. In practice, this meant that questions which were controversial on the academic level, such as regulations on instruction language, could to some extent be handled by the very same persons but at political or ministerial levels.

CHAPTER 5

"Foreign Elements"
Demarcation and Conflict between Latvian and Jewish Students at the University of Latvia, 1919–1940

An important item on the nationalising Latvian state's agenda was to turn state institutions into vehicles for the core nation. In terms of higher education, this meant the creation of a Latvian university using the Latvian language. At the same time, Latvia contained a number of minorities: Baltic Germans, Jews, Russians, Belarusians, and Poles, constituting altogether about 25 per cent of the population. They were citizens, but not part of the core nation. Following Brubaker's terminology, the Latvian nationalisation policy was primarily 'dissimilationist', granting cultural rights to the minorities but at the same time institutionalising ethnic categorisation and separateness.[1] Assimilation of the ethnic minorities was not on the nationalising agenda. How did the minorities and their interest in higher education fit into the national agenda connected with the university?

The previous chapters have primarily dealt with the recruitment policies for academic staff, and have touched on the substantial problems, especially for those who were not Latvian-speakers, to obtain posts at the new university. However, prospective students who belonged to the ethnic minorities in Latvia faced a more tangible problem. How could they reasonably be included in a national project that was primarily intended to produce *Latvian* academics and professionals? To what extent were students from the ethnic minorities included or excluded?

Among most European universities, the prevalent notion after World War I was that higher education should be open to all applicants with adequate high school grades. This stand was clearly embodied in the enrolment regulations of

---

[1] Brubaker, Rogers (1996b): *Nationalism reframed. Nationhood and the national question in the New Europe*, pp. 88–89. Viewing society as composed of separate national and ethnic groups was at least partly a legacy of late Tsarist times. Voluntary associations of various kinds, primarily concerning culture and education, were organised along ethnic lines. In the same way, politics in the early 20th century and relief organisations during the war were also organised according to ethnicity. See Bolin Hort, Per (2003a): "Zeme un tauta: Conceptions of the Latvian Territory and the Latvian Nation", pp. 45–47.

Latvijas Augstskola. Young people with the required school-leaving grades were not to be barred from enrolment due to class background, ethnicity or – an innovation in the Baltic territories when the *augstskola* opened in 1919 – gender. The only relevant admission criteria were completion of high school examinations and the ability to afford the tuition fees. To what extent, then, could a national requirement to primarily educate *Latvians* at the university co-exist with the notions of open enrolment that characterised the modern academic system?

Prior to 1914, Baltic Germans had participated in university education to a much greater degree than the other ethnic groups in the area. After the Russification of Tsarist universities in the 1890s, however, most Baltic Germans preferred to enrol at universities in Germany proper. After 1919, they retained this possibility of choosing between different paths of higher education. Besides the newly founded Latvian university, they had full access to the universities in Germany, as well as to the German-speaking Herder Institute in Riga.

For students belonging to other ethnic minority groups, however, the situation was far less favourable. For Russians, Belarusians, Poles, and Jews, there was no viable institution of higher education in Latvia, and the foreign alternatives were not easily attainable. Youths from Polish-speaking families could, admittedly, to some extent rely on universities in the newly established Polish state, but it seems likely that ethnic Russians and Russian-speaking Jews in Latvia were less prone to seek admission to universities in the Soviet Union. The Russian universities were in deep turmoil and increasingly subjected to political pressure during the years after the Civil War.[2]

The situation of Jewish students in particular highlights some of the problems when forming a university as a 'national' project. Jews were accepted as citizens of Latvia but were not considered to belong to the core nation. Who, then, were regarded as Jews? Which criteria were used in this process? In the societal context of the Baltic provinces before 1914, Jews were defined, not primarily on the basis of language, descent, or 'race' but by religious affiliation. Censuses during the Imperial period seem to have preferred categorisation by religion rather than by ethnicity, since religion was perceived as a more unequivocal and, perhaps, less changeable category. This mode of categorisation made no essential distinction between Russian-, German- and Yiddish-speaking Jews, but certainly served as a demarcation of the Jewish population as a whole.

Historically, Jewish people had been virtually banned from Swedish Livonia in the seventeenth century, and were long kept out of Riga by the German merchants. They had a chance of settling in areas of Polish political domination,

---

[2] David-Fox, Michael (1997): *Revolution of the Mind. Higher Learning among the Bolsheviks, 1918–1929*, pp. 43–55.

that is, present-day Kurzeme and Latgale.³ The Baltic provinces of Estland, Livland and Kurland lay outside the Pale of Settlement, the area of the Romanov Empire where Jews were legally allowed to settle. The Jews of Kurland and Riga were primarily German- and Yiddish-speakers, and formed a more 'Western' or German Jewry than those residing in the Pale. Latgale, however, was a part of the Vitebsk province and situated within the settlement territory. Here, Russian- and Yiddish-speaking Jews constituted an important part of the population in towns and villages.⁴ The region's major city, Dvinsk/Daugavpils, became a very important centre for the Latgale Jewry.

Forbidden to own land in the Baltic provinces in the Imperial era, Jews had primarily become associated with retailing, inn-keeping and business, and with towns rather than the countryside. After the mid-nineteenth century Jews were able to settle more extensively in Riga, and by 1914 they constituted more than ten per cent of the city's population.⁵ In the Baltic provinces of the early twentieth century, the relatively modern economy and political society co-resided somewhat uneasily with retention of the restrictions on the Jewish population regarding settlement and land ownership. After the unrest of 1905, for instance, even the basically conservative political parties established by the Baltic Germans advocated – unsuccessfully – the removal of all legal restrict-tions based on religion or 'nationality'.⁶

During World War I, pogroms directed at Jews and looting of Jewish property became a common feature in the contested western borderlands. Army units, especially Cossacks, seem to have been the main instigators. Widespread anti-Semitism among the Russian General Staff was clearly one predominant factor here. These persecutions, however, were practiced primarily in the Polish and Ruthenian lands.⁷ Jews in Riga were apparently spared this experience by the actions of the local Imperial military command, determined to retain public order.⁸

When the independent Latvian state emerged in 1919/20, the position of the resident Jewish people within the national project was, as I have indicated, questioned and uncertain. Some signs of trouble had emerged during the War of

---

³ Dribins, Leo (2001b): "The History of the Jewish Community in Latvia. A Brief Chronological Survey", pp. 11–17; Gordon, Frank (1990): *Latvians and Jews between Germany and Russia*, p. 5.
⁴ Gitelman, Zvi (2001): *A Century of Ambivalence. The Jews of Russia and the Soviet Union, 1881 to the Present*, p. 2.
⁵ *Beiträge zur Statistik der Stadt Riga und ihrer Verwaltung* (1909), I, p. 335; Ezergailis, Andrievs (1999): *Holokausts vācu okupētajā Latvijā 1941–1944*, pp. 77–82.
⁶ *Baltische Monatsschrift*, 1905, 11. As late as 1900, however, *Rigasche Rundschau* argued for a stricter enforcement of the prohibition of Jews to acquire land. See *Rigasche Rundschau*, 1900/01/05.
⁷ Holquist, Peter (2011): "The Role of Personality in the First (1914–1915) Russian Occupation of Galicia and Bukovina", pp. 52–68.
⁸ Lohr, Eric (2011): "1915 and the War Pogrom Paradigm in the Russian Empire", pp. 41–49;

Liberation. In the spring of 1920, two Jewish men were killed by Latvian troops entering the small town of Kārsava in Eastern Latgale. The provisional Ulmanis government was forced by Britain and France to make an inquiry, but its report laid the blame entirely on 'Jewish plunderers'. In Rēzekne, also in Latgale, more than thirty Jewish people were injured when the Latvian military opened fire with machine-guns on a shop, long after hostilities had ceased. Latvian soldiers continued to harass and plunder Jews in Latgale all through the summer of 1920. Similarly, repeated cases of Jews being assaulted and beaten occurred in Riga. The main perpetrators appear to have been persons associated with the Latvian army and police.[9]

The territory that became Latgale had previously belonged administratively to Vitebsk province, not to the Baltic territory where the Latvian national movement had its centre. The non-Latvian inhabitants of Latgale were therefore probably somewhat unprepared for a situation where they became part of a nationalising Latvian state. Jews in this area were primarily Yiddish- and Russian-speakers and belonged culturally to the Lithuanian or Litvak Jewry. They had formed a sizable Jewish community in Tsarist times but were spread across the states of Lithuania, Latvia, Poland and the Soviet Union after 1919. As historian Ezra Mendelsohn has argued, if this territory had been defined instead according to a Jewish conception of territoriality, it would have included the cities of Daugavpils, Kaunas, Vilnius, and Minsk.[10]

When the national Latvian forces during the War of Liberation managed to secure Latgale for the new Latvian state, they also acquired a population of Litvak Jewry which they apparently perceived as alien, perhaps even hostile to the national ambition of transforming this multi-ethnic territory into a Latvian province. At the same time, the disruptions caused by the war led to a migration of Jews from the Eastern provinces of Latvia to the capital Riga, almost doubling their proportion of the city's inhabitants.[11]

In the new Latvian republic the discriminatory Imperial legislation directed against Jews was finally abolished, but Jews became a distinct and separate 'nation' or *tautība* in the midst of a budding Latvian national state. The extent to which they should be included in the new national and political setting was a

---

[9] Dribins, Leo (2001a): *Antisemītisms un tā izpausmes Latvijā. Vēstures atskats*, p. 84; Stranga (1997), pp. 38–39. Stranga puts part of the blame for these occurrences on the Minister for the Interior, Arvēds Bergs, whom he holds responsible for the spreading of anti-Semitic notions. Rēzekne had been the site of an anti-Jewish pogrom already during the war, in July 1917, when Latgale was still part of Vitebsk province. See Buldakov, Vladimir P (2011): "Freedom, Shortages, Violence: The Origins of the 'Revolutionary Anti-Jewish Pogrom' in Russia, 1917–1918", p. 81.
[10] Mendelsohn, Ezra (1987): *The Jews of East Central Europe between the World Wars*, p. 33; 242.
[11] Skujenieks, M (1925): "Rīgas iedzīvotāju tautība", p. 577. According to Skujenieks, the Jews in Riga constituted 13.6 per cent of the city's population in 1920 and 11.7 per cent in 1925.

matter for debate. Admittedly, the Jewish population was treated as one of the acknowledged minorities, and was allowed to form a separate 'national' school system receiving government funding.[12] Ethnic categorisation was primarily based on self-definition.[13]

It is debatable, however, whether this should be seen as a clear sign of tolerance and recognition on the part of the Latvian majority.[14] A somewhat less benign interpretation is that nationalist Latvian politicians preferred several small minority groups to fewer and larger ones. Since most of the Jews in Latvia were – apart from Yiddish – primarily Russian- or German-speakers, their non-recognition as an official minority would have substantially increased the ranks of these other, previously very powerful, minority groups. Also, it should be remembered that this 'official' ethnic categorization was not synonymous with experienced ethnicity. A moot point was, for instance, whether Christianised or atheist Jews should still be regarded as Jews.[15] Another question was whether the traditionally subordinate group of Jews, now formally included in a liberal *Rechstsstaat*, would cease to be a target of crowd violence motivated by older and xenophobic notions of Jewish inferiority. Such had definitely been the case in Imperial Russia, and also in newly independent Poland.[16]

While the nationalising Latvian state was not prone to assimilate the Jewish population to the core nation, the adoption of a certain degree of 'cultural autonomy' for the ethnic minorities still gave the Latvian Jews some possibility of publicly defining and developing their cultural distinctiveness.[17] While Jewish schools had certainly existed before, they now became part of a state-funded

---

[12] The 'cultural autonomy' of the ethnic minorities was, however, never included in the Constitution. See Stranga, Aivars (1997): *Ebreji un diktatūras Baltijā (1926.–1940. gads.)*, p. 40. It is somewhat strange, therefore, to find that Andrievs Ezergailis claims that the Latvian state granted the minorities the rights of cultural autonomy in the 1922 Constitution. See Ezergailis (1999), pp. 86–87. It appears that Ezergailis is a bit too anxious to show that anti-Semitism was rare in Latvia during the First Republic.

[13] The national minorities received funding in proportion to their number, which meant that the activists were eager to convince 'fellow-nationals' to enlist.

[14] The nature of 'minority' politics and the prevalence or absence of anti-Semitic notions in Latvia during the First Republic are fiercely contested issues among Latvian historians. For an overview, see Onken, Eva-Clarita (1998): *Revisionismus schon vor der Geschichte. Aktuelle Kontroversen in Lettland um die Judenvernichtung und die lettische Kolloboration während der nationalsozialistischen Besatzung*, pp. 51–61.

[15] For instance, the Latvian nationalist ideologue and journalist Ernests Blanks maintained that Christianised Jews still retained the 'spirit of their nation' and were not able to experience the Latvian sense of community in the same way as ethnic Latvians. See Blanks, Ernests (1926): *Nācija un valsts*, p. 5.

[16] Engel, David (2011): "What's in a Pogrom? European Jews in the Age of Violence", pp. 19–35.

[17] A similar process took place in Lithuania. In Germany, there was also a tendency towards a more pronounced Jewish culture in the 1920s when a considerable part of the Jewish population sought to reaffirm their 'roots' after several decades of attempted assimilation. See Brenner, Michael (1996): *The Renaissance of Jewish Culture in Weimar Germany*, pp. 69–152.

system along with the schools established by Baltic Germans, Russians and Poles. At the same time, the Jewish population in Latvia was, as we have seen, hardly homogeneous. Although united by religion and custom, they were clearly divided into the primarily Yiddish- and German-speaking Jews in Riga and Kurzeme, and the Yiddish- and Russian-speaking Jews of Latgale.[18] Since the ethnic categorisation of Jews rested on religion and culture rather than language, the Jewish schools established in the 1920s used a wide range of tuition languages: Yiddish, Hebrew, German and Russian.[19] The choice of instruction language appears to have rested with the parents at each school.[20]

On a political level, the Jewish minority was split into a variety of parties, ranging from the Radical Bundists with close connections with the Social Democrats to the Conservative and Orthodox party of Mordecai Dubins.[21] They, too, differed markedly on the national question. Socialist Jews were mainly international in outlook and viewed 'national' state-building with suspicion. Zionist Jews regarded Palestine as the only viable 'homeland' for the Jews, while Orthodox Jews desired integration but not assimilation in the new Latvian state.

Jewish students

The legal restrictions imposed on the Jewish population in the Russian Empire naturally reduced their possibility of receiving higher education. However, with the expansion of the Russian university system during the nineteenth century, and the establishment of new universities in Kiev, Kharkov, and Kazan, an increasing number of Jewish young men applied for enrolment. Since most careers in the Imperial bureaucracy were closed to them, Jewish students appear to have gone in for technical and medical subjects.[22]

The presence of Jewish students at the Russian universities seems, however, to have been a contested issue. Around 1880, severe restrictions were imposed on the Jewish population regarding access to higher education. This should probably be seen in the context of the Slavophile movement's insistence on a

---

[18] In a census in 1925 investigating the 'first language' of the Latvian Jewry, 85 per cent responded Yiddish, 9.4 per cent German, 5 per cent Russian, and 0.6 per cent Latvian. Naturally, most of the Latvian Jews were bi-, tri- or multilingual. Mendelsohn (1987), p. 246, table 6.1.
[19] In 1928–1929, 48 per cent of the pupils at Jewish schools in Latvia studied in Yiddish, 31 per cent in Hebrew, 14 per cent in German and 7 per cent in Russian. Mendelsohn (1987), p. 251, table 6.2. While Latvian was not the language of instruction, courses in the Latvian language were of course taught at all Jewish schools.
[20] See Levin, Dov (2001): "Some Basic Facts on Latvian Jewry – Before, During and After World War II", p. 136.
[21] Dribins (2001b), pp. 33–36.
[22] On the expansion of the Russian university system, see Meyer, Klaus (1987): "Die Universität im Russischen Reich in der ersten Hälfte des 19. Jahrhundert", pp. 37–50.

thorough Russification of the Empire. Moreover, Jews from the Western *gubernijas* were also suspected of disloyalty towards the tsarist regime. Imperial authorities perceived connections between Jews and revolutionary movements, and wanted to suppress such notions at the universities. In 1887 a *numerus clausus* was imposed on Jewish students, limiting their proportion at the Moscow and St Petersburg universities to a mere three per cent of the student body.[23] Consequently, Jewish youths' access to universities in Russia proper were drastically reduced.[24]

When these restrictions were imposed, many Jewish students chose to move to Dorpat in the Baltic provinces, the only university within the Empire that was relatively autonomous and therefore not yet affected by these regulations.[25] Census material from Dorpat University in the late 1880s shows that Jews, defined by religion, constituted as much as nineteen per cent of the matriculated students.[26] However, during the imposed Russification of the university between 1889 and 1905, Dorpat – now renamed Jur'ev – was required to abide by the rules of the other Imperial universities, not allowing more than five per cent of the newly enrolled students to belong to the Mosaic faith. Only after the turbulence of 1905 were these restrictions gradually disregarded.[27] When the restrictions were finally removed in 1916, the proportion of Jewish students immediately more than doubled, reaching almost 23 per cent of the regular student body, and 56 per cent of the pharmaceutical students.[28]

The proportion of Jewish students at the Riga Polytechnical Institute seems to have been well above twenty per cent in the 1890s. One important reason for this was evidently the aforementioned set of restrictions on Jewish youths applying for enrolment at universities in Russia proper. In the Baltic provinces, however,

---

[23] Philipson, Joakim (2008): *The Purpose of Evolution. The 'struggle for existence' in the Russian-Jewish press 1860–1900*, p. 133. The quota for universities within the Pale of Settlement was 10 per cent, and at other Russian universities 5 per cent.

[24] In contrast, in the Habsburg Empire Jewish youths did not encounter such obstacles in the early 20th century. In 1910, for instance, Jewish students comprised 17.3 per cent of the total student body in institutions of higher education, while their proportion of the total population was a mere 4.4 per cent. This made the Jewish group by far the most 'education-prone' in the empire. See Pálfy, Zoltán (2003): *National Controversy in the Transylvanian Academe: The Cluj/Kolozsvar University, 1900–1950*, table 5, p. 71.

[25] Amburger, Erik (1987): "Die Bedeutung der Universität Dorpat für Osteuropa. Untersucht an der Zusammensetzung des Lehrkörpers und der Studentenschaft in den Jahren 1802–1889", pp. 177–178.

[26] Siilivask (1987): "Über die Rolle der Universität Tartu bei der Entwicklung der inländschen und internationalen Wissenschaft", p. 115; Tankler, Hain (1996): "Dorpat, a German-speaking International University in the Russian Empire", p. 95.

[27] *History of Tartu University, 1632–1982* (1985), p.141.

[28] *History of Tartu University, 1632–1982* (1985), table 4, p. 141. Admittedly, these figures may be somewhat misleading, since the operation of Dorpat/Tartu University was very disorganised by the war. For this or other reasons, by 1925 the proportion of Jewish students at Tartu was no higher than 3.9 per cent. See Raun, Toivu U (1991): *Estonia and the Estonians*, p. 135.

the institutions of higher education did not apply such discriminatory means before 1890.[29]

When the new Latvian university opened in 1919, the aim was clearly to establish a national university. Latvian youths of both sexes were for the first time to be given the chance to partake in higher education conducted in Latvian. The organisation committee decided in August 1919 that in the first place, admission should be restricted to Latvian citizens, with special preference for former soldiers from the War of Liberation.[30] However, the ethnic dilemma soon became evident. Accounting for the first crop of applications, vice-principal Paulis Lejiņš warned that 'far too many Jews', especially German (-speaking) Jews, had applied, and asked for measures to limit their enrolment. The prospect of receiving a substantial number of Jewish students seems to have surprised and dismayed the members of the committee. It was decided that the preference for Latvian citizens should be strictly implemented. As a secondary consideration, students from 'friendly neighbours', i.e. Lithuania and Estonia, were also welcomed. Applications from other 'foreigners', however, should be turned down with reference to the lack of university premises.[31] As a result of these restrictions, only twenty-six 'foreign' students, mainly Russian or Belarusian citizens, were enrolled in 1919.[32]

Naturally, these policies were not in accordance with the university principle of open admission. The academic tradition was to enrol all applicants who could produce relevant school-leaving grades and pay the tuition fees. In restricting admission to Latvian citizens, however, the organisation committee did *not* impose limits on the number of students belonging to the minority ethnic groups in Latvia – Germans, Russians, Poles, and Jews – who held Latvian citizenship. The only 'ethnic' restriction in force was the official requirement that lectures should be held in Latvian. However, since this proved impracticable in some faculties due to a persistent lack of academics knowledgeable in Latvian, lectures were to a considerable extent delivered in Russian or German during the first academic years.

---

[29] *Latvijā 19. gadsimtā. Vēstures apceres,* pp. 320–321. The restrictions on Jews at Tsarist universities meant that a majority of Russian Jewish students in the early 20th century received their education instead at universities in Western Europe, most of them in medicine. See Karady, Victor (2004): "Student Mobility and Western Universities: Patterns of Unequal Exchange in the European Academic Market, 1880–1939", p. 388; 398.

[30] LVVA. Latvijas Universitātes fonds, 7427/6/1, Organisation Committee Minutes, 1919/08/29.

[31] LVVA. Latvijas Universitātes fonds, 7427/6/1, Organisation Committee Minutes, 1919/09/16. Lejiņš belonged to the Faculty of Agronomy, the most ethnically Latvian as regards both teaching staff and student body. However, medical professor Zariņš also complained that the number of 'foreign Jews' was particularly high in his faculty.

[32] LVVA. Latvijas Universitātes fonds, 7427/6/54, Gadu statistiskās ziņas par studentu un mācības spēku sastāvu. They constituted 4 per cent of the student body.

A glance at the ethnic composition of the first student body in December 1919 shows that the organisers' expectations were not fulfilled. Very few Baltic Germans and ethnic Russians had applied. At the same time, the number of students from the Jewish minority was far higher than anticipated, almost 22 per cent of the student body.

Table 1. Students at the University of Latvia, 15 Dec. 1919, according to 'nationality'.

Faculty	Latvian	Russian	German	Jewish	Other
Architecture	9	1	2	9	0
Engineering	32	2	0	8	0
Law/Economics	58	0	1	16	0
Chemistry	36	2	0	36	2
Agronomy	59	1	1	0	0
Natural science/Maths	37	0	0	11	1
Mechanics	18	2	0	29	1
Medicine	66	0	0	17	2
Philosophy/Linguist.	143	0	2	5	0
Veterinary studies	0	0	0	2	0
Total	458	7	6	133	6
Percentage	75.1	1.1	1.0	21.8	1.0

Source: LVVA. Latvijas Universitātes fonds, 7427/6/54, Gadu statistiskās ziņas par studentu un mācības spēku sastāvu.

The conspicuous lack of ethnic Lithuanian and Estonian students was a great disappointment to the organisation committee. Of the first 610 students, only one was Lithuanian and two were Estonian. This result was explained initially in terms of insufficient advertising, and further attempts were made to attract applicants from the two neighbouring Baltic states. In 1921, for instance, tuition fees for these students were made the same as for Latvian students.[33] This was to no avail. Estonian and Lithuanian students continued to constitute a negligible share of the student body at the University of Latvia during the entire First Republic.[34]

The reduction of tuition fees for Estonian and Lithuanian students did *not* apply to Jewish applicants who were citizens of Estonia or Lithuania. When a group of Jewish students holding Lithuanian passports in 1922 asked for a

---

[33] LVVA. Latvijas Universitātes fonds, 7427/6/1, Organisation Committee Minutes, 1919/09/19; 1921/09/21. The University of Lithuania made similar concessions to Latvian students. Ibid., 1922/06/30.
[34] In 1924, students from Lithuania and Estonia constituted a mere 0.5 per cent of the student body at the University of Latvia. LVVA. Latvijas Universitātes fonds, 7427/6/54, Gadu statistiskās ziņas par studentu un mācības spēku sastāvu

reduction of fees to match the other Lithuanian students at *Latvijas Augstskola*, their supplication was simply rejected.[35] Obviously, only *ethnic* Lithuanians were to receive favourable treatment – not Lithuanian citizens of Jewish descent.

The enrolment figures at *Latvijas Augstskola* during the first years reveal a striking predominance of Jewish youths among the students from the ethnic minorities. Apparently there was a substantial demand for higher education among the urban Jewish middle-class in Latvia. Most of these Jewish students were to be found in the technical faculties, the natural sciences, medicine, law, and economics, precisely the faculties where Russian and German were still used to some extent as tuition languages.[36] In the Faculty of Mechanics, the Jewish students actually formed a clear majority, and in chemistry they equalled the number of ethnic Latvians. On the other hand, Jewish students were almost non-existent in the Faculty of Philology and Philosophy, and the Faculty of Agronomy, which even in the decades to come remained the most thoroughly 'Latvian' faculties in terms of students.

The obviously undesired outcome of the 1919 enrolment appears to have prompted the organisation committee to sharpen its attitude on 'national' matters. As shown in chapter 4, in September 1920 a mandatory language test was introduced for all newly-enrolled students: an oral examination of proficiency in Latvian in the presence of faculty representatives.[37] Since records of these examinations have not been kept, it is rather difficult to tell just how many students belonging to the minority nationalities were actually barred by this test. However, there is a clear discrepancy between the first, 'pre-test' enrolment figures, where 33 per cent of the applicants were designated as *svešs*, or 'foreign', and actual enrolment, where this proportion fell to 21 per cent.[38] This indicates that the language test barred about a third of the 'minority' students. In the Faculty of Medicine, where applications exceeded the intake, the language barrier appears to have been applied even more strictly. In the first round, 'foreign' applicants constituted 45 per cent, whereas their proportion of the enrolled students was only 27 per cent. This was surely also connected to the

---

[35] LVVA. Latvijas Universitātes fonds, 7427/6/1, Organisation Committee Minutes, 1922/09/06.
[36] LVVA. Latvijas Universitātes fonds, 7427/6/37a. Pārskats par Latvijas augstskolas, vēlāk Universitātes, nodibināšanu un viņas darbību. Report from the vice-principal to the Ministry of Education, 1920/03/31. See above, chapter 4.
[37] LVVA. Latvijas Universitātes fonds, 7427/6/1, Organisation Committee Minutes, 1920/09/08. As shown in a previous chapter, vice-principal Paulis Lejiņš, an active force on the 'national' side of the committee, actually advocated a stricter test.
[38] LVVA. Latvijas Universitātes fonds, 7427/6/1, Organisation Committee Minutes, 1920/09/01; LVVA. Latvijas Universitātes fonds, 7427/6/54, Gadu statistiskās ziņas par studentu un mācības spēku sastāvu.

perceived 'Jewish question', since a huge majority of the 'foreign' medical students were Jewish.[39]

For the university leadership, the prevalence of Jewish applicants was an obvious dilemma. They apparently saw it as a 'problem' that had to be solved and from their previous experience at Russian universities, where quotas had been imposed, were perhaps mentally quite prepared to find a means to restrict the proportion of Jewish students. At the same time, they were now operating in a state that had not only a nationalising agenda but also pretensions to constitute a democracy where equality before the law was an essential characteristic. The main ethnic 'minorities' – Germans, Jews, and Russians – also formed separate political parties with seats in the provisional Parliament. These 'minority' politicians would not tolerate any overt discrimination of Latvian citizens on ethnic grounds only. Imposing formal quotas on Jewish students was politically impossible. A language test, therefore, was seen as the only politically viable method to reduce the enrolment of Jewish students.[40]

These language tests seem to have reduced the proportion of Jewish students at the University of Latvia during the following years. Applicants from the Russian-speaking Jewish communities in Latgale, especially, found the language requirements difficult to meet; even so, their requests to have the language tests postponed were turned down by the organisation committee.[41]

The influx of ethnic Latvian males after the War of Liberation, and perhaps also an increased enrolment of Baltic German youths, also contributed to this trend. The students enrolled in the autumn of 1920 consisted of 78.5 per cent Latvians, 4.7 per cent Germans, and 14.4 per cent Jews.[42] In a deliberate move to facilitate the recruitment of young Latvian men to the university, many former soldiers in the War of Liberation were exempted from tuition fees.[43] Still, Jewish students remained a predominant and conspicuous group among those

---

[39] LVVA. Latvijas Universitātes fonds, 7427/6/1, Organisation Committee Minutes, 1920/09/01; LVVA. Latvijas Universitātes fonds, 7427/6/54, Gadu statistiskās ziņas par studentu un mācības spēku sastāvu. Among the 'foreign' medical students finally enrolled in 1920, 77 per cent were Jewish.

[40] Within the organising committee, the principal Ernsts Felsbergs seems to have been most perceptive of political and societal realities. In 1920, he proposed to alter the commonly derogatory label of Jew, "žīds", to the more neutral "ebrejs" in all official publications, whereas his fellow linguists Endzelīns and Šmits argued that "žīds" was the 'historically correct' term and therefore should be maintained. See LVVA. Latvijas Universitātes fonds, 7427/6/1, Organisation Committee Minutes, 1920/09/15.

[41] LVVA. Latvijas Universitātes fonds, 7427/6/1, Organisation Committee Minutes, 1920/09/15.

[42] LVVA. Latvijas Universitātes fonds, 7427/6/54, Gadu statistiskās ziņas par studentu un mācības spēku sastāvu.

[43] By May 21, 1921, 612 Latvian soldiers had been wholly exempted from tuition fees, and a further 137 partially exempted. LVVA. Latvijas Universitātes fonds, 7427/6/54, Gadu statistiskās ziņas par studentu un mācības spēku sastāvu.

categorised as non-Latvians.[44] By October 1922, the ethnic composition of the students was as follows:

Table 2. Students at the University of Latvia, 17 October 1922, according to 'nationality'.

Faculty	Latvian	Russian	German	Jewish	Other
Architecture	95	4	18	15	1
Engineering	378	18	21	55	7
Law/Economics	835	13	47	87	6
Chemistry	332	10	51	141	5
Agronomy	539	0	10	6	3
Natural science/Maths	283	5	6	63	3
Mechanics	328	14	33	88	11
Medicine	580	9	36	145	7
Philosophy/Linguist.	683	7	16	11	2
Theology	64	0	16	1	0
Veterinary studies	96	0	2	10	0
Total	4,213	80	256	622	45
Percentage	80.1	1.5	4.9	11.9	0.9

Source: LVVA. Latvijas Universitātes fonds, 7427/6/54, Gadu statistiskās ziņas par studentu un mācības spēku sastāvu.

Generally, the proportion of Baltic German students increased substantially and the proportion of Jews clearly fell. However, even after this marked decline, Jewish students were still by far the most conspicuous of the ethnic minority groups. They also remained more prominent in some of the faculties, primarily chemistry, where they constituted 26 per cent of the student body, Mechanics (nineteen per cent), and Medicine (nineteen per cent). Not surprisingly, these faculties were also among the slowest to apply Latvian as the language of tuition. In 1921, 71 per cent of the lectures in Mechanics were still being held in Russian, while in Chemistry 42 per cent of the lectures were held in Russian and thirteen per cent in German. In the Faculty of Medicine, partly due to the fact that the professor of anatomy was recruited from Sweden, 48 per cent of the lectures were held in German.[45]

However, there is an important difference here between 'nationality' or *tautība* and Latvian citizenship that should be emphasised. The great majority of

---

[44] In his official report, printed in the monthly journal of the Ministry of Education in 1921, the principal Ernsts Felsbergs calculated that Jewish youths constituted 15.7 per cent of the students, primarily concentrated in the faculties of Chemistry, Mechanics, and Medicine. See Felsbergs, Ernsts (1921a): "Dažas ziņas par Latvijas Augstskolu", pp. 305–306.
[45] LVVA. Latvijas Universitātes fonds, 7427/6/54, Gadu statistiskās ziņas par studentu un mācības spēku sastāvu. Calculation of languages used at lectures during one week in 1921.

the students belonging to non-Latvian *tautības* were in fact Latvian citizens. University records in the early 1920s show that almost 93 per cent of the students designated as Jews possessed Latvian citizenship, a proportion that was almost exactly the same in December 1922.[46] In spite of being Latvian citizens, however, in the university records the Jewish students were still registered as belonging to a 'foreign' *tautība*, together with the other non-Latvian minorities.

The 1st December riot

The formal demarcation between Latvian and 'foreign' students was also mirrored in the structuring of student corporations and associations. Latvian students organised corporations primarily by geographic regions, while the Jewish students immediately formed a society for mutual economic assistance. In 1921 some Jewish students formed a more self-conscious and assertive association, *Vetulija*, which sported the motto 'Friendship, Honour, Nation'.[47] Moreover, in the student elections in the autumn of 1922, socialist Jewish students who had previously formed a 'progressive bloc' with Latvians now established their own political party. Organisationally and politically, Jewish students had become more conspicuous than before.

At the same time, nationalist sentiments among the Latvian students were fanned by the newly started student weekly *Students*, whose editors were apparently connected to the extreme nationalist organisation *Latvju Nacionālais Klubs*.[48] In the first issue of the weekly, the editors proclaimed that they wanted to unite all the studying Latvian youths who supported Latvia's independence and expressed a love of the Latvian *tauta un zeme* – nation and territory.[49] Apparently, students from the ethnic minorities were not included in this scenario. The paper expressed particular hostility to Jewish students, descending in some instances into outright anti-Semitism. For instance, deriding some Jewish students' lack of proficiency in Latvian, the paper declared that they could be easily recognised by "their bent noses and their smell of garlic".[50] The editors were also clearly eager to publish instances of Jewish students being arrested for

---

[46] LVVA. Latvijas Universitātes fonds, 7427/6/37a. Pārskats par Latvijas augstskolas, vēlāk Universitātes, nodibināšanu un viņas darbību. Statement from the Vice-Principal to the Ministry of Education, 1920/03/31; Overview of the University, 1922/11/16; LVVA. Latvijas Universitātes fonds, 7427/6/485. Ebreju studentu saraksts. 621 Jewish students are recorded, matriculating in 1920–1922.
[47] LVVA. Latvijas Universitātes fonds, 7427/6/83, LU Studentu organizācijas reģistrācijas žurnāls, 1922–1939; 7427/6/1, Organisation Committee Minutes, 1921/03/09.
[48] *Students* started in September 1922, and gave LNK a wide coverage in spite of the fact that this was by no means a student organisation. See *Students* 1922/11/22; 1923/01/17.
[49] *Students* 1922/09/22.
[50] *Students* 1922/09/22.

possessing forbidden – i.e. communist – books, thus emphasising a 'connection' between Jews and Communism.[51]

The emergence of right-wing nationalist student movements was actually rather common among European countries in the early 1920s. In Finland, for instance, many students in this period adhered to a conservative agrarian ideology, primarily connecting them with the farming population in their native regions and portraying Communists, urban Liberals and Russians as enemies of the Finnish nation.[52] The experience of war, either the civil war in Finland, the wars of liberation in the newly emerged Baltic states, or naturally the tragedies experienced in World War I, certainly had an impact on the young male population entering universities in the early 1920s. According to right-wing nationalist ideology, the universities should be reserved for the sons (and to a much lesser degree, the daughters) of the titular nation.

In December 1922, the growing polarization between nationalist Latvian and Jewish students manifested itself openly. On 1 December Jewish students were forcibly evicted from the lecture halls in the main university building. According to many witnesses, a crowd of Latvian students roamed the building shouting "Get the Jews out!" forcing Jewish students out of the lecture halls and into the street. Some fighting also ensued, but there appear to have been no major injuries.[53]

Outraged by these incidents, the Jewish students demanded an official investigation by the university, but the university council initially decided to view this as an internal student matter to be handled by the Student Court.[54] Apart from this, Ernsts Felsbergs, acting principal, tried to alleviate the situation somewhat by issuing a circular pleading for tolerance and asking for the cooperation of all students to restore order.[55] Obviously not satisfied with these measures, the Jewish students turned directly to the *Saeima*. On 13 December, seven Jewish students sent a letter to the *Saeima*, citing the violence and verbal abuse directed at Jewish students in the university buildings. The violence had not ceased, they maintained, it had only moved from the university premises into the streets. They also criticised the principal for not taking any forceful

---

[51] See *Students* 1922/09/22; 1922/11/08.
[52] Kolbe, Laura (1996): "Rural or urban", pp. 52–60.
[53] See, for example, LVVA. Latvijas Universitātes fonds, 7427/6/363. Studentu ziņojumi par konfliktiem ebreju un latviešu studentu starpā. Letter from Joffe, a Jewish student, to the investigation committee, 1923/01/04. His description of events is not materially different from the Latvian students' version.
[54] LVVA. Latvijas Universitātes fonds, 7427/6/2, University Council Minutes, 1922/12/06.
[55] LVVA. Latvijas Universitātes fonds, 7427/6/363. Studentu ziņojumi par konfliktiem ebreju un latviešu studentu starpā. Circular from Felsbergs, 1922/12/09.

action to prevent these incidents, and for not imposing sanctions or penalties on the perpetrators.[56]

On 15 December the anti-Semitic paper *Latvijas Sargs* published an article supporting the student fraternities that had staged the riot.[57] The incident was now on the political agenda, with the Cabinet imposing a heavy fine on *Latvijas Sargs* for publishing what was seen as an inflammatory article.[58]

Obviously under pressure, the university council now decided to appoint a formal commission of inquiry headed by vice-principal Juris Plāķis, with a mandate to investigate the events that had taken place. The students were to be represented by the chairman of the Students' Council, Rozentāls.[59] Actually, the choice of Plāķis as chairman was somewhat ominous, since only one week previously he had expressed anti-Semitic opinions in Felsbergs's presence at a faculty meeting.[60]

Officially, the incidents were described primarily as an internal student matter, since they concerned alleged violence between students. Still, it was all too obvious that everything which had transpired reflected a wider issue of ethnic boundary-drawing and friction within the university, and also the thorny issue of 'nationality' and citizenship in Latvia at the time.[61]

When the commission started to question students, several interpretations of the occurrences emerged. Jewish students protested against what they saw as clear expressions of anti-Semitic hostility.[62] The Latvian students giving evidence to the commission did not deny that some violence had been perpetrated against

---

[56] LVVA. Izglītības ministrijas fonds, 1632/2/660. Latvijas Satversmes Sapulces ziņojumi un lēmumi, Saeimas deputātu raksts ministram par vardarbību pret ebreju studentiem. Letter to the delegates of the Saeima, 1922/12/13.

[57] *Latvijas Sargs*, 1922/12/15.

[58] See Ezergailis (1999), p. 96, note 26. Ezergailis, however, is keener to see this as proof of the absence of anti-Semitic notions in the Cabinet than to investigate the incident itself. Leo Dribins likewise primarily stresses the stand taken by the Cabinet on this issue. Dribins (2001a), pp. 90–91.

[59] LVVA. Latvijas Universitātes fonds, 7427/6/2, University Council Minutes, 1922/12/20. The commission, 'Studentu starpgadījuma izmeklēšanas komisija', interviewed witnesses in January–February 1923, and delivered its findings in April of the same year. The testimonies will be extensively used in this section to analyse the relations between nationalist Latvians and Jews at the university. Copies of the testimonies can be found in LVVA. Latvijas Universitātes fonds, 7427/6/268. Studentu ziņojumi par konfliktiem ebreju un latviešu studentu starpā.

[60] LVVA. Latvijas Universitātes fonds, 7427/6/363, Minutes of the Faculty of Philology and Philosophy, 1922/12/16. During a faculty meeting, Plāķis argued against open competition as a way to recruit academic staff, since in such a procedure "a Jew might crop up".

[61] Perhaps because matters of 'nation' and 'nationality' have continued to be problematic during the Soviet period and the Second Republic, Latvian historians have not written anything substantial about the 1st December riot in the University building.

[62] LVVA. Latvijas Universitātes fonds, 7427/6/268. Studentu ziņojumi par konfliktiem ebreju un latviešu studentu starpā. Letter from an association of Jewish students to the Principal, 1922/12/05.

Jews, but claimed that a number Jewish students had acted provocatively. According to one version, a Jewish student armed with a knife had instigated the whole riot. However, this person remained unidentified and the story must be regarded as unsubstantiated.[63]

Other testimonies reveal different aspects of the events. According to several of the Latvian students being questioned, the issue was more political than national. The riot took place immediately before the Student Council elections, and the main reason, it was claimed, was the deep animosity between Jewish socialists in the student association "Vetulija" and Latvians in the corporation "Fraternitas Arctica".[64] However, it could not be denied that every Jewish student who could be found was forcibly evicted from the university building on 1 December, not just members of "Vetulija".

Several of the Latvian students put forward another reason for the unrest. They claimed that the incident was caused by what they saw as persistent 'misconduct' on the part of the Jewish students. The Jews, they alleged, always hogged the best tables in the drawing rooms, kept to themselves and were impossible to cooperate with. They flaunted the established rules of conduct, made a lot of noise, whistled, sang, smoked, threw fag-ends everywhere, and refused to take off coats and caps in the lecture halls. As a result, they had become very unpopular with the other students.[65] According to these testimonies, some Jewish students acted very provocatively – such as smoking below 'No smoking' signs, and, when being asked to stop making a noise, deliberately starting to whistle the hymn 'Christ is My Life'.[66]

It is important to see the ethnic and religious element in some of these perceived 'provocations' – they were not simply irritating instances of disorder. While in the last instance it is fairly easy to see the religious provocation in the gesture of a Jewish student whistling a Christian hymn, flouting smoking regulations requires some extra thought. The provocation here, I suspect, was less the discomfort of the smoke, or the disregard of an official sign, but the fact that the sign was written in *Latvian*. To disobey regulations in Latvian symbolically implied that that language was of no consequence. Likewise, the refusal

---

[63] LVVA. Latvijas Universitātes fonds, 7427/6/268. Studentu ziņojumi par konfliktiem ebreju un latviešu studentu starpā. Testimony of Strauss, a caretaker, 1922/12/03; Arturs Melbards 1923/01/17; Jēkabs Krūze 1923/01/24.
[64] LVVA. Latvijas Universitātes fonds, 7427/6/268. Studentu ziņojumi par konfliktiem ebreju un latviešu studentu starpā. Testimony of Arturs Melbards, 1923/01/17; Alfreds Linde, 1923/01/17.
[65] LVVA. Latvijas Universitātes fonds, 7427/6/268. Studentu ziņojumi par konfliktiem ebreju un latviešu studentu starpā. Testimony of Sergejs Aleksejevs, 1923/01/24; Jēkabs Krūze 1923/01/24; Nikolajs Plato 1923/01/24; Arturs Lābans 1923/02/14; Rudolfs Bols 1923/02/19.
[66] LVVA. Latvijas Universitātes fonds, 7427/6/268. Studentu ziņojumi par konfliktiem ebreju un latviešu studentu starpā. Testimony of Arturs Lābans 1923/02/14; Rudolfs Bols 1923/02/19.

to remove caps should probably be seen in the light of many Jewish students apparently wearing what was described as 'national' headwear.⁶⁷

Naturally, one should be wary of accepting the Latvian students' testimonies at face value, especially since the commission showed very little interest in hearing evidence from Jewish students. What was seen as 'provocative' may to a very large extent have been in the eye of the beholder, and the occurrences and gestures described may have been isolated instances rather than general practice. It is still interesting, however, to see exactly what actions and gestures the Latvian students described as 'provocations', and also to consider whether these actions could be interpreted differently.

As early as the Autumn of 1922 there existed strong notions among nationalist Latvian students that the Jews at the university acted disruptively and 'primitively' in the lecture halls, and 'babbled' provocatively in Russian.⁶⁸ However, making allowance for some of the hostile overtones, we can still detect some traces of a symbolic act of ethnic division in the lecture halls. Apparently, this demarcation process was strongest between Jews and ethnic Latvians, but the pattern is not clear-cut. In fact, some of the testimonies indicate a separation along *religious* lines, between Christians and Jews. For example, some of the witnesses to the December riot preferred to describe it as 'Christians' chasing Jews.⁶⁹

No doubt, religious affiliation tended to reinforce ethnic boundaries specifically towards the Jewish population. Ethnic Latvians could in fact be either Lutherans, Catholics, and Orthodox, which to some extent 'blurred' the demarcations from other nations and ethnic groups in the Baltic territory. Jews, on the other hand, had since Imperial times been especially singled out and excluded on religious grounds. The Jewish students constituted by far the largest and most conspicuous minority group at the university, and their visibility was enhanced by the fact that student corporations and associations were organised primarily along ethnic lines.

Indeed, some of the actions that the Latvian students disparagingly described as 'misconduct' and 'provocations' could be seen instead as calculated expressions of ironic distancing and resistance to the pressures of 'Latvian-ness' at the university. Just two weeks before the riot, the university had proudly declared that it steadfastly held to its national character, and that its main aim was to

---

⁶⁷ *Students*, no 1, 1922/09/25; no 10, 1922/11/22.
⁶⁸ See *Students*, no 9, 1922/11/15. Interestingly, the student referring to such complaints among Latvian students also argued *against* the common notion that the Jewish students could not command Latvian.
⁶⁹ LVVA. Latvijas Universitātes fonds, 7427/6/268. Studentu ziņojumi par konfliktiem ebreju un latviešu studentu starpā. Testimony of Strauss, a janitor, 1922/12/03. It should perhaps be noted that "Fraternitas Arctica" enrolled both Latvian and Russian students.

foster a new generation of Latvian scholars and scientists.[70] Many of the Jewish students could hardly have felt included in this project.

On the Latvian side, hostility to the Jewish students seems to have been strongest among those who had participated in the recent War of Liberation. Explaining his animosity to Jews before the commission, the engineering student Nikolajs Plato vented his anger about the actions of Jews during the war. While he was in the provisional Latvian army, he claimed, the Jews were citizens of Belarus. On returning to Riga after the war, he found that the same Jews had by some miracle become Latvian citizens, and were also attending the university in large numbers. This, he asserted, had given rise to much bitterness among the Latvian students.[71]

Jewish students were also accused of associating only with Russians, for attending only lectures given in Russian, for taunting teaching staff lecturing in Latvian, for using Russian and Yiddish in a 'provocative' manner, and for writing their names in Russian on their cupboard doors.[72] The defiant gesture of using Russian to demarcate ethnic identity has its ironic parallel in the old nationalist Krišjānis Valdemārs' likewise defiant gesture of officially proclaiming himself a Latvian at the German-speaking Dorpat University in the 1850s. In the context of the events at the University of Latvia, such actions were perceived as provocations directed against the national aims of Latvia.

It is also apparent that the ethnic conflicts were more evident in certain faculties. Practically all the ethnic Latvian students giving evidence to the committee, and also admitting some involvement in the occurrences, belonged to the Faculty of Mechanics or the Faculty of Chemistry. As mentioned earlier, it was in these faculties that the proportion of Jewish students was greatest during the first years of the university, and had probably been most able to develop a distinct student culture. A further indication of ethnic tensions in the Faculty of Mechanics is that the Association of Mechanics students, on 19 December, decided to bar all Jewish students from membership due to their alleged 'persistence in disrupting academic life'.[73] Also, it is interesting that the proportion of Jews not holding Latvian citizenship was much higher in these faculties than in the others: fourteen per cent of the Jewish students in

---

[70] LVVA. Latvijas Universitātes fonds, 7427/6/37a. Pārskats par Latvijas augstskolas, vēlāk Universitātes, nodibināšanu un viņas darbību. Overview of the state and achievements of the University of Latvia, 1922/11/16.
[71] LVVA. Latvijas Universitātes fonds, 7427/6/268. Studentu ziņojumi par konfliktiem ebreju un latviešu studentu starpā. Testimony of Nikolajs Plato 1923/01/24.
[72] LVVA. Latvijas Universitātes fonds, 7427/6/268. Studentu ziņojumi par konfliktiem ebreju un latviešu studentu starpā. Testimonies of Alfreds Linde 1923/01/17; Arturs Lābans 1923/02/14; Alberts Alksnis 1923/02/14.
[73] *Students*, 1923/01/17.

mechanics, and thirteen per cent in chemistry, were not Latvian citizens as compared with only one per cent of the Jewish students in medicine.[74]

Indeed, it is noteworthy that students in the Faculty of Medicine do not appear to have taken any similar action, although the proportion of Jewish students in the Faculty of Medicine was virtually the same as in Mechanics and Chemistry. One possible explanation is that the Jewish medical students were primarily German-speaking from the more 'Latvian' areas of Kurzeme and Riga, while those in mechanics and chemistry were primarily Russian-speaking from Daugavpils and the Latgale region. Apart from the difference in citizenship noted above, there was a clear difference between these faculties in the proportion of students who failed the Latvian language tests. Jewish students in medicine appear to have been far more proficient in Latvian.[75]

Consequently, the 1st December riot may be seen in the light of a demarcation process along ethnic lines, where Jewish students in some faculties may have adopted a line of ironic detachment from the university's national aims. This may have occasioned friction with extreme nationalist Latvian students, perhaps particularly among those who had fought for the new Latvian republic during the War of Liberation. As a part of their war experience, they had no doubt been exposed to the endemic anti-Semitism among the military previously associated with the Tsarist army.

Reactions from ethnic Latvian students

One important question here, naturally, is how widespread these anti-Jewish notions were among the ethnic Latvian students. Only a small minority of the Latvian students seem to have openly advocated violent measures against the Jewish minority.[76] Among the nationalists who dominated the Student Union, two lines of argument emerged: first, that the animosity shown was simply due to some pre-election turbulence, and should not be seen as an anti-Jewish pogrom; and second, that the Jewish students had themselves caused the riot by their allegedly provocative manner.

---

[74] LVVA. Latvijas Universitātes fonds, 7427/6/54, Gadu statistiskās ziņas par studentu un mācības spēku sastāvu. The reason for this was probably that the Latvian state was not very forthcoming in granting citizenship to Jews in the Latgale region who had been evacuated during the war.
[75] LVVA. Latvijas Universitātes fonds, 7427/6/54, Gadu statistiskās ziņas par studentu un mācības spēku sastāvu. Records of Latvian language tests, September 1922. The failure rate among new students in Mechanics and Chemistry was 15 per cent, while in medicine none of the 185 new students failed the test.
[76] LVVA. Latvijas Universitātes fonds, 7427/6/268. Studentu ziņojumi par konfliktiem ebreju un latviešu studentu starpā. Letter from the chairman of 'Latvju studentu apvienotais centrs' to the Vice-Principal, 1922/12/05.

The nationalist editors of the weekly *Students* declared emphatically that no pogrom against Jewish students had actually taken place – this was depicted as the invention of the Jewish and Social Democratic press. The matter was seen as merely a piece of election fracas. These accounts must surely be questioned. One of the editors was accused of making inflammatory speeches during the riot, while another was canvassing for one of the nationalist student parties.[77]

The Student Union leadership declared soon after the incident that the Jewish students had only themselves to blame. Apart from having provoked the whole incident, the loyalty and patriotism of the Jewish population were also questioned. Jews were portrayed as 'primarily internationalists', and as 'elements hostile to the Latvian state'.[78] Obviously, the nationalist rhetoric here descended into sheer anti-Semitism. A great majority of the Student Union assembly supported the leadership in this matter, and addressed several far-reaching demands to the university council, aimed at reducing the number of Jewish students at the university: First, the number of Jewish students should be reduced to match the Jewish population's proportion in Latvia. Second, the further enrolment of Jewish students should cease until the first demand had been fulfilled. Third, Jews who had not passed the high school exam in the Latvian language would be required to undergo examinations encompassing the full high school curricula in Latvian before being enrolled at the university. Fourth, the teaching staff should be asked to communicate with Jewish students in the Latvian language only.[79]

These demands clearly originated among the students belonging to the nationalist and anti-Semitic organisation *Latvju Nacionālais Klubs*, who claimed that they had collected 2,109 students' signatures to the demand that the university should adopt stricter regulations in order to strengthen its 'Latvianness'. They also demanded, somewhat unrealistically, a definite ban of the use of "Jewish jargon" on university premises.[80] How the university could effectively ban the use of the Yiddish language within its buildings was not discussed. The number of signatures, however, is an indication that anti-Jewish sentiments were

---

[77] *Students*, 1922/11/22; 1922/12/06.
[78] LVVA. Latvijas Universitātes fonds, 7427/6/268. Studentu ziņojumi par konfliktiem ebreju un latviešu studentu starpā. Letter from the Presidium of the Student Council to the Principal, 1922/12/16.
[79] According to the weekly *Students*, the assembly supported this measure with only six 'progressivist' votes against. See *Students*, 1923/01/17; LVVA. Latvijas Universitātes fonds, 7427/6/2, University Council Minutes, 1922/12/20.
[80] LVVA. Latvijas Universitātes fonds, 7427/6/268. Studentu ziņojumi par konfliktiem ebreju un latviešu studentu starpā. Letter from the student section of 'Latvju Nacionālais Klubs' to the University Council, 1922/12/20. The actual signatures can be found in LVVA. Izglītības Ministrijas fonds, 1632/2/661. Studentu starpgadījuma izmeklēšanas komisijas sēžu protokolu noraksti... On the anti-Semitic character of 'Latvju Nacionālais Klubs', see Stranga (1997), pp. 40–41, and Krēsliņš, Uldis (2005): *Aktīvais nacionālisms Latvijā, 1922–1934*, pp. 60–62.

indeed strong among the Latvian students. Given that each signature actually represented a particular student – a debatable issue, no doubt – it would mean that about forty per cent of the non-Jewish students had signed the circular. The *Nacionālais Klubs* followed up this initiative by organising an anti-Jewish automobile demonstration in Riga in March 1923.[81]

Measures by the university leadership

For the university leadership, dealing with the 1st December riot appears to have been a delicate matter. As mentioned earlier, the matter was first transferred to a disciplinary court devised to settle conflicts between students. However, two weeks later the university council decided to appoint a formal investigation committee.[82] The demands from the Student Council for restrictions on the enrolment of Jewish students were, however, rejected on the grounds that decisions of this kind could only by taken by the *Saeima*, not on the university level.

Nevertheless, the university council apparently discussed possible steps that could be taken by the university in order to reduce what was seen as the 'disproportionate' number of Jewish students.[83] The other proposals by the Student Council – that all students should have taken the high school course in Latvian and that the teaching staff should be instructed to use only Latvian in discussions with students – were received more positively by the university leadership. It was, for instance, pointed out that the official language of examination and lecturing should always be Latvian.[84]

Possibly under increasing political pressure, the university leadership obviously felt some need to reinforce the official line on the primacy of Latvian. In January 1923, principal Ernsts Felsbergs issued instructions to the teaching staff, pointing out that all communication with students should – to the best of their ability – be conducted in Latvian.[85] The qualification was probably necessary, since some lecturers and professors, especially in the medical and technical faculties, still had little command of Latvian. Moreover, all courses where lectures were held in Latvian should also require high school qualifications in

---

[81] Krēsliņš (2005), p. 93.
[82] LVVA. Latvijas Universitātes fonds, 7427/6/268. Studentu ziņojumi par konfliktiem ebreju un latviešu studentu starpā. Letter from the Vice-Principal to the Student Court, 1922/12/07; 7427/6/2, University Council Minutes, 1922/12/06; 1922/12/20.
[83] LVVA. Latvijas Universitātes fonds, 7427/6/2, University Council Minutes, 1922/12/20.
[84] LVVA. Latvijas Universitātes fonds, 7427/6/268. Studentu ziņojumi par konfliktiem ebreju un latviešu studentu starpā; 7427/6/8, Council of Deans Minutes, 1922/12/18.
[85] LVVA. Latvijas Universitātes fonds, 7427/6/2, University Council Minutes, 1923/01/10; 7427/6/268. Sarakste ar fakultātēm, profesoriem par mācību pasniegšanu valsts valodā. Letter from Felsbergs to the Student Council, 1923/01/12.

that language.⁸⁶ More 'radical' suggestions that *all* students lacking high school qualifications in Latvian should be required to sit a language test appear to have been shelved, but in future, newly-enrolled students lacking formal qualifications in Latvian would have to pass a more strict language examination.⁸⁷ It should be noted that the language question was always discussed in terms of admission and exclusion – adopting supportive measures such as Latvian language courses for minority students was clearly never a consideration.

The university council soon moved even closer to the nationalist demands. On 17 January 1923 the council decided to implement further measures to restrict the enrolment of Jews. The committee investigating the 1st December riot had started to hear witness statements on that very day, but both the committee and the university leadership appear to have already concluded that the main problem lay in the 'disproportional' number of Jewish students enrolled. The university council now clarified its position that subjects lectured on in Latvian must also be examined in Latvian. It also tightened the regulations on the pre-enrolment examination in Latvian. More radical, however, was the ruling that persons belonging to a 'foreign' nationality, including those holding Latvian citizenship if this had been obtained *after* the founding of the university in 1919, would only be allowed to enrol if the faculty courses were not already filled.⁸⁸

This was a remarkable measure, since it would deny some Latvian citizens access to higher education irrespective of qualifications and language skills. In effect, it amounted in particular to discrimination of the substantial number of Kurzeme and Latgale Jews who had been forcibly evacuated to Russia during the war and had therefore not been able to claim Latvian citizenship as early as 1919. These people would henceforth face serious obstacles when trying to enrol at *Latvijas Universitāte*.

Besides adopting these measures, the university leadership approached the Ministry of Education to obtain further legislative means to curtail the recruitment of Jewish students. Prompted by the official demands of the Student Union, the committee investigating the 1st December riot had prepared a memorandum on the Jewish 'problem' well *before* hearing any witnesses. On 17 January this memorandum was unanimously approved by the university council, which resolved to send it as an official missive to the State President, the *Saeima*, and the Minister of Education.⁸⁹

This missive, officially signed by Ernsts Felsbergs on the behalf of the university council, is indeed remarkable. Felsbergs and the Council evidently

---

⁸⁶ LVVA. Latvijas Universitātes fonds, 7427/6/2, University Council Minutes, 1923/01/10.
⁸⁷ LVVA. Latvijas Universitātes fonds, 7427/6/8, Council of Deans Minutes, 1923/01/09; 7427/6/2, University Council Minutes, 1923/01/10.
⁸⁸ LVVA. Latvijas Universitātes fonds, 7427/6/2, University Council Minutes, 1923/01/17.
⁸⁹ LVVA. Latvijas Universitātes fonds, 7427/6/2, University Council Minutes, 1923/01/17.

considered that a proper investigation was unnecessary, and that the real cause of the disturbances was the 'excessive' presence of Jewish students at the university. This opinion was also formulated remarkably bluntly. The main problem, Felsbergs stated, was that the university had been subjected to a 'massive inflow' of students whose "spirit and culture were foreign to Latvia". During the plight of Latvia's struggle for independence, he maintained, these people had disregarded their duties to the state, and had applied for citizenship only to be able to live in peace and prosperity in Latvia. Consequently, Latvia had seen an inflow of 'foreigners' with only weak moral ties to the state, who had acquired citizenship all too easily. This 'abnormal' situation, Felsbergs continued, was not the fault of the university, since students had been enrolled in accordance with strictly objective principles under the University Constitution. However, if these circumstances were changed, the university would gladly give preference to students who had done their duty and made sacrifices for Latvia's independence.

Felsbergs's target is all too clear, even though he abstained from referring to the Jewish population by name. These 'foreign' students, he went on, came from very affluent circles that had not been materially hit by destruction during the war to the extent Latvians had. Another reason why they had managed to be enrolled at the University of Latvia in such great numbers, Felsbergs maintained, was that the Jewish high schools systematically awarded higher grades to their pupils than their Latvian counterparts. These circumstances, Felsbergs concluded, constituted the vital background to the student disturbances in December 1922.[90]

This document is surprising in many ways. First, the statistics in table 2 above show that ethnic Latvian students actually constituted eighty per cent of the student body, slightly above the proportion of Latvians in the general population. It is therefore difficult to claim that Latvians were disadvantaged by the enrolment of Jewish students. The main 'under-represented' group was in fact ethnic Russians. Second, how could Felsbergs and the university council make these blunt declarations about the reasons for the 1st December riot without awaiting the results from the investigating committee? Finally, and perhaps more seriously, what made them resort to unproven allegations against Latvia's Jewish population, and such sweeping accusations of 'foreign-ness' and 'disloyalty' to the Latvian state?

---

[90] LVVA. Izglītības ministrijas fonds, 1632/2/661. Studentu starpgadījuma izmeklēšanas komisijas sēžu protokolu noraksti... Letter from Felsbergs to the Minister of Education, 1923/01/19. This letter was also printed by *Students*, 1923/01/24, and was therefore commonly known. However, even if this letter was officially signed by Felsbergs in his role as principal, it should be remembered that it was probably drafted by the chairman of the investigation committee, vice-principal Plāķis.

The obvious dismay which the academics in the organisation committee had already expressed in 1919, when it became clear that a substantial number of the enrolled students were Jews, indicates that some degree of anti-Semitism was a part of the perceived national agenda. That impression is strengthened by the actions of Felsbergs and the university council in the aftermath of the 1st December riot. Clearly, the university leadership also felt the pressure from the nationalist Latvian students, and was looking for legal means to limit the enrolment of Jewish students in ways that ran counter to the University Constitution. The admission regulations followed modern academic praxis, allowing the enrolment of all students, male and female, who had completed their high school education. This left no room for limiting the enrolment of students from certain ethnic minorities.

Instead, the university leadership obviously wanted a political solution to the problem, with the *Saeima* politicians taking final responsibility. In this context it should perhaps also be pointed out that the Jewish students did not have any strong support among the established academics. The teaching staff at the university was a mixture of nationalist Latvians, especially prevalent within the humanities and the Faculty of Agronomy, and a substantial body of Baltic German academics, predominantly employed within the scientific and technical faculties. Nobody in the university's influential academic circles appears to have been inclined to defend the rights of Latvian citizens belonging to the Jewish *tautība* in the name of equal rights and academic freedom. While Jewish students were already viewed with some concern from the start in 1919, they appear to have been tolerated initially because of the lack of applicants. By 1923, however, school-leavers from Jewish high schools were evidently seen as a threat to the recruitment of ethnic Latvian students – in spite of the fact that the actual enrolment of students from Jewish high schools was very insignificant.[91]

In mid-February, vice-principal Plāķis and the other academics in the committee investigating the 1st December riot, together with representatives from the Student Union, actually met the Minister of Education to discuss ways of reducing the proportion of Jewish students at the university. Apparently, the parties agreed that a limit of this kind should be imposed, but disagreed as to whose responsibility it was to introduce it. The Minister of Education was firmly of the opinion that this matter should be handled by the university itself, and

---

[91] It should be pointed out, though, that according to the university's own statistics less that 2 per cent of the students enrolled in the autumn term of 1922 had actually graduated from Jewish high schools. How the university council could view the alleged over-generous grading at these schools as a problem is indeed a mystery. On student enrolment, see LVVA. Latvijas Universitātes fonds, 7427/6/54, Gadu statistiskās ziņas par studentu un mācības spēku sastāvu.

within the bounds of the University Constitution. A more political and legislative procedure would, he claimed, be an infringement on the university's autonomy.[92]

The university representatives clearly disliked this interpretation of the situation. Instead, they maintained that this was a matter that could not be regulated by the university, since its Constitution did not contain any clause allowing it to limit the access of students of a certain 'nationality'. Therefore, some kind of legislative measure was required.[93]

It seems that the Minister of Education was not very eager to submit such a proposal to the *Saeima*. A couple of weeks before, he had received a letter from the *Saeima's* Jewish delegates, in which they very incisively questioned the arguments previously put forward by Felsbergs. Refuting the principal's sweeping allegations of the reputed 'disloyalty' and 'abnormal' over-representation of Jewish students, the delegates argued that their relatively high number at the University of Latvia was mainly due to the fact that the Jewish minority was predominantly urban, and the university recruited its students to a far greater extent from Riga and the Latvian towns than from the countryside.

Moreover, the Jewish delegates could not see why Jewish people who had been forcibly evacuated to Russia during the war should have their loyalty questioned while Latvians with the same experience of forced exile should not. With some shrewdness, they pointed out that the great majority of the teaching staff at the university had also 'returned' to Riga after the Peace Treaty with the Soviet Union had been signed in the summer of 1920. Finally, they could not see why one of Latvia's minorities, being Latvian citizens, should in this way be singled out and subjected to limiting measures when applying to the state university.[94]

Apparently, this view had been upheld by the *Saeima's* Education Committee, which indicates the political delicacy of bringing the proposed amendment of the University Constitution before the *Saeima* with the aim of reducing the proportion of students belonging to one of the minority groups. Apart from upsetting political

---

[92] LVVA. Izglītības ministrijas fonds, 1632/2/661. Studentu starpgadījuma izmeklēšanas komisijas sēžu protokolu noraksti... Protocol from a meeting on a percentage norm for Jewish students, 1923/02/19.

[93] LVVA. Izglītības ministrijas fonds, 1632/2/661. Studentu starpgadījuma izmeklēšanas komisijas sēžu protokolu noraksti... Letter from the university representatives to the Minister of Education, 1923/03/20.

[94] LVVA. Izglītības ministrijas fonds, 1632/2/661. Studentu starpgadījuma izmeklēšanas komisijas sēžu protokolu noraksti... Letter from the *Saeima's* Jewish delegates to the Minister of Education, 1923/01/30. They also sent a protest directly to the university council. See LVVA. Latvijas Universitātes fonds, 7427/6/2, University Council Minutes, 1923/02/28. During the war, more than half of the Jewish population living in the Latvian territory was evacuated to Russia proper, and in the early 1920s some 10,000 of these refugees returned, claiming Latvian citizenship. See Levin (2001), pp. 134–135.

deals with minority political parties, the proposed measure was clearly discriminatory and very difficult to reconcile with basic democratic principles.[95]

Indeed, in this matter the university's national agenda obviously conflicted with the democratic framework of the Latvian state, with its insistence on citizenship and citizen rights. The Minister of Education therefore appears to have preferred these troublesome issues to be dealt with by the university itself rather than trying to push a legal amendment through a hostile or divided *Saeima*. Moreover, it should perhaps be pointed out that by spring 1923 the Cabinet was dominated by the Social Democrats, who were unlikely to introduce discriminatory 'ethnic' legislation.[96]

The role of the Minister of Education, the pedagogue and former *jaunstrāvnieks* Aleksandrs Dauge, is somewhat uncertain. Like so many other Ministers of Education during the First Republic, Dauge also belonged to the teaching staff of the university, and appears to have had relatively loose ties with the newly developed party system. Dauge, in fact, was a member of the same Faculty of Philology and Philosophy as the vice-principal negotiating with him on legal restrictions on Jewish students. This may explain the amiable tone of these negotiations, in spite of the fact that the suggested remedies were quite different. While Dauge in the Cabinet discussions had strongly criticised the 'baseness' of Latvian students when 'beating Jews', he seems to have been quite content to see the university implement informal measures to limit the number of Jewish students.[97] The clearly undemocratic notion that the number of Jewish applicants to the university had to be 'controlled' was evidently not questioned. It was only a matter of whose responsibility it was to introduce such measures. According to the Ministry of Education, the main way to restrict the number of Jewish students was to tighten the university regulations on language proficiency; i.e. a more strict test of Latvian skills before enrolment.[98]

Finding it politically impossible to instigate legislative changes in the desired direction, the university leadership was left to handle the 'Jewish problem' as it saw fit. They do not appear to have been very happy about this, complaining that

---

[95] It should perhaps also be pointed out that the demand that the number of Jewish students should be reduced in order to match their proportion of the population in Latvia might well backfire on the Latvians, who in fact were also 'over-represented' at the university.

[96] The well-established ties between the Social Democrats and the Jewish Bundists probably made it quite unthinkable to introduce legal restrictions directed at the Jewish ethnic group. It should perhaps also be noted that Zigfrīds Meierovics, Foreign Minister between 1920 and 1925, came from a partly Jewish family. See Gordon (1990), p. 15. This may have helped to make overtly anti-Jewish discussions less likely at Cabinet meetings.

[97] See Ezergailis (1999), p. 96, note 26; LVVA. Izglītības ministrijas fonds, 1632/2/661. Studentu starpgadījuma izmeklēšanas komisijas sēžu protokolu noraksti... Protocol from discussions between the Education Minister and an LU deputation on a 'percentage norm' for Jewish students, 1923/02/19.

[98] LVVA. Latvijas Universitātes fonds, 7427/6/2, University Council Minutes, 1923/04/04.

according to its constitution, the university could only reprimand students of 'foreign culture and spirit', it could not expel them on the grounds of low proficiency in Latvian or bar them from enrolling if they met the standard entrance requirements.[99]

The university leadership also had to address the apparent malcontent among many Latvian students, whose elected representatives had demanded that measures be implemented without delay. In March, some of the nationalist student organisations proclaimed a strike in protest against what was seen as the 'unfavourable' decision by the *Saeima's* Education Committee, demanding a fully 'national' university. Nationalist activists barred the entrances to the main university building and demanded concrete measures to limit the number of Jewish students.

This seems to have been too much for the university leadership. Felsbergs immediately closed the university and threatened to impose sanctions on the strike leaders.[100] Possibly, student disturbances had been tolerated while the university leadership still hoped for legislative changes, but when this option was closed, the activism of the extreme nationalist students had to be checked. Also, the March strikers had prevented teaching staff as well as students from entering the building, which was seen as an infringement of the academic freedom of the lecturers.[101] This could clearly not be tolerated.

However, in spite of the demands brought forward by the Jewish *Saeima* delegates, the university council refused to withdraw its decision to severely limit the enrolment of students who were not Latvian citizens in 1919.[102] This is indeed remarkable, bearing in mind that its own representatives had previously argued that this decision had no foundation in the University Constitution. In effect, this meant that the university persisted in having a definition of Latvian citizenship that differed from the one used by the state. It is obvious, though, that the university leadership had the tacit support of the Minister of Education to implement measures which would reduce the number of Jewish applicants while at the same time not being too politically embarrassing. In a letter a week later, the Minister announced that he was convinced that the university would in

---

[99] Izglītības ministrijas fonds, 1632/2/661. Studentu starpgadījuma izmeklēšanas komisijas sēžu protokolu noraksti... Letter from Vice-Principal Plāķis et al. to the Minister of Education, 1923/03/20.

[100] LVVA. Latvijas Universitātes fonds, 7427/6/2, University Council Minutes, 1923/03/07; Izglītības ministrijas fonds, 1632/2/661. Studentu starpgadījuma izmeklēšanas komisijas sēžu protokolu noraksti... Letter from the Vice-Principal to the Minister of Education, 1923/03/22. Perhaps significantly, no sanctions were imposed on the strike organisers.

[101] LVVA. Latvijas Universitātes fonds, 7427/6/2, University Council Minutes, 1923/03/07.

[102] LVVA. Izglītības ministrijas fonds, 1632/2/661. Studentu starpgadījuma izmeklēšanas komisijas sēžu protokolu noraksti...Letter from the University Council to the Minister of Education, 1923/03/23.

future scrutinize the applicants' command of the Latvian language in order to reject all 'abnormal specimens'.[103] Apart from the other regulations, the language tests were obviously seen as an ideal tool to ensure that only an 'appropriate' number of students belonging to the 'foreign' *tautības* would be accepted in future.[104]

The official verdict

After all these negotiations behind closed doors between politicians and the university leadership, the committee investigating the 1st December riot finally delivered its report in April 1923. However, the committee's objectivity and impartiality must be seriously doubted. As shown above, the committee seems to have made some very vital conclusions before even hearing witnesses. Not surprisingly, the final report therefore appears to have been heavily influenced by 'national' and political concerns, rather than a serious appraisal of ethnic tensions at the university.

The committee offered some vital conclusions about the origins and character of the 1st December riot. First, they decided that the riot had been primarily politically motivated, and not due to ethnic tensions. The main force behind the disturbances, they alleged, was the conflict between the left-wing Jewish student association "Vetulija" and the Latvians and Russians in "Fraternitas Arctica". They acknowledged that Jewish students had actually been evicted from the university building, but claimed that this had been done without violence. This is somewhat surprising, since at least one Jewish student had needed medical treatment after the event. Even more surprisingly, the

---

[103] LVVA. Izglītības ministrijas fonds, 1632/2/661. Studentu starpgadījuma izmeklēšanas komisijas sēžu protokolu noraksti... Letter from the Minister of Education to the Principal, 1923/03/28. The Minister, for his part, promised that the Ministry would check the Jewish high schools to make sure that they would not award higher school-leaving grades than the Latvian schools. Interestingly, the University Constitution actually did not contain any clause mentioning language tests as a part of the enrolment process. The Constitution only proclaimed that the tuition language was Latvian, and that enrolled students had to provide evidence of their high school – *vidusskola* – examination grades. *Latvijas Universitātes Satversme*, §§ 3 and 81. Andrievs Ezergailis has recently argued that the Latvian government during this period always took sides with the Jews against anti-Semitic propaganda and violence. This conclusion is based on a cabinet meeting in December 1922, when the violence against Jewish students was condemned and the anti-Semitic writings in the paper *Latvijas Sargs* on these incidents were subjected to a fine. See Ezergailis (1999), pp. 84 and 96, note 26. However, this means that Ezergailis clearly underestimates the way anti-Jewish notions among university staff and students were transformed into discriminatory regulations without involving the Ministry or the *Saeima*.

[104] Evidently, the first generation of students at the University of Latvia had not been subjected to language tests. An inquiry in 1920 showed that 102 students (8 per cent) claimed they were unable to understand lectures in Latvian. LVVA. Latvijas Universitātes fonds, 7427/6/37a. Pārskats par Latvijas augstskolas, vēlāk Universitātes, nodibināšanu un viņas darbību.

commission uncritically accepted the testimony of some Latvian students involved in the riot who stated that some left-wing Jewish students armed with knives had in reality provoked the whole incident. In fact, no such persons were ever identified; neither was the evidence of the Latvian activists corroborated by other witnesses examined by the commission.

As shown above, the investigation committee can hardly be seen as having acted impartially or independently. Due to political considerations, the committee obviously chose to accept the explanations for the riot offered by the Latvian nationalist students who were actually involved in the incident. The committee also laid its weight behind the allegations that there had been widespread 'misconduct' among the Jewish students, such as the 'hogging' of attractive seats in lecture halls and drawing rooms, disturbances in the form of illicit smoking, whistling, and singing, the refusal to remove caps inside the lecture halls, and, finally, the persistent and allegedly provocative use of Russian or Yiddish instead of Latvian. This, opined the committee, was an important explanation for the hostility showed by some Latvians towards the Jewish students.

While describing the riot as primarily a political conflict, the committee nevertheless admitted that it contained an element of "racial antagonism", primarily due to the "disproportional" number of Jewish students in some of the faculties, and to the dissatisfaction among Latvian students due to the "uncivilised" behaviour of Jewish students, as described above. Finally, the committee alleged that there were strong links between Latvian Jews and Russia. In order to substantiate this claim, the commission quoted one sentence from a Russian paper published in Berlin (!).[105]

Scrutinizing the report, it is striking that the committee chose to almost completely accept the reasons for the 1st December riot put forward by the nationalist Latvian students, even though supporting evidence was clearly lacking. The committee did not hesitate to accept questionable evidence and interpretations of the alleged 'misconduct' of Jewish students, and appears to have had no qualms about viewing these phenomena in collective ethnic or "racial" terms rather than as actions of individual students. The problem, as defined by the committee, was the 'excessive' presence of Jewish students at a university with distinctly national Latvian aims, not the violence that was perpetrated against them on 1st December. Perhaps not surprisingly, these conclusions agree very well with the line taken by the committee *before* hearing any witnesses, conclusions that were readily accepted by Felsbergs and the university council already in January. The report was, again not surprisingly,

---

[105] LVVA. Latvijas Universitātes fonds, 7427/6/363. Studentu ziņojumi par konfliktiem ebreju un latviešu studentu starpā. Final report of the investigating commission, 1923/04/19.

favourably received by the university council, which decided to pass it on to the Ministry of Education and the press after final editing.[106]

The aftermath

The anti-Jewish riot and student strikes in 1922–1923 may perhaps be seen as relatively isolated instances of ethnic conflict, and the degree of violence used by the perpetrators was comparatively low. To some extent these incidents can probably be explained as a reaction to the war experiences of many Latvian youths, making 'sacrifices' for the nation, yet not reaping the expected rewards. These youths found it difficult to accept the presence of Jewish students at the new 'national' university, which they perceived to be their 'own'. They clearly regarded in particular the Yiddish-speaking and Russian-speaking Jewish students as culturally different and 'foreign' from themselves. In this matter, the Latvian students apparently found like-minded people among the university leadership. The university council was quite ready to perceive the Jewish students as an undesired anomaly, as 'foreign elements' whose presence was not really compatible with the university's national agenda.

As shown above, the university council had already decided, prior to the committee investigating the 1st December riot completing its investigation, that future enrolment should be restricted for applicants who were not Latvian citizens in 1919. The effect of this, and possibly also other measures connected with proficiency in Latvian, appear to have markedly reduced the proportion of Jewish students at the University of Latvia. In 1923/24, Jewish students comprised nine per cent of the total student body, compared to twelve per cent the year before.[107]

While the overall pattern is roughly the same, with the highest proportions of Jewish students in chemistry, mechanics, medicine, the natural sciences and mathematics, the general percentage reduction means that fewer new Jewish students had been accepted.[108] This was not a temporary phenomenon. Towards the end of the 1920s, Jewish students remained much less conspicuous than previously. In 1928 they constituted 8.6 per cent of the student body compared to the 4.8 per cent Germans and 1.8 per cent Russians, while those categorised as

---

[106] LVVA. Latvijas Universitātes fonds, 7427/6/2, University Council Minutes, 1923/03/23.
[107] *Valsts statistikas gada grāmatas*, 1922–1924; Feigmane, Tatjana (2000): *Russkie v dovoennoj Latvii*, p. 301
[108] The university leadership seems to have been rather preoccupied with calculations on relative proportions of Jewish students during the spring of 1923. See LVVA. Latvijas Universitātes fonds, 7427/6/54, Gadu statistiskās ziņas par studentu un mācības spēku sastāvu.

belonging to the Latvian *tautība* comprised 83.5 per cent.[109] While not resorting to overtly discriminatory regulations, it appears that enrolment tests of proficiency in the Latvian language were intentionally used to limit the number of Jewish students at the university.[110]

Table 3. Students at the University of Latvia, June 1924, according to 'nationality'.

Faculty	Latvian	Russian	German	Jewish	Other
Architecture	119	4	16	11	2
Engineering	410	17	14	45	8
Law/Economics	1147	14	44	92	5
Chemistry	376	12	47	105	4
Agronomy	694	2	9	4	5
Natural science/Math	396	7	11	61	7
Mechanics	360	16	37	73	11
Medicine	668	18	37	130	4
Philosophy/Linguist.	684	7	16	6	3
Theology	82	0	12	0	0
Veterinary studies	125	0	3	11	2
Total	5,061	97	246	538	52
Percentage	84.4	1.6	4.1	9.0	0.9

Source: LVVA. Latvijas Universitātes fonds, 7427/6/54, Gadu statistiskās ziņas par studentu un mācības spēku sastāvu.

At the same time, there was probably disagreement among the academic leadership about the exact nature of the university's national character. When the university reopened in the autumn of 1923, the new principal, professor Ruberts from the Faculty of Medicine, stressed that the university was a national and autonomous institution, and that all those who worked and studied there must have regard for and loyalty to common national interests. Apparently, this implied that lecturers and students belonging to the ethnic minorities could take part in this "free university in a free Latvia" as long as they respected the

---

[109] LVVA. Latvijas Universitātes fonds, 7427/6/37a. Pārskats par Latvijas augstskolas, vēlāk Universitātes, nodibināšanu un viņas darbību. Overview of the achievement of the University of Latvia during Latvia's first decade of independence, 1929.
[110] This is also the conclusion of a memorandum submitted to the US State Department in 1942, evaluating relations between the Latvian state and the Jewish minority. See Ezergailis (1999), p. 86. Ezergailis, however, does not comment on this since it runs counter his general thesis that the Latvian Jews were granted full political rights during the First Republic. Generally speaking, the implementation of these discriminatory practices already in the early 1920s is a topic that has not been explored by Latvian or exiled Latvian scholars since it too obviously runs counter to the master historical narrative on the freedoms of the First Republic before 1934.

common national agenda. vice-principal Plāķis, on the other hand, turned much more directly to the ethnic Latvian students in his speech, reminding them that from the national awakening in the nineteenth century onwards, Latvian students had consistently fought for the realisation of "the national idea".[111] Here, a more ethnic and exclusionary vision of the university seems to have predominated. This cleavage among the academics on the role of the minority students at the national university is clearly visible in the early 1920s.

The nationalist students for their part continued to stress *their* national version of *Latvijas Universitāte* as an academic institution devised for ethnic Latvian youth and using a Latvian language purified from what was termed "German and Russian barbarisms".[112] It is also obvious that the ethnic demarcations in the form of separate student corporations and associations remained unchanged.[113] The student body remained split between Latvian corporations that openly supported the 'national idea' of both the Latvian state and the university, and corporations designed for the various minority groups. In the student elections in 1927, for instance, there were two Jewish parties, one German, one Russian, and four clearly nationalist Latvian parties.[114]

In spite of the reduced presence of Jewish students at the University of Latvia, the hostility shown towards them by nationally inclined Latvian students did not subside. Indeed, the impatience within these 'patriotic' circles with what was viewed as the insufficient nationalist policies of the *Saeima* appears to have made some of these students disenchanted with democratic principles as such.[115] By the early 1930s the Latvian fascist organisation *Pērkonkrusts* (Cross of Thunder) had infiltrated some student corporations and completely taken over one of them,

---

[111] Both speeches were printed in *Students*, 1923/4.

[112] *Students*, 1923/1; 1923/2 (quote).

[113] Structuring 'nationality' by ethnically composed student corporations and associations was not a new phenomenon. The corporation "Letonija" was formed at Dorpat in 1882 by former students of Kronvalds. See Kurmis, Ansis (1940): "Baltijas skolotāju semināra nozīme latviešu garīgās kultūras celšanā un suverēnas Latvijas tapšanā," p. 12–13. At the Riga Polytechnical Institute before World War I, Latvian students were also organised in this kind of 'national' association. See Spekke, Arnolds (2000): *Atmiņu brīži*, p. 45. For a general view on the Latvian corporations in Dorpat/Tartu and Riga, see Komsars, Andrijs (1968), "Die lettische Korporationen", pp. 49–58.

[114] LVVA. Latvijas Universitātes fonds, 7427/6/479. Statutes of 'Latviešu nacionālo studentu organizāciju savienība, 1927/02/02; Candidate lists to the Student elections in 1927. Interestingly, the Jewish students seem to have been split into two parties, one using the catchword 'national', the other 'progressive-democratic'.

[115] According to the archaeologist Francis Balodis's memoirs, feelings ran high among nationalist students in 1931 and there was much talk of forcibly dissolving the *Saeima* in order to produce a 'national' government. See Balodis, Francis (1941): *Vāld och frihet. En lettisk universitetsprofessors minnen*, p. 157.

'Selonija'.[116] It should perhaps also be pointed out that the national conservative professor Juris Plāķis, the previous vice-principal and head of the investigation committee in 1922, also joined the *Pērkonkrusts* in the 1930s.[117]

In 1933 the Student Union assembly, dominated by delegates from the nationalist Latvian corporations, demanded once more that the number of Jewish students be curtailed. Complaining that the number of students of 'foreign nationality' at the university still exceeded their proportions of the population as a whole, the Student Council demanded that this should now be rectified. They also renewed their demand that Latvian should be the only teaching language in all faculties, and, finally, that Jewish medical students should be forbidden to use Christian bodies as dissection material.[118]

Obviously, the notions of 'otherness' attributed to Jewish people now also had a direct bodily connotation. The refusal to let Jewish medical students handle 'Christian' corpses was probably due to old anti-Semitic delusions about alleged Jewish 'rites' where Christian flesh or blood was used, conceptions now being recycled in *Pērkonkrusts* circles. Perhaps now in more overtly racist terms, Jews were seen as not fully human, having another kind of physical body than 'Christians'.

In his recently published memoirs, the Latvian neurosurgeon Kārlis Arājs has described how the admission of Jews and Baltic Germans to the Faculty of Medicine was regulated in 1933. Besides excellent grammar school results and the mandatory writing of an essay in Latvian, applicants had to pass an oral examination in Latvian literature and Latvian and Latin grammar. Arājs came from an ethnic Latvian family, his father was a farmer in Kurzeme. For him, the oral examination was swiftly over but this was not the case for other applicants. According to Arājs, it was commonly known that an informal *numerus clausa* was in operation, making sure that students admitted from the ethnic minorities did not constitute a greater proportion than they did in the general population. If forty students were admitted to the Faculty of Medicine, no more than four would be Baltic Germans and no more than three would be Jews.[119]

---

[116] Ezergailis (1999), p. 102. Ezergailis also points out that one of the Latvian leaders of killing commandos, Viktors Arājs, was a member of the old student corporation *Lettonia*, and recruited many of its members into his killing squads in 1941. Ibid., pp. 210–211.
[117] See Dribins (2002a), p. 96.
[118] LVVA. Latvijas Universitātes fonds, 7427/6/268. Sarakste ar fakultātēm, profesoriem par mācību pasniegšanu valsts valodā. Letter from the Student Council to the Principal, 1933/11/06. These students seem to have been quite unconcerned that the proportion of *Latvian* students also exceeded their proportion of Latvian citizens.
[119] Arājs, Kārlis (2005): *Latviešu kauli...Atmiņas par anatomikumu un antropoloģijas ziedu laikiem Latvijā*, pp. 27–32. Such measures had probably been applied for some time. During the academic year 1931–1932, 8 per cent of the medical students were Jews, and almost 6 per cent were Baltic Germans. See Vīksna, A (2011), p. 85.

Naturally, it is rather difficult to see why a thorough knowledge of Latvian literature and grammar was vital for the selection of medical students. But the real key here, of course, was the oral examination. While written tests are open to comparison and scrutiny regarding performance, oral examinations are not. The examiners in Latvian literature and grammar could at their own discretion be pleased or displeased with the applicants. Arājs, who was let off easily, relates that this was certainly not the case for Jewish applicants. Even if they were extremely well prepared and knew Endzelīns's standard book on Latvian grammar by heart, including all the exceptions to grammatical rules and all points where the linguists differed in opinion, they still only competed with other Jews. The tacit rule was that only three of the Jewish applicants were to be admitted.

In this context, it is perhaps not surprising that Arājs's examiner of Latvian and Latin grammar in 1933 was no other than professor Juris Plāķis, the linguist who as vice-principal had previously engineered the exclusionary measures directed at Jewish students after the disturbances of 1922. Now a member of the *Pērkonkrusts* movement, he apparently still saw it as one of his duties to limit the access of Jewish students to *Latvijas Universitāte*.[120] Plāķis remained on the examination board of the Faculty of Medicine during the Ulmanis period.[121]

For the Jews who managed to gain admission to the University of Latvia, a further barrier was the student organisations' ethnic structure. The Latvian and Baltic German student corporations refused to cooperate with the Jewish organisations on the pretext that they did not conform to Christian norms.[122] Jewish students were not allowed to join the 'Latvian' student corporations, and this certainly had a wider implication for future employment possibilities. Jobs in public administration were firmly in the hands of the alumni fraternities, and Jewish graduates found that such employment was almost impossible to attain. In spite of the high educational level of the younger Jewish generation, only 1.5 per cent of the employed Jews in 1935 had jobs in the government administrative sector.[123]

Naturally, as in many other parts of Europe, anti-Semitic notions grew in strength during the Depression in the early 1930s. In Latvia, 'nationalist'

---

[120] Arājs (2005), pp. 22–32. In fact, applicants from the ethnic minorities were not the only ones whose chances were deliberately lessened by these oral examinations. Arājs also claims that women were never allowed to constitute a majority of the medical students, even if more merited women than men applied. Also, the examiner of Latvian literature, the pathologist Ernests Paukulis, did not look too kindly on applicants who expressed high opinions of left-wing writers like Jānis Rainis.

[121] Vīksna, A (2011), p. 104.

[122] Cerūzis, Raimonds (2004): *Vācu faktors Latvijā (1918–1939). Politiskie un starpnacionālie aspekti*, p. 145, footnote 69.

[123] See Ezergailis (1999), appendix 3, p. 494.

arguments that part of the economy was in the hands of ' foreigners', together with a distinct anti-capitalist tendency among the Latvian farmers, paved the way for anti-Semitic sentiments. In 1931, the Education Minister Atis Kēniņš called for a *Kulturkampf* against the autonomous minority schools, a line that eventually led to political turmoil in the *Saeima*.[124] Politically, these notions, combined with a more general distrust of the ethnic minorities and their parties, could be used by the circle around Kārlis Ulmanis when preparing the ground for an authoritarian take-over.[125]

After Ulmanis's coup in 1934, the proportion of Jewish students at the university was reduced even further. The authoritarian regime increased the pressure for official 'Latvianization' or *latviskošana*, and the ethnic minorities were more forcefully excluded from the national project.[126] Jewish political parties were forbidden, and the cultural autonomy of a separate Jewish school system was abolished. The Jewish schools were put directly under the Ministry of Education, and the curriculum was refashioned in a more conservative and orthodox manner.[127] Partly as a result of these authoritarian and discriminatory measures, emigration increased in the late 1930s.[128]

At the University of Latvia, formal quotas were finally imposed for Jewish students. But the notion of a "disproportionate" number of Jewish students in higher education continued to haunt nationally-minded Latvian students. For instance, when one of them in 1937 advocated closer collaboration between the university and the Musical Conservatory, he bolstered his argument by stating that Latvians in fact constituted seventy per cent of the students at the Conservatory, Jews only seventeen per cent.[129]

In a comparative context, the measures which the leadership of the University of Latvia introduced in the early 1920s appear to have been somewhat more discriminatory against Jewish students than those of its newly established counterpart, the Lithuanian university in Kaunas. This is somewhat surprising, considering that, prior to independence, Lithuanian

---

[124] Garleff, Michael (2005): "Die baltischen Staaten und die Juden 1918–1940", p. 105.
[125] See Stranga (1997), pp. 43–45.
[126] Plath, Tilman (2009): "Juden unter Ulmanis", pp. 110–115. In 1938/39, the proportion of Jewish students at the University of Latvia was 6.2 per cent. See Feigmane, p. 301.
[127] LVVA. Izglītības ministrijas fonds, 1632/2/565, Ziņas par mazākuma tautību izglītības pārvalžu likvidēšanu un darbinieku atbrīvošanu 1934. g.; 1632/2/566, Mazākuma tautību skolu stāvoklis.
[128] Stranga (1997), pp. 73–74. However, these measures were, as Stranga points out, in most cases primarily anti-democratic rather than anti-Semitic. The other ethnic minorities were also subjected to such restrictions, not just the Jews. Even Ulmanis's own political party was actually dissolved. Stranga, however, does not discuss the special quotas imposed on Jews applying to the University.
[129] Bērziņš, Alfreds (1937): "Latvijas konservatorija ir mūsu universitātes akadēmiskā māsa", p. 41.

national intellectuals seem to have been decidedly more anti-Jewish than their Latvian equals.[130] The emerging Lithuanian petty bourgeoisie in the late nineteenth century also appears to have developed anti-Jewish sentiments, viewing Jews as difficult business competitors.[131]

According to the 1923 census, Jews constituted a mere 7.6 per cent of Lithuania's total population, but were far more prominent in urban settings. In Kaunas, for instance, Jews made up 27 per cent of the inhabitants in 1923.[132] It is interesting that Jewish youths managed to enrol at the Lithuanian university in Kaunas to a far greater degree than in Riga. The proportion of Jewish students in Kaunas actually remained stable at around 27 per cent until at least 1932, but dropped considerably in the later 1930s. By 1939 the proportion had fallen to 9.3 per cent.[133] This decline may have been caused by the adoption of exclusionary practices, but was probably to some extent due to Jewish emigration.[134] Laws restricting the access of Jewish students to higher education were not adopted in independent Lithuania during the inter-war period.[135]

However, there are some indications that at the Lithuanian university, exclusionary measures in the form of language tests were at least seriously considered in the early 1920s. Already in 1922 the dean of the Faculty of Medicine expressed concern that a considerable proportion of the students did not understand Lithuanian, and therefore could not follow lectures in that language. This faculty seems to have had the largest proportion of Jewish students. In 1923 the university council decided on a set of rules that made proficiency in Lithuanian mandatory for new students.[136] Representatives of the Jewish population appear to have protested that the language tests imposed by

---

[130] On anti-Jewish sentiments among leading Lithuanian intellectuals around 1900, see Sirutavičius, Vladas (2000): "Vincas Kudirka's Programme for Modernizing Society", pp. 110–111.

[131] Valantiejus, Algis (2002): "Early Lithuanian nationalism: sources of legitimate meanings in an environment of shifting boundaries", p. 326.

[132] Atamukas, Solomonas (2001): *Lietuvos žydų kelias. Nuo XIV amžiaus iki XX a. pabaigos*, pp. 132–33.

[133] Atamukas (2001), p. 150. Poles, Russians, Germans and 'others' constituted together not more than 6 per cent of the studentship before 1935. Interestingly, in the re-opened *Polish Stefan Bathory University of Vilnius*, the proportion of Jewish students peaked at 33 per cent around 1929–30, which corresponded rather well with their proportion of the entire Vilnius population. As at the Lithuanian University in Kaunas, this proportion fell markedly during the 1930s. See ibid., p.177.

[134] I intend to clarify these issues in a future study, focusing on the ethnic politics of the Lithuanian University in Kaunas during the interwar period.

[135] Sirutavičius, Vladas & Staliūnas, Darius (2011): "Was Lithuania a Pogrom-Free Zone? (1881–1940)", p. 152.

[136] Janužytė, Audronė (2005): *Historians as nation state-builders: The Formation of the Lithuanian University 1904–1922*, pp. 240–241. However, the extent to which these rules were actually implemented needs to be investigated. Janužytė adds that in 1926 Jews still constituted 45.7 per cent of the students in the Faculty of Medicine.

the Lithuanian government constituted an ethnic barrier designed to restrict the enrolment of Jews.[137]

However, the more marked presence of Jewish students at the Lithuanian university in Kaunas may also have caused more serious friction between 'nationalist' Lithuanian students on the one hand, and Jewish and Polish students on the other.[138] Jews, Poles and Lithuanians belonged to very different cultural spheres in the interwar period.[139] There was certainly also a traditional anti-Jewish xenophobia among the Lithuanian peasantry. However, interestingly enough, it seems that these anti-Jewish sentiments were not exploited in the nationalisation of the newly formed Lithuanian state. Historians Sirutavičius and Staliūnas have recently argued that the Jews of Lithuania were seen as allies against Poland, the perceived main enemy after Poland's annexation of Vilnius district. The nationalisation of Lithuania was therefore primarily seen as an anti-Polish project, not an anti-Jewish.[140]

Of great importance for this alliance was the fact that most Jewish leaders supported the establishment of an independent Lithuanian state during the turbulent years between 1917 and 1920, preferring this solution to an enlarged Poland. However, expectations among Jewish leaders of a far-reaching cultural and political autonomy for their people were not fully realised. In 1924 the Ministry for Jewish affairs was abolished, and the self-governing bodies, *kehiles*, met a similar fate two years later.[141] These changes were implemented during Lithuania's democratic period. The transition to authoritarian rule, the establishment of the Smetona-Valdemars regime in 1926, meant that the nationalist Right became predominant in Lithuanian politics. While the authorities remained hostile to open manifestations of anti-Semitism, Jews were largely barred from posts in public administration. They did, however, retain a separate and public-funded school system which formed a basis for a flourishing and separate Jewish culture, albeit not at the prewar level.[142]

Increased economic competition between Lithuanians and Jews in the 1930s, possibly combined with traditional xenophobic sentiments, seems to have

---

[137] Atamukas (2001), p. 150.
[138] According to the Latvian nationalist student journal *Students*, Lithuanian students dissatisfied with what was seen as the large number of Jewish students in Kaunas had formed the corporation "Neo-Lithuania" in 1923. *Students*, 1923/11.
[139] Donskis, Leonidas (1999): "Between Identity and Freedom: Mapping Nationalism in Twentieth-Century Lithuania", p. 486.
[140] Sirutavičius & Staliūnas (2011), pp. 150–152.
[141] Mendelsohn (1987), pp. 217–223.
[142] Mendelsohn (1987), pp. 224–233. Lithuanian Jewry was only a part of the greater community of Litvak Jewry in prewar times but with a large degree of separateness. Compared to other East European countries, the degree of acculturation to the 'core nation' was very low among the Lithuanian Jewry. In 1937, 98 per cent of Lithuanian citizens adhering to the Mosaic religion also claimed to be of Jewish nationality.

gradually worsened inter-ethnic relations and contributed to the erosion of civil liberties for the Jewish population.[143] In the late 1930s, riots and physical violence against Jewish and Polish students in Kaunas appear to have become more common, perhaps a sign of worse things to come.[144] Indeed, with the fall of the Lithuanian republic and the end of the alliance between the government and the Jewish population, anti-Semitic sentiments could develop unchecked.

Compared to the Latvian and Lithuanian cases, discrimination against Jewish students appears to have been considerably more severe in other Central European states. Jews constituted a large part of the student body in late Habsburg universities, primarily interested in gaining entry to the free professions of physicians and lawyers. In greater Hungary, for instance, Jewish students constituted 22 per cent of the enrolment in 1912/13. In several of the Habsburg successor states, regulations were implemented to reduce the number of Jewish students and enhance the prospects of youths from the titular nations. In 1921 Hungary introduced the first legal measure directed at the enrolment of Jewish students, a *numerus clausus* limiting their proportion to less than one-third of the previous level.[145]

In independent Poland, anti-Semitic sentiments were even stronger. While Polish intellectuals in the mid-nineteenth century had been positive about the assimilation of Jews in the Polish nation, after 1907 the relations between Jews and Poles became very strained.[146] By 1919, most Poles were hostile to the Jewish population, viewing them as enemies of the national cause and also as a serious impediment to the emergence of a Polish middle class. Systematic discrimination and recurring anti-Semitic violence became a characteristic of Polish society. In violation of the Minorities Treaty of 1919, the Polish state refused to finance Jewish schools and also ruled that exams from Yiddish- or Hebrew-speaking high schools did not entail the right to enrol at Polish universities. Jewish professors were almost unknown at Polish universities.[147]

During Habsburg times, aspiring Jewish youths from Galicia had primarily gravitated towards Vienna rather than to the Polish-dominated Jagiellonian

---

[143] Sirutavičius & Staliūnas (2011), pp. 153–154. The remnants of the Lithuanian-Jewish alliance was probably also weakened by the political events in 1938, when Lithuania succumbed to German and Polish diplomatic pressure. The struggle to regain Vilnius was apparently lost, and thereby also the main factor behind the alliance.

[144] Stranga (1997), pp. 13–29.

[145] Pálfy, Zoltán (2003): *National Controversy in the Transylvanian Academe: The Cluj/Kolozsvár University, 1900–1950,* table 4, p. 69, p. 413 footnote 24. In the 'Old Kingdom' part of Romania, Jewish students in 1926 constituted 13.6 per cent of the enrolled at Bucharest University, and 28.4 per cent at Iași University. Ibid., table 25, p. 179.

[146] Weeks, Theodore R (2006): *From Assimilation to Antisemitism. The 'Jewish Question' in Poland, 1850–1914,* pp. 4–6; 149–169.

[147] Mendelsohn (1987), pp. 36–42.

University in Cracow.[148] After the re-establishment of the Polish state, however, those with educational aspirations had to apply to the national universities in Warsaw, Cracow and Lvóv, where they were less than welcome. Students from Jewish families were increasingly discriminated during the 1920s and 1930s, and their proportion fell drastically during the interwar years, from 24.6 per cent in 1921/22 to 8.2 per cent in 1938/39.[149] Jewish applicants were rejected by informal measures, for instance by giving them unanswerable questions at entrance exams. Besides this informal *numerus clausus* restricting the entry of Jewish students to Polish universities, in the 1930s they were forced to comply with segregated seating in the lecture halls, making them targets of abuse and sometimes physical violence perpetrated by students belonging to the national Right.[150]

In Romania, the presence of a large number of Jewish students, particularly in the country's medical faculties, became the focus of political agitation and violence from Rightist student organisations. Here, the entrance of ethnic minorities to the universities seems initially to have been curtailed primarily by mandatory examinations in the Romanian language. However, in 1939 the proportion of students from ethnic minorities at Bucharest University was halved as part of the general policy of favouring the ethnic Romanian majority.[151]

* * *

After the Nazi occupation in 1941, most of the Jews in Latvia and Lithuania were murdered in the Holocaust. This is not the place to discuss the extent to which ethnic Latvians and Lithuanians were involved in this atrocity, a highly controversial issue that still at times casts its shadow over the international relations of these newly independent states. A specific bone of contention is whether a part of the Jewish population actually welcomed the Soviet invasion in 1940 as a lesser evil than a Nazi German presence.[152] There is also still some disagreement

---

[148] Gellner, Ernest (1998): *Language and Solitude. Wittgenstein, Malinowski and the Habsburg Dilemma,* pp.138–139.
[149] Mendelsohn (1987), p. 42.
[150] Connelly, John (2000): *Captive University. The Sovietization of East German, Czech, and Polish Higher Education, 1945–1956,* p. 82.
[151] Pálfy (2003), pp. 190–191; 208; 238; 243. As early as 1922 there was a riot at Cluj University directed at the Jewish students in the Faculty of Medicine. Later, the student national Right was more pervasive at the Iași and Cernăuti universities, forming a movement that was eventually transformed into the infamous Iron Guard.
[152] The allegedly 'pro-Soviet' views of the Latvian Jews, and the connection between Jews and 'Bolsheviks', were really part of Nazi German and *Pērkonkrusts* propaganda, but continued to be propagated by some Latvian refugees after World War II. As Andrievs Ezergailis has shown, these notions are not compatible with facts. See Ezergailis (1999), pp. 120–123. Ezergailis, however, is not prepared to see that such ideas were prevalent in Latvia before

on the extent to which ethnic Latvians collaborated with the Germans in the Holocaust, and whether this participation was voluntary and 'spontaneous' or fully orchestrated by the local German *Einsatzgruppe*.[153]

However, in the context of the present investigation it must be said that the official minorities policy of the Latvian government served to demarcate between ethnic groups and emphasise their separate status compared to ethnic Latvians. While this, in fact, was in accordance with minority politicians defending their own cultural autonomy, in the long run it still meant that Jews and other minorities were not fully included as legitimate citizens of an increasingly 'national' Latvian state.[154] At the University of Latvia, this propensity to separate the Jewish students as a specific, coherent group and, increasingly, possessing certain 'racial' qualities, is a clear example of a demarcation process. Also, it must be said that the university leadership's stance that the Jewish population constituted a 'foreign element' with little loyalty or sympathy for the Latvian state, appears to have opened a door for discriminatory practices. Since formal legislation restricting the proportion of Jewish students at the university was, for many reasons, politically unacceptable during the First Republic, the university leadership appears to have introduced special barriers and language tests with the clear intention of limiting the enrolment of Jews.

Another aspect of the discrimination against Jewish students and academics is that very few of them were able to make academic careers at the University of Latvia during the First Republic. Throughout this period there was a conspicuous lack of teaching staff belonging to the Jewish *tautība*. In spite of the impressive number of Jewish students enrolled, hardly any of them appear to have been given grants and scholarships enabling them to go on to post-graduate studies, or be appointed to junior academic positions. The university leadership, in fact, openly declared that it was not desirable to have the institution primarily filled with 'foreigners', and took determined steps to provide promising Latvian students with international scholarships.[155]

During the First Republic the university appointed only three Jewish professors: Mečislavs Centneršvērs in Chemistry, Naum Lebedinski in Zoology,

---

1941; as shown above, the supposed link between Jews and Bolshevism was an important propagandistic device in the paper *Students* already in 1922.
[153] See Onken (1998), pp. 63–80; Ezergailis, Andrievs (2001): "Folklore versus History: A Problem in Holocaust Studies", pp. 106–119, Levin, Dov (2001), p. 138; Stranga, Aivars (2008): "Holokausts vācu okupētajā Latvijā: 1941–1945", pp. 21–27, and Ezergailis, Andrievs (2008): "Štālekera ziņojumi: holokausta vēstures pirmavots un atslēga", pp. 30–46.
[154] For a similar analysis, see Stranga, Aivars (2001): "Ebreju bēgļi Latvijā. 1933–1940", p. 321.
[155] LVVA. Latvijas Universitātes fonds, 7427/6/37a. Pārskats par Latvijas augstskolas... nodibināšanu un viņas darbību. Overview of the University, 1922/11/16.

and Paul Mintz/Pauls Mincs in law.[156] The most controversial of these appointments seems to have been that of Pauls Mincs. He was employed as a lecturer in the Faculty of Law and Economics in 1919, in a situation when there was a conspicuous lack of ethnic Latvians qualified to teach law.[157] In 1921, however, when Mincs was elected professor by his faculty, the appointment met with some resistance in the organisation committee. While not questioning his ability, several members of the committee maintained that Mincs was far too involved in politics to have the time to exercise the duties of a professor.[158] While it is true that Mincs at this time held the office of State Controller, this was probably just an excuse to vote against his appointment. It is evident from the discussions that some of the most 'nationally' inclined members of the committee, Paulis Lejiņš and Pauls Dāle, argued against Mincs's appointment. However, after some deliberation a clear majority of the committee decided to offer Mincs the professorship.[159]

Pauls Mincs's faculty, Law and Economics, was popular among students belonging to the Jewish *tautība*. In 1922 the proportion of Jewish students in this faculty was 8.8 per cent, considerably lower than in the technical faculties and the Faculty of Medicine, but definitely higher than in the humanities.[160] It should be noted, though, that the opportunity to make an academic career seems to have been practically non-existent for these students. None of Pauls Mincs's many Jewish students in Law were apparently given the chance of promotion in the Latvian academic system.

The same pattern is evident in other faculties. Ethnic Latvians were predominately chosen for all junior academic positions, and Jewish students in particular seem to have been consciously barred. The only minor exception seems to have been the Faculty of Medicine, where some of the assistants belonged to the Jewish *tautība*.[161] What chance they had of promotion, however, remains doubtful. The official university history from 1939 only records two

---

[156] *Latvijas Universitāte divdesmit gados 1919-1939* (1939), I, p. 30.Between 1926 and 1929 only three or four Jewish academics were employed in the entire university.
[157] LVVA. Latvijas Universitātes fonds, 7427/13/1162. Staff records. The situation at the Lithuanian University in Kaunas seems to have been somewhat different. At least six distinguished Jewish professors, especially in Medicine, Psychology, and Law, were appointed, and a Department of Jewish studies was created in 1922. See Atamukas (2001), pp. 150-51.
[158] LVVA. Latvijas Universitātes fonds, 7427/6/1, Organisation Committee Minutes, 1921/02/16. Evidently, Ernsts Felsbergs, the principal, found these objections shallow and embarrassing, since he too was deeply involved in politics while at the same time fulfilling his academic duties.
[159] LVVA. Latvijas Universitātes fonds, 7427/6/1, Organisation Committee Minutes, 1921/02/23. Mincs was elected with 19 votes in favour, 4 against, and 1 abstaining. See also above, chapter 3.
[160] LVVA. Latvijas Universitātes fonds, 7427/6/54, Gadu statistiskās ziņas par studentu un mācības spēku sastāvu.
[161] Stradiņš, Jānis (2004): "Totalitāro okupācijas režīmu represijas pret Latvijas zinātni un akadēmiskajām aprindām", p. 146.

Jews among the teaching staff, Mincs and Lebedinski. Obviously there were no Jewish academics whatsoever below professorial rank.[162]

Pauls Mincs's brother Vladimirs was later appointed professor of surgery, but that was during the period of Soviet rule in 1940. When the Germans occupied Riga in 1941, Vladimirs Mincs was instantly struck from the university lists.[163] Significantly for the tragedy of the Baltic Jews, none of the Jewish professors survived the wartime repression. Zoologist Naum Lebedinski tried to leave Riga after the German occupation, but failed to get the necessary permits. He was forced to move to the Riga ghetto, and in 1942 committed suicide together with his family. Pauls Mincs was deported by the Soviets in June 1941 to a Gulag camp in Kansk, Siberia, where he died the same year. His brother Vladimirs, who had organised an infirmary in the Riga ghetto, was later murdered in Buchenwald.[164] Mečislavs Centneršvērs, professor in Chemistry, moved to Warsaw University and was one of the many Polish Jews who were murdered by the Gestapo.[165]

Conclusions

The main findings in this chapter concern the problems and conflicts that ensued when a newly created university invested with a national agenda had to face a situation in which a considerable proportion of the students were perceived as not belonging to the core nation. Since the prevailing nationalisation policy emphasised difference rather than assimilation, students belonging to the minorities were not fully included. Those of Baltic German extraction were very few during the early years of the University of Latvia, and had access to alternative academic routes, either in Germany or at the Herder Institute in Riga. Young people from primarily Russian-speaking Jewish families, however, did not have those options. Still, Jews constituted an important part of the urban middle-class in Latvia, and had for decades shown a great propensity to take part in higher education.

The university leadership in the formative years was apparently surprised and dismayed by the unexpectedly high number of Jewish applicants. Their presence at the university co-existed very preciously with the institution's national

---

[162] *Latvijas Universitāte divdesmit gados 1919–1939* (1939), I, p. 30.
[163] LVVA. Latvijas Universitātes fonds, 7427/13/1163. Staff records.
[164] Gordon (1990), pp. 16–17. Pauls Mincs had taken part in the provisional government as a representative of the Jewish bloc. He had also taught at the German-speaking Herder Institute. This record may have made him extra suspect in the eyes of the Soviet authorities. Apparently, the Soviet officials saw him as a 'Zionist' and leader of a 'national-democratic' Jewish party. Stradiņš (2004), pp. 137–138. See also Šilde (1976), pp. 705–707; von Hehn (1987), p. 267, and Dribins (2001b), p. 61.
[165] Stradiņš (2004), p. 146.

agenda. While clearly averse to the enrolment of these 'foreign' students, the academic leadership found the ensuing tensions between Latvian and Jewish student groups a very delicate matter to handle. When forced by circumstances to take a public stand in the spring of 1923 in the aftermath of a riot in the main university building, they chose to see the problem in terms of an 'excessive' presence of Jewish students, who they alleged were guilty of misconduct, seclusion, and disloyalty to the Latvian state. Instead of insisting on the primacy of academic endeavour, equality between students, and tolerance, they tried to persuade the government to introduce legislation curtailing the presence of Jewish students at the university.

When this proved politically impossible, the university leadership instead implemented various restrictive regulations specifically aimed at reducing the proportion of Jewish students, notwithstanding that these measures had no foundation in the University Constitution. Taking this course of action, the principal and the university council clearly gave the nationalist aims of the university priority over its academic ones. Paraphrasing the motto of Latvia university; *Patria* was seen as more important than *academia*. In this way the concept of a 'national' university was given a decisively ethnic meaning.

However, interpreting the actual nature of the conflicts between Latvian and Jewish students is a complex matter. The conflicts appear to have had a political element, most apparent in the hostility between left-wing Jewish societies and right-wing nationalist Latvian student organisations. These nationalist students were evidently disturbed by the mere presence of Jewish students at the university. At least partly this was due to the conspicuousness of these Jews, constituting by far the largest ethnic minority at the university. Especially the Russian- and Yiddish-speaking Jews from the eastern part of Latvia were obviously seen in terms of distinct religious and ethnic 'otherness'.

There are indications that at least some of the Jewish students displayed an ironic detachment towards Latvian nationalising ambitions. By persisting, perhaps demonstratively, in using Russian and Yiddish, and symbolically flouting regulations in and about the Latvian language, these students may have participated in the creation of an arena of ethnic friction between themselves and the nationalist Latvian students. However, the reaction of Latvian students and the university leadership in transferring these practices and gestures to the whole group of ethnic Jews at the university shows how prone they were to interpret issues and categorise people according to 'nationality'. Also, the propensity to interpret differences in terms of ethnic and religious 'foreignness', perhaps even bodily 'otherness', ensured that ethnic demarcations were reinforced rather than dissolved. On the matter of Jewish students at the university, the national project became intertwined with currents of anti-Semitism.

Besides the implementation of written and oral language tests in order to reduce the proportion of Jewish students at the university, it is indisputable that those belonging to that minority who managed to enrol found themselves completely barred from making academic careers at *Latvijas Universitāte*. The three Jewish professors, Centneršvērs, Mincs and Lebedinski, had all been educated and formed their early careers at other universities. Not a single Jewish student at the University of Latvia was given that kind of opportunity during the entire First Republic. In this area, the national policies of the university leadership clearly became discriminatory and incompatible with democratic rights. The *tautība* in which you were categorized clearly determined your chances of academic promotion.

In a wider sense, this was part of the conflicts and contradictions of a nationalising state, trying to enhance the titular nation's position while at least formally defending the democratic rights of minorities. At the same time, it is obvious that the categorizing of people according to *tautība* took precedence over citizenship. In the same way as in national politics, students at the University of Latvia organised along ethnic demarcations in student corporations, associations, and parties. This undoubtedly served to demarcate and emphasise boundaries between 'nationalities' in the Latvian state during the First Republic. In the case of student corporations, ethnic exclusiveness also clearly contributed to the growth of anti-Semitic notions and networks among some of these organisations.

Using Rogers Brubaker's terminology, the Latvian nationalisation policy towards the Jews and other minorities was 'dissimilationist', emphasising difference rather than assimilation. However, it should be pointed out that this demarcation process was neither wholly instigated from above nor devised entirely one-sidedly by the Latvian majority. Ethnic politics in Latvia during the First Republic focused on the 'cultural autonomy' of the minorities, or the right of the separate ethnic minorities to control their own school systems, publish papers in their own language, fund their own theatre companies, etc. Government funding of the cultural spheres of the minorities was based on their official number, making it imperative for the minorities to register as many people as possible as belonging to their *tautība*. Therefore, the politicians representing the minorities became preoccupied with the task of defining and demarcating the members of their *tautība* from others. This is indeed one of the tragic ironies of ethnic politics during Latvia's First Republic.

Riga. Univerzitāte — Universität

Principal, Professor Augusts Tentelis
Rektors prof. Augusts Tentelis

Professor Pēteris Šmits
Prof. Pēteris Šmits

Principal, Professor Ernsts Felsbergs
Rektors prof. Ernsts Felsbergs

Professor Kārlis Balodis
Prof. Kārlis Balodis

Professor Francis Balodis
Prof. Francis Balodis

Professor Jānis Endzelīns
Prof. Jānis Endzelīns

Professor Kārlis Straubergs
Prof. Kārlis Straubergs

Principal, Professor Martiņš Zīle
Rektors prof. Martiņš Zīle

(Printed with the kind permission of the University of Latvia Museum, Riga)

Principal, Professor Jānis Ruberts
Rektors prof. Jānis Ruberts

Professor Pauls Dāle
Prof. Pauls Dāle

CHAPTER 6

Making an Impression
the Official University Journal

One of the new university's main aims was to produce scholarly and scientific work of high academic standard. This was necessary to get the new University of Latvia recognised in the international academic world. At the same time, the university was to aim to strengthen national identity. Some of the subjects taught and researched were expected to explore and reconstruct vital characteristics of the Latvian *tauta* or 'nation'. This aim was closer to the university's role as a producer and codifier of a new conception of Latvian-ness.

One of the major tasks facing the new *augstskola* in 1919 was, therefore, to strike a balance between these national and academic agendas. In this chapter I will investigate how these agendas influenced the new university's official academic image. The starting point is a scrutiny of the series of official university publications, *Latvijas Augstskolas Raksti (LAR)*, in order to see to what extent the above-mentioned national aims played a part in the selection of articles for this journal.[1]

In December 1920 the organisation committee elected the prestigious linguist Jānis Endzelīns as chief editor of the projected series of university publications, and also decided that articles could be published in Latvian, German, French or English.[2] Clearly, this meant that the *LAR* was intended partly for an international academic readership. Also, as we have seen in chapter 3, in the committee Endzelīns appears to have been the main proponent of high academic standards. For these reasons, it is perhaps hardly surprising that the official journal's first issue in 1921 contained little material directly connected with the national agenda. Ten out of the thirteen contributions concerned science and medicine, while in the humanities section the piece written by the newly elected principal, Ernsts Felsbergs, was devoted to analysing the pattern on an ancient Greek urn.[3]

In fact, the only contribution with some connection to national concerns was written by Leonid Arbusow, an historian belonging to the Baltic German

---

[1] Numbers I–V were named *Latvijas Augstskolas Raksti (LAR)*, since full university status was only obtained in 1922. Thereafter it was renamed *Latvijas Universitātes Raksti (LUR)*.
[2] LVVA. Latvijas Universitātes fonds, 7427/6/1, Organisation Committee Minutes, 1920/12/22.
[3] See Felsbergs, Ernest (1921b): "A Hieron Kylix", pp. 72–75.

ethnic minority.[4] Moreover, only three of the articles were written in Latvian, compared with nine in German and one in English. Thus it seems that national concerns were not a primary feature of the first issue of the *augstskola's* official journal. The editors apparently found it more important to promote a picture of scientific excellence at the new university for the wider international academic community.

However, this first issue elicited an immediate negative reaction in the organisation committee. Spricis Paegle, the external member from the Latvian Society, expressed his disappointment with *LAR*'s long-awaited début. Since most of the articles were in German, Paegle stated that he felt very uneasy about the journal's reception among members of the Latvian Society, and recommended that it should not be sent abroad to other universities since in his opinion it did not constitute an 'honourable production'.

The agronomist Kirhenšteins concurred, criticising the *augstskola* for producing what he saw as 'a journal in the German language'. The committee eventually decided that first issue of *LAR* should *not* be distributed to foreign universities and that, in future, the journal's contents must be presented to and approved by the Council of Deans. The appointment of a new chief editor was also suggested, but the election was postponed until a later meeting. It should be noted that Endzelīns, the chief editor, was not present during these discussions.[5]

After some delay, the election of a new chief editor was held in September 1921. Pēteris Šmits, ethnographer and linguist, won comfortably with fourteen votes to Endzelīns's five.[6] A month later the distribution of the problematic first issue of the *LAR* was again discussed – once more in Endzelīns's absence. Representatives of foreign universities had requested copies of the journal, which called for a decision on circulation. Felsbergs, the principal, suggested that before being distributed, the journal should be augmented with committee chairman Dāle's overview of the first years of *Latvijas Augstskola*, translated into French, together with the Faculty of Architecture's printed lecture plans. This would provide, in Felsbergs's view, a more correct impression of the new university's 'true character'. After some debate the committee decided that the first number of *LAR* should indeed be circulated, but that the next issue must contain a historical account of the new university's creation, in French or English. It was also decided that articles in future numbers of *LAR* could be printed in Latvian, French, English, German, Italian or Latin. Paegle's proposal

---

[4] Arbusow, Leonid (1921b): "Studien zur Geschichte der lettischen Befölkerung Rigas im Mittelalter und 16. Jahrhundert", pp. 76–100. The case of Arbusow is explored more fully in chapter 7.
[5] LVVA. Latvijas Universitātes fonds, 7427/6/1, Organisation Committee Minutes, 1921/05/25.
[6] LVVA. Latvijas Universitātes fonds, 7427/6/1, Organisation Committee Minutes, 1921/09/14.

that at least half of the contributions should be in Latvian did not find favour with the committee majority.[7]

It should be noted that Russian was *not* included among the languages to be used in the *LAR*, in spite of the fact that the great majority of the academics at the *augstskola* had received their training at Russian-speaking universities and that Russian was a *lingua franca* for all the academics of the previous Imperial territories. The preference for French and English indicates that the main objective was to orient the new university towards Western Europe.

The main conflict was clearly about the use of German. As shown in a previous chapter, many members of the organisation committee were highly sensitive about the matter of Baltic German cultural predominance. The recruitment of Baltic German academics, and the proposed appointment of lecturers and professors from Germany proper, were often blocked by the committee's more 'nationalist' members. The same sensitivity apparently applied to the presentation of the *augstskola* to Latvian society and the outside academic world.

Equally sensitive was probably the demotion of Jānis Endzelīns as chief editor. Endzelīns enjoyed a solid reputation as a linguist and was one of the main architects behind the standardization of the Latvian language. He should probably be seen as one of the new university's star academics, and the decision to demote him as editor cannot have been easy. Not surprisingly, the organisation committee appears to have been split on this issue. When Pēteris Šmits, the newly-elected chief editor, soon resigned due to illness, Endzelīns's name was again brought forward, but he lost to the eminent economist Kārlis Balodis by eleven votes to nine.[8] It must be concluded the committee's majority viewed Endzelīns as not sufficiently diligent in gate-keeping against German cultural influence. However, Balodis's rather narrow election victory is perhaps an indication that many committee members did not find him completely reliable on the German question either. As mentioned in a previous chapter, there had been some turmoil the year before when it was disclosed that Balodis actually held German citizenship. Perhaps for this very reason, Balodis as new chief editor seems to have adopted a very defensive attitude towards the committee. He frequently consulted them on matters that were seen as editorial decisions, and soon handed over the practicalities of the journal to the philosopher Pēteris Zālīte.[9]

---

[7] LVVA. Latvijas Universitātes fonds, 7427/6/1, Organisation Committee Minutes, 1921/10/12; 1921/10/19. Summaries of the articles in Latvian could be printed in French, English, or German.
[8] LVVA. Latvijas Universitātes fonds, 7427/6/1, Organisation Committee Minutes, 1921/11/09.
[9] For instance, before printing the second issue of the *LAR*, he asked the committee to appoint a commission to examine his historical narrative of the creation of the *augstskola*. The com-

Nevertheless, policies on language were clearly modified to fit the guidelines laid down by the committee. The second issue duly contained a short description in French of the forming of *Latvijas Augstskola,* and the third issue a piece by Balodis on Latvia itself, also in French.[10] A look at subsequent issues of the *LAR/LUR* shows that articles in Latvian, English and French predominated, especially in the humanities, while contributions in German remained the established norm in medicine and the natural sciences. In fact, during the first four years, slightly more articles were printed in German than in Latvian.[11] Thus, in spite of the controversial position of German within the university, its academic use was not easily dispensed with.

The anti-German tendency is also evidenced by the university's selection of honorary fellows, with a predominance of French and British academics among those nominated, while Germans were conspicuously absent. When the Latvian academics went abroad for research purposes, however, the great majority went to Germany, not to England or France. While Latvian scholars and scientists certainly tried to establish wider international contacts, Germany's leading role in many branches of academia could not be ignored.

The *LAR/LUR* was clearly intended as a forum for academics at *Latvijas Universitāte*. Only in exceptional cases were contributions from others accepted.[12] The journal was meant to provide the Latvian educated public and the international academic world with the latest findings of Latvian scientists and scholars. The director of the university library was given the task of distributing the journal to universities and research institutions abroad.[13]

Concerning the actual contents of the journal, it should first be noted that contributions from the former chief editor Jānis Endzelīns, are conspicuously absent. It was not he who provided the journal's articles on linguistics, but his less distinguished colleague Juris Plāķis. Plāķis was uncommonly diligent in

mittee, however, did not find this at all necessary. Zālīte took over responsibility for issue 3 and 4. Indeed, it is possible that Balodis's influence at the new university had diminished due to the affair of his German citizenship: he was not elected by the faculty to sit on the new university council, established in 1922. LVVA. Latvijas Universitātes fonds, 7427/6/1, Organisation Committee Minutes, 1922/03/15; 1922/08/26; University Council Minutes 1922/09/13.

[10] Ballod, C [Balodis, Kārlis] (1922): "La Latvie".

[11] *Latvijas Augstskolas Raksti/Universitātes Raksti,* no. II–XII. Between 1922 and 1925, the *LAR/LUR* published 100 articles: 40 in German, 36 in Latvian, 16 in French, 5 in English and 3 in Latin. In the last editions of the *LUR*, before it was replaced by publications from the various faculties in 1930, the numbers were roughly similar: 14 articles in German, 13 in Latvian, 5 in French, 3 in English and one in classical Greek. See *LUR*, no XVIII–XX.

[12] LVVA. Latvijas Universitātes fonds, 7427/6/1, Organisation Committee Minutes, 1921/12/14.

[13] LVVA. Latvijas Universitātes fonds, 7427/6/1, Organisation Committee Minutes, 1922/08/26; 1922/08/30. The actual sending list – a matter that evoked some discussion – was to be put together by the editor and the director of the library, and confirmed by the principal and vice-principals.

publicising articles on various aspects on the Latvian language, especially phonetics. In the first twenty issues of the journal he contributed no less than twelve separate pieces.

Apart from Latvian linguistics, however, there were initially very few contributions from the 'national' disciplines expressing a more national agenda. One exception is perhaps the philosopher Pēteris Zālīte's article on the Latvian 'soul' in a comparison with such phenomena among other nations.[14] In view of the reactions to the previous Baltic German cultural hegemony, it is perhaps a bit ironic that Zālīte's contribution relied very much on romantic German conceptions of *Volk* and nationhood.

By 1924, however, the *LUR* was publishing contributions from an entirely new field of nationally motivated research: physical anthropology. This discipline had an academic status in the late nineteenth and early twentieth centuries, but its scientific credentials vanished after 1945. In a European society increasingly obsessed with perceived racial differences, this branch of science tried to establish 'objective' and measurable differences between races, often in terms of pigmentation of skin, hair and eyes, or skull and facial proportions. These endeavours were clearly tied to various national projects, with Germanic-Nordic types juxtaposed to Celtic or Slavic types.[15]

In the Latvian academic context the main introducer of physical anthropology was actually a Swede, the professor of anatomy Gaston Backman. Apparently he was much influenced by the Swedish school of physical anthropology developed by Anders and Gustaf Retzius, giving prime importance to the measuring of skull proportions as a means of distinguishing scientifically between different 'races'. Backman had previously worked as a physician, while simultaneously participating in various expeditions and excavations for the Stockholm Ethnographical Museum. When appointed professor of anatomy in Riga, he brought with him his supply of anthropological instruments and soon initiated various projects on the measurement and classification of ethnic Latvians and Livonians, alive or dead. Finding here a comparatively under-researched 'race', Backman's averred goal was to establish the anthropological

---

[14] See, for instance, Zālīte, Pēteris (1923) "Latviešu tautas dvēsele ar iepriekšēju dvēseles jēdziena un tautu dvēseles apskatu", pp. 17–32. The main figure in philosophy recruited to the *augstskola*, however, was Walter Frost, an ethnic German expert on Immanuel Kant.

[15] McMahon, Richard (2009): "Anthropological race psychology 1820–1945: a common European system of ethnic identity narratives", 576–583. Physical anthropology seems to have been most popular in Germany, Sweden, France and Britain, with some contributions from Poles and Romanians. While helping to underpin various national and imperial ambitions, these 'scientists' naturally could not agree on the hierarchic order of these perceived 'races'.

characteristics of the 'true' Latvians before the supposed deleterious 'mixing' of various peoples in the region went any further.[16]

With the support of the Latvian General Staff, Backman organised an anthropological examination of all ethnic Latvian soldiers, with thirteen army doctors measuring the skulls and noting the colours of hair and eyes as well as parental parishes of birth. These results were then combined with measurements performed on skulls excavated from what was perceived as ancient Latvian funeral sites.[17]

A number of articles on the height, hair and eye colour, skull proportions, and brain weights of Latvians and Livonians were subsequently published in *LUR* between 1924 and 1928 by Backman and his Latvian associates in the Faculty of Medicine.[18] The main conclusion from these investigations was that the contemporary Latvian population was a form of blending between blonde and long-skulled primordial Latvians and brown-haired, short-skulled Livonians.[19] This meant that in anthropological terms, 'pure' Latvians were rather close to the Nordic type.

While these results were probably fairly compatible with contemporary nationalist notions, others were perhaps less palatable. Jānis Vilde's finding that the mean weight of Latvian brains was considerably lower than that of German brains was perhaps not particularly popular in all quarters, even if nationally-minded Latvians could find some comfort in the finding that Latvian brains were on average heavier than English or French.[20]

Initially, Backman's anthropological investigations were supported by Kārlis Kasparsons, the first Latvian Minister of Education, but the government's overall

---

[16] Arājs, Kārlis (2005): *Latviešu kauli...Atmiņas par anatomikumu un antropoloģijas ziedu laikiem Latvijā*, pp. 87–93. Livonians are an ethnic minority speaking a Finno-Ugric language that is rather close to Estonian. Most Livonians have today been assimilated into the Latvian population, and the remaining Livonian-speakers are very few. On Backman's Swedish background and his involvement in the pseudo-scientific discipline of race biology, see Kott, Matthew (2009): "Antropologen Gaston Backman och den uppsaliensiska rasbiologins spridning i tid och rum", pp. 59–74.
[17] Arājs (2005), pp. 94–98.
[18] See Vilde, Jānis (1924): "Materiali par lībiešu antropoloģiju", pp. 93–181; Backman, Gaston (1925): "Anthropologische Beiträge zur Kenntnis der Bevölkerung Lettlands", pp. 367–379; Prīmanis, Jēkabs (1925): "Pāles galvas kausi", pp. 429–476; Vilde, Jānis (1926): "Materiali par latviešu smadzeņu svaru", pp. 251–270; Jerums, N & Vītols, T M (1928): "Beiträge zur Anthropologie der Letten", pp. 279–375. On Backman's work and associates in the Faculty of Medicine, see Vīksna, Arnis (2011): *Latvijas Universitātes Medicīnas fakultāte 1919–1950*, p. 33.
[19] See Backman (1925), p. 378. These findings are perhaps taken too seriously by present-day Latvian archaeologists. See Grāvere, Rita (2006): "Lībiešu problēmas risinājuma aizsākumi Latvijas antropoloģijā (19. gs. beigas – 20. gs. pirmā puse", pp. 5–15.
[20] See Vilde (1926), pp. 267–268.

interest in these endeavours seems to have dwindled quite rapidly.[21] Moreover, with the departure of the *primus motor,* Gaston Backman, from Riga in 1925, this branch of research seems to have lost most of its impetus.[22] An additional factor may well have been that some of Backman's findings did not fit in with received popular and academic opinion on the nature of the Latvian nation. He claimed, for instance, that one of the traditional Latvian *ciltis* or tribes, the *kurši*, was in anthropological terms actually not Latvian but instead an ancient Finno-Ugric tribe. These conclusions were clearly not appreciated by leading Latvian linguists and historians. Especially Jānis Endelīns was very sharp in his rebuttal of Backman's ideas. For Endzelīns, as well as for other Latvian academics working within the 'national' disciplines, it was virtually impossible to view the *kurši* tribe as non-Latvian. Endzelīns had in 1911 rebutted the claims of some Finnish researchers that the old *kurši* had spoken a Finno-Ugric dialect, and he and the other Latvian linguists were clearly not ready to revise their position.[23] This may be one reason why physical anthropology, compared to its prominent position in some other European countries, did not become an important part of the national Latvian intellectual discourse during this period.[24]

Still, the journal's main character remained solidly academic in a rather a-national way: at least half of the issues were made up of articles on science and medicine, and foreign languages continued to be used far more often than Latvian. Even in potentially 'national' disciplines like linguistics, archaeology, and history, the articles seldom dealt with problems connected with Latvian history or culture. In history, after his initial fairly 'Latvian'-oriented piece in 1921, Leonid Arbusow subsequently only published articles with rather insignifi-

---

[21] LVVA. Izglītības ministrijas fonds, 1632/2/612, Sarakste ar Latvijas Universitāti par mācību spēkiem… 1921. g.– 1922. g. Letter from Backman to the Principal, LU, 1922/10/13; letter from the Principal to the Education Minister, 1922/10/19.

[22] On Backman, see LVVA. Latvijas Universitātes fonds, 7427/13/114. Staff records. The reasons for Backman's departure are difficult to establish for certain. The contemporary press speculated that increased pressure to lecture in Latvian could have been one of the causes. Ibid. However, university records also show that Backman's demands for extra emoluments on top of his ordinary salary as professor met with increasing coldness in the university council. Apparently, the Council decided to stop these extra payments from 1925. LVVA. Latvijas Universitātes fonds, 7427/6/2, University Council Minutes 1924/04/25. Professor of surgery Jēkabs Alksnis claimed in a letter to a Latvian colleague that Backman's unfortunate departure was due to personal intrigues masked as patriotism. See Vīksna, A (2011), pp. 58–59

[23] Blese, Ernsts (1937): "Seno kuršu etniskā piederība", pp. 65–78. Blese, however, deviated somewhat from the standard national narrative by claiming that old *kurši* was in linguistic terms much closer to the extinct old Prussian than the 'Latvian' Semgallian dialect.

[24] Arājs (2005), p. 99. However, Backman's successor as professor of anatomy, Jēkabs Prīmanis, was still asked by Endzelīns to contribute an anthropological piece on the physical stature of ancient Latvians in the new codified edition of the national folksongs, the *dainas*. See Prīmanis, Jēkabs (1929): "Latviešu ķermeņa uzbūve latvju daiņās", pp. 1–46. Prīmanis's conception of ancient Latvians as predominantly tall, strong and well-proportioned was not controversial.

cant 'national' themes – also primarily in German.[25] His ethnic Latvian colleague Augusts Tentelis published only one piece in the *LUR* during the 1920s: a medieval Latin text translated into Latvian and German.[26] The eminent linguist and folklorist Pēteris Šmits, who was one of the main driving forces behind the systematization of Latvian folklore collections, used the *LUR* merely to publish linguistic articles on minor tribal languages from the Amur region in Eastern Siberia.[27] Similarly, his colleague Francis Balodis in archaeology, who later became the driving force behind a more 'national' approach in his discipline, nevertheless published only on Egyptian and Mongol topics in the *LUR* during the 1920s.[28]

Conclusions

The creation of *Latvijas Universitāte* materialised the aspiration of an academic institution for the Latvian nation. While this national agenda was certainly prevalent among the academics in the university leadership, the extent to which the national aims should predominate in the official journal was more open to debate. The university leadership was also driven by a need to prove and make public to the wider academic world the high scholarly and scientific standard of the new university. A closer look at the university's official journal, *Latvijas Universitātes Raksti*, shows that this caused some turbulence when the journal was first launched. The first chief editor, professor Jānis Endzelīns, a linguist with a solid reputation in both academic and national circles, chose to give priority to communication with the predominantly German-speaking academic world. This was clearly too much for the organisation committee's majority, and Endzelīns was replaced as chief editor after the first issue. Having long been under Baltic German cultural hegemony, a majority among the Latvian academic leadership gave priority to a break with the past.

---

[25] See Arbusow, Leonid (1923): "Kirchliches Leben der Rigaschen Losträger im 15. Jahrhundert", pp. 185-224; Arbusow, Leonid (1924): "Ein Verzeichnis der bäurlichen Apgaben im Stift Kurland (1582/83)", pp. 163-286; Arbusovs, Leonīds (1926): "Die handschriftliche Überlieferung des 'Cronicon Livoniae' Heinrichs von Lettland", pp. 189-341; Arbusovs, Leonīds (1929): "II. Römischer Arbeitsbericht", pp. 475-657.
[26] Tentelis, Augusts (1924). "Curlandiae quaedam notabilia".
[27] See Šmits, Pēteris (1923a): "The Language of the Negidals", pp. 3-39; Šmits, Pēteris (1923b): "The Language of the Olchas", pp. 229-288; and Šmits, Pēteris (1928): "The Language of the Oroches", pp. 17-62. Admittedly, Šmits also published an epitaph over Krišjānis Barons, the Grand Old Man of Latvian folklore, in *LUR*. See Šmits, Pēteris (1923c): "Krišjāņa Barona Latvju Dainas", pp. 217-27.
[28] See Balodis, Francis (1924): "Mākslas reforma Echnatona laikā", pp. 182-266; Balodis, Francis (1926): "Alt-Sarai und Neu-Sarai, die Hauptstädte der Goldenen Horde", pp. 3-82. On Balodis and archaeology, see chapter 7.

The main concern was apparently that articles in German should not be allowed to predominate: French and English were preferred, apart from Latvian. While this change was duly implemented in the humanities, the same could not be said in medicine and the natural sciences: here German continued to predominate as the major academic language. This meant that, in spite of the priorities of the university leadership, in the first four years slightly more articles were actually printed in German rather than Latvian.

In this context, it should be noted that Russian was not among the languages used in the official journal, in spite of the fact that practically all Latvian academics had been educated at Imperial Russian universities and were familiar with this language. This should probably be seen as a conscious strategy to orient the new university towards Western Europe.

Apart from a great many articles on Latvian linguistics, the main 'national' topic developed in the journal was Human Anthropology. However, the leading academic behind these contributions was not a Latvian. This perhaps doubtful honour fell to a Swede, the anatomist Gaston Backman, who implemented his native country's skull-measuring methodology and conceptions of race in the Latvian context. These endeavours seem to have fizzled out, at least partly because the results were not quite in accordance with other parts of the national project. Backman's conclusions about the physical characteristics of ancient Latvian tribes were not compatible with popular and academic notions of the nature of the Latvian nation.

Summing up, it seems safe to conclude that during the first decade, the editors of the *LAR/LUR* put academic and international aims before the more strictly national ones. The main conflict seems to have been about the use of the German language, a sensitive issue due to the perceived need among Latvian academics and national intellectuals to distance themselves from the previous Baltic German cultural hegemony. During the rest of the 1920s, the journal was primarily devoted to meeting these general academic requirements, publishing articles predominantly in foreign languages and devoting little space to more narrowly 'national' topics. The journal should probably be seen as the new university's window on the outside academic world, spreading the results of Latvian science and scholarship to the international learned community.

For expressions of more overtly national goals and undertakings in academic work, we must evidently look elsewhere. Traditionally, such 'national' projects within the field of academia are most prevalent in four scholarly fields: language, folklore, archaeology, and history. It is therefore necessary to take a somewhat closer look at the academics employed during the first decade in the Faculty of Philology and Philosophy, to which all of these disciplines belonged.

CHAPTER 7

Developing 'National Disciplines' Archaeology, Folklore, History, Latvian Linguistics and Literature, 1919–1934

While the creation of *Latvijas Universitāte* (*LU*) was in itself a national project, forming an arena of conflicts and compromises around the recruitment of academics and the choice of teaching language, some academic disciplines were closer than others to the cultural meaning of the national project. Above all, they were subjects close to the nation's history, language and culture. Earlier research has shown that these areas were of prime concern for nationalist intellectuals, and were also given high priority at universities in the successor states of Eastern and Central Europe that emerged after World War I. The prime 'national' disciplines of interest here are folklore, archaeology, history, and Latvian linguistics and Literary studies. In this chapter, I will take a closer look at the faculty to which these disciplines belonged, the Faculty of Philology and Philosophy, during the democratic period between 1919 and 1934. More specifically, I will examine the faculty's academic work, appointments, and recruitment policies in this period. My objective, however, is *not* to present a general overview of the faculty's development as a part of university history, but rather to focus on the tensions and frictions occasioned by the simultaneous existence of the national and academic agendas.

The main questions are: to what extent was the faculty able to find qualified Latvian academics in the various subjects? Were Baltic German academics invited to join the staff of these 'national' disciplines – or were they generally barred? Were foreign academics appointed and, if so, to which nationalities did they belong? What kind of tensions and conflicts evolved within the faculty on the appointment of 'foreign' academics – and how were these conflicts resolved? Moreover, to what extent did these disciplines undergo a 'national turn' during the 1920s, developing national grand narratives and codifications of Latvian history, culture, and language? Was this 'turn' more perceptible in some disciplines than in others?

As a methodological tool for analysing the Latvian academics, I use a generational perspective. The categorization will be as follows: an 'older' group connected to the first generation of Latvian nationalist intellectuals educated at Dorpat/Jur'ev, St Petersburg and Moscow Universities, a 'middle' generation of

Latvian academics who were fully established within the Imperial university system before World War I, a 'younger' generation that had received the basic scholarly training at Russian universities but later formed careers at *Latvijas Universitāte*, and, finally, the 'youngest' generation, the academics who received their entire training at *LU* during the interwar period.

To render a coherent narrative of changes over time in several disciplines is difficult. I will start by focusing on the Faculty of Philology and Philosophy in more general terms and then analyse the 'national turn' in the separate disciplines. Finally, I will try to make some comparisons with similar developments at the universities in Lithuania and Estonia.

Putting a faculty together: recruitment in the initial years

When the Faculty of Philology and Philosophy was established in July 1919, it had only five academics: the temporary dean, pedagogue Kārlis Kundziņš, psychologist Pauls Dāle, also chairman of the university's organisation committee, philosopher Pēteris Zālīte and two linguists and literary scholars, Jēkabs Lautenbahs and Ernsts Blese. Their immediate task was to recruit a set of suitable academics in order to make the faculty operational in terms of teaching. Two main principles were formulated right from the start. First, the recruited academics should, if possible, be thorough specialists in their respective area, and, second, they should, if possible, be ethnic Latvians.[1] The question is: how were these principles reconciled?

A year later, university records show that in the questionnaire, fifteen of the faculty's teaching staff had defined themselves as 'Latvian', three as 'German', and one as 'Swiss'.[2] Ten professors of Latvian extraction had received their scholarly training and early career at Russian universities, while a further two had been educated in Germany. Most of them had returned to Latvia either during the war or in the early 1920s. Some of the younger generation of academics, such as psychologist Pauls Dāle and the classical scholar Kārlis Straubergs, had fought for Latvian independence in the war of 1918–1919, while members the 'middle' and 'older' generations, for instance, art historian Ernsts Felsbergs and the linguists Jānis Endzelīns and Juris Plāķis, had generally not

---

[1] *Latvijas Universitāte divdesmit gados 1919–1939* (1939), I, pp. 179–180. Unfortunately, the faculty's minute book for 1919–1922 has been lost.
[2] LVVA. Latvijas Universitātes fonds, 7427/6/37a. Pārskats par Latvijas augstskolas, vēlāk Universitātes, nodibināšanu un viņas darbību. Overview of the teaching staff, 1919/1920. The *augstskola* kept a careful check on the ethnicity of the teaching staff, requiring all academics to state their *tautība*.

returned to Riga until 1920 after having been detained in Soviet Russia.[3] The previously mentioned Pēteris Šmits, a professor of Chinese in Vladivostok, had to travel around the world by sea in order to take up his post in Riga in 1920 – unfortunately losing much of his Asian folklore collection in the process.[4]

Those who had worked at universities in southern Russia, in particular, endured many hardships on their way to Riga. Contagious diseases, lack of food and water, and great difficulties in procuring the necessary travel permits made the journey very hazardous. Travelling from Kazan on a train with many passengers who developed typhus, Juris Plāķis and his young family had to wait for several weeks in very exposed conditions before being issued with all the necessary permits. Finally, Plāķis and his colleague Jānis Endzelīns were held hostage for a time at the border before being exchanged for some Bolsheviks imprisoned in Latvia.[5] Some academics did not survive the journey. One very notable loss for the projected faculty was the philosopher Jēkabs Osis. A professor at Dorpat University, where he had previously provoked the Baltic German academics by delivering some lectures in Russian, during the war Osis was evacuated to Voronezh, where he died in a typhoid epidemic at the age of fifty-nine.[6] A forceful character and experienced professor of philosophy, he would certainly have been a great asset to the faculty.

There were just a few trained Latvian academics in the humanities. As indicated in chapter 3, in the nineteenth century most Latvians who managed to join an intellectual profession had become Germanized in the process. Social and ethnic divides had previously obstructed the emergence of a distinctly Latvian middle class. It is therefore hardly surprising that most of the faculty's professors who were labelled 'Latvian' came from rather modest social backgrounds. During the formative years, between 1919 and 1922, eight ethnic Latvian professors were appointed in the faculty; five of them were the farmers' sons, two had fathers who were foresters and game-keepers, while only one, the youngest, Arnolds Spekke, was the son of an elementary school teacher. Three of these professors, Felsbergs, Plāķis and Tentelis, had also had relatively long

---

[3] LVVA. Latvijas Universitātes fonds, 7427/13/342; 7427/13/475; 7427/13/447. Staff records; 7427/6/42 Filoloģijas un filzofijas fakultātes darbības pārskats no 1919. g. līdz 1938. g.
[4] *Latvijas Universitāte 1919–1929* (1929), pp. 148–195. For the past twenty years Šmits had been in Riga only for some summer vacations but he was an active corresponding member of the Riga Latvian Society's 'scientific' committee, especially on orthographic matters. On arrival in Riga, he duly assumed the post of president of the RLS committee. See Stradiņš, Jānis (1998) *Latvijas Zinātņu akadēmija: izcelsme, vēsture, pārvērtības*, pp. 71–82.
[5] Kļaviņa, Sarma (2010): "LU profesora Jura Plāķa dzīves un ciešanu ceļi (1869–1942)", pp. 37–39. In this article, Kļaviņa edits and publishes some autobiographical fragments by Plāķis, probably written in the 1930s.
[6] Bērziņš, Ludvigs (1935): *Mūža rīts un darba diena. Atmiņu grāmata*, pp. 104–105.

careers as elementary school teachers before returning to more advanced university training at a mature age.[7]

Ernsts Felsbergs, for instance, the son of a gamekeeper outside Cēsis, worked as a schoolteacher in the late 1880s before going to Jur'ev/Dorpat University as a student of art history and Classical Philology. After a career at St Petersburg, Berlin, Dorpat/Jur'ev and Voronezh, he returned to Riga in 1920 to become the first principal of the new *augstskola*. Primarily a classical scholar and expert on ancient Greek art history, he did not produce any major scholarly work on 'national' Latvian topics.[8]

Of this first group of eight Latvian professors, only three had had fairly straightforward academic careers: linguists Lautenbahs and Endzelīns, and Sinologist Pēteris Šmits. In 1914 they were all firmly established at Russian universities. One of the eight, philosopher Pēteris Zālīte, had not been a part of Imperial academia, having worked primarily as a journalist and writer before joining the *augstskola* in 1920.[9]

The problem with Baltic Germans

The perceptible lack of trained Latvian academics in the faculty's subjects naturally made it necessary to look elsewhere for recruits. Considering the long cultural predominance of Germans in the Baltic provinces, it is noteworthy that ethnic Germans were very rare among the teaching staff at the Faculty of Philology and Philosophy at *Latvijas Augstskola*. Of the fifty-four recruits to the faculty between 1919 and 1922, only five were Baltic Germans and two were academics from Germany proper. Of these seven, only three were retained as permanent staff: historian Leonid Arbusow, philosopher Walter Frost, and classical linguist Erich Diehl.

German academics were appointed only in subjects for which it was particularly difficult to find reasonably competent Latvians.[10] Frost was obviously recruited in the wake of the tragic death of the Latvian philosopher Jēkabs Osis. Similarly, the lack of scholarly trained Latvian historians paved the way for the solid Baltic German medievalist Arbusow. As shown in more detail below, the need to develop Latvian archaeology led to the appointment of Karl Löwis of

---

[7] *Latvijas Universitāte 1919–1929* (1929), pp. 162–195
[8] LVVA. Latvijas Universitātes fonds, 7427/13/475. Staff records; *Latvijas Universitāte 1919–1929* (1929), pp. 166–167.
[9] LVVA. Latvijas Universitātes fonds, 7427/13/447; 7427/13/978; 7427/13/1698. Staff records; *Latvijas Universitāte 1919–1929* (1929), pp. 193–195. Zālīte had previously been the editor of the important Latvian newspaper *Mājas viesis*. See Zelče, Vita (2007): "The Establishment and Early Activities of the Weekly '*Mājas viesis*' in the Second Half of the 1850s. A Declaration of Latvian Nationalism", p. 142.
[10] The only exception here was the classicist linguist Erich Diehl. See below on linguistics.

Menar and Max Ebert. In the case of Frost and Arbusow, however, it is apparent that the organisation committee was anxious to complement them with two swiftly promoted Latvian professors: Pēteris Zālīte in Philosophy and Augusts Tentelis in history. The academic record of Tentelis, especially, did not really motivate his appointment as professor. Clearly, the faculty leadership considered that the important 'national' discipline of history could not be left solely in the hands of the Baltic German Arbusow.[11]

Most of the other German academics were appointed on a yearly basis. This was the case with, for instance, the Baltic Germans Philipp Schweinfurth in art history, the Germanic linguist Oskar Masing, who lectured on 'the German spiritual culture of the eighteenth century' and the autodidact archaeologist Karl Löwis of Menar.[12] None of them were retained as permanent staff.

Philipp Schweinfurth, or Filips Šveinfurts to use his Latvian name, belonged to the Baltic German *tautība* and held Latvian citizenship. Schweinfurth had obtained a doctorate at Heidelberg, but returned to Riga before World War I as a high school teacher in art history. In 1919 he was elected *docents* at the Faculty of Philology and Philosophy, and later also at the Art Academy. Schweinfurth's position seems to have been rather stable in the initial years, one important reason being, I suspect, that he had participated on the Latvian side in the War of Liberation and thus proven his loyalty to the new Latvian state.[13] When his appointment was extended in 1922 he was allowed to lecture in *Russian*, but not in German.[14] This is perhaps an indication that the use of German as the language of instruction was still a very sensitive issue. A few years later, Schweinfurth was criticised at a faculty meeting for publishing his articles in German.[15] Finally, in 1926 Schweinfurth's appointment was no longer extended – according to the official history the reason for this was that he was not able to meet the requirement to lecture in Latvian.[16]

---

[11] I will go into these matters in more detail later in this chapter when dealing with the discipline of history.
[12] LVVA. Latvijas Universitātes fonds, 7427/6/37a. Pārskats par Latvijas augstskolas, vēlāk Universitātes, nodibināšanu un viņas darbību. Overview of the teaching staff, 1919/1920/1921. It should perhaps be noted that 'nationality' was not synonymous with teaching language. Schweinfurth lectured in Russian, and Arbusow in Latvian, Russian and German.
[13] LVVA. Latvijas Universitātes fonds, 7427/13/1746. Staff records.
[14] LVVA. Latvijas Universitātes fonds, 7427/6/1, University Council Minutes, 1922/10/25. In 1925, however, he was granted the right to lecture in German. 7427/13/1746. Staff records.
[15] At a faculty meeting in 1923, art historian Ernsts Felsbergs criticised Schweinfurth for publishing his articles in German. Felsbergs saw this as a reason for rejecting Scweinfurth's application for funds for a research trip. Historian Arbusow and the dean, linguist Endzelīns, supported Schweinfurth's application, but the faculty majority turned it down. See LVVA. Latvijas Universitātes fonds, 7427/6/363, Minutes of the Faculty of Philology and Philosophy, 1923/03/24.
[16] *Latvijas Universitāte divdesmit gados 1919–1939* (1939), I, p. 175.

Oskar Masing's sojourn at *Latvijas Augstskola* was even shorter. Sharing in many ways Schweinfurth's background, apart from not having taken part in the War of Liberation, Masing was first employed as a lecturer in German in the Faculty of Law and Economics in 1919 after being on the teaching staff of the Riga Polytechnical Institute since 1912.[17] He was transferred to the Faculty of Philology and Philosophy, which turned down his application for a yearly extension by a narrow majority in 1922. The matter seems to have been sensitive. The influence of Baltic German academics in the Faculty of Law and Economics had apparently prevented that faculty from refusing to renew Masing's appointment.[18] The law students had issued a formal protest on Masing's behalf, to no avail.[19] A clearly disappointed Masing had to leave the university; instead he found a new position at the Herder Institute.[20]

Indeed, as highlighted in a previous chapter, there seems to have been a decided reluctance to employ academics who either belonged to the Baltic German *tautība* or were German citizens. It was much easier for Austrians, Swiss, Swedes and Finns to find favour with the organisation committee, even if they had no previous knowledge of Latvian and their language of instruction therefore had to be German. Before the formal creation of the university in 1922, the committee's voting procedure, requiring a two-thirds majority, also made it easier for the 'national' Latvian wing to block the appointment of academics they perceived as 'undesirable'.

In the Faculty of Philological and Philosophical, recruiting academics in the disciplines of German linguistics and German literature therefore seems to have been a very delicate matter. The first appointed professor of German linguistics was a Finn, Karl Tiander, who was given a two-year contract in 1921.[21] However,

---

[17] There was a clear continuity of staff between this faculty and the previous Department of Commerce at the Riga Polytechnical Institute.

[18] According to Endzelīns, dean of Law and Economics, Jānis Kārkliņš, did not want to have a vote on Masing in his own faculty due to the "many Germans there". LVVA. Latvijas Universitātes fonds, 7427/6/363, Minutes of the Faculty of Philology and Philosophy, 1922/04/29. At this faculty meeting, the only tenured Baltic German academic, historian Leonid Arbusow, was not present.

[19] LVVA. Latvijas Universitātes fonds, 7427/6/363, Minutes of the Faculty of Philology and Philosophy, 1922/05/13. Arbusow now tried to find a compromise, but Masing's appointment was again turned down with only three out of ten faculty members voting in his favour.

[20] LVVA. Latvijas Universitātes fonds, 7427/13/1108. Staff records; LVVA. Latvijas Universitātes fonds, 7427/6/363, Minutes of the Faculty of Philology and Philosophy, 1922/05/27, Letter to the faculty from Masing; Izglītības ministrijas fonds, 1632/2/699, Herdera institūta lieta. Masing answered staff questionnaires in Russian, which may be an indication that he did not command Latvian. Masing's great work during the interwar period was to assemble material for a Baltic German dialect dictionary. See Wörster, Peter (2007): "Vor 60 Jahren. Nachruf Reinhard Wittrams auf den 1947 verstorbenen Germanisten Oskar Masing", pp. 182–185.

[21] LVVA. Latvijas Universitātes fonds, 7427/6/1, Organisation Committee Minutes, 1921/09/07.

Tiander did not hold this position for long. In October 1922, the dean, Jānis Endzelīns, informed the faculty that the Foreign Office had sent him a memo stating that Tiander had acted against the interests of the Latvian state. Apparently, Tiander, who was also a Finnish parliamentarian, had published some articles in the Baltic German press that expressed some criticism of the far-reaching Latvian land reforms.[22] This was a very sensitive issue in Latvian politics, since the Baltic German politicians and landowners – whose estates would be much reduced by the land reforms – tried to arouse international opinion against these perceived 'confiscations'. Here, Tiander had apparently stepped into a hornets' nest.

Tiander declared at the faculty meeting that his prime loyalty naturally lay with Finland, and denied that his writings had contained anything slanderous about Latvia. He then left the meeting and the ensuing discussion was turbulent. Philosopher Pēteris Zālīte defended what he saw as Tiander's right as a foreigner to be critical of the Latvian land reforms. Moreover, he argued, freedom of expression ought to be a paramount consideration. Romanist Arnolds Spekke and the Baltic German historian Arbusow agreed that this was hardly a matter for the faculty. Linguist Juris Plāķis was much more critical, claiming that Tiander in words and writings had shown animosity to Latvia. Endzelīns, trying to find a compromise, suggested that the faculty should decide to ask Tiander to refrain from further journalistic writing, if these articles could be interpreted as being unfriendly to Latvia. This suggestion found favour with everyone except Arbusow, who voted against it.[23]

When the matter reached the university council, the tone was considerably harsher. It was found that Tiander had engaged in political actions that were 'contrary to Latvian interests' and also 'cast a shadow on *Latvijas Universitāte*'. He was therefore barred henceforth from lecturing. Jānis Endzelīns and Pēteris Zālīte, the faculty's delegates, argued against the council majority and declared that they would abstain from voting on this issue.[24] What was especially reprehensible in Tiander's writings was never really specified, and it is note-

---

[22] LVVA. Latvijas Universitātes fonds, 7427/6/363, Minutes of the Faculty of Philology and Philosophy, 1922/09/02; 1922/10/07. It is also possible that Tiander had played some role in the Finnish parliament's decision not to ratify the proposed defence treaty between Finland, Estonia, Latvia and Poland earlier the same year. 'Germanophile' Finnish parliamentarians were among those who opposed this treaty. See *20. gadsimta Latvijas vēsture II. Neatkarīgā valsts 1918–1940* (2003), pp. 565–567.

[23] LVVA. Latvijas Universitātes fonds, 7427/6/363, Minutes of the Faculty of Philology and Philosophy, 1922/10/07. Arbusow maintained that the faculty had no right to require this of a foreign academic.

[24] LVVA. Latvijas Universitātes fonds, 7427/6/2. University Council Minutes, 1922/10/25. Zālīte added to the minutes that in his opinion, Tiander should not be penalised without having had the opportunity of being heard.

worthy that he was never given the opportunity to explain himself. The sensitivity of this issue is perhaps indicated by the fact that Tiander's name is absent from the printed overview of the academic staff in the 1920s.[25]

Endzelīns clearly deplored the university council's stand, stating that it had not examined the allegations against Tiander in a reasonable manner. At the same time, he realised that it would be futile to suggest an extension of Tiander's contract, which was due to expire in the summer of 1923. The faculty, he concluded, would simply have to find another Germanist.[26]

Meanwhile, Endzelīns and the faculty were involved in a drawn-out conflict with the organisation committee on the proposed appointment of a German professor in Romanist linguistics.[27] This spoke against proposing the recruitment of yet another academic from Germany. Eventually, Tiander's successor as professor in the German language and literature, Max Nussberger, was not of German or Baltic German extraction; his candidature was not taken seriously until the faculty had received confirmation of his Swiss citizenship.[28] A *dozent* in German literature at Basel University, and a specialist in German poets born in Switzerland, he was summoned to *Latvijas Universitāte* in 1923.[29]

Since Germany was in economic and political turmoil at the time, the recruitment of a well-qualified German professor would probably have been an easy task. The decided preference for Swiss over German academics must therefore have had political reasons. It seems quite certain that Nussberger's credentials as a 'non-national' Germanist weighed at least as heavily in this matter as his scholarly merits.[30] When the faculty considered Nussberger's appointment, only

---

[25] *Latvijas Universitāte 1919–1929* (1929). It should also be noted that the records of his appointment and the memo from the Foreign Office have been removed from his personal file. Only some papers of economic character remain. LVVA. Latvijas Universitātes fonds, 7427/13/1763. Staff records

[26] LVVA. Latvijas Universitātes fonds, 7427/6/363, Minutes of the Faculty of Philology and Philosophy, 1922/10/21; 1922/12/02. Zālīte, who previously had argued strongly in favour of Tiander's right of expression, suggested that the faculty should re-elect him just to prove a point. The faculty, however, does not seem to have seen this as very constructive. Ibid., 1922/12/06.

[27] See the case of Neubert below.

[28] LVVA. Latvijas Universitātes fonds, 7427/6/363, Minutes of the Faculty of Philology and Philosophy, 1922/12/16.

[29] LVVA. Latvijas Universitātes fonds, 7427/6//2, University Council Minutes 1923/02/07; 7427/13/1230. Staff records; *Latvijas Universitāte 1919–1929* (1929), p.173. I find it decidedly less likely that the University of Latvia had a special demand for Nussberger's expertise on poets born in Switzerland.

[30] Nussberger appears to have been completely unknown among the Latvian linguists until October 1922, when he was recommended by a colleague at Basel University. LVVA. Latvijas Universitātes fonds, 7427/13/1230. Staff records. Letter from Niedermann to Blese, 1922/10/29. Another Swiss in the faculty was Ernst Schneider, appointed docent in psychological pedagogy in January 1920. See *Latvijas Universitātes piecgadu darbības pārskats 1919–1924* (1925), p. 291.

Austrian and Swedish alternatives were brought forward – and were found to be much less interesting. Nussberger's candidacy consequently received very substantial backing in the faculty, and his appointment was confirmed by a solid majority in the university council.[31]

The matter is, however, perhaps more complicated than it would seem at first sight. The exclusion of Germans and Baltic Germans was not total. Linguist Jānis Endzelīns acted as dean in the formative years and was, as we have seen in a previous chapter, less negative towards German academics than many of his colleagues.[32] In 1920, for instance, he successfully proposed the recruitment of philosophy professor Walter Frost from Bonn University. This was, in fact, one of the very few exceptions to the prevailing 'anti-German' preference that the organisation committee accepted.[33] Two years later, Endzelīns moved that Frost be permanently employed at the *augstskola* with an unlimited right to continue lecturing in German. The committee accepted the appointment but not Frost's right to lecture in German indefinitely.[34] The faculty's continued support, in spite of Frost's persistent difficulties in mastering Latvian, enabled him to stay on at *Latvijas Universitāte* and lecture in German until his death in 1936.[35]

Also in 1922, Endzelīns was bold enough to propose the appointment of yet another German academic, the *privat-dozent* Neubert, Leipzig University, as professor of Romance linguistics. This caused some heated discussions in the faculty. The principal, Ernsts Felsbergs, argued strongly against Neubert's election, claiming that he was too young and could hardly be considered a prominent scholar. Felsbergs maintained that it was better to support the academic training of 'one of our own' scholars, and added that in his opinion "we orientate ourselves too strongly towards Germany". However, Endzelīns persisted, claiming that none of the younger Latvian linguists could gain expertise in 'old French' within a reasonable time. The faculty, interestingly

---

[31] LVVA. Latvijas Universitātes fonds, 7427/6/363, Minutes of the Faculty of Philology and Philosophy, 1923/01/08; 7427/6/2, University Council Minutes, 1923/02/07. 25 'ayes', 3 against, 1 abstaining. Like other 'foreign' professors, he was permitted to lecture in German for five years before being required to shift to Latvian.

[32] Endzelīns was dean of faculty until 1 July 1923, when he was replaced by Pēteris Šmits. See *Latvijas Universitātes piecgadu darbības pārskats 1919–1924* (1925), p. 290.

[33] LVVA. Izglītības ministrijas fonds, 1632/2/633. Sarakste ar Latvijas Augstskolu par mācības spēku pieņemšanu darbā. Letter from the Cabinet to the Education Minister, 1920/11/12, granting permission to appoint Frost.

[34] LVVA. Latvijas Universitātes fonds, 7427/6/1, Organisation Committee Minutes, 1922/04/05; 1922/04/22; 1922/05/31.

[35] LVVA. Latvijas Universitātes fonds, 7427/6/268. Sarakste ar fakultātēm, profesoriem par mācību pasniegšanu valsts valodā. Application 1927/01/08; Copy of Council of Deans minutes 1927/02/14; Copy of University Council minutes, 1927/02/16; *Latvijas Universitāte divdesmit gados 1919–1939* (1939), I, p. 194.

enough, voted solidly for Endzelīns's proposal.³⁶ The majority clearly preferred a wider selection of academics in order to maintain scholarly levels rather than a more narrow ethnic preference for less qualified Latvians.

When the matter reached the organisation committee, however, the conflict between Endzelīns and Felsbergs was resumed. Perhaps to stave off opposition, Endzelīns added to his proposal that Neubert would be required to lecture in French, not German, but this was insufficient to satisfy the committee. The principal, Felsbergs, again opposed Neubert's recruitment and demanded an investigation to see if a more suitable candidate could be found in France or Italy. The committee called on Endzelīns to seek the assistance of the Latvian ambassadors in Rome and Paris to achieve this before a decision was made.³⁷

The controversy continued on the faculty level, with Felsbergs arguing strongly for the recruitment of a French or possibly Italian academic. To achieve this, Felsbergs was even prepared to pay the professorial salary in foreign currency, a practice which the organisation committee had previously criticised strongly. Endzelīns, in turn, argued that continued prevarication would only result in the loss of Neubert, which was clearly not in the interest of the students. Plāķis agreed with Felsbergs, but a substantial faculty majority – eight to four – sided with Endzelīns.³⁸

Consequently, Endzelīns as dean continued to delay the appointment of Neubert in the new university council, declaring that the Latvian ambassadors in Rome and Paris had not been able to supply him with any suitable candidates. A petition from the students in Romance linguistics was also presented, in which they supported Neubert's recruitment. After several weeks of prevarication, Neubert was finally elected with the smallest possible majority. He was appointed for a period of five years, with the requirement to lecture in French.³⁹

Apparently, Endzelīns had managed to rally the faculty behind him – with the notable exceptions of Felsbergs and Plāķis – and after a protracted process secured the appointment of a well-qualified German Romanist. However, his victory was short-lived. A month later the Latvian government, which had the final say in the recruitment of foreign academics, refused to condone Neubert's

---

[36] LVVA. Latvijas Universitātes fonds, 7427/6/363, Minutes of the Faculty of Philology and Philosophy, 1922/09/02. The vote was 10 in favour, 2 against and 1 abstaining. Felsbergs, it seems, was not very influential within his own faculty.
[37] LVVA. Latvijas Universitātes fonds, 7427/6/1, Organisation Committee Minutes, 1922/09/06.
[38] LVVA. Latvijas Universitātes fonds, 7427/6/363, Minutes of the Faculty of Philology and Philosophy, 1922/09/23. When Endzelīns took the matter to a new vote a fortnight later, in Felsbergs's absence, only Plāķis voted against. Ibid., 1922/10/07.
[39] LVVA. Latvijas Universitātes fonds, 7427/6/2, University Council Minutes, 1922/10/25. Naturally, this was under the new voting rules that required just a simple majority in the university council to secure an appointment. Endzelīns was certainly aware of this.

appointment.[40] Forced to find a new solution, and probably reasoning that it would be pointless to propose yet another German, the faculty now suggested a Finnish academic, Dr O. Tallgren from Helsinki University.[41] Perhaps not unexpectedly, the university council found the recruitment of a Finn decidedly more palatable than a German, and Tallgren was duly elected with a very solid majority.[42] For unknown reasons, however, Tallgren never accepted the invitation.[43] After all these trials and tribulations, Endzelīns finally managed to recruit an academic from an 'acceptable' country: the Austrian Dr Josef Brüch from Vienna University.[44]

The Neubert case clearly illustrates the general resistance to recruiting German academics, particularly in the organisation committee and on governmental levels. Only if no viable alternative could be found and there was a clear need for a prominent academic in the field, could a German be seriously considered.

In view of the disputes between Endzelīns and Felsbergs over the suggested election of Neubert, it is perhaps somewhat surprising that it was the latter who lay behind the appointment of another ethnic German, Erich Diehl, a classical philologist, as *privātdocents* in September 1922. In this case, however, there may have been other considerations. Diehl, born in Daugavpils and the son of a Baltic German engineer, had studied classical philology in 1908–1913 at St Petersburg University, where he became a *privātdocents* in 1916. In 1917 he was appointed professor of classical philology at Tomsk University. By 1921, however, it seems that his position in Tomsk was becoming increasingly difficult. Diehl's in-laws, Baltic Germans in Riga, approached the principal, Felsbergs, asking for the formal election of Diehl as *privātdocents* at the university. He apparently needed a formal appointment in order to gain permission to leave Soviet Russia. His in-laws emphasised not only his precarious situation in Tomsk, but also his strong desire to 'serve his native country'. Sensing that the language question was a

---

[40] LVVA. Latvijas Universitātes fonds, 7427/6/2, University Council Minutes, 1922/11/15.
[41] LVVA. Latvijas Universitātes fonds, 7427/6/363, Minutes of the Faculty of Philology and Philosophy, 1923/01/08. Tallgren was elected unanimously.
[42] LVVA. Latvijas Universitātes fonds, 7427/6/2, University Council Minutes, 1923/01/17. The vote was 27 'ayes', one against and one abstaining.
[43] Possibly, this was due to unsatisfactory conditions. The university council refused to grant Tallgren more than the regular salary, a matter that was later criticised by Spekke in the faculty. LVVA. Latvijas Universitātes fonds, 7427/6/363, Minutes of the Faculty of Philology and Philosophy, 1923/01/19.
[44] LVVA. Latvijas Universitātes fonds, 7427/6/2, University Council Minutes, 1923/03/07; 1923/04/11. Brüch was appointed without discussion for a term of five years, and with the requirement to lecture in French. However, he left *Latvijas Universitāte* in September 1926, for a position at Innsbruck University. See *Latvijas Universitāte divdesmit gados 1919–1939* (1939) I, p. 175.

major issue, they claimed that Diehl was knowledgeable in Latvian and would be able to lecture in that language within a year's time.[45]

In the faculty, Felsbergs advocated Diehl's appointment and was supported by fellow linguists Ķikauka and Straubergs. Plāķis and Tentelis were openly against, the latter allegedly for undefined 'political reasons'. Endzelīns apparently lay low and in the election procedure, all faculty members except Plāķis and Tentelis voted for Diehl.[46]

Why Felsbergs, normally so opposed to the appointment of Baltic Germans, assumed this position is not altogether clear. The faculty does not seem to have had any real need for Diehl's specific expertise, as Pēteris Zālīte actually pointed out during the discussion. Perhaps Diehl's difficult situation in Tomsk – together with some sense of solidarity with a fellow classicist scholar – made Felsbergs positively inclined to his appointment. It should perhaps also be noted that Diehl's specialty – classical philology, Latin and Greek – was fairly neutral ground compared to subjects closer to the national agenda. Classical philology was essentially a transnational discipline.

With the principal, Felsbergs, clearly in favour of Diehl's election, the organisation committee did not voice any objections. Like other *privātdocenti* unfamiliar with Latvian, Diehl was initially allowed to lecture for three years in German or Russian.[47] Diehl appears to have had the faculty's continued support; he was retained at *Latvijas Universitāte* and was finally appointed full professor in 1939.[48]

Diehl was, however, the last academic with a German or Baltic German background to be appointed by the faculty in the interwar period. Apart from that, it should be noted that the faculty never appointed any Jewish scholars. In fact, when the faculty discussed whether further recruitments should be made by appointment or open competition, the linguist Juris Plāķis argued strongly

---

[45] LVVA. Latvijas Universitātes fonds, 7427/13/376. Staff records. Letter from Diehl's mother-in-law Augusta Eduarda Waldenberg to Felsbergs, 1921/11/04; letter from the sister-in-law Gerda Augusta Waldenberg to the Foreign Office requiring assistance, 1921/11/12. According to Diehl's own statement, he had visited Jekaterineburg in 1918 in an attempt to ascertain the fate of the Romanov family. If this was true, it probably made his situation in Soviet Russia even more precarious. The fact that it was his Baltic German in-laws who pleaded for his appointment rather than himself can be interpreted in various ways: according to traditional gender patterns, letters of supplication were preferably written by women rather than men. However, it may also have been the case that it was dangerous for Diehl to communicate directly with the university leadership in Riga – if his letter had been intercepted by the Bolshevik regime, he and his family might have been in serious trouble.

[46] LVVA. Latvijas Universitātes fonds, 7427/6/363, Minutes of the Faculty of Philology and Philosophy, 1922/09/02.

[47] LVVA. Latvijas Universitātes fonds, 7427/6/2, University Council Minutes, 1922/09/27.

[48] *Latvijas Universitāte divdesmit gados 1919–1939* (1939), II, p. 52. LVVA. Latvijas Universitātes fonds, 7427/13/376. Staff records. Diehl retained solid support in the faculty: eleven out of twelve members voted for his promotion to professor.

against the practice of open applications, claiming that in such a procedure "a Jew might crop up". Nobody in the faculty appears to have questioned this argument, an indication that such anti-Semitic sentiments were widely shared by his colleagues. The policy of recruitment by appointment was retained.[49]

Ethnic Russian academics appear to have fared somewhat better. Endzelīns made several attempts to have Konstantin Arabasjin, professor of Russian literature, appointed *privātdocents*. Arabasjin had in fact lectured at the *augstskola* since 1920. In the faculty, Endzelīns's first proposal in 1922 was supported by Jēkabs Lautenbahs, a literary historian of the 'older' generation, as well as by Šmits, Zālīte and Straubergs. Plāķis was, as usual, the most vociferous opponent. However, while Endzelīns managed to get a narrow faculty majority for the election of Arabasjin, his appointment was eventually turned down in the organisation committee.[50] A similar attempt the following year also failed. In spite of Endzelīns's efforts, in the end Arabasjin had to leave the faculty.[51] After this, Slavic literature was generally taught by Polish academics, not Russians.[52]

The main ethnic Russian addition to the faculty was the historian Robert Wipper in 1924; later his son, Boris Wipper, an art historian, was elected professor in 1932.[53] Apart from these two, no more ethnic Russian academics were added to the faculty. Not counting the lecturers in modern languages, the foreign academics appointed later were primarily Swedes: Harry Wallin in Swedish history and language, Tor Helge Kjellin in art history, and Dag Trotzig in ethnology.[54] While Endzelīns certainly tried to widen the range of 'foreign' recruitments and emphasise the weight of scholarly merit, faculty appointments seem in the end to have been largely guided by the general university and

---

[49] LVVA. Latvijas Universitātes fonds, 7427/6/363, Minutes of the Faculty of Philology and Philosophy, 1922/12/16.

[50] LVVA. Latvijas Universitātes fonds, 7427/6/363, Minutes of the Faculty of Philology and Philosophy, 1922/04/29; 7427/6/1, Organisation Committee Minutes, 1922/05/10.

[51] LVVA. Latvijas Universitātes fonds, 7427/6/363, Minutes of the Faculty of Philology and Philosophy, 1923/04/21; 1923/05/05; 1923/12/08. The last attempt was made by Endzelīns's successor as dean, Pēteris Šmits.

[52] Primarily Julian Kšižanovski between 1930 and 1934, and Stanislav Kolbuševski between 1934 and 1939. See *Latvijas Universitāte divdesmit gados 1919–1939* (1939), I, pp. 195–196; II, pp. 61, 65–66.

[53] The case of Robert Wipper/Vipers will be dealt with more fully below. See *Latvijas Universitāte divdesmit gados 1919–1939* (1939), I, pp. 194–195, II, pp. 84–85. Boris Wipper was initially a in the Faculty of Architecture between 1924 and 1930. This faculty had quite a few Russian academics. See *Latvijas Universitāte divdesmit gados 1919–1939* (1939), I, pp. 134–136.

[54] *Latvijas Universitāte divdesmit gados 1919–1939* (1939), II, pp. 64, 92. Kjellin taught at the University of Latvia between 1929 and 1931. Trotzig was appointed docent in 1938. Harry Wallin taught courses in the Swedish language and history between 1928 and 1936. Ibid., I, p. 293. Wallin was actually appointed *privātdocents* on a permanent basis in 1932, and seems to have been well received in the faculty. He nevertheless chose to return to Sweden in 1936. LVVA. Latvijas Universitātes fonds 7427/13/1832. Staff records.

government line to favour Swedes, Finns, Austrians and Swiss and exclude Germans, Russians and Jews.

The actual number of academics recruited from the former small and supposedly friendly countries was never very substantial. Apart from those mentioned earlier – the Finn Tiander, the Austrian Brüch, the Swiss Nussberger and the Swedes Wallin, Kjellin and Trotzig – there was a Swiss expert in child psychology, Schneider. The only ones who stayed in Riga on a permanent basis were Nussberger and Wallin: all the others spent a limited period at *Latvijas Universitāte,* in some cases, such as Tiander's, very limited. As we have seen, Tiander's recruitment ended in a complete fiasco, primarily for political reasons.

Another recruitment that was somewhat complicated concerned the previously mentioned professor in child psychology, the Swiss Ernest Schneider. His appointment had caused some irritation in the organisation committee since he had demanded his salary in foreign currency.[55] In the faculty, he created something of a scandal when he presented a work based on psychoanalysis, *Über das Stottern,* to the faculty for his *habilitation* in order to be promoted to full university professor.[56] This was clearly more than the faculty could stomach. Philosopher Pēteris Zālīte was especially critical, seeing the psychoanalytical ideas about children's sexuality as the 'fruits of a morbid fantasy'. Zālīte claimed that it was erroneous to draw general conclusions from single pathological cases, especially when such inferences were applied to 'our healthy Latvian youth'. Suggestions were made that Schneider's work, since it primarily concerned pathological behaviour, should instead be sent to the Faculty of Medicine for assessment. However, fears that this would create a scandal and become an embarrassment for the Faculty of Philology and Philosophy led eventually to the decision not to send it elsewhere for evaluation. The faculty unanimously decided not to accept the *habilitation,* and by a large majority resolved to take the unusual step of prohibiting Schneider from referring to psychoanalytical theory in future psychology courses.[57] Apparently, psychoanalytical theory did

---

[55] Some of the first recruited foreign academics demanded their salaries in foreign currency, partly because the financial capacity of the newly emerged Latvian state was uncertain. Apart from Scheider, this was the case with the German professor Frost in Philosophy and the Swedish professor Backman in anatomy.

[56] LVVA. Latvijas Universitātes fonds, 7427/6/363, Minutes of the Faculty of Philology and Philosophy, 1923/09/08. The work apparently concerned the problem of stuttering among children. In 1923, Schneider also published a piece on psychoanalysis in the official Ministry journal: Šneiders, Ernsts (1923): "Kas ir psichanalīze", pp. 233–243, which he ended by expressing his wish that the free Latvia and its university would extend their hospitality to psychoanalysis. In view of the faculty's reception of the psychoanalytical theory, this was perhaps rather optimistic.

[57] LVVA. Latvijas Universitātes fonds, 7427/6/363, Minutes of the Faculty of Philology and Philosophy, 1923/09/08; 1923/09/13. Schneider's only defender was the German philosopher Walter Frost, who tried to convince the faculty that psychoanalysis had already gained some

not fit the faculty members' conceptions of 'healthy' Latvian children and youth as the embodiment of the Latvian nation.

The recruitment of foreign citizens was not an easy matter; it entailed considerable costs, some academic complications, and also some problems connected with what was seen as a lack of loyalty to the newly created Latvian state. The need for these foreign academics was naturally greatest during the university's early years. During the course of the 1920s, the 'younger' generation of Latvian academics, who had received their basic training at Imperial universities, could acquire merit and pursue their academic careers. This was clearly the predominant university policy, and it certainly had full support at faculty level. As early as 1922, it is evident that the faculty had lined up some of the younger Latvian academics for promotion to professorships.[58] Still, when there was no viable Latvian alternative, the need to find lecturers and develop key disciplines sometimes made it necessary to consider the recruitment of foreign academics.

On the specific issue of Germans and Baltic Germans, it should still be noted that after the resignation of Jānis Endzelīns as dean in 1923, academics belonging to these ethnic backgrounds were never again appointed by the faculty.[59] By then, naturally, most of the pressing recruitments had been made and some of the 'younger' generation of academics had qualified themselves for positions. The next two deans, Šmits and Spekke, appear to have shared Endzelīns's general views on recruitment, giving precedence to academic merit rather than favouring narrow ethnic appointments. However, by 1927 these three took little interest in faculty matters. Endzelīns devoted himself entirely to Baltic linguistics, and never served again as dean during the First Republic. Šmits clearly did not relish administrative duties, and Spekke eventually joined the Latvian Foreign Office. This left the faculty's academic leadership to deans more in favour of a more narrowly ethnic meaning of the university: linguist Juris

---

academic acceptance at other European universities. The Swiss Germanist Nussberger distanced himself from psychoanalytic theory, but warned that *Latvijas Universitāte* might get a bad reputation and be less able to recruit academics abroad if it were known that the university was hostile to the free pursuit of knowledge. Schneider narrowly avoided being barred from teaching altogether.

[58] LVVA. Latvijas Universitātes fonds, 7427/6/363, Minutes of the Faculty of Philology and Philosophy, 1922/04/29. The faculty's decision was to move for the promotion of the *docenti* Spekke, Blese and Dāle in that order, trying to obtain the consent of the organising committee. Spekke was appointed professor in 1922; Dāle had to wait until 1927 and Blese until 1928. *Latvijas Universitāte divdesmit gados 1919–1939* (1939), I, pp. 194–195.

[59] Endzelīns appears to have had very substantial backing in the faculty until his final resignation, in spite of his recurring conflicts with the principal, Felsbergs, and his somewhat impetuous manner. He frequently offered or threatened to resign as dean, but was regularly persuaded to accept re-election. See, for instance, LVVA. Latvijas Universitātes fonds, 7427/6/363, Minutes of the Faculty of Philology and Philosophy, 1922/04/29; 1923/01/08; 1923/01/19.

Plāķis between 1927 and 1929, and then archaeologist Francis Balodis and historian Augusts Tentelis in turns from 1929 to 1937.[60]

The Latvian character of the faculty was further enhanced by the ethnic composition of the students. While students from Jewish, Baltic German and Russian backgrounds were quite prevalent in the technical faculties, Medicine, Architecture and Law, they were very few in the Faculty of Philology and Philosophy. University records from 1922, for instance, show that ethnic Latvians constituted 95 per cent of this faculty's students.[61]

In terms of politics, there were very close connections between the Faculty of Philology and Philosophy and the Ministry of Education. Several of the faculty's academics served in the Cabinet as Ministers of Education: linguist Juris Plāķis, 1920–1921, pedagogue Aleksandrs Dauge, 1921–1922, linguist Kārlis Straubergs in 1924, art historian Ernsts Felsbergs in 1925 and finally historian Augusts Tentelis in 1926 and again in 1935–1938. Moreover, psychologist Pauls Dāle served as the Ministry's representative and chairman of the *augstskola's* organisation committee between 1919 and 1922, and the first principal, Felsbergs, chaired the first *Saeima's* Education Committee.[62] The connections between politics and academia were therefore strong, and some of the academics of this specific faculty could exert considerable political leverage – but were perhaps also open to government pressure.

Summing up, in the initial years there was clearly a general recruitment policy at *Latvijas Augstskola* to avoid, if possible, the appointment of German or Baltic German academics. Instead, there was a decided preference for Austrians, Swiss, Finns, and Swedes, even if they too could only lecture in German. Considering the historical and political context, these findings are perhaps not very surprising. Among many nationally inclined Latvian intellectuals, the struggle against the long tradition of German cultural predominance was clearly a top priority. This was in a sense an academic consequence of the 'ethnic reversal' that characterized the Latvian state. While some appointments of Russians could be considered, Jewish academics were seldom chosen.

---

[60] LVVA. Latvijas Universitātes fonds, 7427/6/42. Filoloģijas un filozofijas fakultātes darbības pārskats no 1919. g. līdz 1938. g., pp. 1–2.

[61] LVVA. Latvijas Universitātes fonds, 7427/6/54, Gadu statistiskās ziņas par studentu un mācības spēku sastāvu. In the Chemistry faculty the corresponding figure was 62 per cent; in Medicine 75 per cent. The only faculty with a higher percentage of ethnic Latvian students was Agronomy: almost 97 per cent.

[62] *Latvijas Universitāte 1919–1929* (1929), p. 167; *Latvijas Universitāte divdesmit gados 1919–1939* (1939), I, pp. 205–206. Dāle was also the editor of the Ministry's official journal, *Izglītības Ministrijas Mēnešraksts*, a task that was taken over by linguist Ernsts Blese. Dauge had previously belonged to the Leftist *jaunstrāvnieki* group that had published the collection *Pūrs* at Dorpat/Jur'ev University in the early 1890s.

In the Faculty of Philology and Philosophy, however, the picture is somewhat more complex. The dean during the formative first three years, Endzelīns, appears to have several times promoted the appointment of German academics in the humanities in both the organisation committee and the university council, sometimes successfully, sometimes not.

That there was, however, a decided political and academic determination on university level to demarcate against German academics is evident from the fact that not a single one of the nineteen honorary fellows elected by the university between 1919 and 1939 was German or, for that matter, Russian.[63] French and English academics were primarily chosen, in spite of the fact that academic contacts with these countries were really very sparse. At the same time the election of some Latvian intellectuals close to the 'national' disciplines in the humanities were very important symbolic acts. Especially the election of the legendary nationalist and folklorist Krišjānis Barons as the first honorary fellow was made a national manifestation. At the inauguration ceremony, the grizzled Barons's entrance was greeted with ovations.[64] In Latvian literature, the election of the celebrated national playwright and poet Jānis Rainis was also clearly a part of the national agenda – even though Rainis as an active Social Democrat was doubtless a politically more controversial person.

It is now time to turn to an analysis of the separate 'national' disciplines. What were the recruitment patterns like in each subject in terms of academic generations and ethnic backgrounds? Is a 'national turn' in the scholarly production in these disciplines discernible in the 1920s?

Latvian linguistics

The codification and standardization of the Latvian language naturally had high priority for both nationalists and linguists – a language which Baltic Germans had long seen as inappropriate for cultural communication. Somewhat ironically, though, it was Baltic German pastors who had first transformed Latvian peasant dialects into a written and printed form, thus saving the Latvian language from being completely submerged by German. One of them, August

---

[63] *Latvijas Universitāte divdesmit gados 1919–1939* (1939), I, pp. 15–16; LVVA. Latvijas Universitātes fonds, 7427/6/37a. Pārskats par Latvijas augstskolas, vēlāk Universitātes, nodibināšanu un viņas darbību. Overview of the achievements of the University of Latvia during its first ten years. The list of honorary fellows elected during the first ten years comprised three Latvians (Barons, the poet and playwright Jānis Rainis, and the former Minister of Education Kārlis Kasparsons), five Frenchmen, three Englishmen, one Finn, and one Swiss.

[64] *Latvijas Universitāte 1919–1929* (1929), p. 24.

Bielenstein, published the first Latvian grammar in 1863.[65] On the other hand, early nationalist intellectuals like Kaspars Biezbārdis sharply criticised the German 'distortions' of Latvian when it was first transformed into a literary language.[66] Pursuing this view, Biezbārdis was something of a pioneer when he published the first scholarly work on Latvian in the Latvian language, *Mūsu valoda un viņas rakstība*, in 1869.[67]

The work of standardizing Latvian, purging it of germanisms and constructing a new common orthography, replacing the Gothic script with Latin letters, was continued by a group of linguists, publishers, writers and schoolteachers under the auspices of the Riga Latvian Society. A 'linguist department' within the Society's scholarly commission was created in 1904, and this group continued to operate during the First Republic as a joint platform for academic linguists, *literati*, publishers and teachers resolved to expand and codify the Latvian language.[68]

These vital national undertakings were naturally pursued by the Latvian linguists appointed at the new university. While Baltic linguistics had existed in Tsarist times as an acknowledged sub-discipline of Philology, it had been very much subordinated to the study of Russian and Slavic linguistics. Now priorities were changed. The Latvian language was to be standardized and restored to its original 'purity'. However, just what this 'pure' form should be seems to have occasioned some heated discussions among Latvian linguists.[69] In 1922, the government set up a committee, consisting of linguists, schoolteachers, journalists and publishers, to work out the new orthography. The university professors and linguists Jānis Endzelīns, Pēteris Šmits and Juris Plāķis played a very important role in this committee in advocating the need for a radically new orthography. Publishers, on the other hand, voiced some misgivings, fearing that unduly dramatic changes would create a double standard, not the language's desired homogenization. The more 'radical' view of the linguists Šmits and

---

[65] It was naturally printed in German with the title *Die lettische Sprache nach ihren Lauten und Formen erklärend und vergleichend dargestellt*. See Kļaviņa, Sarma (2008): *Latviešu valodas pētnieki. No klaušu laikiem līdz savai valstij*, pp. 25–28.

[66] Biezbardis, Kaspar (1865a): *Die Sprach- und Bildungskampf in den baltischen Provinzen Russlands*, pp. 8–9. Like many Latvian nationalist intellectuals of the first generation, Biezbārdis was seen as *persona non grata* by the ruling Baltic German nobility and wrote this treatise during a period of enforced Russian exile. See Kļaviņa (2008), p. 54.

[67] Kļaviņa (2008), p. 56. The title means "Our language and how to write it".

[68] Kļaviņa (2008), pp. 123–131.

[69] Spekke, Arnolds (2000): *Atmiņu brīži*, p. 93. No doubt connected to this issue, there was also dissension among Latvian linguists in the faculty over whether a common 'proto-Latvian' language had existed in ancient times, or if there had always been dialectal differences between the Latvian 'tribes' or *ciltis*. Endzelīns and Šmits supported the first view, Blese and Plāķis the latter. See Breidaks, Antons (1999): "Latviešu valodas dialektu un izlokšņu grupu cilme un teritoriālā izplatība", p. 26.

Plāķis, won the day, and the committee decided to base the new standard orthography on their suggestions.[70] The previous German-inspired mode of printing Latvian was replaced by a new version, primarily inspired by Czech orthography and using Latin letters.[71]

Conscientious efforts were also made to expand Latvian's range by devising new terms, especially in the fields of Science and Technology. The Ministry of Education organised a special committee with the task of selecting and introducing such neologisms. The idea, naturally, was to make Latvian equally versatile and usable as the more established cultural languages German and Russian. This was necessary in order to make Latvian a fully applicable academic language.

There was also a need for a new standardized grammar, as well as a modern dictionary that would build on Kārlis Mīlenbahs's work from the early twentieth century. Among the early professors at the University of Latvia, it was in particular the professor of Baltic Philology, Jānis Endzelīns, who shouldered this task. Heading a group of linguists, publishers and schoolteachers connected to the Riga Latvian Society, Endzelīns edited, complemented and published the expanded dictionary in four volumes between 1923 and 1932.[72]

As we have seen, Endzelīns was clearly one of the faculty's most forceful personalities. A farmer's son from the Valmiera region, Endzelīns had made his academic career at Dorpat/Jur'ev, St Petersburg and Charkov. Before coming to *Latvijas Augstskola* in May 1920, he had been a professor of linguistics at Charkov University for eight years.[73] Even during his 'exile', he had participated in the linguistic projects of the Riga Latvian Society.[74] Endzelīns belonged to the 'middle' generation of Latvian academics, being firmly established in the Imperial university system and yet only forty-seven years old when he took up his position in Riga. He was elected dean of faculty almost immediately.

Endzelīns *Lettische Grammatik* was published in 1922 as one of the first scholarly monographs from the University of Latvia but, as the title shows, it was written in German.[75] Possibly, this could be seen as a typical compromise between the urgent political need to achieve some nationalist aims, and the

---

[70] LVVA. Izglītības ministrijas fonds, 1632/2/795. Prof-a Šmita, Ed. Paegļa u.c. raksti Izglītības Ministrijai ortogrāfijas jautājumos… Minutes from the Commission on Orthography, 1922/06/16. The new orthography was to be based on the text *Izrunas un rakstības vadonis* written by the linguists Pēteris Šmits and Jānis Endzelīns.
[71] Endzelīns, Jānis (1930): "Latvieši un viņu valoda", p. 53.
[72] Kļaviņa (2008), pp. 129–135; 143–150.
[73] LVVA. Latvijas Universitātes fonds, 7427/13/447. Staff records; *Latvijas Universitāte 1919–1929* (1929), p. 162.
[74] Stradiņš, Jānis (1998): Latvijas Zinātņu akadēmija: izcelsme, vēsture, pārvērtības, p. 67.
[75] Johansons, Andrejs (1987): "Die Lettländische Universität in Riga 1919–1940", p. 259; *Latvijas Universitāte 1919–1929* (1929), p. 46. Endzelīns, Jānis (1922): *Lettische Grammatik*.

academic need to publish in a more 'distinguished' language – in this case, ironically, in one of the very languages that the Latvian nationalists strove to contain. Endzelīns was one of the academic world's foremost specialists in Baltic languages, and therefore naturally felt the need to publicise in a language accessible to other grammarians. Still, his decision to publish his Latvian grammar in German seems to have been somewhat controversial in nationalist circles. Shortly after its publication, Endzelīns accused his faculty colleague Felsbergs for spreading 'incorrect views' about his grammar in the *Saiema's* education committee, and also strongly denied being 'unpatriotic'.[76]

In his memoir, the historian Arnolds Spekke portrays Endzelīns as a forceful and sometimes arrogant promoter of strictly academic ideals, and in perpetual conflict with the more national and political agenda of some of his colleagues.[77] Indeed, in a previous chapter we have seen that Endzelīns was clearly one of those members of the organisation committee who consistently emphasised the importance of academic qualifications in the selection of new staff. As dean between 1920 and 1923, he also seems to have been relatively open to the recruitment of foreign specialists in key areas when no reasonable Latvian candidates could be found.

Much respected in both nationalist and academic circles, Endzelīns was certainly in a position to follow his own mind and inclinations. In Imperial times he was already a member of the Riga Latvian Society's orthographic committee, and much involved in the Society's project to standardize the Latvian language. Together with Kārlis Mīlenbahs of the previous generation, Endzelīns published Latvian grammars and dictionaries.[78] During the 1920s and 1930s, he directed the work of the Riga Latvian Society in its continued endeavour to develop and standardize the Latvian language.[79] These contributions certainly earned Endzelīns a solid reputation among the nationalist intellectuals.

At the same time, belonging to the generation of academics who were firmly established in the Imperial university system, and certainly one of the most prestigious professors at the new university, Endzelīns seems to have been pragmatic about the sensitive German question. As shown above, he supported the appointments of Walter Frost in Philosophy and the Baltic German linguist Erich Diehl as *privātdocents* in Classical Philology. Also, in 1921 he promoted the Königsberg professor Adalbert Bezzenberg as an honorary member of the

---

[76] LVVA. Latvijas Universitātes fonds, 7427/6/363, Minutes of the Faculty of Philology and Philosophy, 1923/01/19.
[77] Spekke (2000), p. 92. Spekke describes this as a personal conflict between Endzelīns and Ernsts Felsbergs, who was voted the university's first principal, a conflict that according to Spekke went back to their years at Dorpat/Jur'ev.
[78] Kļaviņa (2008), p. 128. Mīlenbahs, however, died in 1916.
[79] Kļaviņa (2008), pp. 192–193.

Philological Society at the *augstskola*.[80] Another indication that Endzelīns would not let his commitment to the national agenda turn into ethnic exclusion is that he chose Edīte Hauzenberga as his long-term assistant and co-worker on the dictionary project. Hauzenberga was raised in a German-speaking family in the Valmiera region.[81]

Of the faculty's professors, Endzelīns appears to have had the widest network of academic contacts, being attached to universities in Czechoslovakia, Germany, Holland, Sweden, Lithuania and Estonia.[82] When Endzelīns was offered a chair in linguistics at Königsberg University in 1926, a great many students petitioned the dean to convince him to decline the offer and remain in Riga – which he eventually did.[83] This incident clearly says something about Endzelīns' international standing – and also about his popularity among the students.

Also one of the 'middle' generation of Latvian linguists, but not quite possessing Endzelīns' shining academic reputation, was Juris Plāķis. He had been a schoolteacher who, having been active in the 1905 popular revolt in the Baltic provinces, had taken refuge in Siberia to avoid persecution. In 1908 he enrolled at Kazan University, and after receiving his *Magister* remained as *docents* and later professor of comparative linguistics.[84] Returning to Riga at the age of fifty-one he, as indicated above, became much involved in the codification of the Latvian language, especially the expansion of Mīlenbahs's unfinished dictionary. However, his scholarly production is not very impressive. Plāķis never submitted a doctoral dissertation.[85] He wrote mainly on phonetic issues during the 1920s, more specifically on the pronunciation of various Latvian dialects, and later developed a special interest in Latvian ancient history, joining archaeologists and folklorists in the investigation of the proto-Latvian tribes, the *ciltis*.[86] These endeavours were naturally very close to national academic concerns. His teaching mainly concerned the linguistic properties of Lithuanian, Sanskrit, Latin and ancient Greek.[87]

Kazan University was certainly less renowned than St Petersburg, Moscow, and Dorpat/Jur'ev, so in terms of academic prestige Plāķis was certainly inferior to Endzelīns. However, while perhaps not belonging to the top layer of Latvian linguists, Plāķis was definitely an important figure in politics and university

---

[80] Kļaviņa (2008), p. 88.
[81] Kļaviņa (2008), pp. 205–207.
[82] *Latvijas Universitāte divdesmit gados 1919–1939* (1939), II, p. 54.
[83] LVVA. Latvijas Universitātes fonds, 7427/13/447. Staff records; Kļaviņa (2008), p.192.
[84] Kļaviņa (2010), pp. 25–29; *Latvijas Universitāte divdesmit gados 1919–1939* (1939), II, p. 71.
[85] LVVA. Latvijas Universitātes fonds, 7427/13/1329. Staff records. It should be noted that in her recent monograph on Latvian linguists, Sarma Kļaviņa hardly mentions Plāķis.
[86] See, for instance, his contribution to the anthology "*Latvieši*: Plāķis, Juris (1930): Baltu tautas un ciltis", pp. 45–49. On his articles on phonetics, see chapter 6.
[87] *Latvijas Universitāte divdesmit gados 1919–1939* (1939), I, p. 287.

administration. He was Minister of Education between June 1920 and April 1921, a very formative year for *Latvijas Augstskola*. In 1922 he was elected vice-principal responsible for student and educational matters, a position he retained for four years.[88] In this context, as shown in a previous chapter, he played an important role in devising exclusionary measures directed against Jewish students.[89] Pļāķis belonged politically to the nationalist Right, becoming in the 1930s a member of the authoritarian *Pērkonkrusts* movement.

Another academic belonging to the 'middle' generation was literary historian Ludvigs Bērziņš, in 1922 appointed *docents* at *Latvijas Universitāte* at the age of fifty-two. Bērziņš had a background in school teaching and Theology[90], and can hardly be said to have had a very impressive scholarly production. However, deeply interested in Latvian folk songs and poetry, he served as an important transmitter of a 'national' codex in literature between the university, the teacher-training seminary and the general public.[91] Bērziņš also explored the earliest examples of printed Latvian religious catechisms from the sixteenth century.[92] Jānis Kauliņš should probably also be included in this 'middle' generation. He became a *docents* at the *augstskola* in 1920 at the age of fifty-seven. However, he does not seem to have had any position in the Imperial university system, and during the First Republic his main duty was to administer the State Cultural Fund.[93]

There were also some representatives of an 'older' generation. A very important figure among the first generation of Latvian philologists was Jēkabs Lautenbahs, who had been appointed lecturer in the Latvian language at Dorpat/Jur'ev in 1898, and was later promoted to professor of both Latvian and Lithuanian.[94] As such, he was of great symbolic importance for nationally inclined Latvian students at Dorpat/Jur'ev.[95] As we have seen, the organisation

---

[88] LVVA. Latvijas Universitātes fonds, 7427/13/1329. Staff records; 7427/6/1, University Council Minutes, 1922/09/13; 1923/05/16; *Latvijas Universitāte divdesmit gados 1919–1939* (1939), I, p. 205. Pļāķis was vice-principal between 1922–1924 and 1925–27.
[89] On the role of Pļāķis in the implementation of exclusionary measures, see chapters 5 and 8.
[90] Bērziņš (1935), pp. 27, 90, 110–111. He actually aspired to become a Lutheran pastor, but found it very difficult as an ethnic Latvian to obtain a position in a Church so heavily dominated by Baltic German clergy.
[91] Bērziņš was the Director of the Teacher Training Institute between 1922 and 1934, and frequently contributed articles on Latvian literature to cultural journals. *Latvijas Universitāte divdesmit gados 1919–1939* (1939), II, pp. 39–41. On his appreciation of the Latvian folksong heritage, see Bērziņš, Ludvigs (1930a): "Tautas dzejas nozīme latviešu tautas dzīvē", pp. 235–254.
[92] Bērziņš, Ludvigs (1930b): "Latviešu rakstniecība svešu tautu aizbildniecībā", pp. 277–301. His main point is to criticize the many germanisms and erroneous grammar in these texts, written under Baltic German tutelage.
[93] *Latvijas Universitāte divdesmit gados 1919–1939* (1939), II, pp. 60–61.
[94] LVVA. Latvijas Universitātes fonds, 7427/13/978. Staff records.
[95] According to the memoirs of both Ludvigs Bērziņš and archaeologist Francis Balodis, the Latvian student corporation "Lettonia" required its members to attend Lautenbahs's lectures –

committee had gone to great lengths to ensure that Lautenbahs would come to Riga. Professor Lautenbahs was clearly seen as an important figurehead at the new Latvian *augstskola*, belonging to an older generation of firmly established Latvian academics. Being, however, seventy-two years of age when he took up his new duties in Riga, his importance was perhaps more symbolical than scholarly.[96] He took very little part in faculty matters, refusing for instance to serve as dean. In spite of wavering health, though, he did produce a short Latvian grammar and some works in literary history in the early 1920s.[97]

Another link with the older generation of Latvian nationalist academics was Jēkabs Velme, previously a lecturer in German at Moscow University. Velme had been a very important figure among Latvian nationalist academics in Moscow, a founder of the local Latvian Society and also the publisher and editor of the journal *Austrums*.[98] Velme was appointed first as lecturer in German in 1923, and later as both *privātdocents* and honorary doctor. He was, however, sixty-eight years of age when he took up his duties at the University of Latvia.[99] Lautenbahs and Velme both died in 1928.

The Latvian linguists also included a 'younger' generation of scholars. Ernests Blese, a candidate of German and Comparative Philology at St Petersburg University in 1914, was attached to *Latvijas Augstskola* as early as 1919, and became a professor in 1928. He was deeply involved in the project of developing and standardising the Latvian language.[100] His colleague Pēteris Ķiķauka had studied Classical Philology at Dorpat/Jur'ev during the World War I, and was a Latin and Greek schoolteacher in Russia before returning to Riga and *Latvijas Augstskola* in 1921.[101] Together with Anna Ābele, one of the very few female academics allowed to make a career in the humanities during the First Republic, they constituted a younger generation of linguists who had received basic academic training at Imperial Russian universities and could later pursue academic careers at *Latvijas Universitāte*.[102]

---

otherwise they would be penalized. According to Bērziņš, such measures were necessary since Lautenbahs's lectures were in fact rather boring. See Bērziņš (1935), pp. 106–107; Balodis, Francis (1941): *Våld och frihet. En lettisk universitetsprofessors minnen*, p. 36.

[96] LVVA. Latvijas Universitātes fonds, 7427/13/978. Staff records.

[97] *Latvijas Universitātes Filoloģijas un filosofijas fakultātes Bibliografisks pārskats, 1919–1925.* (1926), pp. 4–5.

[98] For Velme's own account of the Latvian circle in Moscow and the founding of *Austrums*, see Velme, Jēkabs (1922): "Atmiņas no manas Maskavas dzīves", pp. 1,233–1,241.

[99] LVVA. Latvijas Universitātes fonds, 7427/13/1876. Staff records

[100] *Latvijas Universitāte divdesmit gados 1919–1939* (1939), II, pp. 41–42; Blese, Ernsts (1930): "Latviešu valodas attīstības posmi", pp. 54–60.

[101] *Latvijas Universitāte divdesmit gados 1919–1939* (1939), II, pp. 61–62.

[102] Ābele specialised in phonetics and was appointed *privātdocents* in 1924. Unlike Blese and Ķiķauka, however, she did not become a professor before World War II in spite of obtaining a doctorate already in 1923. There were no women professors at the University of Latvia during the First Republic. LVVA. Latvijas Universitātes fonds, 7427/6/363, Minutes of the Faculty of

In generational terms, it has to be concluded that the Latvian linguists at the new university constituted a comparatively large group, comprising academics of all generations: the 'older' one connected to Latvian nationalist circles at Dorpat and the Russian universities (Lautenbahs, Velme), a 'middle' generation of academics with positions within the Imperial university system (Endzelīns, Plāķis) and finally a 'younger' generation, educated at Russian universities but developing careers at *Latvijas Universitāte* (Blese, Ķikauka, Ābele). In terms of academic record and prestige, as well as in sheer numbers, they clearly dominated the Faculty of Philology and Philosophy.

Baltic and comparative linguistics was also by far the most popular subject among the faculty's students. With the creation of their own student organisation *Ramave* in 1929, the students of linguistics became an important part of the cultural life of both the university and Latvian society in general.[103]

All things considered, this meant that the Latvian linguists were in a good position to implement the national project. As we have seen, the codification of standard Latvian as a 'national' undertaking had begun in the early twentieth century under the auspices of the Riga Latvian Society. Some of the prominent academics at *Latvijas Augstskola*, most notably Jānis Endzelīns, had been involved in these language projects for more than a decade before the new university was created. To continue this work was naturally a priority for the academic linguists of the University of Latvia. Endzelīns, Plāķis and Blese, in cooperation with the wider network of the Riga Latvian Society, strove to develop a standardised, expanded and grammatically consistent Latvian, using a new orthography. After the publication of the fourth and final volume of Mīlenbahs's expanded dictionary in 1933, concerted efforts were made to disseminate the new standard Latvian in the school system.[104]

Conflicts about what constituted the 'real' Latvian language, however, continued during the 1930s. In publishing circles especially, there was a strong notion that the academic linguists had gone too far, devising a language that was very different from that of everyday usage. When the orthography of Latvian became a national concern and a matter for the Cabinet during the Ulmanis dictatorship, some of the 'pragmatist' objections were acknowledged, though on

---

Philology and Philosophy, 1923/04/06. *Latvijas Universitāte divdesmit gados 1919–1939* (1939), II, pp. 85–86; Kļaviņa (2008), pp. 197–202. Apart from Ābele, the linguist Alīse Karlsone was one of the very few women academics in the faculty who was given a scholarship enabling her to receive a doctorate from Münich University in 1925. *Latvijas Universitāte divdesmit gados 1919–1939* (1939), II, p. 98.

[103] Kļaviņa (2008), p. 218; *Latvijas Universitāte divdesmit gados 1919–1939* (1939), I, pp. 241–243.
[104] Kļaviņa (2008), pp. 193–194.

the whole the main linguistic structure devised by Endzelīns and his colleagues remained intact.[105]

A special problem confronting Endzelīns and his colleagues was the difference between standard Latvian spelling and orthography and that used when writing in the Latgallian dialect. Latgale, the easternmost province in Latvia, had not been part of the German-dominated Baltic Provinces of Imperial Russia. It had previously been part of the Polish-Lithuanian Commonwealth and, after the latter's dissolution in the late eighteenth century, a part of the Russian *gubernija* of Vitebsk. In terms of culture and religion, Latgale differed markedly from the rest of Latvia. Catholicism, Judaism and Orthodoxy predominated, and Russian and Yiddish were commonly used alongside the Latgallian dialect. The predominance of Catholicism had also meant that the Latgallian dialect had never been used for a Bible translation in the same way as a version of Latvian had in Protestant Livland and Kurland.

For these reasons, the Latgallian dialect differed markedly from the standard Latvian developed by the linguists of the late nineteenth century, actually making it difficult to circulate Latvian newspapers in Latgale.[106] Latgallian, although belatedly, was eventually also used as a print-language and a literary language. Moreover, it used a Polish-influenced orthography, thus increasing the difference between the two language versions.[107] This clearly posed a substantial problem for the linguists endeavouring to standardise and homogenise the Latvian language.[108] During the Ulmanis regime, as will be shown in a later chapter, this matter acquired strong political significance. In order to unify the Latvian *tauta*, a separate print-language or orthography could no longer be allowed. Printing in Latgallian was banned in order to achieve a full standardisation of the Latvian language.

---

[105] Vanags, Pēteris (2004): "Language Policy and Linguistics under Ulmanis", pp. 126–136. As early as 1923, a group of publishers protested against the changes to Riga street names proposed by the linguist Pēteris Šmits. See LVVA. Latvijas Universitātes fonds, 7427/6/2, University Council Minutes, 1923/05/23.

[106] Apparently, the important nationalist journal *Pēterburgas Avīzes* was never circulated in the Latgale area since Lettgallians did not find it readable. See Goba, Alfrēds (1929): *Pirmās "Pēterburgas Avīzes" un viņu nozīme tautas atmodas gaitā*, p. 59; Zelče, Vita (2009): *Latviešu avīžniecība. Laikraksti savā laikmetā un sabiedrībā, 1822–1865*, pp. 430–432.

[107] See Endzelīns, Jānis (1930): "Latvieši un viņu valoda", p. 53.

[108] The Estonian nationalist intellectuals faced a similar problem with two distinct Estonian print-languages: northern and southern Estonian. Eventually the northern variant was favoured, and printing in the southern variant virtually ceased in the late 19th century. During Estonia's First Republic, forms of the Estonian language other than the established standard were considered incorrect or marginal. See Taagepera, Rein (2011): "Albert, Martin, and Peter Too: Their Roles in Creating the Estonian and Latvian Nations", p. 133; Koreinik, Kadri (2011): "Public Discourse of (De)legitimation: The Case of South Estonian Language", pp. 241–242.

Folklore and ethnography

In the area of folklore, the first Latvian collectors of such material were clearly integrated with an Imperial Russian knowledge regime. Mythology and folklore attracted a great deal of interest in the nineteenth century, primarily among Russians but also among smaller nations in the Imperial context.[109] Ethnographic expeditions exploring the folklore heritage of the Empire's peoples became an important undertaking for the scholars attached to the Imperial Geographical Society.[110] The scholars at the new Latvian university could therefore fall back on these early attempts to collect folklore material, for instance, Fricis Brīvzemnieks's work in the late 1860s and early 1970s, and the efforts by the academic committee of the Riga Latvian Society (RLS). Many of those who gathered and edited material for the RLS committee were Latvian students at the Riga Polytechnical Institute (RPI).

The most impressive collection of folksongs and poetry, however, was assembled by Krišjānis Barons and his associates during the last decades of the nineteenth century. However, Brīvzemnieks and Barons both operated from Moscow, and with some support from Russian academic ethnographers. Brīvzemnieks was a member of the Anthropological and Ethnographic Society of Moscow University, and also translated a substantial number of the typical Latvian folk-poems, *dainas,* into Russian. At St Petersburg University, a programme for the collection of Latvian folklore material was launched in 1892.[111] These folklore collections were therefore made in *both* a national and an Imperial context. By 1893 Barons had amassed 54,000 *dainas,* all written out on separate cards and stored in a specially constructed archival cupboard. When his *magnum opus* was finally completed in 1912, Barons listed nine hundred contributors to his collections – farmers, teachers, clergymen, and others.[112]

These collections of folk culture, especially the *dainas,* involved a great many Latvians in various positions in society and contributed materially to the mobilisation of nationalist sentiments. Since Latvians, unlike Lithuanians, could not realistically refer to a previously existing 'national' state and a repertoire of

---

[109] Byford, Andy (2007): *Literary Scholarship in Late Imperial Russia. Rituals of Academic Institutionalisation,* pp. 28–29.

[110] Petronis, Vytautas (2007): *Constructing Lithuania. Ethnic Mapping in Tsarist Russia, ca. 1800–1914,* pp. 109–173.

[111] The programme was led by Eduard Vol'ter, one of the ethnographers connected to the Imperial Geographical Society. See Šmits, Pēteris (1923d): "Programma tautas gara mantu krājējiem", p. 178. Vol'ter later became a naturalized Lithuanian citizen under the name Volteris, and was the main ethnographer at the Lithuanian University in Kaunas.

[112] See Vīksna, Māra (1996): "The History of the Collection of Folklore in Latvia" pp. 85–90; *Latviešu literatūras vēsture,* Vol. 1, (1998), pp. 124–126. Barons' famous cupboard with all the handwritten *dainas* is in the safekeeping of the Folklore Archive in the Academy of Sciences' building in Riga.

historical symbols connected with former statehood, their folk culture and language constituted the main definers of the Latvian nation. The subsequent publishing of the *dainas* collection in several volumes, starting in 1894, was therefore a crucial national undertaking. The *dainas,* it was believed, captured the very essence of Latvian-ness. The notion that the traditional folksongs were a collective cultural product that reflected the nation's soul and worldview influenced not only folklorists proper but also literary and cultural historians.[113] In a sense, the *dainas* collected and edited by Barons *were* the nation. He was later cast in the role of a national redeemer – *Barona tēvs* or Baron the Father.[114] Here we clearly have an intellectual in the role of national hero.

The importance of the folklore heritage did not diminish after independence. As a part of the ethnic categorisation that characterised the First Republic, Latvian intellectuals tended to define and demarcate their *tautība* by referring to its folklore heritage.[115] The folklore repertoire was to some extent used to separate the Latvian *tauta* from ethnic minorities, 'us' from 'them', using the formula: 'we' are a part of this culture, 'you' are not.[116] Also, the Song Festivals based on the *daina* material, already a tradition in Imperial times but even more important after independence, constituted orchestrated occurrences where participants could *perform* their common Latvian-ness.

Carrying on the tradition of Barons and his associates, folklore and ethnography became very important fields of endeavour for the first generation of Latvian academics. One of the most central figures here was the previously mentioned linguist and Sinologist Pēteris Šmits, who joined the academic staff in Riga in 1920 after an arduous journey from Vladivostok. Šmits belonged to the 'middle' generation of Latvian academics, fifty years old at the time and with a solid scholarly record from St Petersburg University and the Eastern Institute in Vladivostok. He had, however, apart from recurrent summer vacations in the Baltic provinces, spent twenty-four years in the Far East. Still, Šmits's dedication to the national cause cannot be doubted. During his Siberian 'exile' he had studied and reviewed Barons' published *dainas* and other folklore literature, and strove diligently to keep himself informed about developments in this field.[117] He

---

[113] Among Latvian historians of literature, Ludvigs Bērziņš, for instance, claimed that the nation's "spiritual face" and "soul" were reflected in the *dainas*. See Bērziņš, Ludvigs (1930), p. 235. Historian Arveds Švābe was in his early writings very interested in the *daina* heritage, and used this material for instance to investigate notions of legal rights among Latvian peasants. See Švābe, Arveds (1932): "Latviešu tautas tiesiskie uzskati", pp. 15–25.

[114] Lindqvist, Mats (2003): "Giving Voice to the Nation. The Folklorist Movement and the Restoration of Latvian Identity", p. 199.

[115] Bula, Dace (1996): "The Singing Nation: The Tradition of Latvian Folk Songs in the Self-Image of the Nation", pp. 4–20.

[116] Bula, Dace (2000): *Dziedātājtauta. Folklora un nacionālā ideoloģija,* chapter 3.

[117] Pakalns, Guntis (forthcoming 2011): "Pēteris Šmits".

also managed to retain a steady connection with the Riga Latvian Society's academic committee, and after his return to Riga he was immediately voted its chairman.[118] Šmits also enjoyed considerable confidence among his fellow academics. In 1921 he was, for instance, elected both chief editor of the official journal *Latvijas Augstskolas Raksti* and vice-principal on student and educational matters.[119]

After his return to Riga, Šmits initially finalised some of his ethnographic research on Siberia, publishing a few articles on the languages of ethnic groups in the Amur valley. Soon, however, he turned to national issues, devoting his time to the study of Latvian mythology and the Latvian language. In 1923 he launched a programme for the systematic collection of Latvian ethnographic material, a 'sacred task' primarily involving teachers and pupils at Latvian schools.[120] Together with the archaeologist Francis Balodis, Šmits codified the received scholarly opinion on Latvian society and culture before the arrival of the German Crusaders in the early thirteenth century. Šmits also organised ethnographical investigations in the early 1920s, and his reputation as an ethnographer is perhaps indicated by him being selected as academic supervisor for this department at the State Historical Museum in 1932.[121] Apart from these undertakings, he was deeply involved in the publication of Latvian folklore literature, editing numerous volumes of collected tales and fairy stories.[122]

Šmits, however, was well aware of the dilemmas connected with the scholarly study of folk culture when the results of such studies did not entirely correspond with tenets within nationalist ideology. One such crucial issue was the antiquity and authenticity of Latvian folk culture. According to nationalist mythology, the Latvian *dainas* and other expressions of folk culture were genuine, unadulterated remnants of a very distant past, an echo of 'Latvian-ness' from the time before Baltic German and Russian domination.

Especially on the matter of Latvian pagan mythology, Šmits pointed to the need for more research since to his mind there were many misconceptions and distortions in this field.[123] Here he had to navigate carefully between a nationalist

---

[118] See Stradiņš (1998), p. 76.
[119] LVVA. Latvijas Universitātes fonds, 7427/6/2. Organisation Committee Minutes, 1921/09/14; 1921/12/14. However, he soon resigned from both positions due to poor health.
[120] Šmits (1923d), pp. 178–187; 278–288; 398–415; 559–570; 703–712. Šmits issued a questionnaire containing 1,369 questions on a wide variety of issues, for instance Latvian houses, household implements, clothing, food, drink, life courses, popular traditions, festivals, language, poetry, and popular conceptions of gods, spirits, history and geography.
[121] LVVA. Latvijas Universitātes fonds, 7427/6/363, Minutes of the Faculty of Philology and Philosophy, 1923/03/24; 7427/13/1698. Staff records; *Latvijas Universitātes Filoloģijas un filosofijas fakultātes Bibliografisks pārskats, 1919–1925* (1926), p. 5.
[122] *Latvijas Universitāte 1919–1929* (1929), p.189; Šmits, Pēteris (ed.): *Latviešu pasakas un teikas*, published in 15 volumes between 1925 and 1937.
[123] Šmits, Pēteris (1930c): "Latviešu mitoloģija", p. 161.

perspective, emphasising the importance of Latvian folklore and the heritage from Barons and his associates, and a scholarly perspective, which was considerably more sceptical about the 'ancient' past and the *daina* supposedly 'unchanged' character.[124] Later, however, Šmits seems to have been more prone to project the *dainas* backward in time, arguing that 'enslaved nations' could only repeat their culture, not materially change it.[125] Šmits was also initially rather sceptical about notions of a specific, ancient place of origin of the Balts, but here too he was later more prone to accept the idea of a specific *Urheim* of the Baltic peoples.[126]

While certainly very dedicated to the study of Latvian folklore and mythology, Šmits was possibly somewhat unfamiliar with recent scholarly developments in this area. Arveds Švābe, a main promoter of a 'national turn' in academic history writing, wrote in his autobiography about meeting Šmits in Vladivostok in 1916. Švābe, at that time a young intellectual completely self-taught in folklore studies, was surprised to find that Šmits apparently had no knowledge of recent work in this field, and that his library contained just a handful of elementary German handbooks in folkloristics. According to Švābe, Šmits was at that time completely unaware of recent important scholarly contributions like Frazer's *The Golden Bough*.[127]

Organisationally, the study of folklore was given a firmer structure by the establishment of a state-funded archive, *Latviešu folkloras krātuve*, in 1924. Here, the collecting efforts of a vast number of Latvian schoolteachers, journalists and amateur folklorists were assembled. Formally subordinated to the Antiquities Commission, *Pieminekļu valde*, it had four academics from the university on its Steering Committee: chairman and linguist Jānis Endzelīns, ethnographer Pēteris Šmits, linguist Jānis Kauliņš and literary historian Ludvigs Bērziņš. While not organisationally a part of the university, the archive definitely played a major role in Latvian society by emphasising the folklore heritage as a part of the national project. To this very day, the folklore archive displays Krišjānis Barons's mythologized cupboard, containing his vast collection of *dainas*. As we have seen in chapter 6, the transfer of the ageing Barons from Moscow to Riga in the early 1920s was a very important symbolic event.

---

[124] See Šmits, Pēteris (1923e): "Par mūsu tautas dziesmu vecumu"; Šmits, Pēteris (1930b): "Valodas liecības par senajiem baltiem", pp. 61–62.
[125] Šmits, Pēteris (1932): "Dažādi laikmeti tautas dziesmās", p. 13; Pakalns, Guntis (forthcoming 2011).
[126] I am grateful to Toms Ķencis at the Latvian Folklore Archives for these observations.
[127] Švābe, Arveds (1947): *Mana dzīve*, p. 175, cited in Ķencis, Toms (forthcoming 2011b): "Kārlis Arveds Švābe". However, this may be a reflection of earlier disagreements. Already in his book *Raksti par latvju folkloru* from 1923, Švābe was critical of Šmits's work on Latvian mythology.

However, there are some indications that the collection of folk traditions was not high on the national agenda during the 1920s. The reasons for this are debatable. Pēteris Šmits maintained in 1930 that it was the radical intellectuals among the *jaunstrāvnieki* who had been responsible for the low level of support for further folklore collections. According to him, these intellectuals ridiculed folk traditions, "propagated for internationalism and dreamed about the cosmos".[128] Here, it should be born in mind that some previous members of the *jaunstrāvnieki* group seem to have dominated the *augstskola's* organisation committee as well as the Ministry of Education in the early 1920s. Possibly, they viewed the folklore collections of the first generation of nationalist intellectuals as an outmoded development. Adjusting Latvia to modernity was seen as more important than its supposedly ancient traditions. Šmits, on the other hand, pleaded for a renewed scholarly study of folklore: songs, myths, riddles and tales.[129]

Towards the end of the 1920s, however, there seems to have been renewed emphasis on the importance of the *Latviešu folkloras krātuve*. The folklore archive was to become more academic – but perhaps also more male-dominated. The first female director, Anna Bērzkalne, was a Riga schoolteacher who had studied linguistics and folklore at the University of Kazan, Russia, as a pupil of the Baltic German philologist Walter Anderson. As director of the new Folklore Archive she had visited similar institutions in Denmark, Germany, Estonia, and Finland, and seems to have formed strong scholarly ties with her counterpart in Estonia, Oskar Loorits.[130] Bērzkalne initiated a very broad collection effort by students and schoolchildren in the 1920s. She also worked out the programme for the folklore archive, making a special point of organising collections from those parishes in Latvia that had not previously contributed to Barons's collection of *dainas*. The folk culture of the whole of Latvia's territory was to be mapped.[131]

A specific problem seems to have been the charting of the folklore of Latgale, the Eastern province of Latvia that had not previously been a part of the Baltic provinces of Livland and Kurland in Imperial times. Here, the proto-national project of folklore collection had been pursued less intensely than in the Baltic provinces proper. According to an estimate in 1924, only three per cent of the

---

[128] Šmits, Pēteris (1930d): "Tautas tradīcijas", p. 231. Šmits claimed that Jānis Rainis's play "Pusideālists" (Half-idealist) had played a major role, with its ridiculing of Latvian folk traditions.
[129] Šmits, Pēteris (1930d), pp. 232–234. Another problem for the scholarly study of Latvian folklore was that its pagan mythology was also used to construct a new Latvian religion, *Dievturība*, whose main propagator Ernests Brastiņš had a background as an academic folklorist. See *20. gadsimta Latvijas vēsture II. Neatkarīgā valsts 1918–1940* (2003), p. 761.
[130] Treija, Rita (forthcoming, 2011): "Anna Bērzkalne (1891–1956)". I am very grateful to Rita Treija for allowing me to take part of her as yet unpublished article on Bērzkalne.
[131] Vīksna, M (1996), pp. 93–95. According to Toms Ķencis at the Folklore Archive, Bērzkalne's main model for this work was that developed by the Finnish school of folkloristics.

dainas in Barons's collection emanated from Latgale.[132] Also, the important cultural manifestations during the late Imperial period, the song festivals based on the traditional *dainas*, never really spread to the Latgale area.[133] Moreover, the low level of literacy there in Imperial times meant that there was a much smaller group of Latvian intellectuals who could take part in the previous national undertaking of folklore collection. In 1924, therefore, a specific campaign was directed at schoolteachers in Latgale, urging them to become involved in the collection of the rich local folksong heritage and help promote what was seen as a common national culture.[134] Here, the national project seems to have involved the full cultural integration of Latgale in the common Latvian context.

Another problematic issue seems to have been the folklore of the Livonian population. The Livonians were a remnant of a Finno-Ugric group, and lived primarily in the coastal areas of Kurzeme and Vidzeme. While the ethnographic study of the Livonians was a central issue among Estonian and Finnish academics during the 1920s and 1930s, their Latvian colleagues seem to have been decidedly less interested.[135] This may have been an area where different national projects collided in the 'reconstruction' of a national or ethnic past. While it was generally accepted that the Latvian territory defined in 1920 had long been inhabited by people speaking Finno-Ugric dialects this notion fitted rather uneasily with the national imagining of the land as the ancient abode of proto-Latvian tribes. Therefore, the still-existing Livonian minority was a politically sensitive issue. National projects in ethnography tend to be directed at regional varieties of the majority population, or ethnic communities of the titular nation living abroad – not ethnic minorities of 'others' within the 'national' state itself.

In 1929, however, Anna Bērzkalne was unexpectedly replaced as director of the Folklore Archive.[136] There may have been many reasons for this. Bērzkalne, it seems, was involved in some kind of conflict with the chairman of *Pieminekļu*

---

[132] Rupjais, Jūlijs (1924): "Dziesmas un dziedāšana Latgalē", pp. 172–173. Most of these songs were collected in the communities close to the Livland border.

[133] Bērzkalns, Valentīns (1965): *Latviešu dziesmu svētku vēsture, 1864–1940*, p. 115.

[134] Rupjais (1924), p. 176. In this article, Rupjais tried to mobilise the Latgale teachers, claiming that it was the duty of every educated Latgallian to collect this folklore material before it disappeared entirely.

[135] Tankler, Hain & Rämmer, Algo (2004): *Tartu University and Latvia, with an Emphasis on Relations in the 1920s and 1930s*, pp.184–194. Bērzkalne was clearly the most important Latvian contact for the Estonian and Finnish ethnographers researching the Livonians.

[136] Māra Vīksna finds the treatment of Bērzkalne "unjustifiable" in the light of her dedicated work to establish the Folklore Archive. Vīksna, M (1996), p. 96. However, it has to be said that Bērzkalne did not publish any major work during the 1920s, apart from shorter articles and guides to the Folklore Archive collections.

valde, Pauls Gailītis.[137] However, it should be remembered that Bērzkalne was a woman and did not yet have a doctoral degree, in a scholarly setting totally dominated by men. At the same time, she may have been seen as too closely attached to the Estonian ethnographers. During the 1920s she published several articles on Estonian and Finnish folklore, and already in 1922 inquired about the possibility of her obtaining a degree at Tartu University where her old professor from Kazan, Walter Anderson, was now teaching. Bērzkalne also consulted with Anderson and Finnish ethnographers, especially Karl Krohn, on the methods for folklore collection to be implemented at the archive. In general terms, she appears to have been the Estonian and Finnish ethnographers' most important scholarly contact in Latvia.[138] While these connections certainly provided her with a wider scholarly network, they may have made her less appreciated among Latvian conservative nationalist circles.

Anna Bērzkalne clearly did not receive much support for her academic development from professor Pēteris Šmits and the faculty. When she applied for a stipend from the Cultural Fund in order to complete her doctoral thesis, the faculty decided not to support her application after having heard an assessment prepared by Šmits on Bērzkalne's scholarly work.[139] After this setback she had to continue as a high school teacher in Riga, pursuing her folklore studies as a private scholar. Eventually she managed to make use of her Estonian contacts, passing her doctoral exams at Tartu University in 1935 and defending her thesis there in 1942.[140]

Bērzkalne's successor as director of the Folklore Archive was Kārlis Straubergs, an expert in classical philology and ancient Greek and Latin literature. Judging by his academic record, his appointment was hardly due to any substantial merits in folklore studies. Straubergs had belonged to the circle of younger Latvian academics at Moscow University, and joined the staff in Riga already in 1919 at the age of twenty-nine. He initially taught classes in

---

[137] Treija, Rita (forthcoming, 2011). Treija maintains that Gailītis's personal dislike of Bērzkalne played a role in her dismissal. In the *Saeima* debate on the leadership of the Folklore Archive, Anna Bērzkalne was defended by the Social Democrat Kārlis Dēšens. This may be an indication that it was primarily politicians belonging to the national conservative wing who wanted her to be dismissed.

[138] Treija, Rita (forthcoming, 2011); *History of Tartu University, 1632–1982* (1985), p. 187; Tankler & Rämmer (2004), pp. 191–192. Tankler and Rämmer, however, are more interested in documenting *positive* relations between Estonian and Latvian academics and therefore tend to stress the cooperation between the Tartu and Riga folklorists rather than the more problematic issues.

[139] LVVA. Latvijas Universitātes fonds, 7427/6/363, Minutes of the Faculty of Philology and Philosophy, 1935/08/31. The minutes do not give any details on Šmits's assessment, but it can hardly have been very positive. According to Treija, the faculty had already in 1932 refused to acknowledge that Bērzkalne's diploma from Kazan University equalled a diploma in Slavic linguistics from *LU*. Treija, Rita (forthcoming, 2011).

[140] Tankler & Rämmer (2004), pp. 191–192.

Latin literature and classical Greek. Straubergs served a number of times as secretary to the faculty, and as delegate to the university council. He even had a short spell as Minister of Education in 1924, and was later also voted the university's delegate to the *Saeima's* Education Committee in 1928. Just before his appointment at the Folklore Archive, Straubergs had defended his doctoral dissertation on the Latin poet Horace. Shortly afterwards he was elected professor of classical philology.[141]

Straubergs was certainly a merited academic classicist. There is little evidence, however, that he developed any substantial competence in folklore studies before the late 1930s, and he clearly never became an accomplished ethnographer. Practically all his publications, as well as his teaching, were in the field of Latin literature and classical philology.[142] His only publications in folklore studies before his appointment as director of the Folklore Archive were a short piece on Latvian conceptions of the afterlife and a few articles on magic spells, but even here the references to classical sources predominate.[143] After his appointment, Straubergs contributed to the anthology *Latvieši* in 1930 with a piece on prehistoric Latvian clothing – probably in collaboration with the archaeologists in the group around Francis Balodis. It was probably strategically important for Straubergs to appear in this anthology: it actually represented a 'national turn' in several of the academic disciplines in the faculty.[144] Still, one cannot escape the feeling that Straubergs was given the post at the folklore archive primarily as a result of networking and as a reward for faithful services rendered to the state and the university.

Only towards the end of the 1930s did Straubergs write more extensively on folklore matters. In 1939 he published a substantial work on Latvian spells and witchcraft, but present-day sources within the folklore archive maintain that this

---

[141] LVVA. Latvijas Universitātes fonds, 7427/13/1642. Staff records; Kļaviņa (2008), p. 176; Ķencis, Toms (forthcoming 2011a): "Kārlis Straubergs". Straubergs was Minister of Education when the Folklore Archive was founded in 1924.

[142] See *Latvijas Universitātes Filoloģijas un filosofijas fakultātes Bibliografisks pārskats, 1919–1925* (1925), and *Latvijas Universitātes Filoloģijas un filosofijas fakultātes Bibliografisks pārskats, II, 1925–1930* (1930). In the overview of the faculty's academics published in 1939, Straubergs is still recorded as professor of classical philology, not folklore studies. His teaching was also entirely directed towards classical subjects. See *Latvijas Universitāte divdesmit gados 1919–1939* (1939), I, p. 201; 288.

[143] Straubergs, Kārlis (1923): "Piezīmes pie dažām latviešu burvju grāmatām", pp. 804–816; 935–944; 1029–1041, three short articles based on some books on sorcery in the State Historical Archive; Straubergs, Kārlis (1926): "Burvju grāmatas", pp. 227–431. See also Ķencis, Toms (2011a, forthcoming), on Straubergs's writings on folklore issues.

[144] Straubergs, Kārlis (1930): "Latviešu tērps un viņa raksta ornamentika", pp. 322–356. On archaeology and Francis Balodis, see below.

book was to written mainly by his assistants.[145] Apart from that, he published some works on beliefs in werewolves in the Baltic provinces.[146]

The faculty's main academic expert on Latvian folklore was naturally Pēteris Šmits, who continued to lecture on the subject during the 1930s. Šmits was, however, also heavily involved in linguistics and publishing. In fact, in terms of teaching, Šmits seems to have done more lecturing in linguistics and Chinese than in ethnography or folklore studies. Ethnography is not even listed among the subjects taught in the faculty before 1938, when the Swedish ethnologist Dag Trotzig was recruited.[147] Folklore and ethnography did have a professorial chair but in fact never became a separate department within the faculty. In terms of academic 'empire-building', Šmits clearly failed to create an organisational setting for academic folklore and ethnography.[148] Moreover, there are no indications that he managed to gather a group of younger academics in these disciplines prepared to continue his work. After Šmits's death in 1938 the faculty had no representatives of a younger generation of academics who were fully qualified to teach Latvian folklore and mythology: it fell to Straubergs to deliver these lectures.[149] Only at this point, it seems, did Straubergs change his academic priorities and start to focus on folklore.

The reasons for this apparent lack of a younger generation of academic folklorists and ethnographers are not clear. To some extent, naturally, it was a result of priorities within the faculty: linguistics, history, philosophy, pedagogy and psychology swiftly established themselves as the main disciplines there, leading to separate departments. If historian Arveds Švābe was correct in the criticisms he published later, it is also possible that Šmits was a bit old-fashioned in his theoretical approach, and therefore failed to make use of contemporary developments in academic folklore studies.[150]

Moreover, it should be borne in mind that the performative aspects of Latvian folklore in the form of song and dance festivals largely took place outside

---

[145] I am grateful to ethnographer Aldis Pūtelis at the *Folkloras Krātuve* for this information. In this book, Straubergs combines the notions of witchcraft in ancient Greece and Rome with folklore material and records from witch trials. See Straubergs, Kārlis (1939–1941): *Latviešu buŗamie vārdi*, Volumes I & II. Some of this work, especially the classical aspects, goes back to the articles Straubergs published in 1923. One of Straubergs's assistants was probably the local historian Lauma Sloka, whose article on a late witch trial was more or less copied by Straubergs in his volume from 1939. See Sloka, Lauma (1923): "Kāda raganu prāva Latvijā 19. gadu simtenī,", pp. 1262–1264; Straubergs (1939a), pp. 102–104.

[146] Straubergs, Kārlis (1939b): "Vilkaču ideoloģija Latvijā", pp. 98–114.

[147] *Latvijas Universitāte divdesmit gados 1919–1939* (1939), I, pp. 288; 292. LVVA. Latvijas Universitātes fonds, 7427/13/1797. Staff records.

[148] Typically, these disciplines are not even mentioned in the 1938 official university celebration of 'science for the fatherland': *Zinātne tēvzemei divdesmit gados 1918–1938* (1938).

[149] LVVA. Latvijas Universitātes fonds, 7427/13/1642. Staff records; 7427/6/363, Minutes of the Faculty of Philology and Philosophy, 1938/09/03.

[150] Ķencis, Toms (forthcoming 2011b).

academia. These public concerts and exhibitions were an important part of the Latvian national project but perhaps for that very reason, subjecting the hallowed folklore heritage to critical academic scrutiny could be a sensitive issue. Modern scholarly analyses have shown, for instance, that Barons's edition of the *dainas* was a somewhat sanitised version, where bawdy allusions and perceived borrowings from other genres were deliberately omitted. Moreover, the symbolic weight of the folklore tradition and the very central position of Krišjānis Barons personally in the national project in the interwar period probably complicated the presentation of such critical perspectives. This, I would argue, may have hampered the 'academisation' of folklore studies.

Another reason for the modest position of folklore within the faculty may have been that the study of Latvian *dainas* was also a matter for the more prestigious linguists and literature scholars. While Šmits focused on Latvian folktales and mythology, the symbolically important work of continuing Barons's editing and publishing of *daina* material was headed by linguist Jānis Endzelīns. Under Endzelīns's supervision, an expanded and commented collection of *dainas* was published in nine volumes between 1928 and 1931 using the new orthography.[151] It therefore seems that the Latvian linguists managed to stake their claim to the 'national treasure' of the *dainas*, making it part of their academic territory.

However, yet another reason for folklore's relatively slow development within the faculty may have been Šmits's very negative attitude to female academics. During a faculty meeting in 1923, for instance, he stated that he was strongly against women being included among the teaching staff; this, he argued, would erode scholarly standards.[152] At the same time, a large majority of the faculty's students were actually young women.[153]

In a similar manner, women predominated among the staff of the *Folkloras Krātuve*. As shown above, the academic career of its female director Anna Bērzkalne was thwarted in Latvia. Although promising male students were

---

[151] *Latvju tautas daiņas*, 9 vols, (1928–31); Endzelīns, Jānis (1928): "Ievads", p. v. Apart from the *dainas* themselves, each volume contained essays in Latvian cultural history on matters such as trees, folk dress, building styles, family forms and traditional jewelry designs, mostly written by faculty colleagues and curators from the national museums.

[152] LVVA. Latvijas Universitātes fonds, 7427/6/363, Minutes of the Faculty of Philology and Philosophy, 1923/12/01. He made similar statements at other faculty meetings. See ibid., 1923/03/24.

[153] The proportion of female students in the Faculty of Philology and Philosophy during the 1920s and 1930s was around 80 per cent – a quite remarkable figure compared with other European universities during this period. See *Latvijas Universitāte divdesmit gados 1919–1939* (1939), I, p. 231. Female students were admitted alongside males from the very beginning of *Latvijas Augstskola*. In Imperial times, separate courses had been organised for women at the universities. Some aspiring female academics were educated instead in Switzerland. See Zelče, Vita (2002): *Nezināmā. Latvijas sievietes 19. gadsimta otrajā pusē*, pp. 161–165.

certainly given priority over female students in the other disciplines in the faculty, none of the other prominent professors was so clearly against the preparation of female academics as Pēteris Šmits.[154] Here, naturally, Bērzkalne's close association with the theoretical and methodological approach of the Finnish school of folklore studies may have been an additional reason for Šmits's refusal to support her academic career at *Latvijas Universitāte*.

The rejection of Bērzkalne is indeed remarkable, since no other young academics in the faculty were heading for a doctoral exam in Ethnology. Šmits seems to have preferred to cooperate with the literary historians in the faculty, Ludvigs Bērziņš and the young Jānis Jansons, rather than form a new generation of academic folklorists and ethnographers.[155]

The recruitment of the Swede Dag Trotzig in 1938 in fact demonstrates the perceptible lack of a younger generation of scholarly Latvian folklorists who could firmly establish the discipline in the faculty and continue the work of Šmits. Moreover, the recruitment of Trotzig was hardly a matter of appointing an established and experienced ethnographer. When offered a position in Riga he was twenty-three years old and had not even produced a *licenciat* thesis. His appointment was clearly based on the recommendation from his ethnology professor, Sigurd Erixon at Stockholm University, to dean Straubergs.[156] In spite of Trotzig's very modest academic record, the faculty appointed him by a very substantial majority. This indicates that there were no feasible Latvian candidates.[157]

Summing up, mainly through the efforts of Pēteris Šmits, folklore seems to have re-emerged as an important 'national' scholarly discipline during the early

---

[154] Among the prominent professors at the faculty, Jānis Endzelīns appears to have been most open to the advancement of women academics. He clearly supported the academic careers of linguists Anna Ābele and Edīte Hauzenberga, and also the Germanist Alīse Karlsone. Endzelīns also seems to have been the main academic supporter of folklorist Anna Bērzkalne. See Treija, Rita (forthcoming, 2011). Taking a wider look at the faculty, there was at least a handful of women in the other disciplines who were allowed to make academic careers: Milda Liepiņa in Psychology, Olga Rudovska in art history, and Elvīra Šnore in archaeology. *Latvijas Universitāte divdesmit gados 1919–1939* (1939), II, pp. 85–87; 97–100; 111–112. For an overview of the research of women in academia, see Carls, Lina (2004): *Våp eller nucka? Kvinnors högre studier och genusdiskursen 1930–1970*, pp. 49–67.

[155] On Bērziņš and Jansons and their interest in Latvian folk poetry and songs, see *Latvijas Universitāte divdesmit gados 1919–1939* (1939), II, pp. 39–40; 95–96.

[156] LVVA. Latvijas Universitātes fonds, 7427/13/1797. Staff records. Letter from professor Sigurd Erixon to dean Straubergs, 1938/10/09. Straubergs had apparently over the course of several years had discussions with Erixon on the possibilities of recruiting a Swedish ethnographer to Riga. LVVA. Latvijas Universitātes fonds, 7427/6/363, Minutes of the Faculty of Philology and Philosophy, 1938/09/03.

[157] The vote was 14 for, 2 against and 1 abstaining. LVVA. Latvijas Universitātes fonds, 7427/13/1797. Staff records.

1930s, codifying crucial aspects of national culture.[158] However, the absence of a younger generation of scholars in folklore and ethnography meant that the 'national turn' in these disciplines was clearly uncertain. What remained was the semi-academic institution of *Folkloras krātuve*. In Kārlis Straubergs, it is evident that the folklore archive had a good classicist but hardly a fully competent folklorist during the national project's formative years.

Archaeology

The discipline of archaeology often has a central place in national academic agendas. In the case of Ireland, for instance, archaeology played an important part in 'reconstructing' an imagined Gaelic past before the coming of the English.[159] In the Imperial Russian context, however, such 'proto-national' tendencies were not very pronounced. Archaeology was an important subject at St Petersburg and Moscow University during the nineteenth century, but the focus was rather on two major topics: the ancient remains of Greek, Scythian and Mongol civilisations in Southern Russia, and, under the influence of Pan-Slavism, the excavation of old Slavic settlements.[160]

In the Latvian context, however, it seems that archaeology got off to a rather slow start. None of the Latvian academics called to the new *augstskola* had solid scholarly training in this specific discipline. As a temporary solution, the task of teaching archaeology was initially given to Karl von Löwis of Menar, a *privātdocents* on yearly contracts who could only lecture in German.[161] Löwis of Menar actually belonged to one of the more prominent Baltic German noble families, the name indicating Scottish origins. At the time of his appointment he was sixty-six years old.[162]

Löwis of Menar was an unconventional choice in many ways. His formal academic record was slim: he had primarily studied at Stuttgart *Technische Hochschule*, and definitely had no academic training in archaeology. As a Livonian nobleman he initially served in a junior position in one of the Riga district courts, but in 1888 he was given the post of head librarian of the Livland

---

[158] In the important work *Latvieši*, published in two volumes 1930–32, folklore matters were given considerable attention. See Šmits (1930c); Šmits (1930d); Bērziņš, Ludvigs (1930): "Tautas dzejas nozīme latviešu tautas dzīvē", pp. 235–254; Šmits, Pēteris (1932): "Dažādi laikmeti tautas dziesmās", pp. 7–14.
[159] Hutchinson, John (2001): "Archaeology and the Irish rediscovery of the Celtic past", pp. 505–519.
[160] Trigger, Bruce G (1993): *Arkeologins idéhistoria*, pp. 250–254.
[161] LVVA. Latvijas Universitātes fonds, 7427/6/2. Organisation Committee Minutes, 1921/09/21.
[162] Whelan, Heide W (1999), *Adapting to Modernity. Family, Caste and Capitalism among the Baltic German Nobility*, p. 22; LVVA. Latvijas Universitātes fonds, 7427/13/1013. Staff records.

Diet. He served in this position until the political transformations and the Diet's dissolution in 1920 suddenly rendered him unemployed.[163]

During his time as librarian, Löwis of Menar became a self-taught archaeologist and cartographer with a special interest in the castles and maps of medieval Livland. He was a member of several learned societies, and played a major role in two Baltic German historical associations: *Der Vereinigung für Heimatkunde in Livland* and *Der Gesellschaft für Geschichte und Altertumskunde des Ostseeprovinsen*. Historical societies such as these became very important for the Baltic German elite in the late nineteenth century, under pressure from Russification programmes.[164] Karl Löwis of Menar contributed materially to the conception of a German *Heimat* in the Baltic provinces, writing a substantial number of articles on local history and archaeology in journals connected to these societies.[165]

Consequently, Löwis of Menar had for three decades been deeply involved in the cultural world of the Baltic Germans. How can we explain his recruitment to the new *augstskola* with its national Latvian ambitions? First, as we have seen above, the organisation committee simply could not find any trained archaeologist with an ethnic Latvian background. Second, he received a very positive evaluation from the faculty's main historian, the Baltic German Leonid Arbusow. In this assessment, Arbusow admitted that Karl Löwis of Menar was entirely self-taught and completely lacked formal qualifications in archaeology. Nevertheless, he was the only available expert in Latvia on ancient hill forts and medieval castles. Arbusow stressed that these fortifications had played a very important role in Latvian history, and that Löwis of Menar was the only person who possessed profound knowledge of these matters. Arbusow also stressed Menar's practical experience of conducting excavations.[166] The committee's solid support for the appointment of Löwis of Menar was clearly facilitated by this very positive assessment from Arbusow.[167] However, it should also be noted that the appointment as *privātdocents* did not give a permanent position: it had to be

---

[163] LVVA. Latvijas Universitātes fonds, 7427/13/1013. Staff records. He gained the position of *assessor* in the Riga court without ever having studied law: such positions were seen as a noble prerogative. Whelan (1999), p. 195.
[164] Whelan (1999), pp. 237–239.
[165] LVVA. Latvijas Universitātes fonds, 7427/13/1013. Staff records. Curriculum Vitae. His main publication was *Livland im Mittelalter* (1907).
[166] LVVA. Latvijas Universitātes fonds, 7427/13/1013. Staff records. Assessment of Karl von Löwis of Menar by Leonid Arbusow, 1921/09/05. On Arbusow, see the section on history below.
[167] LVVA. Latvijas Universitātes fonds, 7427/6/1. Organisation Committee Minutes, 1921/09/21. The vote resulted in 26 'ayes' and 3 abstentions.

extended annually. Also, it is clear that the faculty kept Löwis of Menar's teaching assignment at a minimal level.[168]

A more academically trained archaeologist was nevertheless required. The need for a specialist in this field was repeatedly voiced at faculty meetings. When contacts with the Finnish professor Mikkola did not provide a solution, Endzelīns, with the support of Arbusow, in 1922 suggested the election of Dr Max Ebert, then at Königsberg University in East Prussia.[169]

Historian Augusts Tentelis was chosen to prepare an assessment of Ebert's academic record. Tentelis again emphasised the faculty's needs for the discipline of archaeology and since there was no ethnic Latvian scholar with expertise in this field, Ebert should be elected. Arbusow, who was obviously more acquainted with Ebert's work than Tentelis was, described him as 'one of the most prominent contemporary archaeologists' available. Arbusow also pointed to the important organisational work that was acutely needed in Latvian archaeology, and that it was of prime scholarly importance that Ebert could be associated to the university. Ethnographer Šmits also supported the election of Ebert, pointing to the necessity of establishing the discipline and also the difficulties of finding a suitable candidate in Sweden, Finland, England or France. Only linguist Juris Plāķis grumbled somewhat about general German 'narrow-mindedness'. In the end, the faculty elected Ebert unanimously.[170]

During these discussions, however, philosopher Pēteris Zālīte had raised the question: would the organisation committee accept the election of another German academic? A fortnight earlier the faculty had proposed the election of the Baltic German linguist Erich Diehl and this matter was still pending. Moreover, the contested election of the German Romanist Neubert had not yet been resolved.

However, a restructuring of the academic leadership apparently facilitated the proposed appointments. On 13 September 1922, the organisation committee was replaced by the newly formed university council. As shown in a previous chapter, the new Council did not contain any external members tied to Latvian organisations, and also applied a voting procedure that required just a simple majority for academic appointments. This surely made it easier to

---

[168] In 1922, for instance, Löwis of Menar was assigned two hours' teaching per week – he had applied for six. LVVA. Latvijas Universitātes fonds, 7427/6/363, Minutes of the Faculty of Philology and Philosophy, 1922/04/29.

[169] LVVA. Latvijas Universitātes fonds, 7427/6/363, Minutes of the Faculty of Philology and Philosophy, 1922/09/02; 1922/09/08.

[170] LVVA. Latvijas Universitātes fonds, 7427/6/363, Minutes of the Faculty of Philology and Philosophy, 1922/09/16. One week later, however, Plāķis had reconsidered and suggested that the faculty should have another vote on the election of Ebert. Nobody seems to have supported his proposal, though. Ibid., 1922/09/23.

obtain confirmation of faculty elections, especially when they were made with solid majorities.

In October 1922, dean Endzelīns informed the university council that since it had proved impossible to find a Latvian candidate for a professorship in archaeology, he and the faculty had decided to propose the election of the German Max Ebert. In spite of the earlier described reluctance to appoint German academics, the Council eventually elected Ebert, albeit by a rather slim margin.[171] In this case, the Latvian government accepted the appointment of a German citizen, and Ebert was duly eleced for period of five years and granted the right to lecture in German.[172]

The successful recruitment of Ebert was certainly a consequence of the strongly perceived need, within the faculty and the university, to establish archaeology as a discipline, and also to promote the important work of excavating ancient Latvian sites. Ebert had a solid academic background, having studied at the universities of Innsbruck, Heidelberg, Halle and Berlin before becoming a *privatdozent* in Königsberg in 1918. In spite of some early misgivings about his possible 'German' tendencies in archaeological research, he seems to have been much respected and appreciated by his faculty colleagues – perhaps with the single exception of linguist Juris Plāķis.[173]

Ebert organised excavations at ancient 'Latvian' sites, and took the initiative to devise an archaeological terminology in the Latvian language.[174] When Ebert was appointed to a chair in Königsberg in 1923, deans Endzelīns and Pēteris Šmits made strenuous efforts to find a compromise whereby Ebert would continue in Riga, at least on a part-time basis.[175] In a letter to the Council of Deans, for instance, Šmits stressed that such a compromise was absolutely necessary; otherwise the university would lose "a very prominent archaeologist

---

[171] LVVA. Latvijas Universitātes fonds, 7427/6/2. University Council Minutes, 1922/10/04. The vote was 17 'ayes', 7 against, and 6 abstaining. This means that Ebert would *not* have been elected under the two-thirds majority rule in the previous Organisation Committee.

[172] LVVA. Latvijas Universitātes fonds, 7427/6/2. University Council Minutes, 1922/10/18. Ebert does not seem to have been entirely happy with this arrangement. Apart from demanding a salary well above that of the other professors in the faculty, he wanted to be elected for *twenty* years, not five. However, Endzelīns seems to have been able to reason with him, promising to approach the Miniistry of Education to secure funds for excavations. LVVA. Latvijas Universitātes fonds, 7427/6/363, Minutes of the Faculty of Philology and Philosophy, 1922/11/04.

[173] Plāķis appears to have been hostile to all recruitment of 'foreign' academics, especially Germans and Russians. In the case of Ebert, Plāķis remarked that his decision to move to Königsberg University was caused by archaeology's failure to recruit students – a remark that was immediately rebutted by dean Šmits. LVVA. Latvijas Universitātes fonds, 7427/6/363, Minutes of the Faculty of Philology and Philosophy, 1923/03/01.

[174] LVVA. Latvijas Universitātes fonds, 7427/6/363, Minutes of the Faculty of Philology and Philosophy, 1923/10/06.

[175] LVVA. Latvijas Universitātes fonds, 7427/6/363, Minutes of the Faculty of Philology and Philosophy, 1923/02/24; 1923/04/21; 1924/03/08.

and scholar".[176] However, in the end it proved difficult to retain both professorships and Ebert left *Latvijas Universitāte* towards the end of 1924.[177]

The loss of Ebert was clearly a blow to the faculty, and a discussion ensued on how best to replace him. The aged Baltic German Karl Löwis of Menar was clearly not seen as an alternative. He had been kept on as a *privātdocents* in cartography and numismatics but his qualifications as an archaeologist had been increasingly questioned. Arbusow and Šmits appear to have been his main supporters in the faculty, while art historian Felsbergs several times argued against the extension of Menar's contract.[178] Even Jānis Endzelīns, who seldom agreed with Felsbergs on anything, grew increasingly critical, questioning Löwis of Menar's competence to lecture in his assigned courses. Max Ebert concurred in this assessment, stating that Menar was incompetent as an archaeologist.[179] In the spring of 1925, the faculty finally decided not to renew his appointment.[180]

When discussing the problem of replacing Ebert, the faculty turned instead towards the possibility of preparing some of the most promising Latvian archaeology students by sending them for further training to Ebert in Königsberg. On this question the faculty seems to have been practically unanimous. The only question was: which students were to be selected – and how many could the university be persuaded to finance? In the meantime, Ebert could possibly be persuaded to stay for another year.[181]

However, these considerations took a somewhat surprising turn with the appearance of an unexpected Latvian academic: Francis Balodis. In the autumn of 1923, a letter from Balodis had arrived, expressing a wish to be appointed professor at *Latvijas Universitāte* – on condition that the university provided the means for him and his family to travel from Moscow, where he was presently situated. This letter seems to have taken the faculty completely by surprise. In all previous discussions in the faculty and the organisation committee on the great difficulties in finding a Latvian archaeologist, Balodis's name had never been mentioned. Only the classicist Kārlis Straubergs, previously affiliated to the

---

[176] LVVA. Latvijas Universitātes fonds, 7427/13/420. Staff records. Letter from Šmits to the Council of Deans, 1924/03/10. The faculty was supported by the university council. The principal, Jānis Ruberts, informed the Ministry of Education that Ebert was "irreplaceable". Ibid., Letter from Ruberts to the Ministry of Education, 1924/09/24.
[177] *Latvijas Universitātes piecgadu darbības pārskats 1919.–1924* (1925), p. 293.
[178] LVVA. Latvijas Universitātes fonds, 7427/6/363, Minutes of the Faculty of Philology and Philosophy, 1923/03/24.
[179] LVVA. Latvijas Universitātes fonds, 7427/6/363, Minutes of the Faculty of Philology and Philosophy, 1924/03/01.
[180] LVVA. Latvijas Universitātes fonds, 7427/13/1013. Staff records. Löwis of Menar had by then also reached the official retirement age of seventy, and furthermore faced the obstacle of being required to teach in Latvian.
[181] LVVA. Latvijas Universitātes fonds, 7427/6/363, Minutes of the Faculty of Philology and Philosophy, 1924/03/01; 1924/03/29.

Moscow Archaeology Institute, seemed knowledgeable about Balodis, commenting tersely 'he is an Egyptologist'.[182]

Straubergs was at least partially correct. Trained as an archaeologist at Dorpat/Jur'ev and Moscow, and as an Egyptologist in Munich, Francis Balodis belonged to the generation of Latvian scholars who had become firmly integrated in the Russian Imperial academic system. In the early 1920s he devoted himself to the excavation of the old Mongol capital of Saraj on the Volga.[183] As recounted in a previous chapter, he had previously not shown any inclination to return to Latvia. Only after the Soviet government pressed him to leave the University of Saratov and return to Moscow, it seems, did he resolve to leave the Soviet Union. However, he had to wait until the summer of 1924 until he had received the necessary permits, allegedly to travel to a scholarly conference abroad. When he arrived in Riga that summer, he was forty-two years old.[184] In generational terms, he belonged to the 'middle' generation of academics fully established at Imperial universities before World War I.

As we have seen in the faculty discussions, Balodis was at first perceived primarily as an Egyptologist rather than an archaeologist. His letter still caused considerable enthusiasm among the more 'national' members of the faculty. While Endzelīns expressed some doubts about the costs involved in transporting Balodis and his family to Riga, Felsbergs argued that Balodis must be assisted to return to his 'native country' irrespective of the expense. Pauls Dāle pointed to the 'national opportunity' of adding Balodis to the faculty. Felsbergs and Plāķis motioned that Balodis should be appointed immediately, but the faculty majority found that the regular procedures must be observed: an assessment must first be made of Balodis's scholarly work.[185]

The assessments of Balodis were written by theologian Imanuels Bencingers and archaeologist Max Ebert. While Bencingers was very positive in his evaluation, Ebert, interestingly enough was considerably more critical. In this situation the faculty decided that since Balodis would be appointed professor of

---

[182] LVVA. Latvijas Universitātes fonds, 7427/6/363, Minutes of the Faculty of Philology and Philosophy, 1923/09/01; Ķencis, Toms (forthcoming 2011a). Still, Straubergs did not mention Balodis at all in his short article on excavations in Southern Russia a few years previously. See Straubergs, Kārlis (1921): "Izrakumi Dienvid-Krievijā", pp. 1150–1162. Balodis, it seems, had been summoned by the Organisation Committee already in 1919, but no reply apparently reached Riga. After that, there is no evidence that his name was ever raised again. See Dāle, Pauls (1921): *Vēsturisks pārskats par Latvijas Augstskolas nodibināšanu un viņas darbību pirmā (1919/20.) mācības gadā*, p. 22.

[183] Mugurēvičs, Ēvalds (1997a): "Arheologam Dr. phil Dr. hist profesoram Francim Aleksandram Balodim 125", p. 185.

[184] LVVA. Latvijas Universitātes fonds, 7427/13/123. Staff records.

[185] LVVA. Latvijas Universitātes fonds, 7427/6/363, Minutes of the Faculty of Philology and Philosophy, 1923/09/01.

Austrumu vēsture (Eastern history) not archaeology, Ebert's rather negative appraisal should not be given much weight. Balodis was duly elected.[186]

Balodis was primarily neither seen as an archaeologist or a possible successor to Max Ebert. His inaugural lecture as professor, and his first scholarly articles in Latvian, were also entirely on ancient Egyptian themes.[187] The faculty continued to discuss the possibilities of having some of the promising Latvian archaeology students sent abroad for further scholarly training, and in the meantime, an attempt would be made to persuade the Finnish archaeologist Tallgren to lecture in Riga for one year. Ebert's own suggestion, to appoint a young German archaeologist, Ernst Wahle, however, found no support in the faculty.[188]

Adapting himself to the new circumstances and opportunities in Riga, Balodis appears to have shifted rapidly from Egyptology and the exploration of Mongol settlements to archaeological investigations of early Baltic cultures.[189] As early as 1925 he started excavation projects at ancient 'Latvian' settlements in the Eastern province of Latgale.[190] Continuing Ebert's work, Balodis was especially interested in the excavation of ancient 'Latvian' hill-forts.[191] This turn towards ancient proto-Latvian topics was an undertaking he continued to pursue for the next fifteen years.

The symbolic importance of this 'national' turn of archaeology is evident from the fact that Francis Balodis was chosen to hold the celebratory lecture when the university celebrated its first decade in 1929. The title of his lecture was *Senlatvieši – zemkopji*, "The Old Latvians: farmers".[192] Balodis had clearly managed to re-cast himself as one of the university's most profiled national academics.

Around 1930 it becomes possible to see a 'national turn' in both archaeology and ethnography. In 1930 Balodis together with Šmits edited a very influential

---

[186] In the end he was actually appointed professor of 'Eastern philology' by 10 votes in favour, 1 against and 2 abstaining. LVVA. Latvijas Universitātes fonds, 7427/6/363, Minutes of the Faculty of Philology and Philosophy, 1923/10/27.
[187] Balodis, Francis (1924a): "Otrā Tebu laikmeta Ēģiptes garīgā kultūra", pp. 605–613; Balodis, Francis (1924b): "Mākslas reforma Echnatona laikā".
[188] LVVA. Latvijas Universitātes fonds, 7427/6/363, Minutes of the Faculty of Philology and Philosophy, 1924/03/01; 1924/03/29. Typically, the right-wing Plāķis pointed out that one of the proposed archaeology students was politically on the left and therefore undesirable – but this did not influence the faculty decision. Wahle was a young German archaeologist who excavated some ancient Latvian burial sites in the summer of 1924. See Mugurēvičs (1997a), p. 15.
[189] *Latvijas Universitātes Filoloģijas un filosofijas fakultātes Bibliografisks pārskats, 1919–1925* (1925), and *Latvijas Universitātes Filoloģijas un filosofijas fakultātes Bibliografisks pārskats, II, 1925–1930* (1930). However, he continued to lecture on ancient Egyptian culture and archaeology during the 1920s and 1930s. See *Latvijas Universitāte divdesmit gados 1919–1939* (1939), I, pp. 282–283.
[190] Balodis (1938): "Vēsture un vēstures palīgdisciplīnas", p. 383.
[191] Vasks, Andrejs (2005): "Latvijas pilskalnu izpētes gaita", pp. 11–16.
[192] Šnē, Andris (2009): "Latvijas Universitātes rektors profesors Augusts Tentelis", p. 20.

scholarly anthology, *Latvieši* (the Latvians), in which the established national-academic understanding of early Latvian culture and society was codified.[193] As Šmits declared in the foreword to the first volume, it was seen as a priority to explore the ancient history of the Latvians since such scholarship had previously been in the hands of Baltic Germans, who were only interested in the chronicles and other documents produced by the German elite. A new generation of Latvian specialists should now take over, broadening and deepening research on the ancient past.[194] In Balodis's contribution to the anthology, he claimed that the Baltic German archaeologists had based their conclusions on the territorial conception of the Baltic provinces, not on a national one connecting the different Latvian 'tribes'. This meant, according to Balodis, that important aspects of the Latvian ancient past had previously been neglected.[195]

Later, writing his memoirs in exile during World War II, Balodis emphasised that the development of the discipline of archaeology at the University of Latvia in the late 1920s had been inspired by nationalist enthusiasm. He and his co-workers in the first generation of academic Latvian archaeologists strove to use their "patriotic ideals" in the exploration of the Latvian past.[196] He wrote:

> It seemed to us archaeologists that we also should take part in the work to enrich and deepen the Latvian spirit and Latvian ideals. Latvia's ancient past would re-emerge from sand and ashes to help our people love and cherish their land and their fathers...[197]

Balodis's work appears to have focused on four major issues. First, the ancient past of the Latvian people had previously been misrepresented by 'foreign' scholars, and should now be rectified by a 'patriotically' inspired archaeology.[198] Second, Balodis claimed that it was possible to distinguish ethnic boundaries and territories from the archaeological remnants in hill forts and burial sites. In this way, one could map the ethnic territory of 'Latvian' tribes during the Iron Age.[199] Third, evidently inspired by human anthropology, Balodis was keen to distinguish the characteristics of Latvian people and culture before they 'mingled' with Finno-Ugric tribes, and later with Germans, Swedes, Poles, and Russians. The 'original' Latvians, he claimed, were very tall and powerfully built and had typical long skulls. These physical characteristics proved that they belonged to what he saw as a "Nordic race". Culturally, they were also clearly

---

[193] *Latvieši. Rakstu krājums.* 2 Vol. (1930–1932)
[194] Šmits, Pēteris (1930a), "Priekšvārdi", pp. 5–6.
[195] Balodis, Francis (1930): "Latviešu aizvēsture", p. 76.
[196] Balodis (1941), pp. 135–136.
[197] Balodis (1941), p. 139. My translation.
[198] Balodis, Francis (1947): "Latvia and the Latvians", pp. 246–247.
[199] Mugurēvičs (1997a), pp. 13–18.

distinct from the Finno-Ugrians and the Slavs.[200] Third, in spite of allegations from German scholars, the Latvians had already developed 'modern' regal state structures in the ancient period. Fourth, such Latvian states had existed, Balodis claimed, in the ninth century. His most important archaeological work was on Jersika, the capital of the supposed kingdom of 'Lettia' in present-day Latgale.[201] Much of the archaeological investigation of 'Latvian' settlements under Balodis's supervision was geared in this direction. He summarized in 1947:

> The sites of the ancient Latvian forts testify to the excellence of the construction and the overall planning of the entire system of defence. They would indicate a corresponding development in political and social organization. /.../ Assuredly, too, a powerful and orderly state authority must have existed in order to allow such important constructions as fortresses to be undertaken. It is evident that the peoples were developing a sense of unity and common purpose.[202]

In this manner, Balodis obviously projected a more modern, state-centred Latvia backwards in time, fully in tune with the nationalist agenda of the 1920s and 1930s. Understandably, Balodis's archaeological endeavours were firmly supported by both the university and the government. Archaeology had become a national priority.[203]

Balodis was clearly a charismatic figure. Developing this brand of 'national' archaeology in brilliant, well-attended lectures, Balodis gathered around him a group of scholars fostered at *Latvijas Universitāte*.[204] The more experienced of them had been pupils of Max Ebert, and had followed him to Königsberg University. Valdis Ģinters and Eduards Šturms both received their PhDs in archaeology at Königsberg, and later returned to Latvia to become main associates in excavations led by Balodis. They also assumed important positions at the Historical Museum and the Commission of Antiquities, *Pieminekļu valde*.[205]

There was also a slightly younger group of Latvian archaeologists, primarily Rauls Šnore and Elvīra Šnore.[206] Certainly, to some extent due to gender issues, it was Rauls rather than Elvīra who received academic assignments and scholar-

---

[200] Balodis (1947), pp. 246–247.
[201] Balodis, Francis (1940): *Jersika un tai 1939. gadā izdarītie izrakumi*.
[202] Balodis (1947), p. 249.
[203] Balodis (1941), pp. 140–141.
[204] Mugurēvičs (1997a), p. 17.
[205] LVVA. Latvijas vēstures institūta fonds, 1865/1/46. LVI Darbinieki. Raksturojumi un biogrāfijas, 1936. Biographical notations of the academics associated with the Latvian Historical Institute. Ģinters became the Director of the Historical Museum in 1934, while Šturms continued to work within the *Pieminekļu valde*.
[206] Šturms was born in 1895, Ģinters in 1899, Rauls Šnore in 1901 and Elvīra Šnore in 1905.

ships, specialising above all in numismatics.[207] Elvīra had to work outside academia as a schoolteacher, but still managed to take part in the excavation of ancient Latvian sites under Balodis. In the early 1930s she was eventually allowed to conduct independent archaeological investigations, and she also developed contacts with the Swedish archaeologists around professor Birger Nerman, one of Balodis's closest international colleagues.[208] Her main interest was the ethnogenesis of Latvian 'tribes' in pre-German times, a topic well in line with the national agenda.[209]

Pursuing their careers within the arenas of academia, at the *Pieminekļu valde* and historical museums during the 1930s, Ģinters, Šturms and the two Šnores were very important codifiers and disseminators of the newest direction of archaeology for public display and consumption. The new 'national' archaeology and its conceptions of the past of Latvian *tauta* were structured and popularized through the creation of new museums. In 1928 the open-air museum, *Brīvdabas muzejs*, displaying primarily buildings and folk-art from the Latvian regions, was inaugurated. Similarly, in 1932 the new State Historical Museum was created, where one of the most important collections consisted of the findings from Balodis's various excavations of ancient Latvian settlements. Balodis himself played a key role in these endeavours, being scholarly director at the Historical Museum and also director of the open-air Museum between 1934 and 1940. Moreover, he played a prominent part on matters concerning historical sites, archives and monuments as chairman of the *Pieminekļu valde*.[210]

Besides promoting a 'national turn' in Latvian archaeology, Balodis strove to establish cooperation with academics in the other two Baltic states. In 1930 he organised the Second Baltic Archaeology Conference in Riga, inviting the most prominent colleagues from Tartu University.[211] In a similar manner, Balodis contributed materially to the development of a 'national' archaeology in Lithuania. In the 1930s he frequently lectured at the university in Kaunas, and

---

[207] Šnore, Rauls (1997): "Raula Šnores dzīves un zinātniskās darbības apraksts (autobiogrāfija)", pp. 40–41. Rauls Šnore and Valdis Ģinters were appointed to junior academic positions in the faculty during the late 1920s and early 1930s. See *Latvijas Universitāte divdesmit gados 1919–1939* (1939), II, p. 199. Rauls Šnore was, for instance, awarded a scholarship to England in 1933. LVVA. Latvijas Universitātes fonds 7427/13/1705. Staff records.
[208] LVVA. Latvijas Universitātes fonds, 7427/13/1704. Staff records; Guščika, Elīna (2010): "Elvīra Šnore un Latvijas agrā dzelzs laikmeta pētniecība", p. 112.
[209] Mugurēvičs, Ēvalds (1997b): "Elvīras Šnores dzīves un zinātniskās darbības apraksts", pp. 9–10.
[210] LVVA. Latvijas Universitātes fonds, 7427/13/123. Staff records; Mugurēvičs (1997a), p. 17; Balodis (1941), p. 148.
[211] Tankler & Rämmer, (2004), p. 173; *Latvijas Universitāte divdesmit gados 1919–1939* (1939), I, p. 191.

participated in some excavations of ancient settlements in 1934.²¹² In official recognition of his services to the Lithuanian university, he received an honorary doctorate in 1936.²¹³ Indeed, contacts with historians and archaeologists at the university in Kaunas seem to have deepened perceptibly during the 1930s.²¹⁴

Balodis emerged in the 1930s as the most influential academic in the faculty, serving several times as dean. He also gained a considerable international reputation, receiving offers to lecture at many European universities.²¹⁵ Exporting national Latvian archaeology in this international context, Balodis gradually filled the role of a national academic 'hero', a symbol of Latvian scholarship.

History

Compared with the work of Šmits and Balodis, the contributions of historians to the Latvian 'national' project in academia seem to have been rather slim, at least during the 1920s. Here, it should perhaps be noted that after 1889 the discipline of history at Dorpat/Jur'ev was clearly dominated by Russian academics who saw little reason to pursue substantial research on the history of the Baltic provinces.²¹⁶ These matters were largely left to the Baltic German historians, *literati* and historical societies, who had formed their own conception of these provinces' history. Very few of the Latvian nationalist intellectuals wrote on historical subjects.²¹⁷

Still, the new 'national' university was surely expected to deliver scholarly research more in tune with national prerogatives. One of the most obvious tasks would be to rewrite and re-research history in order to make it more compatible

---

²¹² LVVA. Latvijas Universitātes fonds, 7427/6/363, Minutes of the Faculty of Philology and Philosophy, 1934/09/01; 1935/05/28.
²¹³ Janužytė (2005), pp. 280–281.
²¹⁴ In 1934, for instance, professor Mikola Biržiška from Kaunas was voted honorary doctor by the faculty. LVVA. Latvijas Universitātes fonds, 7427/6/363, Minutes of the Faculty of Philology and Philosophy. The Lithuanians also sent a large and prestigious delegation to the Baltic History Conference in Riga in 1937, including Volteris, Jonynas, Puziņas, Jablonskis, Ivinskis and Janulaitis. In comparison, the Estonians were primarily represented by Hans Kruus. See *Pirmā Baltijas vēsturnieku konference Rīgā 16. – 20. VIII. 1937* (1938), and below chapter 8.
²¹⁵ LVVA. Latvijas Universitātes fonds, 7427/6/363, Minutes of the Faculty Philology and Philosophy, 1934/12/08; 1935/04/06; 1937/04/17; 1937/10/09.
²¹⁶ *History of Tartu University, 1632–1982* (1985), pp. 148–149. However, it must be said that history was not a central discipline at Dorpat University before the Russification period. Most Baltic German historiography took place under the auspices of learned societies rather than at the university.
²¹⁷ Kaspars Biezbārdis, whose main work was actually on Latvian linguistics, published a pamphlet in 1865 on the history of the Baltic provinces. However, his main point was that the Latvians did not yet constitute a nation, and they achieved full societal recognition mainly by joining the Russian nation. Biezbārdis, Kaspars (1865b): *Zustände und Eigenthümlichkeiten in den baltischen Provinzen Russlands*.

with the new political context. The history of the Latvian nation, hitherto neglected and disregarded by Baltic German and Russian scholars, would now be written. How was this achieved at the University of Latvia after 1919? What kinds of conflict and dissent did this occasion with historians of a non-Latvian background?

A brief glance shows that the first generation of historians at the University of Latvia comprised very few people, and not all of them were ethnic Latvians. However, as in all these contexts, the question of ethnicity is hardly straightforward. Professor Leonid Arbusow, first employed in 1919 at the age of thirty-seven, appears to have been by far the most merited of the historians. He was the grandchild of a Russian army officer, but his family had resided in Latvian territory since at least the 1840s and seems to have become firmly Baltic German both culturally and ethnically. Arbusow's mother's maiden name indicates that she was Russian. His father was a schoolteacher in Jelgava and an historian of the Baltic provinces. He devoted much of his time to the study and editing of Baltic German medieval records.[218]

Indeed, Arbusow's case illustrates the difficulties in distinguishing between ethnicity, class and culture in the Baltic provinces in Imperial times. Although he perhaps had a primarily Russian ethnic background, Arbusow was included among the Baltic Germans on grounds of class, culture and education. Being 'Baltic German' was not, therefore, primarily an ethnic question. Moreover, there was a large element of both assumed and prescribed ethnicity. At the same time, this combination of class, cultural capital and ethnic belonging meant that the boundaries between *tautības* were jealously guarded; the Baltic Germans in particular were intent on demonstrating their separateness from the 'uncultured' Latvians and Estonians.[219]

This ethnic structuring remained intact during the First Republic. In the Latvia that emerged from the War of Liberation, ethnic belonging or *tautība* became a basic dimension for categorizing its citizens. At the university, the ethnic identity of the teaching staff was not seen as a private matter. On the contrary, regular overviews were made of the 'nationality' of teaching staff in the various faculties; academics were requested to define their *tautība*. In such records from 1919–1920, Arbusow unequivocally described himself as 'German', and furthermore noted that he lectured in German and Russian even in his courses on early Latvian history.[220]

Apart from his family origins, Leonid Arbusow was firmly situated in a German cultural context. He had received a thorough German academic

---
[218] *Latviešu konversācijas vārdnīca* (1927–28), Vol. 1, col. 816–817.
[219] See Whelan (1999), p. 33.
[220] LVVA. Latvijas Universitātes fonds, 7427/6/37a. Pārskats par Latvijas augstskolas, vēlāk Universitātes, nodibināšanu un viņas darbību. Overview of the Faculty of Philology and Philosophy, 1919–20; 7427/13/123. Staff records.

training, studying theology in Dorpat/Jur'ev and history in Göttingen. He obtained a doctoral degree in Göttingen in 1909 with a thesis on the Teutonic Order after 1400. His research primarily concerned German topics in the Baltic area in the medieval and early modern period, and he published his main works in the German language.[221] However, after his appointment as *docents* at the University of Latvia in September 1919, Arbusow also wrote in – or was translated into – Latvian on some typically 'national' subjects such as the earliest handwritten manuscripts in Latvian, and Latvians engaged in the Reformation.[222]

None of these texts appears to have been notably scholarly. Instead, the impression is that, as an acknowledged member of the Baltic German *tautība*, Arbusow had to prove that he was able to address Latvian historical issues. No doubt he was fully aware of his sensitive position as one of the very few Baltic Germans in the faculty. A narrower and not entirely implausible interpretation is that this was Arbusow's strategy in order to qualify for tenure and a full professorship. When he obtained a chair in 1922, the scholarly evaluation duly noted his attempts to pursue these Latvian issues. The assessment contains no indication that Arbusow's ethnic background had influenced his scholarly work. On the contrary, his main work on the Reformation in the Baltic provinces was seen as methodologically sound and 'devoid of tendencies'. The faculty's decision to promote Arbusow to full professor was unanimous.[223]

What is perhaps more remarkable is that the organisation committee was also unanimous in upholding this appointment.[224] This was very unusual: the more 'nationally' inclined members of the committee, such as Spricis Paegle and Paulis Lejiņš, generally voted against the appointment of non-Latvians. The committee was in fact seldom unanimous even when it came to approving ethnic Latvian professors. It should also be noted that the issue of tuition language did not feature in Arbusow's appointment, which probably means that he was perceived to have at least a sufficient command of Latvian. It should also

---

[221] *Latvijas Universitāte 1919–1929* (1929), pp. 148–52.
[222] See, for instance, Arbuzovs, Leonīds (1920a): "Peezīmes par XVI. g.s.vecākajeem latveešu literatūras peeminekļeem. Visagrakee rokraksti latveešu valodā kopš 1558. g."; Arbuzovs (1920b): "Latveešu tēvreize senos textos"; Arbuzovs (1921a): Reformācijas kustība latviešu starpā"; Arbusow (1921b): "Studien zur Geschichte der lettischen Bevölkerung Rigas im Mittelalter und 16. Jahrhundert".
[223] LVVA. Latvijas Universitātes fonds, 7427/6/363, Minutes of the Faculty of Philology and Philosophy, 1922/04/29; 7427/13/88. Staff records. In his evaluation of Arbusow's work, his colleague Augusts Tentelis remarked that it only to a small extent dealt with 'Latvian matters', but he was nevertheless positive and signalled his approval.
[224] LVVA. Izglītības ministrijas fonds, 1632/2/612, Sarakste ar Latvijas Universitāti par mācību spēkiem, mācību darbu, budžetu u. c., 1921. g. – 1922.g. Letter from the principal to the Minister of Education, 1922/05/26; LVVA. Latvijas Universitātes fonds, 7427/6/2. Organisation Committee Minutes, 1922/05/24.

be noted, however, that having been appointed, Arbusow's interest in specific Latvian topics in medieval history seems to have swiftly declined.

Meanwhile, Arbusow's central position in an academic discipline so close to national concerns had become a matter of dispute. Already in 1920 there had been signs that some Latvian intellectuals outside the faculty questioned his interpretation of history. His main work on the Reformation in the Baltic provinces, which the faculty assessed very favourably, had been reviewed rather critically by R. Klaustiņš in the official journal of the Ministry of Education. Klaustiņš claimed that Arbusow adhered much too firmly to a Baltic German perspective on history. Far from being the 'positive' event described by Arbusow, Klaustiņš argued that the Reformation had strengthened the power of the Baltic German nobility, making the local clergy dependent on noble patronage. From a 'Latvian' perspective, therefore, this was a lamentable development. Formulating these criticisms, Klaustiņš several times applied the term *vācu zinātne* (German scholarship) to Arbusow's interpretations.[225]

In his rejoinder, Arbusow maintained that Klaustiņš's objections were based on opinions and conjectures, not established historical facts. He insisted that his work was wholly based on a scholarly evaluation of a number of such facts verified with historical methods. Klaustiņš main criticism, that Arbusow operated within a specifically Baltic German interpretation of history, was therefore never answered or discussed.[226]

It is interesting that the Klaustiņš debate does not seem to have had any effect on the faculty's assessment of Arbusow's work; he remained firmly established at *Latvijas Universitāte*. In 1925, for instance, he received a prize for his book on the legal rights of the Livonian peasantry in the sixteenth century.[227] Occasional publications on Latvian issues seem to have sufficed. However, he appears to have become less and less interested in submitting articles to the ministry's journal.[228] Towards the end of the 1920s, as we shall see, the notion of contrasting 'German' and 'Latvian' historical perspectives re-emerged, this time in a more academic setting.

As the years passed, however, Arbusow's position appears to have become increasingly difficult. He seems to have tried to straddle the divide between

---

[225] Klaustiņš, Roberts (1920a): "Die Einführung der Reformation in Liv-, Est- und Kurland. Bearbeitet von Dr. L Arbusow", pp. 181–188.
[226] Arbuzovs, Leonīds (1920c): "Atbilde uz R. Klaustiņa kga recenziju", pp. 586–592. See also Klaustiņš's reply, Klaustiņš, R (1920b): "Peezimes pee Arbuzova kunga atbildes", pp. 592–593. After this exchange, the editors ended the debate, concluding that the two contenders did not seem to find any common ground.
[227] See *Latvijas Universitāte divdesmit gados 1919–1939* (1939), I, p. 207. The prize was awarded by the government-funded *Kultūras fonds*.
[228] Arbusow contributed frequently to *Izglītības Ministrijas Mēnešraksts* in 1920 and 1921, but very rarely after that.

Latvian and Baltic German cultural circles in Riga, publishing in both German and Latvian (and Estonian) journals. From 1925 onwards, he also chose to combine his teaching at the University of Latvia with lecturing at the German-speaking Herder Institute in Riga, which was exceptional among his faculty colleagues. He did obtain the faculty's formal permission to teach at the Herder Institute, but this line of action hardly made him more popular among his more 'nationally' inclined colleagues.[229] Gradually, many of his fellow academics in the faculty began to see him as being far too influenced by Baltic German conceptions of the Latvian past. In particular, some of the prominent Latvian academics who had been recruited to the university more recently appear to have been more critical of his work. Francis Balodis, for instance, publicly criticized Arbusow's views of Baltic society on the arrival of German crusaders.[230] A further indication of Arbusow's growing isolation is that, in spite of his professorship, he was never elected to a leading post within the faculty or at university level.[231]

There is also some doubt about the extent to which Arbusow actually managed – or chose – to lecture in Latvian. Faculty records from 1921 indicate that Arbusow was then lecturing in German and Russian only.[232] However, he did not belong to the group of old Riga Polytechnical Institute professors who had an unlimited right to lecture in those languages. Neither is he mentioned among the professors who were given a grace period, usually five years, before being required to lecture in Latvian. There are no indications that he ever applied for leave or extended permission to lecture in Russian or German. If Arbusow continued to lecture in German and Russian – which seems probable – this may have contributed to his problematic situation in the faculty.

Still, while clearly being somewhat undesirable from the 'nationality' point of view, in the initial years Arbusow was unquestionably by far the most qualified historian on the teaching staff. None of the historians with an ethnic Latvian background could match his academic record and experience. Indeed, his professorship can only be fully understood in the light of the obvious lack of scholarly trained historians among ethnic Latvians.

A few writers of 'national' history had indeed emerged among the intellectuals of the Latvian national movement in the late nineteenth and early twentieth centuries, though most of them clearly lacked formal academic

---

[229] LVVA. Latvijas Universitātes fonds, 7427/13/88. Staff records. See also von Hehn, Jürgen (1987): "Deutsche Hochschulaktivitäten in Riga und Dorpat zwischen den beiden Weltkriegen", p. 275.
[230] Spekke (2000), p. 94.
[231] LVVA. Latvijas Universitātes fonds, 7427/13/88. Staff records.
[232] LVVA. Latvijas Universitātes fonds, 7427/6/37a. Pārskats par Latvijas augstskolas, vēlāk Universitātes, nodibināšanu un viņas darbību. Overview of the teaching staff, 1919/1920/1921.

training as historians. In the turmoil of 1917–1919, some members of this 'first generation' of Latvian historians were "lost" for political reasons. Kārlis Landers, author of a pioneering three-volume 'History of Latvia' in 1905–1908, ended up on the Bolshevik side and remained in the Soviet Union until his death in 1937. The same appears to have happened to Fricis Roziņš, who was on the staff of the *augstskola* during the spring of 1919, the brief spell of Bolshevik rule.

However, the most prominent representative of the first generation, Jānis Krīgers-Krodznieks, sometimes labelled 'Latvia's first historian', did join *Latvijas Universitāte*. He clearly belongs to the university's 'older' generation of Latvian academics, having reached seventy years of age when elected by the faculty.[233] He had previously belonged to the circle of young Latvian intellectuals in Moscow who had produced the important nationalist journal *Austrums*. Krodznieks held a history degree from Moscow University, but like many other Latvian intellectuals had earned his living primarily as a language teacher.[234] He wrote a large number of articles in *Austrums* on older Latvian history, challenging what he saw as a predominant Baltic German interpretation of the past.[235] In 1919 he returned to Riga to be appointed the first Director of the Latvian State Archives, and became a *privātdocents* at the university in 1921. However, his actual faculty teaching in history amounted to a mere two hours per week between 1921 and 1923, mainly on feudalism and the agrarian question.[236]

In Riga, Krodznieks published two short textbooks, two collections of printed sources and a few shorter articles, often characterized by a sharp nationalist edge directed at Baltic Germans.[237] Being without regular scholarly training, he does not seem to have made much of a mark on the faculty and hardly ever attended its meetings. Some of the more prominent academics there seem to have had reservations about his writings.[238] Instead, Krodznieks appears to have used his

---

[233] LVVA. Latvijas Universitātes fonds, 7427/13/877. Staff records. Krodznieks's appointment was based on an evaluation by Arbusow. See LVVA. LU fonds, 7427/6/1, Organisation Committee Minutes, 1921/02/23.
[234] Šalda, Vitālijs (2000):"Jaunlatvieši Maskavā", pp. 55–57.
[235] Plakans, Andrejs (1999):"Looking Backward: The Eighteenth and Nineteenth Centuries in Inter-War Latvian Historiography", pp. 294–295; Zelče, Vita (2001): "Jānis Krodznieks – Latvijas Republikas pirmā arhīva direktors", pp. 151–155.
[236] *Latvijas Universitāte divdesmit gados 1919–1939* (1939), I, p. 292.
[237] On his output, see *Latvijas Universitātes Filoloģijas un filosofijas fakultātes Bibliogrāfisks pārskats, 1919–1925* (1925), p. 6. On the nationalist edge, see, for instance, Krodznieks, Jānis (1920): "Kā zaudēta zeme", pp. 536–543, Krodznieks, Jānis (1921a): "Līgumi ar kuršiem 1230. gadā", pp. 12–16, and Krodznieks, Jānis (1921c): "Iz nesen pagājušiem laikiem", pp. 842–844, which with their theme of the eviction of Latvian peasants from their land by the Baltic German nobility were at the same time a contribution to the fierce contemporary debate on land reform.
[238] Krodznieks reacted with obvious irritation when his textbook on early Latvian history received some scholarly criticisms from professor Pēteris Šmits in 1921. See Krodznieks, Jānis

position at the Historical Archive and its journal *Valsts Arhīva Raksti* (*VAR*) as a platform for a more openly 'nationalist' perspective on the Latvian past.[239] His symbolic stature at the university is evident from his election as honorary doctor by the faculty in 1924, shortly before his death.[240]

As one of the first generation of Latvian nationalist intellectuals and historians, Krodznieks was indeed of very substantial importance for the development of a 'Latvian' perspective of history. However, his influence on academic historiography in the 1920s was limited by a weak scholarly record, his general abstention from faculty meetings, and ultimately by his death in 1924. Only a decade later did this trend reassert itself.

The more openly 'national' direction of *Valsts Arhīvi Raksti* continued to some extent after Krodznieks's death, but the journal was geared towards the publication of Latvian archival sources, not scholarly and analytical articles.[241] However, the *VAR* did play a seminal role in the furthering of a national Latvian perspective on history in the late 1920s when it published Juris Vīgrabs's articles on the legal position of the Latvian peasantry in the eighteenth century. This occasioned one of the first major academic battles over national perspectives on history.[242] Instead of continuing at the faculty as a codifier of a 'national' Latvian history, Vīgrabs joined the Latvian diplomatic service.

There was, in fact, one ethnic Latvian academic who was appointed professor of history before Arbusow: Augusts Tentelis. Tentelis did not belong to the 'first' group of prominent academics whom the organisation committee took great pains to recruit in 1919/20, but the 'second'.[243] The son of a Latvian farmer son who had taken the long road via elementary-school teaching before becoming a professional academic, Tentelis had received his scholarly training in St Petersburg, primarily in philology and history; he passed the *Magister* exam in 1913 and became a *privat-docent* at that university in 1916. He specialised in Western Europe's medieval history and taught some minor courses at St Petersburg University. His main occupation was teacher of history and Latin in various St Petersburg schools.[244]

(1921b): "Paskaidrojumi", pp. 202–206, and Šmits's answer; Šmits, Pēteris (1921): "Piezīmes pie J. Krodznieka kunga paskaidrojumiem", pp. 207–208.
[239] See, for instance, Krodznieks, Jānis (1924): "Vidzemes muižnieku un zemnieku adreses ķeizaram Aleksandram II", pp. 3, 28–41; Plakans (1999), pp. 295–296.
[240] LVVA. Latvijas Universitātes fonds, 7427/13/877. Staff records.
[241] See, for instance, Lauma Sloka's extensive work on Vidzeme and Kurzeme parish chronicles between 1925 and 1934.
[242] Vīgrabs, Juris (1927): "Vidzemes zemnieku tiesiskais stāvoklis XVIII gadusimteņa pirmajā pusē. I daļa."; Vīgrabs, Juris (1930): "Vidzemes zemnieku tiesiskais stāvoklis XVIII gadusimteņa pirmajā pusē. II daļa". For the ensuing so-called 'Rozen-dispute', see below.
[243] Tentelis was formally elected in March 1920. LVVA. LU fonds, 7427/6/1, Organisation Committee Minutes, 1920/03/30.
[244] Šnē, Andris (2009), "Latvijas Universitātes rektors profesors Augusts Tentelis", p. 8.

Formally appointed by the organisation committee in March 1920 and promoted to *docents* six months later, Tentelis apparently remained in St Petersburg until the end of 1920.[245] The records give no indication of the reason for this. Many of the recruited Latvian academics had severe difficulties in departing from Soviet Russia but no such information can be found regarding Tentelis.[246]

It could have been the sudden prospect of gaining a professorial position that encouraged Tentelis to return to Riga. Jānis Endzelīns, dean of the faculty, approached the principal in November 1920, suggesting that the vacant post as professor of history should be filled by the still-absent Tentelis. Knowingly or not, in his letter Endzelīns clearly overstated Tentelis's academic record, describing him as a "history professor at St Petersburg University".[247] This may have prepared the ground for Tentelis's surprisingly rapid promotion: the organisation committee formally appointed him professor in September 1921.[248] This was rather remarkable, since Tentelis had not written any *habilitation* thesis after passing the *Magister* exam. Clearly, this is an indication of the faculty's paramount concern to have an ethnic Latvian professor in the central national discipline of history.

When he arrived in Riga, Tentelis was forty-four years old, and in terms of academic generations he belonged to a 'younger' rather than a 'middle' group, not having been firmly established at St Petersburg University. One would perhaps have expected him to be a relatively young, vigorous promoter of a 'Latvian' perspective in history during *Latvijas Universitāte's* formative years. There are, in fact, some indications that he actually had such ambitions, but for several reasons they do not seem to have materialised.[249] First, Tentelis seems to have been primarily preoccupied with administrative duties. He was vice-principal in 1924–1925, and principal from 1925 to 1927, and again between 1929 and 1932. He was elected dean of faculty three times: 1927, 1931 and 1932. He was also heavily involved in national politics, serving as Minister of Education in 1928 and later in the 1930s.[250]

---

[245] LVVA. Latvijas Universitātes fonds, 7427/13/1760. Staff records.

[246] Tentelis appears to have explained that his delay in coming was occasioned by the difficulties he encountered in transporting his voluminous library. Šnē (2009), p. 9.

[247] LVVA. Latvijas Universitātes fonds, 7427/13/1760. Staff records. Letter from dean Endzelīns to the Principal, 1920/11/10.

[248] LVVA. Latvijas Universitātes fonds, 7427/6/1, Organisation Committee Minutes, 1921/09/21.

[249] On Tentelis's ambitions in 1923–1924 to produce a Latvian history along 'national' lines, providing a 'true' picture of Latvia's past, see Balodis (1938), p. 373; Balodis (1941), p. 134. However, Francis Balodis is describing the achievements of one of his closest associates in the developement of a 'national turn' in history, and his account should not be accepted uncritically.

[250] LVVA. Latvijas Universitātes fonds, 7427/13/1760. Staff records; *Latvijas Universitāte divdesmit gados 1919–1939* (1939), I, pp. 178–179. First appointed to the university council in 1923, Tentelis made very little impression until his election as vice-principal for student and

Tentelis's considerable administrative duties and political involvement certainly hampered his chances of writing scholarly history: a closer look at his publications shows that they were rather sparse, to put it mildly. During his first decade at the University of Latvia he did not in fact produce any major work in history, just a few reviews and some minor articles. However, this is not fully attributable to a heavy administrative workload. Tentelis had published very few contributions to academic history even *before* he was appointed vice-principal in the summer of 1924; indeed, he does not appear to have written anything substantial after his *Magister* thesis in St Petersburg before the war.[251] Later, in the 1930s, his main contribution as a historian seems to have been as an editor of source collections. On the whole, therefore, it must be said that Tentelis's scholarly output was exceedingly slight. Unlike most of the faculty's other professors, he never submitted a doctoral dissertation. Tentelis was therefore hardly the *writing* academic who could play the expected role as synthesiser and codifier of a new national conception of history.

Moreover, Tentelis, at least initially, was not all that well acquainted with the substantial issues and problems of Latvian history. Primarily a classical scholar and a philologist, as a historian he was essentially a medievalist with the focus on Western Europe and Italy. In terms of teaching he mainly lectured on Roman and medieval history, and did not address any 'national' Latvian issues in his seminars. Later, his many administrative duties certainly also reduced his involvement in teaching, making him less able to form a new generation of Latvian history students. His main contribution, as a historian and Minister of Education, seems to have been on educational matters and the implementation of a more 'national' curriculum in Latvian schools.[252] Here, he actually seems to have been rather controversial. A conservative on educational issues, Tentelis was far from popular in the Latvian schoolteachers' association and the left-wing opposition in the *Saeima*.[253]

---

educational matters in May 1924. Before that, the minutes never mention him as taking part in the debates. His support when elected principal in 1925 was very weak: the smallest possible margin in the university council. See LVVA. Latvijas Universitātes fonds, 7427/6/2, University Council Minutes, 1925/05/21.

[251] See the bibliography in *Profesors Dr. honoris causa Augusts Tentelis. Dzīve un darbs* (2009), pp. 122–124; *Latvijas Universitātes Filoloģijas un filosofijas fakultātes Bibliogrāfisks pārskats, 1919–1925* (1925), and *Latvijas Universitātes Filoloģijas un filosofijas fakultātes Bibliogrāfisks pārskats, II, 1925–1930* (1930). Apart from one article on Kurland/Kurzeme in the late 17th century, "Curlandiae quaedam notabilia", actually a translation of a historical document, most of Tentelis's articles dealt with university matters, education, and his views on future tasks for Latvian historians.

[252] Auns, Muntis (2009): "Augusts Tentelis – vēsturnieks", p. 89; Krūze, Aīda (2009): "Augusts Tentelis – izglītības ministrs", p. 100.

[253] Krūze (2009), pp. 102–103.

In strictly academic terms, Tentelis clearly carried far less weight than his colleague Leonid Arbusow. Still, it was Tentelis who, somewhat paradoxically, after his rapid promotion had to make a scholarly assessment of Arbusow's work before the latter's appointment as full professor.[254] Also, it was Tentelis who received all the honorary assignments, such as the academic leadership of the State Historical Museum.[255] Summing up, it appears that Tentelis primarily played the role of an organiser, administrator, and figurehead, not a researcher, tutor, or writing scholar.

In terms of university politics, it was some years before Tentelis joined the 'national' side. In the early 1920s he did not vote with the more 'national' faculty members who regularly opposed the appointment of Baltic German or foreign academics – a group primarily consisting of linguist Juris Plāķis, art historian Ernsts Felsbergs and psychologist Pauls Dāle. In most of that period's debates on recruitment, Tentelis was relatively passive but generally supported the relatively open recruitment policy of the dean, Jānis Endzelīns.[256]

By 1926, however, Tentelis was clearly moving more openly in a 'national' direction. He was not actually writing a 'new' version of Latvian history but indicating the direction in which he believed younger colleagues should go.[257] In 1930–1932 he participated with Francis Balodis and Pēteris Šmits in producing the symbolically important anthology *Latvieši*.[258] He also now openly criticised the works by Arbusow which he had assessed very favourably ten years earlier. He now deplored the perceived lack of a 'national perspective' in Arbusow's writings and offered a brief outline of a historical synthesis based on a typical national master narrative: the gradual development of the Latvian nation, its rise from bondage and desire for freedom.[259]

Also, in more public settings outside the university, Tentelis appears to have positioned himself as a more active promoter of the 'national turn' in historical scholarship. Speaking at a meeting of the Latvian Society's Academic Committee

---

[254] See Tentelis's evaluation in LVVA. Latvijas Universitātes fonds, 7427/13/88. Arbusow's staff records. Arbusow held a doctoral degree from Göttingen, while Tentelis only had a *Magister* from St Petersburg.

[255] LVVA. Latvijas Universitātes fonds, 7427/13/1760. Staff records. He shared this appointment with Pēteris Šmits, ethnography, and Francis Balodis, archaeology.

[256] A major exception was his opposition to the appointment of the Baltic German classicist Erich Diehl – but in this case it was Felsbergs who advocated the appointment, not Endzelīns. LVVA. Latvijas Universitātes fonds, 7427/6/363, Minutes of the Faculty of Philology and Philosophy, 1922/09/02.

[257] His most important contribution was the article "Latvijas vēsturnieku tuvākie uzdevumi" [Future tasks for Latvian historians], published by the Riga Latvian Society in 1926.

[258] Tentelis contributed to the first volume with a short piece on the subjection of the Latvian and Livonian tribes by the German Order in early medieval times; he co-edited the second volume. See Tentelis, Augusts (1930): "Latvieši Ordeņa laikā", pp. 121–138; *Latvieši. Rakstu krājums.*, Vol. II, (1932).

[259] Tentelis, Augusts (1932): "Latviešu brīvības tieksmes", pp. 107–125.

in 1932, he expanded on why Latvians had hitherto participated so little in the writing of their history. The main reason, he concluded, was that the historical archives were still in the hands of 'foreigners' – *sveštautieši* – i.e., the Baltic Germans. These people, he maintained, undoubtedly worked diligently but followed their own interests, documenting only their own history in the Baltic provinces. With *Latvijas Universitāte*, Tentelis concluded, a new era of Latvian history could begin. Krodznieks, he claimed, had laid a foundation for others to follow.[260] While the audience no doubt appreciated this reference to the 'national hero' Krodznieks, it has to be added that there are no indications that Tentelis had actually supported or promoted Krodznieks in the faculty during the latter's lifetime.

Apart from Tentelis, Arbusow and Krodznieks, there was a decided lack of properly qualified teaching staff in history. Faculty records from the formative years at *Latvijas Universitātes* show that the other Latvian historians appointed were mere candidates on annual contracts: Frīdis Zālītis lectured on modern Latvian history and Pēteris Dreimanis, for just one term, on historical method.[261] They had both studied history at Dorpat/Jur'ev, and worked as highschool teachers in Riga. They also wrote history textbooks for Latvian schools. However, neither of them became a permanent member of staff.[262] Zālītis's announcement in 1923 that he would not apply for an extension caused some worry in the faculty. Felsbergs in particular found this deplorable, since, he averred, Zālītis was the only Latvian who could teach Latvian history.[263]

Frīdis Zālītis was replaced in 1923 by Jānis Bērziņš, yet another Latvian historian with comparatively modest scholarly merits.[264] Bērziņš had studied history at Dorpat/Jur'ev and passed the *kandidat* examination in 1911. He had intended to specialise in Russian history, but World War I impeded his scholarly development. In Riga he lectured mainly on historical methodology and Latvian and Lithuanian history and was appointed *privātdocents* in 1929 but his scholarly imprint on the discipline sems to have been faint.[265] Previously a

---
[260] Krūze (2009), p. 112. I will return to the matter of Baltic German control of archives in a later chapter. What Tentelis referred to was probably the archives of the *Gesellschaft für Geschichte und Altertumskunde*.
[261] LVVA. Latvijas Universitātes fonds, 7427/6/37a. Pārskats par Latvijas augstskolas, vēlāk Universitātes, nodibināšanu un viņas darbību. 1921/06/16. Overview of the Faculty of Philology and Philosophy, spring term 1921. 7427/13/1959; 7427/13/395. Staff records. Dreimanis lectured only during the spring of 1921.
[262] LVVA. Latvijas Universitātes fonds, 7427/13/1959; 7427/13/395. Staff records.
[263] LVVA. Latvijas Universitātes fonds, 7427/6/363, Minutes of the Faculty of Philology and Philosophy, 1923/05/19. This may also have been a covert criticism of Tentelis, who in 1923 had not yet shown any inclination to develop into a more 'national' historian.
[264] LVVA. Latvijas Universitātes fonds, 7427/6/363, Minutes of the Faculty of Philology and Philosophy, 1923/11/17.
[265] Bērziņš became *privātdocents* after submitting a handwritten manuscript on the Imperial authorities' attempts to introduce the Cyrillic alphabet when writing in Latvian and Lithuanian. See LVVA. Latvijas Universitātes fonds, 7427/13/174. Staff records. Assessment

librarian at Dorpat/Jur'ev, Voronezh and *Latvijas Universitāte*, his main occupation after 1925 seems to have been as Director of the State Archive. Bērziņš was clearly not counted among the 'younger' generation of promising Latvian scholars; he was never awarded a scholarship enabling him to further an academic career.[266]

With Tentelis primarily occupied with administrative duties, at least by 1924, and with the death of Krodznieks in the same year, the lack of properly trained Latvian historians persisted in the 1920s. No representatives of a 'younger' generation had yet emerged who could develop the discipline in a national direction. At the same time there seems to have been a reluctance to recruit any of the Baltic German historians connected with the learned societies.

The greatest need was for a professor of modern history. Arbusow and Tentelis were both essentially medievalists, even though the former had also written a major work on the Reformation. Neither of them was really competent – or inclined – to lecture on more modern times. Filling this need proved exceedingly difficult. Since no Latvian modern historian could be found, Tentelis tried to secure the appointment of Erwin Grimm, a former colleague and his professor at St Petersburg who at that point held a post at Sofia University in Bulgaria. When Tentelis proposed Grimm, however, art historian Ernsts Felsbergs strongly objected to Grimm's political views, claiming that he was a proponent of a 'Greater Russia' programme that did not include the conception of a free Latvia.[267]

The need for a professor in modern history was repeatedly discussed at faculty meetings, but little progress was made.[268] Felsbergs argued several times for the recruitment of a French academic, but Tentelis was clearly against this: according to him, only a quarter of the students would be able to follow lectures in French.[269] The alternative 'national' option, to rely on the preparation of some of the gifted Latvian students of history, was not considered realistic as it would take too long.

---

by Tentelis. Later, Bērziņš was hardly a prolific or innovative writer but produced some articles on Latvian and Lithuanian issues. See, for instance, Bērziņš, Jānis (1937a): "Livonija un Lietuva 16. gadsimteņa sešdesmitajos gados", pp. 127–144; Bērziņš, Jānis (1937b): "Kurzemes hercogiste XVI. un XVII. gs.", pp. 158–168.

[266] *Latvijas Universitāte divdesmit gados 1919–1939* (1939), I, pp. 197; 216–217; 292; II, pp. 92–93.

[267] LVVA. Latvijas Universitātes fonds, 7427/6/363, Minutes of the Faculty of Philology and Philosophy, 1922/09/02. Grimm had been principal of St Petersburg University between 1911 and 1918.

[268] LVVA. Latvijas Universitātes fonds, 7427/6/363, Minutes of the Faculty of Philology and Philosophy, 1922/09/08; 1922/09/16; 1922/10/21.

[269] LVVA. Latvijas Universitātes fonds, 7427/6/363, Minutes of the Faculty of Philology and Philosophy, 1922/10/21; 1923/01/08.

Endzelīns argued that a prominent foreign historian would have to be recruited as a temporary measure, allowing some of the promising Latvian students to develop. Juris Plāķis was clearly against this, claiming that the teaching of modern history was much too important to be entrusted to foreigners as they would not adhere to Latvia's interests. He claimed that the faculty's medievalists should also be able to teach modern history. Arbusow and Tentelis – the medievalists in question – reacted strongly against this, maintaining that modern history could only be taught by a specialist. At Tentelis's suggestion, the faculty finally voted to elect Erwin Grimm, who received a narrow majority.[270] However, this election was overturned in the university council.[271]

Faced with this situation, Felsbergs, who as principal had argued in the university council against Grimm's election and was therefore to some extent responsible, reiterated Plāķis's suggestion that the faculty's medieval historians ought to be able to teach courses in modern history. He found it completely unreasonable that both history professors were specialists in the medieval period. Tentelis, he suggested, was 'not so deeply buried in medieval times' and should be able to lecture on the French Revolution. Tentelis, who probably quite rightly perceived this as a slighting reference to his practically non-existent scholarly output, retorted angrily: if he could lecture on the French Revolution, so could Felsbergs. The latter replied that as an art historian specialising in ancient Greece, and the only professor of art history in the faculty, this was hardly reasonable.

Despite the pressure from the principal, Felsbergs, Tentelis was clearly not willing to alter course and specialise in modern history or Latvian issues. Unlike the archaeologist Francis Balodis and the folklorist Pēteris Šmits mentioned earlier, Tentelis seems to have lacked the energy and commitment to radically change his field of study and develop an expertise in a new but, from a national perspective, vital area of the historical discipline.

The faculty members, however, generally supported a professional perspective on this issue rather than a narrow national line. Apart from backing by the nationally inclined Juris Plāķis, Felsbergs does not appear to have received much support for his position on this matter. Pēteris Šmits, doubting the scholarly quality of teaching by one of the medievalists, advocated the recruitment of a true specialist in modern history. Philosopher Pēteris Zālīte reminded the faculty that Felsbergs had on three occasions blocked the appointment of a professor in modern history, and remarked with some irony that this made it hard to envisage

---

[270] LVVA. Latvijas Universitātes fonds, 7427/6/363, Minutes of the Faculty of Philology and Philosophy, 1922/11/04.
[271] LVVA. Latvijas Universitātes fonds, 7427/6/2. University Council Minutes, 1922/12/06. Endzelīns's proposal to elect Grimm for a period of three years was decisively rejected: 10 in favour, 17 against, 2 abstaining.

Felsbergs's ideal professor of modern history. Felsbergs retorted that as principal he had always looked to the university's best interest and had never been hostile to foreign academics just because they were foreigners.[272] Here Felsbergs apparently differed from linguist Juris Plāķis, who clearly had no such qualms.

The discussion ended in stalemate. While there appears to have been solid backing in the faculty for the recruitment of a foreign specialist in modern history, the opposition from the principal, Felsbergs, and the vice-principal, Plāķis, to the appointment of Russian or German academics seems to have precluded all such elections in the university council. Not until 1924, under a new university leadership, was the situation eventually resolved. The ethnic Russian professor Roberts Vipers/Robert Wipper was finally appointed professor of modern history at *Latvijas Universitāte*. Vipers, then sixty-five years of age, was a very experienced historian, having been professor at the Odessa and Moscow universities for thirty years. He was primarily an expert on the Reformation in early modern Europe.[273]

Vipers's appointment was nevertheless contested. The faculty board's discussion shows that opinions differed markedly on the practicality of appointing an ethnic Russian historian who was unfamiliar with the Latvian language. The recruitment of Vipers had actually been discussed in 1922, but on that occasion Augusts Tentelis had consistently favoured Erwin Grimm, his professor from St Petersburg. Tentelis was still sceptical about the Viper's recruitment, maintaining that it was not appropriate for the University of Latvia to become what he termed "a sanctuary for foreign professors". Ernsts Felsbergs, the former principal, agreed with Tentelis and reiterated his own position that courses in modern history should preferably be taught by a Latvian academic. Not surprisingly, linguist Juris Plāķis concurred, expressing concern that Vipers would be unsuitable for teaching since he did not know any Latvian and the students' command of Russian was deteriorating.

Against this, Vipers's supporters on the faculty board, especially Romanist Arnolds Spekke, stressed his impressive academic credentials. Spekke also maintained that Vipers's profile would fit the needs of the history department. Archaeologist Francis Balodis added that Vipers was an eminent educator, and only desired to be able to work in a free scholarly setting. Balodis and the classicist Kārlis Straubergs also emphasised Vipers's precarious position and unpopularity with the Bolshevik regime. Linguist Jānis Endzelīns, who

---

[272] LVVA. Latvijas Universitātes fonds, 7427/6/363, Minutes of the Faculty of Philology and Philosophy, 1922/12/16. Only linguist Juris Plāķis supported Felsbergs on this matter, remarking that Grimm's majority in the faculty was small. He also found it reasonable that academics sometimes had to lecture on matters outside their field of expertise; he claimed this was common at Russian universities. He therefore saw no need to appoint foreign specialists.
[273] LVVA. Latvijas Universitātes fonds, 7427/13/1922. Staff records.

7. DEVELOPING 'NATIONAL DISCIPLINES'

previously as dean and also as a member in the organization committee had frequently pressed for the recognition of academic merit and the need for a foreign specialist in modern history, specifically asked Tentelis and Arbusow, as scholarly historians, for their opinions of Vipers. Tentelis, probably grudgingly, concurred that Vipers was good pedagogue. Arbusow supported the idea that Vipers should be appointed for a limited period.

That seems to have been the compromise which most of the faculty members could accept. A clear majority decided to appoint Vipers, but for one year only – an unusually short period for a foreign professor.[274] The vote for Vipers in the university council was equally positive, and should probably be seen as a clear acknowledgement of his substantial academic qualities. However, the fact that the initial appointment was for one year only surely signalled some caution. Normally, 'foreign' professors were elected for five years. However, Vipers's contract was extended several times, which indicates that the faculty valued his services.[275]

Indeed, Vipers appears to have adapted extremely well to the Latvian context, in spite of belonging to a non-Latvian *tautība*. Although at first sight hardly equipped to explore the past in more Latvian 'national' terms, Vipers actually played a very important part in this development. In 1927, as shown previously, the Latvian diplomat and historian Juris Vīgrabs published an important annotated source collection on Latvian serfdom and the legal prerogatives of German landlords in the eighteenth century.[276] His interpretation of some central documents differed materially from that of Baltic German historians, and Vīgrabs was attacked by Arbusow and Hermann Bruiningk, another Baltic German historian and archivist.

In Latvian historiography, this incident is known as the 'Rozen dispute' after the name of the Baltic German *Landrat* that produced one of the key documents.[277] Evidently, this scholarly dispute was heavily steeped in national sentiments and conflicts, and had obvious connections with these two *tautības'* sensitive relations in contemporary Latvia. Vipers joined the dispute on

---

[274] LVVA. Latvijas Universitātes fonds, 7427/6/363, Minutes of the Faculty of Philology and Philosophy Board, 1924/09/06. The final decision was almost unanimous: 13 'ayes' and 2 blanks. Heinrihs Strods maintains in his contribution to the 1994 history of the University of Latvia that Vipers was elected in spite of Tentelis's protests. This is perhaps something of a simplification. The main opponents to Vipers's appointment, it seems, were still Felsbergs and Plāķis. See Strods, Heinrihs (1994): *Latvijas Universitāte (1919–1940)*, p. 53.
[275] LVVA. Latvijas Universitātes fonds, 7427/13/1922. Staff records. The vote in favour of Vipers was 28 votes for, 1 against, 2 abstaining.
[276] Vīgrabs, Juris (1927): "Vidzemes zemnieku tiesiskais stāvoklis XVIII gadusimteņa pirmajā pusē. I daļa", pp. 1–270. A second part was published a few years later: Vīgrabs, Juris (1930): "Vidzemes zemnieku tiesiskais stāvoklis XVIII gadusimteņa pirmajā pusē. II daļa", pp. 1–245.
[277] Zeids, Teodors (1992): *Senākie rakstītie Latvijas vēstures avoti līdz 1800. gadam*, pp. 189–191.

Vīgrabs's side, criticizing Arbusow for his 'German' and 'apologetic' interpretation of the documents.[278]

Indeed, Vipers's obvious popularity among his colleagues in the faculty, manifested later, was probably due as much to his siding with the 'Latvians' on historical issues as to his undoubted academic qualities. A sign of this appreciation is that he was almost the only 'foreigner' who participated in the nationally inspired two-volume anthology *Latvieši* in 1930–1932; contributing articles on early modern Latvian history.[279] When the faculty in 1934 again requested that the university council renew Vipers's appointment, it was argued that he had been of material assistance not only to the development of Latvian scholarship, but also to the entire Latvian nation in spite of the attacks he had allegedly suffered from "some German historians". For this, the request continued, every Latvian scholar should be grateful. It was also pointed out that by then, Vipers had acquired the ability to lecture in Latvian.[280] Somewhat paradoxically, therefore, it seems that the historian who most strenuously supported a 'national turn' in the discipline during the 1920s and early 1930s was an ethnic Russian academic – Roberts Vipers.

Vipers was obviously much appreciated and retained because he supported and developed the emerging Latvian master narrative of history – but it was also a matter of the time required to form a new generation of academic historians. Although well over retirement age, Vipers had his appointment repeatedly extended because no younger Latvian historian was yet ready to replace him. Juris Vīgrabs, seen for a time as a possible prospect, found employment in the Foreign Office.[281] Indeed, in the 1920s and early 1930s there was a perceptible lack of younger historians. One of the few to aim for a doctorate, Gustavs Lukstiņš, somewhat ironically chose to specialise in ancient Roman history, not

---

[278] Vipers, Roberts (1927): "Piezīme prof. L. Arbuzova rakstam".

[279] Vipers, Roberts (1930): "No XV līdz XVIII g. simtenim". In this article Vipers commends the Latvian people for their "extraordinary endurance" during the previous period of Baltic German oppression. Ibid., p. 139. See also Vipers, Roberts (1932): "Vidzemes apgaismotāji XVIII. gadsimtenī", pp. 26–47. Apart from Vipers, the only other foreign contributor to *Latvieši* was the Swedish art historian Tor Helge Kjellin. See Kjellins, T H (1932): "Latviešu māksla", pp. 465–511.

[280] LVVA. Latvijas Universitātes fonds, 7427/13/1922. Staff records. Request from the faculty to the University Council, 1934/05/05. According to his pupil Stepermanis, Vipers already lectured entirely in Latvian in the autumn of 1931. Stepermanis, Marģers (1939b): "Prof. Dr. hist. Roberts Vipers dzīvē un darbos", p. 24.

[281] Vīgrabs was born in 1881, and studied theology at Dorpat/Jur'ev University before World War I, eventually becoming a German teacher. He later studied history at Leipzig and Dorpat/Jur'ev. Returning from the Soviet Union to Riga in 1922, he primarily worked as a journalist and writer before starting a career at the Foreign Office in 1927. He was therefore not really on the academic track at *Latvijas Universitāte*. LVVA. Latvijas vēstures institūta fonds, 1865/1/46. LVI darbinieki. Raksturojumi un biogrāfijas, 1936.

on the more pressing modern and Latvian issues.[282] The main prospect in modern history was undoubtedly Vipers's pupil Marģers Stepermanis, but he was abroad on a scholarship between 1931 and 1934, and appointed *privātdocents* only in 1936.[283] Compared to the situation for linguistics and archaeology, it took considerably longer for the discipline of history to form a new generation of scholars.

In conclusion, history does not seem to have had a prominent role among the 'national' academic disciplines, at least not in the first decade. The main reason seems to have been the lack of established, academically experienced Latvian historians. The most prominent historian at the new university was in ethnic terms a Baltic German, Arbusow, which is strange since the recruitment of Baltic German academics generally met with considerable resistance. At the same time, there were repeated 'national' demands for a historical master narrative that was purely Latvian, uninfluenced by Baltic German notions and perspectives. What was perceived as the Baltic German interpretation of history, personified by Arbusow, was therefore increasingly questioned.[284] This became more apparent towards the end of the 1920s, when the other 'national' academic disciplines, ethnography, folklore and archaeology, gained considerable momentum under the leadership of Pēteris Šmits and Francis Balodis.

As regards history, however, in the first decade there seems to have been little momentum and initiative to contribute to the national agenda. The main ethnic Latvian historian, Augusts Tentelis, clearly lacked the ability to codify a new national history; furthermore, he was soon primarily occupied with administrative duties and political office. In generational terms, ties with the 'older' group of national intellectuals were rather feeble. The only historian in this generation was Jānis Krodznieks; as we have seen, for several reasons his influence was rather limited. Tentelis belonged to a 'younger' generation and, not really a writing scholar, appears to have been less able to form a group of younger, committed Latvian historians than, for instance, his faculty colleague Francis Balodis in archaeology.

---

[282] Lukstiņs received some of his scholarly training in Göttingen, Germany, and completed his doctoral examinations in 1935. See *Latvijas Universitāte divdesmit gados 1919–1939* (1939), Vol. II, pp. 94–95; Lukstiņš, Gustavs (1936): "Rōmula un Rema problēma un tās atrisinājuma mēģinājumi", pp. 19–30.

[283] LVVA. Latvijas Universitātes fonds, 7427/6/363, Minutes of the Faculty of Philology and Philosophy, 1936/01/29.

[284] A further indication of conflict on 'national' interpretations of history is that no German academics were given honorary doctorates in history at the University of Latvia during the First Republic even though the list includes four Swedes, one Pole, one Hungarian, one Estonian and one Dutchman. See *Latvijas Universitāte divdesmit gados 1919–1939* (1939), I, pp. 17–18.

History had not previously been a strong discipline among Latvian academics educated in the Imperial university system. Indeed, a brief glance at the historians of the 1920s and early 1930s reveals that several of them were primarily trained as linguists, not historians. Philology had been by far the most prestigious discipline in the humanities in the early twentieth century. In the 1920s, both Augusts Tentelis and Arnolds Spekke were primarily philologists and historians of literature. Spekke, for instance, started his career at *Latvijas Universitāte* as a lecturer in Italian renaissance literature.[285] Notwithstanding some initial doubts about the weight of his scholarly merits, he was appointed professor in Romanist philology in 1922. He gradually moved towards history but wrote very little on such issues before 1930.[286] It certainly took some time to turn philologists like Spekke, and to some extent even Tentelis, into proper historians.[287]

Perhaps somewhat ironically, the main promoter and codifier of a Latvian perspective of history, and inspirer of a new generation of historians, was the ethnic Russian professor Roberts Vipers. In the 1920s there was no up-and-coming 'younger', nationally committed generation of Latvian historians. The main representative of this 'younger' generation, and the eventual prime codifier of Latvian history, made his academic career outside the Faculty of Philology and Philosophy. Arveds Švābe, and his pupil Edgars Dunsdorfs, were originally legal historians in the Faculty of Law and Economics. Not until 1936 was Švābe appointed professor of Latvian history, whereupon he developed this discipline's national perspective.[288]

---

[285] LVVA. Latvijas Universitātes fonds, 7427/6/37a. Pārskats par Latvijas augstskolas, vēlāk Universitātes, nodibināšanu un viņas darbību. Overview of the Faculty of Language and Philosophy, 1919-1920. Spekke, the son of a schoolteacher, was a student at the Riga Polytechnical Institute. According to his autobiography, he was expelled for attending a forbidden political meeting at the institute. He later received training in classical philology in Moscow. He was actually appointed professor in Romanist philology at the University of Latvia in 1922 before turning to history. *Latvijas Universitāte 1919-1929* (1929), pp. 181-182; Spekke (2000), pp. 45-46.

[286] See *Latvijas Universitātes Filoloģijas un filosofijas fakultātes Bibliografisks pārskats, 1919-1925* (1925), and *Latvijas Universitātes Filoloģijas un filosofijas fakultātes Bibliografisks pārskats, II, 1925-1930* (1930). For his first appointment in 1920 Spekke was clearly less competent than some of the 'foreign' candidates. This was openly admitted even by the 'nationally-minded' vice-principal, Paulis Lejiņš. LVVA. Izglītības ministrijas fonds, 1632/2/632. Sarakste ar Latvijas Augstskolu par mācības spēku ievēlēšanu. Letter from P. Lejiņš to the Ministry of Education, 1920.07.01; P. Lejiņš, "Personīgā leetā". Spekke's bibliograhy can be found in Spekke (2000), pp. 287-296. In 1933, when Spekke was appointed Latvia's ambassador in Rome, his teaching at the university virtually ceased. See *Latvijas Universitāte divdesmit gados 1919-1939* (1939), II, p. 72.

[287] In his autobiography, Spekke claims that this 'need to resaddle' was due to the problem that the Latvian history taught by – primarily – Arbusow was far too much influenced by the historical concepts of 'foreign people'. Spekke (2000), p. 88.

[288] On Švābe's importance for the development of a national narrative in history, see below, chapter 8.

Another indication of the relative initial inertia in the discipline of history is the absence of a major academic historical journal. The only proper journal was issued by the State Historical Archive, merging archival and nationalist issues but lacking academic weight. The historians at the university were apparently unable to produce a journal with a common scholarly agenda. As we shall see in a later chapter, this changed in the mid-1930s, when history emerged as the most forceful of the 'national' academic disciplines under the special protection of the authoritarian leader Kārlis Ulmanis. Summing up the findings in this section, it seems clear that at least during the first decade there was, for various reasons, a conspicuous lack of Latvian historians involved in the task of rewriting the nation's past.

A brief glance at the corresponding situation at the Estonian Tartu University indicates some differences in the conflict there between Baltic German and Latvian scholarship and interpretations of the past. As in the Latvian case, history writing had played a minor role in the Estonian national movement, which was more preoccupied with culture, mythology and language issues.[289] Lacking obvious Estonian candidates, the academic recruited as professor in Estonian and Scandinavian history at Tartu was a Finn from Helsinki, Arno Rafael Cederberg, who became a diligent scholar of the Estonian people's past. Cederberg belonged to the 'Finnish' side in the academic conflict between ethnic Swedes and Finns that had characterised history writing in Finland in the late Imperial era.[290]

However, Cederberg hardly committed himself to producing a radical 'national turn' in Estonian history writing; he rather appears to have stressed the need for scholarly 'objectivity' to temper nationalist feelings. Also, in contrast to their colleagues in Riga, the historians at Tartu University soon established a common Historical Society, staging public lectures and publishing an academic historical journal, *Ajalooline Ajakiri*.[291]

Other Finnish academics also considerably influenced the development of 'national' disciplines at Tartu. Aarne Michaël Tallgren was appointed

---

[289] Raun, Toivo U (2003): "Nineteenth and early twentieth-century Estonian nationalism revisited", p. 140.
[290] The conflict between a 'Finnish' and a 'Swedish' conception of history split the historians into two camps, each producing its own scholarly journal. The controversy continued after Finland's independence, reinforced by the creation of a separate Swedish-speaking university in Åbo/Turku. See Engman, Max (1994): "National Conceptions of History in Finland", pp. 55–57.
[291] Kivimäe, Sirjie & Kivimäe Jüri (1987): "Estnische Geschichtsforschung an der Universität Tartu 1920–1940. Ziele und Ergebnisse", pp. 280–292. On Cederberg's ability to mediate between Estonian and Baltic German historians at Tartu, see also von zur Mühlen, Heinz (1987): "Kontinuität und neue Anstösse der deutschbaltischen Geschichtsforschung in Estland nach dem ersten Weltkrieg", p. 295.

professor of archaeology, and Ilmari Manninen of ethnology.[292] Here, it should be noted that in the late nineteenth century Estonian nationalist intellectuals already saw Finland as a 'blueprint' for their national development, with special attention to the transformation of vernacular Finnish into an academic language at Helsinki University.[293] Finland had no doubt served as a positive external 'Other' for the Estonian national movement, a relationship that continued in the 1920s and 1930s.[294]

The presence of Finnish academics may possibly have modified Estonian attitudes to academics belonging to the 'negative internal Others', the Baltic Germans. Tartu historians appear to have been more inclusionary than their colleagues at the University of Latvia. Several of the Baltic German historians, for instance Georg von Rauch, Arved Taube, and Helmut Speer, presented their *Magister* theses at Tartu and an academic institution there, *Institut für wissenschaftliche Heimatsforschung*, became the scholarly base for Baltic German historians. It is also noteworthy that the Baltic German professor Walter Anderson was the main academic in Estonian folklore throughout the First Republic.[295]

However, Tartu University undoubtedly also had some nationalist priorities when it came to promotion and scholarship. Awarding research scholarships to promising Estonian students was clearly a university policy early on, thereby promoting a coming generation of trained academic staff. The prominent Estonian historians of the 1930s, Peeter Tarvel and Hans Kruus, both received this kind of material support.[296] This selection principle certainly paid off: all those who were awarded doctoral degrees in history in the interwar period were ethnic Estonians.[297]

Finally, Estonian history writing was more open to different national interpretations of history, instead of being tied to a single master narrative. Hans Kruus especially produced a more left-wing version of Estonian national history, emphasising the role of societal factors and openly criticising some prominent figures in the national movement.[298] Kruus had no real counterpart among Latvian historians.

---

[292] Janužytė, Audronė (2005): *Historians as nation state-builders: The Formation of the Lithuanian University 1904–1922*, p. 275. The Swede Birger Nerman was also professor of archaeology in Tartu for a few years. See Mugurēvičs (1997a), p. 15.
[293] Raun (2003), pp. 139–140.
[294] Petersoo, Pille (2007): "Reconsidering otherness: constructing Estonian identity", p. 126.
[295] *History of Tartu University, 1632–1982* (1985), p. 187.
[296] *History of Tartu University, 1632–1982* (1985), p. 176.
[297] Kivimäe & Kivimäe (1987), p. 292.
[298] Hackmann, Jörg (2010): "Narrating the Building of a Small Nation: Divergence and Convergence in the Historiography of Estonian 'National Awakening', 1868–2005", pp. 175–179.

A comparative view: 'national disciplines' at the Lithuanian university

While folklore and the collection of *dainas* was the prime undertaking for Latvian nationalist intellectuals in the late nineteenth century, history as an academic discipline was by far the most important for Lithuanians. There seem to be several reasons for this. Firstly, Lithuanian nationalist intellectuals could look back to the medieval state structure of the Grand Duchy of Lithuania, arguing that independent statehood needed to be reinstated, not created. Reminiscences of a past, independent Lithuania became a central issue for the emerging group of nationalist intellectuals. As American historian Virgil Krapauskas has put it, "History obsessed the activists of the Lithuanian national rebirth".[299]

Secondly, since Polish and Russian had been the predominant print-languages, and used in administration and the education system, language and ethnography were not seen as reliable hallmarks of 'actual' Lithuanians. History as a means to define a *historic* territory supposedly inhabited by ethnic Lithuanians served better: this would make also Lithuanians out of people who currently spoke Polish or Belarusian dialects. Mapping this supposedly historic Lithuania became an important undertaking among national activists towards the end of the nineteenth century.[300]

Thirdly, formulating a separate interpretation of history became a way of drawing a boundary vis-à-vis the culturally hegemonic Poles. The creation of the Polish-Lithuanian Commonwealth in the fourteenth century, and more specifically the actual meaning of the central treaties of Krewo and Lublin, were a source of fierce conflicts between Lithuanian intellectuals and Polish historians. Being a 'true' Lithuanian in this context meant castigating the 'traitor' Jogaila who sold out the Lithuanians in order to become King of Poland, and commending the 'patriot' Vytautas who remained 'true'. In this way, historical arguments and interpretations were used to draw a boundary between Poles and Lithuanians.[301]

For all these reasons, history became a central issue and endeavour for Lithuanian intellectuals. Therefore, historians and history-writers such as Jonas Yčas, Jouzas Purickis, Augustinas Voldemaras, Jonas Basanavičius, Mykolas Biržiška, Petras Klimas and Jonas Šliūpas played a major role in Lithuanian nation-building and state-building.[302]

---

[299] Krapauskas, Virgil (2000): *Nationalism and Historiography: The Case of Nineteenth-Century Lithuanian Historicism*, p. 9.

[300] Petronis (2007), chapter 5.

[301] This historical controversy continued well into the 1920s, partly due to the hostile relations between Lithuania and Poland after the annexation of the Wilna/Vilnius region. See Janužytė (2005), pp. 286–287. For some contemporary historians, the controversy still exists.

[302] For an analysis of these historians as builders of nation and state, see Janužytė (2005), pp. 43–44; 63–131. However, this does not mean that Lithuanian historians aspired to resurrect

Some of the activists connected with the nationalist periodical *Aušra* were historians out of interest and avocation rather than formal academic training. Both Basanavičius and Šliūpas primarily studied medicine at university, not history.[303] For them, writing Lithuanian history mainly had to do with the aim of raising national consciousness among Lithuanians. Academic concerns, and a critical scrutiny of historical sources, appear to have played a very minor role. They both, for instance, toyed with the rather far-fetched notion of a Lithuanian origin in the Balkans, and a supposed descent from the ancient Thracians and Phrygians.[304]

While national activists and history-writers such as Basanavičius and Šliūpas were certainly important in the creation of a Lithuanian state, several of the more academic historians played prominent roles when the university was eventually established in Kaunas in 1922. Augustinas Voldemaras was a member of the organisation committee, led the planning of what became the Social Faculty of Science, and was also its first dean. With two more professors in that faculty, Yčas and Janulaitis, history was clearly the most prominent 'national' academic discipline in the first, formative years of the Lithuanian university, Kaunas.[305] Still, the discipline of history was not entirely reserved for ethnic Lithuanians. Three Russians were appointed professors in the interwar period: Pavel Gronskij, Lev Karsavin and Ivan Lappo. They functioned primarily in the field of general history, where their Lithuanian colleagues seem to have been less qualified. However, they were all required to lecture in Lithuanian within two or three years, a demand that only Karsavin managed to meet.[306]

Conspicuous by their absence are historians associated with the *krajowcy* group. Generally speaking, this group consisted primarily of Polish-speaking intellectuals in the Vilnius region who had tried to resist the demarcation of Poles and Lithuanians along ethnic lines, promoting instead an identity based on the historic Commonwealth. The group's most important historians were Konstancya Skirmuntt, Józef Albin Herbaczewski, and Michał Römer.[307] Only Römer played any part at the new university in Kaunas.

---

the previous Grand Duchy, where most the subjects had been Slavs. Voldemaras, for instance, wrote about a future state based on an *ethnic* Lithuania – but who qualified as ethnic Lithuanians certainly remains debatable. See ibid., pp. 94–95.
[303] Krapauskas (2000), p. 108. They took only undergraduate courses in history. Janužytė unfortunately does not make any distinctions concerning the academic training of Lithuanian historians at the new university in Kaunas.
[304] Krapauskas (2000), pp. 118–131.
[305] Janužytė (2005), pp. 232–234. She also includes Eduardas Volteris among the historians, but this is hardly reasonable. Originally a linguist, Volteris turned eventually towards ethnography and archaeology. It is something of a problem that Janužytė does not really discuss any criteria for those she includes in the group of historians.
[306] Janužytė (2005), pp. 273–277.
[307] Krapauskas (2000), pp. 38–40. The case of Konstancya Skirmuntt seems especially interesting. Writing in Polish, she nevertheless promoted a 'Lithuanian' perspective on history.

While history seems to have been predominant among the 'national' disciplines, the role of archaeology at the Lithuanian university in Kaunas appears to have been very modest. This may be somewhat surprising, since as early as 1884 Jonas Basanavičius pointed to the importance of the ancient castle mounds as vital links with the perceived heroic national past.[308] The first Lithuanian to receive a doctorate in archaeology, Jonas Puzinas, did so as late as 1934. Before that, courses in archaeology were taught by the versatile and multi-talented Eduardas Volteris, who also lectured in folklore studies and the Latvian language and literature.[309]

Volteris belonged to the 'older' generation of Imperial academics, being sixty-six years old when the university opened in 1922. He was part of the Constituent Commission in the Humanities, headed by Voldemaras and set up to organise courses and the recruitment of academic staff.[310] Volteris is actually an interesting example of an academic who did not fit neatly into any of the ethnic categories in the region. Born in Riga as Eduard Wolter, he grew up under Baltic German and Russian cultural influences. He later studied at the Leipzig, Dorpat, St Petersburg and Kharkov universities, becoming a linguist specialising in Slavic and Baltic languages. During the 1880s he did ethnographical research on Latvians and Lithuanians on behalf of the Imperial Russian Geographical Society, under the Russified name Vol'ter. Among Latvians he is known as Volters. He later assumed a Lithuanian identity as Eduardas Volteris, devoting his time to the study of Lithuanian ethnography, folklore, and archaeology.[311] He was pivotal in obtaining government funds for securing the remains of Trakai Castle, a prestigious reconstruction project in Soviet times and a powerful national symbol.[312]

Volteris was at the same time an important advocate of promoting Latvian academia. In Imperial times he used his academic position to support the work of the Latvian linguists Mīlenbahs, Endzelīns and Šmits.[313] In his ethnographic

---

[308] Rindzevičiūtė, Eglė (2010): "Imagining the Grand Duchy of Lithuania: The Politics and Economics of Rebuilding of Trakai Castle and the 'Palace of Sovereigns' in Vilnius", pp. 182, 184.
[309] Janužytė, pp. 258; 272; 361 Appendix D. Jonas Puzinas received his doctorate in Heidelberg on the thesis *Vorgeschichtsforschung und Nationalbewusstsein in Litauen*.
[310] Janužytė (2005), p. 220.
[311] Petronis (2007), pp. 159–160. His collection of Lithuanian folksongs during the IRGS expedition of 1882–87 was, however, somewhat problematical. Many Catholic priests refused to cooperate with him, and Lithuanian peasants were often reluctant to communicate with him since he was accompanied by Russian gendarmes. See also Krapauskas (2000), p. 37.
[312] Rindzevičiūtė (2010), pp. 184–192. During the interwar period Trakai Castle could not become an object of Lithuanian national archaeology, since it was situated in the region occupied by the Poles in 1920. At the same time, Trakai's symbolic weight in the nationalist Lithuanian vision made it difficult to attach any major interest to 'lesser' castle mounds situated on state territory.
[313] Kļaviņa (2008), pp. 153–163.

investigations he also piloted the conception that speakers of Latvian dialects outside the Baltic provinces were part of a common Latvian nation.[314] He therefore provided some scholarly support for the notion that the predominantly Catholic Latgallians belonged to the Latvian nation rather than the Lithuanian.

However, as Volteris's position at the new university in Kaunas might indicate, folklore and ethnography seem to have played a comparatively minor role among Lithuanian national activists. Moreover, no major 'folk-epic' supposedly based on ancient tradition, like the Finnish *Kalevala*, the Estonian *Kalevipoeg* or the Latvian *Lāčplēsis,* ever appeared in Lithuanian. Possibly, an interest in pagan culture and mythology was relatively difficult to reconcile with a strong Catholic identity. The interest in Lithuanian folklore appears to have been stronger among secular nationalists such as Jonas Šliūpas.[315] History, especially research on the previous state structure of the Grand Duchy of Lithuania, remained the prime national academic discipline.

Conclusions

One of the most vital 'national' aims of the new *Latvijas Universitāte* was to provide research on and codification of matters concerning the Latvian language, culture, and history. These subjects, previously developed by Latvian intellectuals outside established academic institutions, would now be given a firm academic footing. Professorial chairs, as well as scholarly journals and monographs from the Faculty of Philology and Philosophy, aimed to place the new Latvian state on the cultural map of Europe.

At the same time, most of the ethnic Latvian humanists who had been trained in the Imperial Russian university system had specialised in disciplines that had been prestigious in that setting but less relevant for more national issues. Most of them were philologists or classicists. In some of the academic disciplines and specialities that had priority in the new national *augstskola* it therefore proved very difficult to find adequately trained Latvian scholars. This was especially the case in history and archaeology, but also in philosophy and German linguistics. Recruitment in these cases often occasioned protracted conflicts within the faculty, the organisation committee and the university council. The questions were: should the new university give priority to the recruitment of prominent foreign academics in certain fields; to what extent should scholars from the ethnic minorities be appointed; or should the university primarily select ethnic Latvian academics with 'satisfactory' qualifications? Yet another option,

---

[314] Vanaga, Lilita (2009): "Eduards Volters (1856–1941) Latvijas etnoloģijas kopainā 19 gs. 80.–90. gados", pp. 41–47.
[315] Krapauskas (2000), pp. 129–139.

requiring a longer time perspective, was to send promising young Latvian students abroad for further training.

In the Faculty of Philology and Philosophy, these matters were frequently debated in the formative first five years. The first dean, linguist Jānis Endzelīns, often advocated the election of prominent foreign academics, giving academic merit priority over ethnicity. This policy seems to have been supported by a solid majority in the faculty, most clearly by folklorist and linguist Pēteris Šmits, his successor as dean, philosopher Pēteris Zālīte, classicist Kārlis Straubergs, linguist Ernests Blese, and Romanist Arnolds Spekke. There was, however, a minority within the faculty that consistently advocated more national and ethnic recruitment, giving a clear priority to Latvian academics. This group consisted primarily of classical art historian Ernsts Felsbergs, linguist Juris Plāķis, and psychologist Pauls Dāle. While often clearly outvoted in faculty sessions, when it came to the organisation committee these three, in their roles as principal, vice-principal and chairman, were able to block several of the proposed appointments of foreign academics.

Due to the previous experience of Baltic German cultural and political hegemony, there was a decided reluctance in the organisation committee, and also among the faculty's 'national' minority, to appoint German or Baltic German academics. This must be seen as an aspect of the 'ethnic reversal' that characterized Latvian society in the early 1920s. Instead, when foreign scholars were acutely needed, professors from small and supposedly friendly countries were given priority; primarily Austrians, Swiss, Finns and Swedes.

Even so, the Faculty of Philology and Philosophy did appoint several German citizens: philosopher Walter Frost, archaeologist Max Ebert, and Romanist Neubert, although Neubert's appointment was eventually overruled by the Latvian government. Several Baltic Germans were also appointed in the initial years: historian Leonid Arbusow, art historian Philipp Schweinfurth, German linguist Oskar Masing, classical linguist Erich Diehl, and the archaeologist Karl Löwis of Menar. By 1925, however, only Arbusow and Diehl remained as permanent faculty members. The appointments of the other Baltic German scholars were not renewed. Of the academics from Germany proper, only Walter Frost remained permanently at *Latvijas Universitāte*.

The option clearly favoured by the organisation committee, to recruit academics from one of the 'smaller nations', can hardly be described as successful. Unlike the case in neighbouring Estonia, no prominent scholars from these countries made any real imprint on *Latvijas Universitāte*. Some of the recruitments, such as that of the Finn Karl Tiander, clearly backfired. Others who accepted the invitation to Riga were relatively unmerited scholars, for instance, the Swedish ethnologist Dag Trotzig. The most successful outside recruitment seems to have been the Swiss professor of German literature Max Nussberger, but even here there are some reasons for doubting the extent of his academic merits.

During the leadership of deans Endzelīns and Šmits, the faculty largely supported the basic notions of the professionalized academic field, and was clearly more open than the organisation committee to recruitment based primarily on academic merit. Even so, the outcome was that Baltic German and foreign academics were appointed primarily on a temporary basis, pending a new generation of ethnic Latvian academics.

During the First Republic the faculty consistently recruited academic staff solely by appointment. The alternative, open competition, was never used: all recruitments therefore depended on the faculty's initiative. In this way, the faculty remained in almost complete control of the process, and hoped to avoid potentially embarrassing situations when well-qualified applicants from the ethnic minorities competed with less merited ethnic Latvians. More overt clashes between the academic and national agendas could thereby be avoided.

From the mid-1920s, however, elected deans of the Faculty of Philology and Philosophy, Tentelis, Plāķis and Balodis, belonged primarily to the 'national' wing. Most recruitment matters had been solved by then but this is an indication that the 'national turn' was underway.

In terms of academic generations, it seems clear that the 'older' generation of Latvian academics played a relatively minor role in forming the Faculty of Philology and Philosophy. They were relatively few and most of them had relatively modest scholarly credentials. Only Jēkabs Lautenbahs, professor in Latvian literature, had a solid scholarly record but he seems to have taken very little interest in academic leadership. Historian Jānis Krodznieks and linguist Jēkabs Velme, on the other hand, had relatively modest academic credentials, being appointed merely as *privātdocenti*. Krodznieks's main achievements lay outside the faculty, in his work at the State Historical Archive and its journal. Finally, the main symbolic figurehead of the 'older' generation, folklorist Krišjānis Barons, did not participate in faculty matters on account of his age.

The group of academics who developed the faculty most forcefully belonged to the 'middle' generation: above all linguist Jānis Endzelīns, the first dean, ethnographer and linguist Pēteris Šmits, the second dean, and archaeologist Francis Balodis. They played a key role in adapting their respective disciplines to the emerging national agenda while at the same time adhering to academia's established scholarly conventions. This trio also became the faculty's most renowned figures, with wide international networks that, somewhat paradoxically, reinforced their emergent status as national 'heroes'.

The actual movement towards a 'national turn' in the various disciplines seems to have been generated, at least in part, by connections between generations of Latvian academics and their respective fields of expertise. In terms of interconnections between generations, the greatest 'overlap' can be seen in linguistics. Lautenbahs and Velme of the 'older' generation worked together with Endzelīns and Plāķis of the 'middle' group, while Blese, Ķiķauka and Ābele constituted a younger generation of scholars. Here, the 'national' project of codifying and 'purifying' the Latvian language seems to have made an early start, continuing work started by the Riga Latvian Society in the early twentieth century. That project was adopted and expanded by the substantial group of Latvian linguists recruited to *Latvijas Augstskola*. Officially sanctioned new grammars and dictionaries were produced and a new orthography was put into operation, albeit with some opposition from publishers. One remaining 'inconsistency' was the Latgallian language/dialect, which was still used as a separate print language until the mid-1930s.

In the other disciplines, however, there was considerably less 'overlap' between generations. Links with the older academic generation were weak or nonexistent, and established academics of the 'middle' generation had to abandon their previous areas of expertise and focus instead on Latvian issues. This is evident in the cases of Šmits and Balodis. Šmits, an expert in Chinese, and Balodis, an Egyptologist, now felt the need to revert to issues that lay closer to the 'national' priorities.

Balodis assumed the task of developing Latvian archaeology, continuing the work of his German predecessor, Max Ebert. Balodis had previously been firmly established in an Imperial academic context, specialising in the cultures of ancient Egypt and the Western Mongol realms. Returning to Latvia, he swiftly developed archaeology into a 'national' project, focusing on the Baltic cultures of pre-German times. From the mid-1920s onwards, he gathered a circle of young Latvian archaeologists who enthusiastically took part in the work of 'recreating' the ancient culture of proto-Latvian tribes. The main tenure of this work was to show that the 'Latvians' had developed advanced and stable state structures well before the German conquest. This reorientation took time, however, and a clear 'national turn' in this discipline cannot be discerned before the late 1920s.

In a similar manner, the many-talented Sinologist Šmits turned towards Latvian folklore and ethnography, which had great symbolical weight. The scholarly collection and publishing of *dainas*, folktales, and riddles had long had a special appeal to Latvian intellectuals and academics in Russian 'exile'. This had been the main preoccupation of many among the 'older' generation of nationalist intellectuals. Šmits therefore had a considerable tradition to draw on, and a large material of folklore collected earlier. But he did have to radically change his focus of research, and largely abandon his previous fields of scholarship.

In contrast, the discipline of history had no established Latvian academics belonging to the 'older' or 'middle' generations. Augusts Tentelis, the only ethnic Latvian professor of history before 1935, had a very meagre scholarly record compared to Endzelīns, Šmits and Balodis. Partly due to his extensive administrative duties, he never really acquired expertise in Latvian historical issues. In the early 1920s, Tentelis was relatively passive in faculty discussions, and primarily sided with Endzelīns and Šmits rather than the 'national' group around Felsbergs and Plāķis. Indeed, his apparent unwillingness or inability to develop an expertise in modern Latvian history seems to have occasioned several conflicts between him and the 'national' group, especially Felsbergs. Only in the mid-1920s, possibly due to his increased involvement in party politics, did Tentelis emerge as an active promoter of a 'national' conception of history. However, he never developed a national historical narrative. Ironically, the historian who did most of the groundwork in this direction in the faculty was an ethnic Russian, Roberts Vipers. Compared to the other disciplines, the faculty's historians were less able to formulate a coherent national master narrative during the democratic era 1919–1934.

The movement towards a 'national turn' in the various disciplines also depended to a large extent on the established academics' ability to train a new generation of ethnic Latvian scholars. Here we can definitely see some differences. For Balodis and Šmits, who were fairly alone in the 'middle' generation of their respective disciplines, the crucial issue was to create a circle of younger academics to assist them in furthering the national academic project. In Latvian archaeology, Balodis seems to have been quite successful in gathering a young group, primarily Valdis Ģinters, Eduards Šturms and Elvīra and Rauls Šnore, to join him in the exploration of Latvian and Livonian culture before the arrival of the Germans. In folklore and ethnography, however, there was no similar development. The faculty did not produce any group of academically trained folklorists, and ethnography did not even emerge as a subject in the faculty curriculum. This is indeed remarkable, considering the symbolical national importance of the Latvian folklore heritage. One possible reason here is the unwillingness of the main academic figure, Šmits, to support the careers of female academics – in a subject where a great majority of the students were women.

In most of the faculty's other disciplines, a younger generation of scholars emerged in the late 1920s and early 1930s: academics who had received their basic training at *Latvijas Universitāte*. A selective use of scholarships, for example from the Morbergs foundation, gave a new generation of primarily male Latvian academics the chance to merit themselves for doctoral examinations. This 'youngest' generation included Alvils Augstkalns in Latvian linguistics, Elvīra and Raul Šnore in archaeology, and Marģers Stepermanis in history. Augstkalns, for instance, was able to improve his academic skills by visiting colleagues at Leipzig, Königsberg, Munich and Vienna. This generation proved vital for the more consistent implementation of the 'national turn' in the 1930s. Elvīra Šnore became director of the archaeological department of the State Historical Museum in 1933, while Augstkalns became the first director of the Latvian Language Archive when this institution was created in 1936.

The main puzzle regarding the 'national turn' in the humanities at the University of Latvia is why it took so long. Only the national project of codifying and 'purifying' the Latvian language started at once. In archaeology, a 'national turn' can be observed in the late 1920s, whereas this tendency was much more delayed in history. Folklore, on the other hand, certainly adhered to a national agenda but failed to develop its academic position within the faculty. These disciplines therefore display very different trajectories concerning the 'national turn'.

The main explanations for these differences in the progress of the national project can probably be found, first, in the generational shifts and interconnections within the disciplines, second, in the time required for those accustomed to the Tsarist universities to develop academic expertise in new and more 'nationally' oriented fields, third, in the presence of academics supporting competing master narratives, and, fourth and finally, in the established scholars' ability to form a younger generation of academics devoted to the national project. With the partial exception of history, however, it is possible to discern the emergence of a new *Denkstil* or 'epistemic community' within the faculty: a conception of national scholarship was gradually established with the emergence of national narratives in several of the disciplines. The initial conflicts between proponents of the academic and the national agendas had abated by the mid-1920s; after that, academics of the 'national' wing gradually became predominant in faculty matters.

In a comparative perspective, one important difference between *Latvijas Universitāte* and the new Lithuanian university seems to have been that historians played a much more important part in Lithuania, both as organisers of the new university and in the Faculty of Humanities. History had been a vital symbolic field of contention between Lithuanian and Polish nationalist intellectuals in Imperial times, thereby helping to form a generation of Lithuanian scholars devoted to a national interpretation of history. Developments at the Estonian University in Tartu were rather similar to those in Riga, with the important exception that Finnish academics played a very important role in the development of 'national' disciplines at Tartu. The Latvian scholars did not have access to a similar group of external positive 'others'.

CHAPTER 8

The University under Dictatorship
Changes in National Policies and the Academics under the Ulmanis Regime, 1934–1940

The 1920s, the first decade of Latvia as an independent state, is frequently depicted as a period of 'generous' treatment of ethnic minorities. Separate schools for German, Russian, Polish and Jewish pupils were allowed, to some extent even encouraged. Ethnic press and associations continued to exist. In the case of Baltic Germans, however, a considerable number chose to emigrate to the German *Reich*, some of them due to the radical land reforms in the early 1920s.

Many ethnic demarcations continued during the 1920s. One perhaps unforeseen effect of democratization was the persistence of ethnic boundaries in the political sphere. Politics was "ethnified". The two major parties, the Social Democrats and the Farmers' Union, became thoroughly Latvian parties. Several parties developed in the German, Russian, Polish and Jewish communities. On top of this, a strong Catholic party emerged in Latgale, adding a regional and religious dimension to national politics.

Since the Farmers' Union and the Social Democrats found it very difficult to cooperate, the smaller parties could gain considerable political leverage. This, however, also led to rather frequent changes in government. With the oncoming economic depression in the early 1930s, this could easily be depicted as a "weak" and inefficient form of government, moreover a system giving "undue" influence to the relatively small ethnic parties.

Naturally, Latvia should not be seen in isolation.[1] A row of newly established states in Central and Eastern Europe fell under authoritarian rule in the 1920s and 1930s. Czechoslovakia alone among the post-imperial successor states remained reasonably democratic. Poland and Lithuania had already shifted to authoritarian rule in 1926, Estonia in early spring 1934.

After a period of growing political and ethnic tension, Kārlis Ulmanis, leader of the Farmers' Union, abandoned democratic institutions and introduced authoritarian rule in Latvia on 15 May 1934. While the ethnic minorities had previously had some 'cultural autonomy', the new regime signalled a much more

---
[1] Stranga, Aivars (1998a): "Liberālisms, demokrātija un autoritārisms Eiropā un Latvijā (20.–30. gadi)", pp. 48–49; Feldmanis, Inesis (1998): "15. maija Latvija un autoritārie režīmi Austrumeiropā (1926–1940): salīdzinošs raksturojums", pp. 82–91.

severe policy of 'Latvianization' or *latviskošana*.² Latvia was to become more of a proper nation-state, culturally and politically dominated by the majority ethnic group. Ulmanis did not adopt the aggressive slogan "Latvia for the Latvians" sported by the fascist organisation *Pērkonkrusts*: indeed, this organisation was prohibited along with all other political parties or movements. For the minorities this put an end to the 'ethnically' based parties which had possessed considerable political power under the democratic regime. With government administration already firmly in ethnic Latvian hands, the public sphere became decidedly more Latvianized in the Ulmanis era.

This is not the place to go into the intricate details of Ulmanis's *apvērsums* (coup) or its breach of constitutional principles.³ However, some reflection on the historiography of Ulmanis is perhaps required. A conference of historians in Riga in 1997 amply demonstrated that the opinions about Ulmanis as a politician differ greatly.⁴ The contributions ranged from Aivars Stranga's ironic depiction of Ulmanis as a homespun dictator with a very limited understanding of societal economics, who constantly interfered in petty issues like Riga's bus timetables, to Emīls Dēliņs's call for a public collection for a commemorative monument over Ulmanis in Riga.⁵

Opinions about the character of the Ulmanis regime also differ substantially. In his biography of Ulmanis, Edgars Dunsdorfs claims that previous renderings are full of errors, and tend to be either hagiographies or 'satanographies'.⁶ No doubt the Soviet occupation in 1940 and the death of Ulmanis in 1942 as a Soviet prisoner are at the root of this. According to the official Soviet version, Ulmanis was a 'fascist', similar to Hitler and Mussolini, and the brave Soviet army had intervened and 'saved' Latvia from fascism. In contrast, for Latvians in exile, Ulmanis remained by and large a symbol of independent Latvia crushed by the Soviet Union. In addition, there seems to have been a reaction in Latvia after liberation in 1991: since Ulmanis was portrayed as a 'bad' figure in the Soviet version, in *reality* he must have been a 'good' figure. Obviously, the very different portrayals of Ulmanis by Soviet historians and exiled Latvians remain important. Indeed, an evaluation of the Ulmanis era is a difficult undertaking,

---

² Stranga (1998a), pp. 52–56.
³ On the constitutional implications of the coup, see Apsītis, Romāns (1998): "Kārlis Ulmanis un Satversme", pp. 65–79.
⁴ The conference was staged to celebrate the 120th anniversary of Ulmanis's birth. The contributions were published in *Kārlim Ulmanim 120* (1998) Caune, Andris et al. (ed).
⁵ Stranga (1998a), pp.54–57; Dēliņš, Emīls (1998): "Prezidents Kārlis Ulmanis un Latvijas trīsdesmito gadu jaunatne", p. 169.
⁶ Dunsdorfs, Edgars (1992): *Kārļa Ulmaņa dzīve. Ceļinieks, politiķis, diktators, moceklis*, p. 9.

since a great number of myths surrounding him as a person and his achievements still circulate in Latvia.[7]

However, the aim of this chapter is not to present a new assessment of the Ulmanis regime. Instead, the focus will be on Ulmanis's policies of *latviskošana* (Latvianization) that evolved during his authoritarian rule. Under the slogan *tauta un valsts* (nation and state), Ulmanis projected the future of a completely Latvian Latvia. The Latvian state, he argued, had room for only one culture – Latvian culture. The state was seen as a tool for implementing Latvianization. The effects are evident in many areas, but primarily in the press, with the prohibition of most of the 'minority' publications, and in education. In the school sector, 'minority' schools lost their cultural autonomy and were put under the direct rule of the Ministry of Education.

In language matters, an attempt was made to standardize and homogenize the Latvian language, probably with the intention of unifying the traditional provinces of Vidzeme, Kurzeme, Zemgale and Latgale in a more homogeneous Latvia. Of special interest here is Ulmanis's attempt to ban literature written in the Latgallian dialect, for fear that it could develop into a competitor for 'standard' Latvian. Latgallians, for their part, claimed that their language was more 'pure', genuine and less influenced by German than the version of Latvian spoken in other regions.[8]

Some cultural spheres appear to have been less affected than others. In spite of the regime's authoritarian character, Latvian literature and theatre seem to have flourished. Although political parties were banned, writers on the left were still allowed to publish their works. Theatres in provincial towns were frequently taken over by the local Latvian associations, and turned into important arenas for expressions of nationalism.[9]

Other arenas were developed as mainstays of *latviskošana*. Ulmanis took a great interest in educational matters, and throughout his political life promoted Latvian schools as a refiner of the Latvian spirit. After the 1934 coup, he frequently visited school examination ceremonies; these occasions were gradually turned into celebrations of official nationalism.[10]

The links between official, state-promoted nationalism and the educational system were very strong. Quite in accordance with similar tendencies in Europe, children were seen as the nation's embodied future. Forming these children into

---

[7] See *Agora*, nr 6, 2007, an issue devoted to the image of Ulmanis; more specifically Zelče, Vita (2007a): "Ievads. Reiz dzīvoja/reiz bija…", pp. 7–13; Naglinska, Evita (2007): "Mīts par Kārli Ulmani latviešu presē, 1989–2004", pp. 30–93.
[8] Zeps, Valdis J (1995): "Latgalian Literature in Exile", p. 313.
[9] Hausmanis, Viktors (1998): "Literatūra un teātris trīsdesmit gados", pp. 147–153.
[10] For examples, see Timšāns, Sigismunds (1998): "Kārlis Ulmanis un tautas izglītība Latvijā", pp. 127–136; Dēliņš (1998), pp. 164–169

loyal and striving Latvians therefore became a crucial task, following Ulmanis's exhortations on the importance of work, nation and state.

The nation was seen as a harmonious cultural entity whose road to full development depended on the avoidance of internal strife and the guidance of the *vadonis*, the Leader. The connections between the Leader and the people were orchestrated in a number of public rituals. Apart from observing the existing days of national celebration, such as Latvia's Independence Day on 18 November, new ones were invented: Harvest Festivals, Labour Celebrations, celebrating the Leader's 60th birthday, and, naturally, the annual commemoration of the coup, the Celebration of National Unity on 15 May. These festive occasions included public parades, competitions of various kinds, theatrical performances and speeches.[11]

The nation was also expressed in more masculine imagery. Apart from the *vadonis* self-evidently being a man, public celebrations increasingly focused on the nation's perceived male heroes. At the symbolically important inauguration of the Freedom monument in central Riga on 18 November 1936, Ulmanis paid special tribute to the male heroes who, as he put it, had regained the honour of the Latvian people in the War of Independence.[12] In a similar manner, another speaker at this ceremony described the united Latvian state as an expression of a 'masculine will'.[13] In accordance with traditional renderings of the nation, the monument itself was cast in the form of a woman, while the statues forming its base primarily depicted Latvian men defending the nation – the most prominent of them an extremely muscular figure representing the mythical hero Lāčplēsis.[14]

The tradition of Song Festivals was also rearranged to fit the new regime's rituals, though only the festival of 1938 actually took place during the authoritarian regime. It was arranged to celebrate the inauguration of Riga's Victory Square, one of the regime's most prestigious building projects. Naturally, the Song Festival culminated in a speech by Ulmanis.[15] In a similar manner, the 20th anniversary of Latvia's independence in 1938 was turned into a spectacular

---

[11] Zelče, Vita (2007b): "'Bēgšana no brīvības': Kārļa Ulmaņa režīma ideoloģija un rituāli", pp. 329–348.
[12] Ulmanis, Kārlis (1936b): "Tautas brīvība un gods", p. 67. Celebrating the dead heroes of the War of Independence, the monument designed by Kārlis Zāle was built between 1931 and 1936. Its construction was opposed for a long time by the political Left in Riga's city council, which saw it primarily as a symbol of the Latvian military and the political Right. For a contemporary 'official' history, see Smilga, V (1936): "Cīņa ap Brīvības pieminekli. Īss vēsturisks atskats", pp. 136–150.
[13] Lapiņš, Jānis (1936): "Brīvība un vienības valsts", p. 78.
[14] For an excellent analysis of gendered depictions of the nation, see Valenius, Johanna (2004): *Undressing the Maid. Gender, Sexuality and the Body in the Construction of the Finnish Nation*.
[15] Zelče, Vita (2008b): "IX Latviešu dziesmu svētki – Kārļa Ulmaņa Latvijas mūžības zvērests", pp. 106–124.

show, demonstrating the main tenets of the authoritarian regime: national unity, a Latvian Latvia, trust in the Leader.[16]

Special campaigns were also launched, often connected with agricultural, forestry or educational issues: matters close to the regime's basically agrarian outlook. In this way, popular support for the regime and mass participation were promoted by and expressed through such ritualised events. Lacking the brutality and racism of the Hitler regime, Ulmanis's brand of authoritarianism was closer to that of Mussolini, but without the latter's dreams of empire. Ulmanis's rule was characterised by a paternalist household ideology, imagining a future, culturally homogeneous, Latvia, basically an agricultural society guided by the benevolent Leader.

Ulmanis's policy of *latviskošana* and the University of Latvia

How did the Ulmanis coup and the subsequent dramatic change in political circumstances influence academic work and priorities in Latvia? Did the policy of *latviskošana* enhance the 'national turn' in some of the academic disciplines? What characterized relations between the university's academics and the regime?

One obvious consequence of the coup was that the German-speaking Herder Institute came under increased political pressure. Apparently, the Baltic German minority was seen as the prime foe of the Latvianization project, still possessing substantial economic and cultural capital while constituting a mere 3.2 per cent of the total population. Moreover, the relationship between ethnic Latvians and the Baltic German minority had deteriorated markedly after Hitler's *Machtübernahme* in 1933. Latvians on both the political Left and Right increasingly questioned the Baltic Germans' loyalty to the Latvian state.[17]

In 1937 the Minister of Education, historian Augusts Tentelis, complained that a large number of students at the Herder Institute were not Latvian citizens. This, he claimed, was contrary to the Institute's constitution. Trying to avert the attack, the Institute produced enrolment lists showing that only six of the 179 students were in fact German citizens, but the Minister refused to be impressed. Instead, he prohibited the employment of German academics as lecturers at the Herder Institute.[18] Clearly, the objective was to force the institution to close. The new regime did not see any need for 'foreign' higher education in a country that

---

[16] Zelče, Vita (2008c): "Svinēšana. Ieskats Latvijas valsts dibināšanas 10. un 20. gadadienas svētkos", pp. 59–105.
[17] Cerūzis, Raimonds (2004): *Vācu faktors Latvijā (1918–1939). Politiskie un starpnacionālie aspekti,* pp. 144–167.
[18] LVVA. Izglītības ministrijas fonds, 1632/2/705. Sarakste ar Herdera institūtu par mācības spēku ... Letter from the Ministry of Education to the Principal, 1937/07/14, 1937/11/27; List of students, 1937/10/15. Apart from the six Germans, a few Czechs, Finns and Swedes were listed.

was to be made completely Latvian, and it no longer needed to keep up democratic pretences or solicit the political support of minority parties. Moreover, the Institute's academic and financial links with Germany met with disapproval in government circles, and there were fears that incoming German students were spreading Nazi propaganda.[19] The Herder Institute was finally closed in 1939, when all ethnic Germans still in Latvia were evacuated and resettled in Poland on Hitler's order.

Latvijas Universitāte naturally did not come under this kind of pressure. Here, the academic leadership seems to have reacted positively to the Ulmanis coup. The principal, Jūlijs Auškāps, immediately sent greetings to the new leader on behalf of the university council, congratulating him on the creation of a new phase in the 'life of the state'.[20] Both Ulmanis and his subordinate president, Alberts Kviesis, were swiftly awarded honorary academic titles.[21] Naturally, dissident voices would not be heard in this situation. The government's general ban on political activity also had some repercussions at the university. The previously elected Student Council was dissolved, supposedly because some delegates had been elected on a 'political' ticket.[22] The government closed some student societies, especially those on the political Left and some Jewish.[23] Also, a small number of academics, primarily those politically active in the Social Democratic Party or the near-Fascist *Pērkonkrusts* movement, were briefly interred. Most of the university academics, however, probably welcomed the coup, viewing the new authoritarian regime as a dedicated supporter of the university as a national institution of science and scholarship. Still, in order to retain their posts, all academics at the university had to sign a pledge of loyalty to the Ulmanis government.[24]

The principal, Auškāps, clearly went beyond the bounds of duty, making several contributions to the regime-friendly journal *Sējējs*.[25] In these articles Auškāps imagined the nation as an organism, a harmonious cultural entity that needed the support of a strong state in order to develop its special characteristics

---

[19] Björklund, Fredrika (2003): "The Rhetoric of the Nation. Baltic Germans in the First Latvian Democracy", p. 99; Cerūzis (2004), p. 192.
[20] LVVA. Latvijas Universitātes fonds 7427/6/4. University Council Minutes, 1934/05/16.
[21] Kviesis was elected Honorary Fellow of the University, while Ulmanis, originally an agronomist involved in the dairy industry, became honorary doctor in agronomy. LVVA. Latvijas Universitātes fonds, 7427/6/4. University Council Minutes, 1934/09/26.
[22] LVVA. Latvijas Universitātes fonds, 7427/6/4. University Council Minutes, 1934/05/30.
[23] LVVA. Latvijas Universitātes fonds, 7427/6/4. University Council Minutes, 1934/12/12.
[24] LVVA. Latvijas Universitātes fonds, 7427/13. Staff records.
[25] *Sējējs*, 1936:1; 1936:3; 1936:6. Several of the prominent academics in the 'national' disciplines frequently contributed to *Sējējs*, for instance Tentelis, Šmits, and Švābe. Auškāps also contributed to the volume congratulating the Leader on his 60th birthday. See also Zelče (2007b), p. 331.

and destiny. The new national state, he claimed, must therefore eject everything 'foreign'.[26] As he put it in a public speech in 1937:

> This ideal has been given to us by our people's leader. That is the Latvian Latvia, Latvian from the beating hearts to the discernible horizon, Latvian in the towns and in the country, Latvian from the ground to the sky.[27]

Auškāps later joined the Ulmanis cabinet as Minister of Education, and helped to formulate the regime's main tenets: unity, leadership and a Latvian Latvia.[28] Professor Ludvigs Adamovičs formulated similar notions with undisguised approval in an essay celebrating the university's 20th anniversary in 1939. According to him, the transformation of *Latvijas Universitāte* into a completely Latvian academic institution had only been made possible during what he called "the Age of Latvian Latvia", beginning on 15 May 1934.[29] Such eulogies, and the multiplication of the term 'Latvian' in all kinds of imaginable and unimaginable contexts, became very frequent after that date. Turning to his fellow academics, Adamovičs went on to say that the new regime was more favourably inclined towards the university than any previous government, and had promised to provide the adequate funding previously withheld by the democratically elected *Saeima*.[30]

At the Faculty of Philology and Philosophy, the official reaction to the coup was positive and filled with expectancy. At the first faculty meeting after the event, much of the discussion centred on formulating a proposal to the Ministry of Education on what were seen as important principles for future educational reforms.[31] Apparently, the faculty members believed that their opinions on educational matters would be received more favourably by the authoritarian government than had been the case in the democratic era.

Naturally, the minutes are silent about dissident opinions and views on some negative implications of the coup. Some faculty academics who had been heavily involved in politics were temporarily barred – among them the professor of

---

[26] Auškāps, Jūlijs (1936): "Latviešu nākotnes ceļi", p. 9.
[27] *Universitas*, 1937:4, p. 73. (My translation) Auškāps belonged to the Faculty of Chemistry, and was elected principal between 1933 and 1937. LVVA. Latvijas Universitātes fonds, 7427/13/105. Staff records.
[28] Stranga, Aivars (1998b): *LSDSP un 1934. gada 15. maija valsts apvērsums. Demokrātijas likteņi Latvijā*, p. 217.
[29] *Latvijas Universitāte divdesmit gados 1919–1939* (1939), I, p. 5.
[30] *Latvijas Universitāte divdesmit gados 1919–1939* (1939), I, p. 19. Adamovičs was a professor of church history, but a prolific writer also on ancient Latvian religion and mythology.
[31] LVVA. Latvijas Universitātes fonds, 7427/6/363. Minutes of the Faculty of Philology and Philosophy, 1934/05/26. These expectations were perhaps not wholly unfounded. According to a later report by Straubergs, the Ministry had been positively inclined to nearly all of the faculty's suggestions. Ibid., 1934/09/01.

linguistics Plāķis, an active member of the *Pērkonkrusts* movement, and the young historian Alfrēds Altements, a Social Democrat. However, they were soon reinstated.[32] Plāķis was given some honorary assignments and also permitted to remain at the university until the age of seventy.[33]

On the whole, the relationship between the authoritarian government and the university appears to have been relatively smooth. The government seems to have largely respected the university's autonomy, and apparently did not interfere with academic appointments or impose any drastic changes involving non-Latvian teaching staff.[34] Government discussions about relocating a part of the university in Jelgava raised a good deal of concern, but in the end only the Faculty of Agronomy actually moved – a faculty certainly strongly supported by Ulmanis.[35] The regime's major innovation, a separate faculty for Roman Catholic theology, was hardly a bone of contention.[36]

For many academics at *Latvijas Universitāte* the authoritarian regime certainly meant a forceful turn towards more 'national' issues. This affected both the form and the content of academic work. The various faculty series of the official university journal, *Latvijas Universitātes Raksti*, henceforth gave priority to contributions on Latvia's nature and Latvian culture.[37] International acclaim also became secondary to national concerns: the printing of dissertations, for instance, obtained financial support only if it was done in the Latvian language.[38]

Many of the fields of academia that were close to 'national' issues clearly received new, forceful support. Latvian archaeology and folklore were boosted. Within folklore studies, the sharper 'national' turn and the stress on *latviskošana* also put a considerable strain on relations with Estonian and Finnish ethnographers researching the culture of the Finno-Ugric speaking Liv

---

[32] *Latvijas Valsts universitātes vēsture 1940–1990* (1999), p. 36. Alfrēds Altements was an active Social Democrat until 1934. He was imprisoned after Ulmanis's coup, but released after Tentelis's personal intervention. See Caune, Andris (1997): "Vēsturniekam Alfrēdam Altementam - 95", p. 165.

[33] LVVA. Latvijas Universitātes fonds, 7427/6/4. University Council Minutes, 1934/09/05; 7427/6/363, Minutes of the Faculty of Philology and Philosophy, 1935/03/02.

[34] For instance, the appointment of the Baltic German professor in mechanics, Gustav von Taube, was extended on condition that one of his subjects and all examinations were conducted in Latvian. LVVA. Latvijas Universitātes fonds 7427/6/4. University Council Minutes, 1934/12/12.

[35] LVVA. Latvijas Universitātes fonds, 7427/6/363, Minutes of the Faculty of Philology and Philosophy, 1935/04/06.

[36] Possibly, the creation of this faculty can be seen as a concession to the inhabitants of the predominantly Catholic Latgale – and perhaps also as a form of compensation for the regime's more heavy-handed approach to Latgallian as a print-language.

[37] LVVA. Latvijas Universitātes fonds, 7427/6/363, Minutes of the Faculty of Philology and Philosophy, 1934/12/08.

[38] LVVA. Latvijas Universitātes fonds, 7427/6/363, Minutes of the Faculty of Philology and Philosophy, 1937/01/16.

minority. The matter came to a head in 1937 when the Estonian ethnographer Oskar Loorits was actually deported from Latvia for his cultural-political activities on behalf of the Livs.[39]

The pseudo-scientific discipline of human anthropology was invigorated in the late 1930s, much due to increased worries about diminishing fertility rates. Demographers and mass media fuelled concerns about lower population growth to an extent that came close to 'moral panic'.[40] These trends naturally ran counter to the authoritarian regime's notion of an "eternal Latvia". At the Faculty of Medicine at *Latvijas Universitāte*, the main proponents of eugenics were professor Ernsts Fērmanis and *privātdocents* Gustavs Reinhards, who both published popular works on this issue. Reinhards, especially, underpinned in his lectures the notion that the Latvian nation was threatened by extinction. In response to these concerns, in 1938 the government founded a research institute for eugenics, *Tautas dzīvā spēka institūts* (The National Life Force Institute), under the direction of anatomist Jēkabs Prīmanis.[41]

The preoccupation with eugenics was common to many European countries in the 1930s. Latvian anatomists had a special connection with Swedish colleagues, since human anthropology had been introduced in Latvia by the Swedish anatomy professor Gaston Backman in the early 1920s. However, while Prīmanis and his colleagues retained very cordial relations with Backman, his conclusions about the 'racial characteristics' of Latvians were perhaps less appreciated. Backman described the Latvians as a 'bastardized mixed race', whose 'original' Nordic type had been degenerated by mixing with East European elements.[42]

Baltic linguistics was also given increased government support through the creation of the Latvian language archive in 1936. Under the direction of the talented young linguist Alvils Augstkalns, this institution was devised to strengthen scholarly research on the Latvian language, especially its dialects.[43] Moreover, as indicated previously, in language matters the Ulmanis regime took

---

[39] Tankler, Hain & Rämmer, Algo (2004): *Tartu University and Latvia, with an Emphasis on Relations in the 1920s and 1930s*, pp. 193–198.
[40] Zelče, Vita (2006): "Vara, zinātne, veselība un cilvēki: Eiģēnika Latvijā 20. gs. 30. gados", pp. 94–96.
[41] Zelče (2006), pp. 100–114; Kott, Matthew (2009): "Antropologen Gaston Backman och den uppsaliensiska rasbiologins spridning i tid och rum", pp. 62–63. Reinhards had been on the staff of the Faculty of Medicine since its inauguration in 1919, and suggested the appointment of a *docents* in 'racial hygiene' already in 1920 – without much success. See Vilde, Arnis (2011): *Latvijas Universitātes Medicīnas fakultāte 1919-1950*, p. 35.
[42] Kott (2009), pp. 68, 73. Surprisingly, Backman's contributions and the method of anthropological measurement are still given some serious scientific consideration in present-day Latvia. See, for instance, Denisova, Raisa (1999): "Latviešu antropoloģija kultūrvēsturisko teritoriju atspulgā", pp. 9–24, and Grāvere, Rita (2008): "Latgales antropoloģija reģionālā griezumā", pp. 62–90.
[43] Kļaviņa (2008), pp. 223–224.

the project of standardizing the Latvian language a step further by trying to ban the Latgallian dialect as a print-language.[44] A new commission to standardize and simplify Latvian was also set up, comprising, just like fifteen years earlier, the prominent linguists Endzelīns, Šmits, and Blese.[45] However, the most important change in academic matters concerned the discipline of history.

The creation of the Historical Institute, and the development of national history

Kārlis Ulmanis coup d'etat on 15 May 1934 and the transformation of Latvia into an authoritarian state had decisive effects on conceptions of the past. In the field of academic history, the turn towards 'Latvian-ness' became a much more pressing issue. Perhaps not all that surprisingly, this meant that the position of professor Leonid Arbusow, the eminent medievalist belonging to the Baltic German 'nationality', became increasingly difficult. Along with his faculty colleagues, Arbusow signed the required pledge of loyalty to the Ulmanis government in the autumn of 1935, but handed in his letter of resignation a few months later. He did not specify his reasons for resigning, but the dean noted that Arbusow's grounds were that his students had not "interpreted him in a positive manner".[46] This would indicate some kind of conflict between Arbusow and 'nationally' inclined history students. It should, however, be borne in mind that in more general terms the relationship between ethnic Latvians and the Baltic German minority had worsened considerably after 1933.[47]

Arbusow's colleagues in the faculty made no attempt to persuade him to stay, and his resignation was evidently accepted with alacrity.[48] It is therefore not too far-fetched to see this as a forced resignation connected with the augmented

---

[44] Zeps, Valdis (1995): "Latgalian Literature in Exile", p. 313; Bukšs, Miķelis (1957): *Latgaļu literatūras vēsture*, p. 558.

[45] LVVA. Izglītības ministrijas fonds, 1632/2/792. Izglītības ministrijas pareizrakstības komisijas atzinumi latviešu pareizrakstības jautājumos. 1938. g. The linguists were now perhaps less enthusiastic about prescribing the 'correct' way to write in Latvian. Augstkalns, who was also a member of this commission, complained that the implementation of 'correct' Latvian was really a task for government inspectors, not researchers. See Kļaviņa (2008), pp. 224–225.

[46] LVVA. Latvijas Universitātes fonds, 7427/13/88. Staff records. Letter from the Dean of Faculty to the Principal 1935/12/30, recommending that Arbusow's letter of resignation be approved.

[47] Cerūzis (2004), pp. 144–165.

[48] LVVA. Latvijas Universitātes fonds, 7427/6/5. University Council Minutes, 1936/01/15; 7427/6/363, Minutes of the Faculty of Philology and Philosophy, 1936/01/18. There was no recorded discussion at this faculty meeting when Arbusow's resignation was announced – in spite of the fact that Arbusow himself was present. It should also be noted that the dean, Francis Balodis, one of Arbusow's previous critics, formally approved of the resignation well before the matter was disclosed to the faculty. See footnote above.

'national' requirements for history teaching and writing.[49] Although Arbusow appears to have become cautious and more or less abstained from writing in the Baltic German press in the late 1920s, in the eyes of his Latvian colleagues he was probably still far too strongly connected with Baltic German society and German academic circles.[50]

A new professorial chair in Latvian history was swiftly established and assigned to Arveds Švābe, who rapidly emerged as the faculty's most forceful promoter of a national Latvian historical narrative.[51] In the *Festschrift* dedicated to Švābe only two years after his appointment, the title page is adorned with one of his programmatic sentences: "The task for scholarly Latvian history is to give back to the Latvian people their lost past".[52]

Švābe had a rather unconventional background for an academic historian. Originally a student of natural sciences in Moscow, he changed to history but only for a short while because the war intervened. His interest in Latvian culture and mythology was awakened by Krišjānis Barons's edition of Latvian folksongs, *dainas,* while working during the war in the Imperial postal service in Siberia.

Like many other Latvian intellectuals in Russian 'exile', Švābe took an active part in local national associations. Back in Riga, he published poetry and some textbooks in history for Latvian elementary schools; works that were in fact not very well-received by historians at the university. He also wrote some analyses of folkloristic themes in the *dainas*.[53]

After 1919, Švābe was a member of the Constitutional Assembly and a major speechwriter for the Social Democrats, supplying them with historical arguments for far-reaching agricultural reforms that were implemented in the early 1920s. Instead of continuing his scholarly career in history, Švābe chose to join the Faculty of Law and Economics.[54] He stopped writing poetry after a personal

---

[49] This is how Arbusow's resignation is interpreted by the Latvian historian Andrejs Johansons. See Johansons, Andrejs (1987): "Die Lettländische Universität in Riga 1919–1940", p. 261. However, some Latvian historians seem reluctant to acknowledge the 'national' dimension of Arbusow's resignation. See, for example, Ronis, Indulis (1995): "Latvijas vēstures institūts laikmeta kontekstā", p. 23.
[50] Apart from his position at the Herder Institute, Arbusow had become Honorary Doctor in Theology at Rostock University. LVVA. Latvijas Universitātes fonds, 7427/13/88. Staff records. On his conspicuous lack of publications in the Baltic German press, see *Latvijas Universitātes Filoloģijas un Filosofijas Fakultātes Bibliogrāfisks Pārskats. II. 1925–1930* (1930), p. 24, where only a single article is listed.
[51] LVVA. Latvijas Universitātes fonds, 7427/6/363, Minutes of the Faculty of Philology and Philosophy, 1936/04/22; 1936/05/16; 1936/05/23. The vote in the faculty was 14 for, 3 abstaining.
[52] *Tautas vēsturei. Veltījums profesoram Arvedam Švābem* (1938), p. 5.
[53] *Vēsturnieks profesors Dr. iur. Arveds Švābe (1888–1959)* (1998), pp. 8–10, 25–26; Švābe, Arveds (1920): "Ozols un liepa latviešu reliģijā". His highly personal combination of sociological history, folklore and linguistics failed to impress the academics at the faculty.
[54] His reasons may have been both academic and political. His early works in history and folklore had been disparaged by Arbusow and Šmits as amateurish, and his Social Democratic

crisis in 1926 but remained a versatile intellectual, among other things becoming editor-in-chief of a Latvian encyclopedia, *Latviešu konversācijas vārdnīca*.[55] As a graduate student in the late 1920s he researched legal history, focusing especially on Latvian peasants' legal position under Baltic German rule. He now left the Social Democrats and became more of a nationalist intellectual, developing a line of "historical justice" for the Latvians against the Baltic German feudal *Ritterschaft*.

In the late 1920s when still a graduate law student, he, rather than one of the academic historians, was given the politically sensitive task of providing an official historical background to the Latvian agrarian reform, a measure that many Baltic Germans perceived as out-and-out confiscation of land. His historical narrative was eventually published in German, French, and English in 1928–1929, primarily with the political aim of placating international opinion.[56] This was a highly sensitive issue, since it dealt with the structures of power, landowning, and jurisdiction that the far-reaching agrarian reforms were devised to rectify.[57] In these matters, Švābe placed himself firmly on the nationalist Latvian side. Such political credentials certainly worked in his favour after the coup of 1934, helped perhaps also by his programmatic article "Latvian history as a national academic subject", published in a newspaper close to the Ulmanis regime in October 1935.[58]

At *Latvijas Universitāte*, Švābe was first employed in the Faculty of Law and Economics as lecturer in Latvian legal history; in 1932 he was promoted to a professorship.[59] In the official version, with some support in his autobiographical writings, Švābe remained in the Faculty of Law and Economics primarily due to Arbusow's opposition to having him elected to the Faculty of Philology and Philosophy. They reputedly disagreed on national issues, as well as on scholarly methodology.[60]

However, this may well be a simplification produced in hindsight. As shown previously, Arbusow's position in the faculty was relatively weak, and it should also be borne in mind that Švābe's early writings on history, folklore, and linguistics had not found very much favour with some of the established Latvian

views were probably not much appreciated by the more national-conservative Faculty of Philology and Philosophy.

[55] Ķencis, Toms (forthcoming 2011b): "Kārlis Arveds Švābe".
[56] See Švābe, Arveds (1928): *Grundriss der Agrargeschichte Lettlands*.
[57] *Vēsturnieks profesors Dr. iur. Arveds Švābe (1888–1959)*, pp. 13–14; Ķencis (forthcoming 2011b).
[58] *Brīvā Zeme*, 1935/10/05.
[59] LVVA. Latvijas Universitātes fonds, 7427/13/1740. Staff records; *Latvijas Universitāte divdesmit gados 1919–1939* (1939), I, pp. 177–178; Tentelis, Augusts (1938): "Arveds Švābe – vēsturnieks", p. 11.
[60] *Vēsturnieks profesors Dr. iur. Arveds Švābe (1888–1959) (1998))*, p. 9.

academics. As a historian, Švābe was essentially self-taught.[61] By 1932, however, he was sufficiently established to be invited to contribute to the second volume of *Latvieši*, the codified version of Latvian folklore and history, with a piece on traditional Latvian conceptions of rights and justice.[62] In 1934, Švābe's recent historical work was very favourably assessed by the faculty when discussing candidates for the Cultural Fund Prize.[63] Clearly, his academic credentials had improved considerably.

After Arbusow's forced resignation, Švābe was swiftly elected professor and incumbent of the newly established chair of Latvian history. In this position, he worked primarily together with the ethnic Russian professor Roberts Vipers, since Augusts Tentelis, the ethnic Latvian professor of history, served as Minister of Education in the Ulmanis government between 1935 and 1938.[64]

Indeed, the retention of Vipers serves as an interesting contrast to the case of Arbusow. While Arbusow was a Latvian citizen belonging to the Baltic German *tautība*, Vipers remained a Soviet citizen of Russian 'nationality'. In the conflict over the Rozen declaration, as shown in a previous chapter, Vipers supported the young Latvian historian Vīgrabs and forcefully promoted a Latvian national perspective on history. This certainly made him very popular among the Latvian colleagues in the faculty, and his tenure was extended several times.

In 1934, for instance, when the faculty applied for yet another extension of Vipers's tenure, it argued that Vipers was involved in research on important Latvian issues and made major contributions both to Latvian scholarship and to the Latvian people. A special quality in Vipers, the faculty request continued, was that he had remained "unaffected" by German scholarship and lectures, and had acquired the ability to teach in Latvian.[65] It should be noted that this request was formulated while Arbusow, one of the academics obviously too affected by 'German scholarship', was still a professor in the faculty.

During the Ulmanis regime, Vipers was retained as the only non-Latvian historian at the university. He received several extensions of the right to teach in Russian, and was allowed to continue as professor well into his eighties, although

---

[61] Zeids, Teodors (1990a): Foreword to Švābe's reprinted textbook for Latvian schools, *Latvijas Vēsture. 1. daļa*, [1925], p. 4. Zeids maintains that this textbook was criticized by the historians of the faculty both for its factual mistakes (Arbusow) and for its didactic shortcomings (Dreimanis). Ibid., p. 6.
[62] Švābe, Arveds (1932): "Latviešu tautas tiesiskie uzskati", pp. 15–25.
[63] LVVA. Latvijas Universitātes fonds, 7427/6/363, Minutes of the Faculty of Philology and Philosophy, 1934/03/10.
[64] LVVA. Latvijas Universitātes fonds, 7427/13/1760. Staff records.
[65] LVVA. Latvijas Universitātes fonds, 7427/13/1922. Staff records. Request from the faculty, 1934/05/05; Letter from the Principal to the Minister of Education, 1934/05/25, advocating an extension or one year for Vipers since there was a lack of younger academics.

the formal retirement age according to the University Constitution was seventy.[66] Together with Balodis and Švābe, Vipers continued to develop and disseminate the Latvian historical perspective in both scholarly and popular versions during the Ulmanis regime.[67]

The year 1936 proved an important turning point in 'national' Latvian history writing. The Ulmanis government provided a new impetus in this direction with the creation of the Latvian Historical Institute under the directorship of Tentelis, and with the archaeologist Francis Balodis as deputy director. Several of the faculty's professors were included among the members of the Institute: Švābe, Spekke, Šmits, and Vipers.[68] The faculty duly responded by awarding honorary doctorates in history to Ulmanis himself, to his close ally general Jānis Balodis, and the faculty's own Minister of Education, Tentelis.[69]

Apart from addressing these markedly 'national' undertakings, the new Latvian Historical Institute served as an important centre and educator for a new generation of professional Latvian historians. Here we can include Marģers Stepermanis, secretary of the Institute and a former pupil of Vipers, Edgars Dunsdorfs, a prolific economic historian who had received some of his training from professor Heckscher at Stockholm University, and Juris Vīgrabs, the Latvian combatant in the Rozen dispute. There was also a 'younger' generation of promising historians in junior academic positions, for instance Alfrēds Altements, Georgs Jenšs, Uldis Ģērmanis, and Teodors Zeids.[70] This was rather different from the situation in the 1920s, when the discipline of history clearly lacked a younger generation of scholars. The Institute's considerable resources were used to finance the research and publications of these younger scholars.[71]

---

[66] LVVA. Latvijas Universitātes fonds, 7427/13/1922. Staff records; *Latvijas Universitāte. Lekciju un praktisko darbu saraksts 1939/40 mācības gadam* (1939), pp. 135–37; *Latvijas Universitāte divdesmit gados 1919–1939* (1939), II, pp. 101–102.

[67] He participated, for instance, in the dissemination of the Latvian historical master narrative to schoolteachers, a project headed by Balodis. See Vipers, Roberts (1937a): "Latviešu zemniecības tiesības un stāvoklis pirms dzimtbūšanas ievešanas", pp. 116–126; Vipers, Roberts (1937b): "Pāreja no zviedru valdīšanas uz krievu laikmetu", pp. 169–188. Ironically, Vipers actually serves as a counter-example to Ulmanis's and Tentelis's notion that only a member of the nation can understand and write that nation's history. Before the appointment of Švābe as professor of Latvian history, Vipers was the main scholarly figure behind the development of the national master narrative.

[68] Graudonis, Jānis (1995): "Latvijas vēstures institūts Latvijas Republikas laikā", p. 10. Spekke, however, was primarily engaged in the Latvian diplomatic service.

[69] LVVA. Latvijas Universitātes fonds, 7427/6/363, Minutes of the Faculty of Philology and Philosophy, 1936/09/19. The vote was, perhaps not surprisingly, unanimous.

[70] Graudonis (1995), p. 10. Vīgrabs's participation in the work of the Institute was only part-time. He had been a civil servant in the Foreign Office since 1927.

[71] LVVA. Latvijas vēstures institūta fonds, 1865/1/1, Director's book, 1938/04/02, 1939/03/30, 1940/07/16; 1865/1/2. Board meeting minutes, 1938/12/01, 1938/12/15.

8. THE UNIVERSITY UNDER DICTATORSHIP

The founding of the Latvian Historical Institute also led to the birth of the important journal *Latvijas Vēstures Institūta Žurnāls* with Tentelis as editor-in-chief. The journal's aim, he stated in the inaugural issue, was to reinterpret the historical sources through the eyes of Latvian historians, and in a 'national spirit'.[72] A brief glance at this journal indicates that Kārlis Ulmanis took great personal interest in the Institute's creation and funding. Indeed, the figure of Ulmanis is inescapably connected with this journal: page one of the very first issue was adorned with a full-page portrait of the authoritarian ruler.[73] This was only the beginning. In the same issue, Ulmanis was given ample space to expound his views on the Latvian nation and its past, and the future work that was expected from academic historians. History, he claimed, was the people's most dedicated guide on the way through life. It gives inspiration, strengthens endurance and pride, and constitutes a road for the increased love of the *tauta*. History also, Ulmanis claimed, clarifies the importance of strong government.[74] Here, Ulmanis referred to a conception that he reiterated frequently in most of his public addresses: the importance of loyalty to nation and state – *tauta un valsts*.

The problem with history and the Latvian *tauta*, according to Ulmanis, was that their history had been neglected for so long. Instead, Latvians had been taught another kind of history, mainly about people and times that did not really concern them, a history that was incapable of infusing them with knowledge and love of their own past. This kind of history, Ulmanis demanded, must be disregarded and forgotten. Instead, Latvians should scrutinize their past, and begin to rewrite a national history that combined a love of the *tauta* with a free and open look at realities.[75]

The task of academic historians, Ulmanis continued, was to develop such a national history, even though this might disturb the serenity of others. The Latvian *tauta* did not live in thin air: it had roots in the past, long and deep, which "could nourish the people's tree". The "sorry sight" of previous historiography, with its "outlandish" teachings, had to be changed in order to strengthen the *tauta* for coming trials. Only a united 'nation', secure in its past, had the strength to defy thunderstorms. This, according to Ulmanis, was the wide and demanding field of work for teachers of history, ranging from history professors to primary-school teachers. Historians were to be the true guides of the *tauta*.[76]

In this way, Ulmanis laid out the prescribed 'national' path for Latvian historians. To a class of graduating history teachers, Ulmanis took this theme a step further. The role of history was to emphasise the bonds between the Latvian

---

[72] Tentelis, Augusts (1937c): "Lasītājiem", pp. 3–5.
[73] *Latvijas Vēstures Institūta Žurnāls*, 1936:1, p. 1.
[74] Ulmanis, Kārlis (1936a): "Tauta un vēsture", pp. 8–9.
[75] Ulmanis (1936a), p. 9.
[76] Ulmanis (1936a), p. 10.

tauta and the land which, he claimed, it had inhabited for "thousands of years". A consciousness of the past must be strengthened to ensure that these bonds would endure in the future. The Latvian *tauta* would remain firmly planted in the soil of their own land, while 'others' would move away.[77] Using Ulmanis's own agricultural manner of expression, the role of history was obviously that of a combined fertilizer and herbicide, nurturing Latvian plants while weeding out others.

The link between Ulmanis's visions of history and the Latvian Historical Institute was his devoted political supporter Tentelis. The latter served as Minister of Education during most of the Ulmanis period, while at the same time directing the work at the Historical Institute. He had firm control of the main research fund, created by Ulmanis in Tentelis's name and supplied with additional donations from Ulmanis personally, the state cultural fund, and banks connected with the state and the farmers' movement.[78] Recognising the important role of Tentelis as a promoter and organiser of a 'national' turn of history, and as a link between academia and the Ulmanis regime, Tentelis was elected honorary doctor of history in 1936. In the letter from the faculty to the principal, Tentelis was especially commended for ensuring that Latvian history "now shone in national-scholarly splendour".[79]

There were occasions when these links between the authoritarian government and the Institute became more than obvious. In 1937, when the *Latvijas Vēstures Institūta Žurnāls* celebrated the Leader's 60th birthday, Tentelis composed a highly flattering account of Ulmanis's importance for the Latvian state, asserting that "the entire history of Latvia is the history of K. Ulmanis's work".[80] He then made flattering comments on Ulmanis's looks and personality, and finally commended him both for his longstanding interest in the past of the Latvian *tauta*, and for his unswerving material support for the writing and distribution of history from a national Latvian perspective. This, Tentelis asserted in an agricultural metaphor probably inspired by his 'Leader', had enabled the members of the Institute to become "workers in the cornfields of history".[81]

The close relationship between Tentelis and Ulmanis was already evident in the late 1920s, when the latter, on the former's proposal, was elected Honorary

---

[77] Ulmanis, Kārlis (1937): "Klausaities vēstures soļos!". This article was a reprint of a speech made by Ulmanis in August 1934.

[78] LVVA. Latvijas vēstures institūta fonds, 1865/1/1. Director's book, 1936/05/28, 1937/03/17; 1865/1/2. Board meeting minutes. Review of the period 27 March–4 May 1938. A personal donation of 20,000 Lats from Ulmanis was acknowledged on 22 December 1938. See also Krūze, Aīda (2009): "Augusts Tentelis – izglītības ministrs", p. 104.

[79] LVVA. Latvijas Universitātes fonds, 7427/13/1760. Staff records. Letter from the faculty to the Principal, 1936/09/22.

[80] *Latvijas Vēstures Institūta Žurnāls*, 1937:3; Tentelis, Augusts (1937d): "Tautas Vadoņa dzīve un personība", p. 331.

[81] Tentelis (1937d), pp. 32–34. Quote on p. 34.

Fellow, *goda biedrs*, of *Latvijas Universitāte*. Both Tentelis and archaeologist Francis Balodis were members of Ulmanis's Farmers' Party in the 1920s. After the coup in 1934, these credentials appear to have made Tentelis a suitable candidate for Ulmanis's Cabinet. He was appointed Minister of Education in October 1935 and held the post until August 1938.[82] This ensured the Historical Institute and the faculty a very direct link with government circles.

This special relationship seems to have endured throughout the Ulmanis era. Several of the Leader's speeches were reprinted in the Institute's journal, even though their scholarly merits must have been negligible.[83] In 1939 Ulmanis was appointed Honorary Fellow of the Institute, and in his eulogy Tentelis further commended the "Leader of our Nation" for his deep understanding of the people as the creators of history, and of history's role in the life of the state and the Latvian *tauta*. In Ulmanis's public speeches, Tentelis claimed, perceptive answers could be found to virtually every question posed by historians.[84] Similarly, when Tentelis wrote a retrospective article on the five years that had passed since the Ulmanis coup, he praised the return to order and the unification of the Latvian *tauta*. The ethnic minorities, he claimed, had obtained unreasonable rights and privileges; these malpractices had now given way to spiritual and material 'Latvian-ness'.[85]

In other words, Ulmanis provided financial means for the Historical Institute, Tentelis and his colleagues provided a legitimisation of the authoritarian regime. Ulmanis and the historians seem to have agreed on the need for a substantial reconstruction of Latvian history using a 'national' perspective. Older versions of the history of the Baltic provinces were seen as indelibly tainted and distorted by German narratives of the past. As Tentelis put it in a student paper in 1937:

> We are well aware that twenty years ago our history was still being researched by those belonging to a foreign *tautība*, who naturally looked for the achievements and interests of their own people. Now we must scrutinize the historical material with Latvian eyes and must process it from the perspective of the Latvian people.[86]

---

[82] Šnē, Andris (2009): "Latvijas Universitātes rektors profesors Augusts Tentelis", p. 16; Krūze (2009), pp. 103–106. On resigning as dean when he became Minister, he was immediately elected faculty delegate to the university council, and also continued to attend faculty meetings. LVVA. Latvijas Universitātes fonds, 7427/6/363, Minutes of the Faculty of Philology and Philosophy, 1935/11/09.
[83] See Ulmanis, Kārlis (1938a): "Valsts un Ministru prezidenta atgādinājums 1938. gadu sākot"; Ulmanis, Kārlis (1938b): "Valsts prezidenta Dr. K. Ulmaņa uzruna 6. Rīgas pulka piemiņekļa atklāšanā 1937. g. 31. oktobrī".
[84] *Latvijas Vēstures Institūta Žurnāls*, 1939:1: "Apskats", pp. 150–151.
[85] Tentelis, Augusts (1939): "Pieci gadi", pp. 166–167.
[86] Tentelis, Augusts (1937b): "Lielo pārvērtību un ideālisma ceļš. Aicinājums akadēmiskai jaunatnei …", p. 181. Tentelis cultivated the links with nationalist students, in the same article commending them for their strong support for 'the ideas of 15 May'.

A dual perspective of scholarship *and* nation was to be applied. Tentelis saw no problems in harnessing the ideas of nationalist authoritarianism – 'the ideas of 15 May' – to the craft of historiography. He approvingly quoted Ulmanis's dictum; 'history can only be written by each nation for itself', and seems to have considered it impossible to write history without or 'outside' a national perspective. A nation's history, Tentelis maintained, could be understood "better and more profoundly" by those who belonged to that nation.[87] At the same time, he repeatedly argued that contemporary Latvian historiography was based on reliable sources and therefore rested on solid scholarly foundations.[88] He refused to admit that a 'national' history could be biased – in his opinion only individual historians could be biased, not a whole nation's perspective.[89] This means that the 'national turn' in history was no longer a matter merely of perspectives and interpretations; it included a change of epistemological fundamentals. Scholarly history during the Ulmanis regime became underpinned by what I would describe as a nation-grounded epistemology. The national 'turn' was taken to a new level.

Tentelis served in this manner as a link between authoritarian nationalist politics and the Institute, and also as an orchestrator of historical research. He simultaneously acted as Minister of Education, Director of the Historical Institute, and editor of its journal, *Latvijas Vēstures Institūta Žurnāls*.[90] As Minister of Education, moreover, he was a driving force behind the state's appropriation of the major Baltic German historical archives in Latvia, thus handing over control of vital sources to Latvian archivists and historians.[91]

As a researcher, however, his contributions remained negligible.[92] While certainly celebrated by faculty colleagues, who hailed him on his 60th birthday as Latvia's "famous father of history" and "the Latvian Herodotus"[93], his own out-

---

[87] Tentelis (1937c), p. 4.
[88] Tentelis (1937c), pp. 4–5; Tentelis (1939), pp. 174–175. Andrejs Plakans describes the 'nationalist' programme of the Institute as 'surprising', since in his view Latvian historical scholarship had shown a trend of moderation after Krodznieks's departure. See Plakans (1999), pp. 298–299. However, Plakans takes little notice of the important Rozen dispute in the late 1920s, or the development of a more 'nationalist' brand of archaeology in this period.
[89] Auns, Muntis (2009): "Augusts Tentelis – vēsturnieks", pp. 93–94.
[90] Šnē (2009), p. 21.
[91] Zvirgzdiņš, Kārlis (2009): "Vācbaltiešu arhīvu pārņemšana valsts glabāšanā (1935. gada rudens)", pp. 52–68.
[92] According to the historian Uldis Ģērmanis's autobiography, Tentelis, apart from the burden of his political and administrative duties, suffered from writer's block. Ģērmanis claims that some of Tentelis's articles in the late 1930s were actually written by one of his young associates, Alfrēds Altements. See Ģērmanis, Uldis (1995): *Zili stikli, zaļi ledi*, p. 106.
[93] Poem by faculty linguist Pēteris Ķiķauka in *Senatne un Māksla*, Nr. IV, p. 5, 1936. Apart from the celebrations in *Senatne un Māksla*, a *Festschrift* was published with contributions from most of the historians at the Historical Institute. See *Veltījums izglītības ministram un profesoram Dr. h.c. Augustam Tentelim* (1936).

put remained sparse. He mainly edited source collections, wrote editorials in *LVIŽ* and published some programmatic articles for a more general readership.[94] Tentelis should therefore be seen primarily as a politician and a figurehead with tremendous influence and considerable power to distribute funds and scholarships, but academically a very mediocre scholar and certainly not a codifier of the new 'national' history. That role was primarily played by Arveds Švābe.

In order to work at the Historical Institute, the other academics there certainly had to adapt to the circumstances. Still, it is not self-evident that they wholly shared Tentelis's reactionary political views. Naturally, they developed research within the Institute's officially prescribed 'national' perspective, but that does not necessarily mean they were all ardent supporters of Ulmanis.[95] Teodors Zeids, one of the very few historians to publish with personal memories from the prewar Historical Institute, has indicated that the researchers received not only clearly political directions about 'approved' areas and problems, but also hints about desired results.[96] The official national agenda was obviously seen as more important than notions of academic freedom.

Besides carrying out research, the Historical Institute fulfilled its national obligations by staging public sessions to present their findings to a wider audience. Ulmanis and some of his Cabinet ministers were often present, as were army generals, schoolteachers, and students. These events appear to have been staged about four times a year, and obviously served as a meeting ground for academics and politicians.[97] Here, the scholarly and political perceptions of the Latvian past were supposed to merge in a politically approved version for immediate propagation through the channels of the regime.

Another 'national' task for the academics at the Institute was to disseminate the approved knowledge of Latvian history and folklore in the elementary school system. Balodis and his associates led a course in Latvian history for schoolteachers in the summer of 1936, and the lectures were published the following year. The aim of the course, Tentelis averred in the foreword, was to 'clarify our nationality issues', and above all correct Baltic German misconceptions of early Latvian society. The task for the schoolteachers, Tentelis continued, was to spread the results of the new and national historical scholarship to ordinary people so that it might bear fruit in the future.[98]

---

[94] Tentelis regularly contributed minor articles to *Sējējs* and other journals close to the Ulmanis regime. See, for instance, Tentelis Augusts (1936b): "Latviešu cīņa par izglītību", pp. 3–8.
[95] Alfrēds Altements, for instance, had previously been an active Social Democrat.
[96] Zeids, Teodors (1990b) "Latvijas Vēstures Institūta nozīme Latvijas vēstures zinātnes attīstībā", pp. 61–62. Still, Zeids maintains that even under these conditions, some work of lasting value was produced.
[97] Graudonis (1995), p. 13.
[98] Tentelis, Augusts (1937a): "Ievadam. Patiesība un nacionālisms vēstures zinātnē un mācīšanā", pp. 7–18. In the recently published biography on Tentelis, historian Muntis Auns

The contributors to this volume included Francis Balodis on early Latvian state structures before the German conquest, the church historian Ludvigs Adamovičs on ancient Latvian pagan religion, and the young historian Marģers Stepermanis on the 'Latvian' character of the Kurland duchy in the sixteenth and seventeenth centuries, and also on 'Latvian' figureheads in the enlightenment of the eighteenth century.[99]

One of the most active participants in these sessions, and clearly the main scholarly figure among the historians at the Institute, was Arveds Švābe. Other academics of the older generation, for instance Spekke and Straubergs, appear to have played minor parts.[100] Both of them, however, were important for the Latvian bonds with Fascist Italy, Spekke as a diplomat, and Straubergs as chairman of the Latvian-Italian Society.[101]

As professor of Latvian history in the faculty, Švābe continued his research on legal history and the judicial position of the Latvian peasantry during the Baltic German domination. However, he also wrote some political history on the formation of Livonian territory in the sixteenth century, tracing the roots of the modern Latvian boundaries.[102] Švābe was clearly the most productive of the established historians at the Historical Institute, editing several source collections and frequently contributing to its journal.[103]

Broadly speaking, the endeavours of historians at the Institute seem to have been spread over four categories. First, one of the most important tasks was to publish source collections and documents on Latvian history. This was seen as a vital prerequisite for the development of Latvian historiography and a new

---

views Tentelis's blend of 'national' history as a "natural reaction" to the previous historiographic predominance of the Baltic German scholars. This, I believe, is to underestimate the specific characteristics of the works produced by Latvian historians in the late 1930s. Rather than a "natural reaction", these works should be seen as contributions to a new official master narrative closely connected with the authoritarian regime. See Auns (2009), p. 94.

[99] Balodis, Francis (1937): "Senās latviešu zemes", pp. 19-26; Adamovičs, Ludvigs (1937): "Senlatviešu reliģija", pp. 45-115; Stepermanis, Marģers (1937a): "Kurzemes starptautiskais stāvoklis hercoga Jēkaba laikā", pp. 145-157; Stepermanis, Marģers (1937b): "Latviešu apgaismotāji XVIII gadsimtenī", pp. 189-204.

[100] Straubergs was responsible for the Historical Institute's contacts with the wider society, but apparently not active as a researcher. See LVVA. Latvijas vēstures institūta fonds. 1865/1/2. Board meeting minutes. Overview of March–May 1938. Spekke, previously active in Ulmanis's Farmers' Union, launched a diplomatic career in 1933. See *Latvijas Vēstures Institūta Žurnāls*, 1937:2, "Apskats", pp. 307-308; Spekke, Arnolds (2000): *Atmiņu brīži*, pp.128-163.

[101] Ķencis, Toms (2011a, forthcoming): "Kārlis Straubergs". Straubergs was also chairman of the Latvian-Polish Society – both these countries having authoritarian regimes with close bonds with Ulmanis.

[102] See Švābe, Arveds (1937a): "Sigismunda Augusta Livonijas politika"; Švābe, Arveds (1937b): "Sigismunda Augusta Livonijas politika. Viļņas sarunas".

[103] Graudonis (1995), p. 12.

consciousness of the past. All in all, twelve such volumes were produced, with particular emphasis on the eighteenth and nineteenth centuries.[104]

Second, some attempts were made to assist the archaeologists in reconstructing the Latvian culture of pre-German times.[105] Of special interest here was the search for evidence of advanced and stable 'Latvian' pre-medieval state structures, which would refute the Baltic German claims that the Baltic peoples were ruled by primitive chieftains and clan leaders before the arrival of German crusaders.[106]

Third, further research into the legal history of the Latvian peasants was encouraged. Here, Švābe was joined by his former students Benno Ābers and Edgars Dunsdorfs. Benno Ābers remained at the Faculty of Law and Economics and continued Švābe's work on legal history and the position of the Latvian peasants under Baltic German rule; Dunsdorfs was a very talented economic historian who specialised in particular on the Swedish era in the seventeenth and early eighteenth centuries. They both belonged to the 'youngest' generation of Latvian historians. Trained in the Faculty of Law and Economics, and also at *Stockholms högskola* (Stockholm college), Dunsdorfs was appointed to a post at the Historical institute in 1937.[107]

One of Dunsdorfs's main points was to demonstrate the legal and material improvements for peasants in the era of Swedish rule.[108] The Latvian participant in the Rozen controversy, Juris Vīgrabs, had been employed at the Foreign Office for almost a decade and now resumed his work on the relations between Latvian peasants and Baltic German nobility.[109] Alfrēds Altements, another 'youngest' generation historian, contributed work on attempts by the Baltic German nobility in Livland to hinder peasants from addressing grievances to Imperial officials.[110] A common theme was that the Baltic German nobility tried to impede reforms initiated by the Imperial centre. Another important research topic was the labour regulations in agriculture after the formal lifting of bondage in 1815, showing that

---

[104] Zeids (1990b), p. 62. In contrast, source collections published by Baltic German historians were predominantly from the medieval pre-Russian period.

[105] This research was published in the collection *Latviešu kultūra X–XII gadsimtenī* in 1938.

[106] See, for instance, Biļķins, V (1938): "Rimberta dati par kuršiem", pp. 225–232, which argues that it is possible to see traces of a unified Couronian state already in the 9th century. Švābe also published minor articles on early 'Latvian'states. *Vēsturnieks profesors Dr. iur. Arveds Švābe (1888–1959)* (1998), p. 16. For archaeology, see Balodis, Francis (1940): *Jersika un tai 1939. gadā izdarītie izrakumi*.

[107] *Latvijas Universitāte divdesmit gados 1919–1939* (1939), II, pp. 556–557.

[108] See Dunsdorfs, Edgars (1937a): "Muižu redukcija Zviedrijā"; Dunsdorfs, Edgars (1937b): "Latvju zemnieka brīvības izredzes Kārļa XI laikā".

[109] See Vīgrabs, Juris (1937): "Vidzemes bruņniecības uzstāšanās pret rakstnieku F. B. Albersu 1805. un 1806. gadā par bruņniecības apvainošanu rakstos"; LVVA. Latvijas vēstures institūta fonds, 1865/1/46. LVI Darbnieki. Raksturojumi un biogrāfijas, 1936.

[110] Altements, Alfrēds (1938): "Vidzemes zemnieku reformas jautājums 1795. – 97. g.", pp. 35–84.

restrictive and authoritarian patterns largely remained in force in spite of this reform.[111] Some work addressed the Russian-dominated peasantry of Latgale, bringing them into the general Latvian narrative.[112]

Fourth, there was strong interest in the Latvian national 'awakening' in the nineteenth century. Here, an important tendency was to portray historiography at the Historical Institute as the latest link in a long tradition of Latvian nationalist intellectuals. Tentelis evoked the examples of Valdemārs and Krodznieks, and Stepermanis the even older Enlightenment figure Garlieb Merkel.[113] The most substantial scholarly contribution, however, was that of Alfrēds Altements in his work on journalists, peasants and school-teachers in this 'awakening'.[114] Two major source collections were published, one on the legendary nationalist paper *Pēterburgas Avīzes*, and the other on documents connected with the national 'awakening'.[115]

Sometimes there was obviously a need to demonstrate the intrinsic, ethnically Latvian roots of the national movement. In 1938, for instance, A. Baumanis investigated the family trees of the nationalist 'heroes' Valdemārs and Kronvalds, and showed that the rumours of their having Russian, Swedish, Danish or German ancestors were groundless. Naturally, their family trees were shown to be full of solid Latvian peasants.[116]

The main task of the Historical Institute's historians was, as we have seen, to find new sources and reconstruct the history of the Latvian *tauta*. In many cases this could be done without much controversy, since many of these themes had not been addressed before. During its four years of existence before the Soviet occupation in 1940, the Institute's journal primarily published articles on vital 'Latvian' issues previously largely neglected by the Baltic German or Russian historians.[117] A part of this process, however, involved the confiscation of central Baltic German archives. This was done in the autumn of 1935 by the Board of

---

[111] See Dunsdorfs, Edgars (1938): "Klaušu beigu cēliens Kurzemē".

[112] See Brežgo, B (1939): "Latgales zemnieku pretošanās dzimtbūšanai krievu laikos", pp. 271–277.

[113] Tentelis (1939), pp. 172, 175; Stepermanis, Marģers (1939a): "Garlība Merķela uzskati zemnieku brīvlaišanas jautājumā", pp. 441–446. In 1797 Merkel published a vitriolic attack on the Baltic German landed aristocracy and their despotic rule over Latvian peasants, *Die Letten vorzüglich in Liefland am Ende des philosophisches Jahrhunderts. Ein Beytrag zur Völker- und Menschenkunde*.

[114] Altements, Alfrēds (1939a): "Studijas nacionālās atmodas vēsturē"; Altements, Alfrēds (1939b): "Studijas nacionālās atmodas vēsturē II". See also Augstkalns, A (1938): "Politiski dzejoļi 1863. gadā un Dinsberģa trimda".

[115] *Dokumenti par "Pēterburgas Avīzēm"* and *Dokumenti par tautas atmodas laikmetu 1856.-1867.g.*, both edited by Tentelis and Altements.

[116] Baumanis, A (1938): "Kronvalda Ata un Krišjāņa Valdemāra senči", pp. 233–246.

[117] See Plakans (1999), pp. 300–303, for an analysis of the contents of *Latvijas Vēstures Institūta Žurnāls* during this period.

Historical Monuments, *Pieminekļu valde*, with the support of Tentelis, Švābe and Valdis Ģinters, director of the Historical Museum.[118]

On some issues, however, there was clearly a need among the Latvian historians to question the scholarly arguments which German or Baltic German historians in particular put forward about the past of 'Latvian' territory. Teodors Zeids has labelled this tendency among Latvian historians the 'Schirren syndrome' after an influential nineteenth century Baltic German historian, Carl Schirren.[119] In general terms, German claims of their far-reaching colonization, and their cultural and political importance in the Baltic Provinces, were criticised as examples of inflated *Gross-Deutschland* thinking.[120]

Especially irritating were, apparently, the German historians' claims that German clergymen, educationalists, and writers had played an important part in the forming of the Latvian nation. The Church historian Ludvigs Adamovičs, for instance, rebutted such interpretations, arguing that the interest in educating Latvian peasantry had varied greatly among the Baltic German elite and quality of schools intended for Latvian children was generally very poor. The credit for raising levels of education should really go to the Latvian parents who had educated their children at home. The national enlightenment and 'awakening', Adamovičs concluded, was a result of the vitality and forcefulness of the Latvian *tauta* itself, not due to patronising Baltic Germans.[121] In this manner, perceived 'German' perspectives were laboriously replaced with 'Latvian'.[122]

One interesting feature of the historiography in this period is a certain propensity to project contemporary notions about the Latvian *tauta*, culture, and territory further back into a distant past. For instance, in his depiction of the Baltic German *Ritterschaft* in the Latvian-speaking part of Livland, Juris Vīgrabs applied the term 'Vidzeme', or even 'Vidzemes *guberņa*', to this territory even though neither that term nor *guberņa* existed at the time in question.[123] Marģers Stepermanis in turn dwelt on eighteenth century prophesies foreshadowing the

---

[118] Zvirgzdiņš (2009), pp. 55–66.
[119] Zeids (1990b), p. 61.
[120] Dunsdorfs, Edgars (1939): Review of Rudolf Schulze's *Der Deutsche Bauer im Baltikum*, pp. 136–40; Tentelis (1939), p. 174, for a criticism of the German historians centred on the journal *Jomsburg*. See also Spekke, Arnolds (1937): "Brēmenes Ādamu lasot ar latviešu tautas vēsturnieka acīm", pp. 11–66.
[121] Adamovičs, Ludvigs (1938a): "Latviešu tautības veidošanās un tautas izglītība latviešu un vācu apgaismojumā"and Adamovičs, Ludvigs (1938b): "Latviešu tautības veidošanās un tautas izglītība latviešu un vācu apgaismojumā. (Beigas)".
[122] Andrejs Plakans in his analysis of the Historical Institute finds the tone of the Latvian researchers relatively sober, and actual arguments with Baltic German historians relatively few. See Plakans (1999), pp. 302–303. The main reason why such open 'flashpoints' were relatively rare was probably that the Latvian historical narrative was still under construction, and therefore not in open confrontation with competing Baltic German or German historical narratives.
[123] Vīgrabs (1937), pp. 256–263.

emergence of a 'Latvian' territory under the Kurland Duke Jacob.[124] Statistical data for the Livland and Vitebsk provinces in the Imperial period were recalculated to obtain figures for the territory within the Latvian borders of 1920, excluding the 'Russian' and 'Estonian' parts.[125] In this way a form of historical 'Latvia' was brought into existence, at least notionally, well before its actual creation.

Apart from codifying the national history of the Latvians, the members of the Historical Institute were involved in international cooperation with scholars in the other Baltic countries, Sweden and Finland. Archaeologist Francis Balodis was clearly the most active in these contacts, developing close collaboration with the Swedish archaeologist Birger Nerman and his associates, and also contributing materially to the development of the discipline in Lithuania. Švābe and Dunsdorfs had close ties with Estonian and Swedish scholars, and Tentelis, finally, had a special bond with Estonia through his wife. These international scholarly exchanges materialised in the important history conference in Riga in August 1937.[126]

Comparing national narratives: *Baltijas Vēsturnieku konference, Rīgā, 1937*

This conference was indeed a prestigious event in which the Historical Institute's historians were eager to show the delegates from other participating countries the advances made in national Latvian history. Somewhat paradoxically, the main tenet of this international conference was to demonstrate the need and relevance of national history. It is perhaps not surprising that this was the main content of Kārlis Ulmanis's inaugural speech, but this line of thought was immediately taken up by the Swedish history professor from Stockholms högskola, Nils Ahnlund. The scholarly need for objectivity, he claimed, does not preclude "a deeply grounded national way of thinking". In fact, Ahnlund continued, they are "hand in glove".[127] National historical narratives apparently still had supporters in Swedish academia, even if these notions had been increasingly questioned in preceding decades.

A closer look at the delegates to the conference shows that the Swedes constituted the largest group among non-Latvians. However, this group consisted almost entirely of historians, archaeologists, museum directors and archivists from Stockholm. The most prominent Swedish delegates, apart from

---

[124] Stepermanis, Marģers (1937c): "Piezīmes par kādu Kurzemes zemnieka pravietojumu hercogam Jēkabam", pp. 424–429.
[125] Plakans (1999), p. 303.
[126] The conference papers are printed in *Pirmā Baltijas Vēsturnieku konference Rīgā 16. – 20. VIII. 1937* (1938).
[127] Ahnlund's inaugural speech, printed in *Pirmā Baltijas Vēsturnieku konference Rīgā 16. – 20. VIII. 1937* (1938), p. 24. For Ulmanis, see ibid., pp. 13–15.

professor Ahnlund, were historian Sven Tunberg, principal of Stockholms högskola, archaeologist Birger Nerman, historian Adolf Schück, and the director of the Swedish War Museum, Theodor Jakobsson. They all had links with the Latvian scholars. Nerman was one of Balodis's closest associates, while Tunberg had previously been appointed honorary doctor at *Latvijas Universitāte*.[128] Tunberg and Schück had also been the prime movers behind the appointment of the Swede Harry Wallin as lecturer in the Swedish language and history in 1928.[129] Wallin, it seems, coordinated the visits of the Swedish delegates in 1937.[130] However, historians from other Swedish universities were conspicuously absent.

At first sight, these connections between Swedish and Latvian historians may seem rather odd, but there was a major common theme: the era of Swedish rule in the Baltic territories in the late seventeenth and early eighteenth centuries. For conservative Swedish historians with nationalist inclinations, this period was certainly one of particular glory. Among those who participated, the conference may well have been an opportunity to expound on a national master narrative that was being increasingly questioned at home.[131] At the same time, Latvian historians often portrayed the Swedish rule in Estland and Livland as something of a Golden Age, with the Swedish state curbing the power of the Baltic German nobility, introducing popular education and improving the legal rights of the peasantry.

The second largest delegation to the 1937 conference was clearly the Lithuanians. Practically all their most prestigious historians took part in the proceedings: Volteris, Jonynas, Puziņas, Jablonskis, Ivinskis and Janulaitis. Their contributions were very similar to that of the Latvian: examples of national history writing. The conference's main flashpoint was actually the strong disagreement between Lithuanian and Polish historians on the meaning and interpretation of the treaties that led to the formation of the Polish-Lithuanian Commonwealth. Here, obviously, different master narratives collided with something of a bang.

The Estonians attending the conference were much fewer, and only professor Hans Kruus contributed a paper. Interestingly enough, this was the only paper

---

[128] *Latvijas Universitāte divdesmit gados 1919–1939* (1939), I, p. 17.
[129] LVVA. Latvijas Universitātes fonds, 7427/13/1832. Wallin's staff records. Letter from Tunberg, Stockholm, to the principal at *Latvijas Universitāte*, 1928/11/02; letter from Tunberg to the faculty at LU, 1928/11/03. Among the Swedish academics at *Latvijas Universitāte*, Wallin was employed for the longest period, lecturing between 1929 and 1936.
[130] LVVA. Latvijas vēstures institūta fonds. 1865/1/22. LVI. Baltijas vēsturnieku conference. Zviedrija. 1937.
[131] Sven Tunberg's article in *Senatne and Māksla* earlier the same year celebrating the genius and vitality of King Gustavus Adolphus would probably have occasioned some critical comments from colleagues at Swedish universities. See Tunberg, Sven (1937): "Gustavs Ādolfs", pp. 13–17.

that called for a *transnational* approach rather than merely adding to the national template. Kruus advocated a joint venture of historians from several countries to make a fresh analysis of the power struggles in the Baltic Sea area.[132]

Estonian historians seem to have been considerably less interested in this conference than their Latvian and Lithuanian colleagues. One possible reason for this is that historiography in Estonia had not developed along quite the same route. At Tartu University, the academic historians devised a common agenda early on, striking a compromise between 'national' needs and scholarly standards. The most productive period in terms of completed *Magister* theses had been between 1927 and 1933, and as early as 1930 the faculty at Tartu possessed a younger generation of Estonian professors in the historical disciplines. With Päts's coup in 1934 and the transition to authoritarian rule in Estonia, however, there was increased pressure to deliver 'national' scholarship. Somewhat similar to the Arbusow case at the University of Latvia, one Baltic German applicant for a vacant chair in history, Paul Johansen, found himself blocked in 1938 on what seem to have been ethnic grounds.

However, unlike the case in Latvia, the Tartu historians apparently split on the national issue. Some of them were quite ready to follow the new regime's call for a more 'patriotic' history, others stuck to previously established conceptions of scholarly standards. In the late 1930s, therefore, two diverging syntheses of Estonian history emerged in Tartu, one more 'patriotic' and the other more in line with the agenda laid down in the 1920s.[133]

Academia, cultural institutions, and the general public: the founding of *Senatne un Māksla*

The academics at the Faculty of Philological and Philosophical were likewise very involved in the launching of a new and influential journal, *Senatne un Māksla* (Antiquity and Art), founded in 1936 with solid support from the Ulmanis regime.[134] This new journal was closely tied to its main editor, archaeology professor Francis Balodis, and to the Board of Historical Monuments, *Piemiņekļu valde*, which Balodis had chaired since 1932. The journal's general aim was to provide a wider Latvian public with popular scholarly essays on the nation's past and culture. Francis Balodis, the new journal's main promoter as well as its editor, had strong connections with

---

[132] Kruus, Hans (1938): "Der Kampf um die Ostsee als Aufgabe der Geschichtsforschung", pp. 31–36.
[133] Kivimäe, S & Kivimäe, J (1987), pp. 289–290.
[134] See Minister of Education Tentelis's declarations in the inaugural issue. Tentelis, Augusts (1936a): "Ievadam", p. 3. As could perhaps be expected, several issues were adorned with pictures of the Leader, Ulmanis.

Ulmanis's party, the Farmers' Union, having joined its 'academic section' in 1925. Later, in his autobiography, Balodis noted with apparent satisfaction that Ulmanis had taken a very special interest in archaeology and research on Latvia's ancient history.[135]

Senatne un Māksla became an important forum, especially for the younger generation of Latvian archaeologists, who contributed a large number of articles on their excavations of prehistoric Latvian hill forts and grave sites. Altogether, Ģinters, Šturms, and Elvīra and Rauls Šnore published 33 articles in *Senatne un Māksla* between 1936 and 1940.[136] Balodis published seven articles, but few of them were on archaeology; they mostly dealt with art, primarily Latvian painters. He also wrote some articles of a more political nature, praising the Estonian authoritarian leader Konstantin Päts and the Swedish King Gustav V. He seems to have left much of the archaeological groundwork to his younger colleagues.

The academic historians were also frequent contributors to *Senatne un Māksla*. Arveds Švābe, in particular, wrote frequently on a variety of topics. Most of the other historians who contributed belonged to the 'youngest' generation: Ābers, Dunsdorfs and Stepermanis.[137] The main themes were generally the same as those that predominated in the more scholarly *Latvijas Vēstures Institūta Žurnāls*, but here they were condensed and written in a style more accessible to the general public. Most articles dealt with proto-Latvian states in the period AD 900–1200, and the legal situation of Latvian peasants during the centuries of Baltic German domination. The general argument in these articles was that before they were forcibly subjected to serfdom, Latvians had managed to form affluent, stable states and societies. This historical narrative was formulated in express opposition to previous Baltic German narratives on the alleged primitiveness of the prehistoric Latvian tribes.

Senatne un Māksla also contained a section on folklore and ethnography. The main contributors here were persons connected with the *Pieminekļu valde*, the Historical Museum and the ethnographic Open Air Museum, primarily Pēteris Ārends and Jānis Jaunzems on Latvian historical buildings and A. Karnups on folklore textiles. Many of these articles mainly concerned these museums' collections and acquisitions, and were less prone to contain national master narratives than the articles on history and archaeology. Among the faculty academics, Kārlis Straubergs contributed a few short articles on folklore themes, which no doubt indicates his gradual shift from the study of classical literature to

---

[135] Balodis (1941), p. 138.
[136] Ģinters published 11 articles, Šturms 8, and Rauls and Elvīra Šnore 7 each. The younger archaeologists, P. Stepiņš and H. Riekstiņš, published 3 and. 2 articles, respectively.
[137] Between 1936 and 1940, Ābers contributed 6 articles, Dunsdorfs and Stepermanis 4 each.

folklore in the late 1930s.[138] Perhaps surprisingly, the 'Grand Old Man' of academic folklore and ethnography, Pēteris Šmits, published only two minor articles in *Senatne un Māksla*.[139] The main reason was probably poor health – Šmits died in 1938.

Senatne un Māksla was also a medium for conveying images of academic 'heroes' of the nation to the general public. Augusts Tentelis, historian and Minister of Education, was extensively celebrated in connection with his 60th birthday. Pictures of him and his rural childhood home, and a reproduction of a commemorative medal were accompanied by a flattering poem in classical Greek.[140] The journal's main editor, Francis Balodis, received even more attention for a perhaps less obvious jubilee: a celebration of his 25 years in academia. Pictures of Balodis and his father Voldemārs, a schoolteacher and amateur archaeologist, were combined with a reproduction of a commemorative medal. Here, however, the theme of a national academic hero was primarily conveyed by having a number of international scholars contribute to the journal in his honour. Thus, international academic acclaim was used to enhance Balodis's stature as a national Latvian figure.[141] Apart from purely academic heroes, the journal celebrated Latvian artists and sculptors. Especially the sculptor Kārlis Zāle, creator of the Freedom Monument and the decorations adorning the *Brāļu kapi* cemetery, was given a truly heroic status.[142]

The journal *Senatne un Māksla* was accordingly used as an important vehicle for presenting the general Latvian public with accessible, condensed versions of the emerging master narratives on prehistoric and historic times. It also served to inform and familiarise the Latvian public with the work and collections of the national museums, and to communicate the images of academic and artistic 'heroes' of the nation.

The academics of the Faculty of Philology and Philosophy: an epilogue

In 1939 practically all the Baltic Germans in Latvia were evacuated in a massive operation and resettled in the border area between Germany and Poland. This entailed the final dissolution of the Herder Institute and the emigration of

---

[138] In *Senatne un Māksla* between 1936 and 1940, Ārends published 10 articles, Jaunzems 9, and Karnups and Straubergs 5 each.
[139] Šmits, Pēteris (1936): "Latvijā atrastas ķīniešu lietas", pp. 117–118, on the finding of a few Chinese objects in Latvian excavations, and Šmits, Pēteris (1937): "Ai, kundziņ bajāriņ", pp. 165–168, a short piece where Šmits argued that the Latvian peasantry were relatively well off before being reduced to serfdom by the Baltic Germans.
[140] *Senatne un Māksla*, IV, p. 5, 1936.
[141] *Senatne un Māksla*, I, 1938.
[142] Siliņš, Jānis (1936): "Latviešu jaunā tēlniecība", pp. 135–157; Siliņš, Jānis (1937): "Brāļu kapi Rīgā", pp. 91–106.

academics who were seen as belonging to the German *tautība*. Historian Leonid Arbusow, who had been eased out of the university in 1935, was evacuated to Posnan together with many other Baltic Germans. After World War II he became a professor in Göttingen.

The faculty's only remaining German academic, the classical linguist Erich Diehl, seems to have faced a difficult situation. His academic career had been made at *Latvijas Universitāte*, where he became a full professor in 1939 with solid backing in the faculty.[143] However, shortly afterwards he wrote a letter of resignation to the principal:

> It is very difficult for me to be separated from my native country and my dear university, but my honourable duty towards my [German] *tautība* does not allow me to decide otherwise.[144]

Consequently, Diehl joined the other Baltic Germans in the evacuation. For historian Roberts Vipers, one of the faculty's few ethnic Russians, things turned out otherwise. During the Soviet occupation in 1940–1941, Vipers was interrogated and forced to leave Riga. Formally a Soviet citizen but certainly not a Communist sympathiser, he was ordered by the Soviet authorities to return to Moscow and the Academy of Sciences.[145]

For others, 'nationality' was less clear-cut. The young economic historian Georgs Jenšs came from a mixed Polish-German-Latvian background, and had received some of his scholarly training at Hamburg University. At the time of the Baltic German evacuation, Jenšs's mother and sisters joined the emigrants but Jenšs saw himself as primarily Latvian and therefore stayed behind.[146]

Among the Latvian linguists, Jānis Endzelīns remained in Riga and managed to continue his academic work even though the Soviet authorities probably

---

[143] LVVA. Latvijas Universitātes fonds, 7427/13/376. Staff records. The faculty voted eleven to one for his appointment as professor, which was confirmed by the Latvian government in May 1939.

[144] LVVA. Latvijas Universitātes fonds, 7427/13/376. Staff records. Letter from Diehl to the principal, 1939/10/13.

[145] LVVA. Latvijas Universitātes fonds, 7427/13/1922. Staff records. Vipers wrote in a Soviet enquiry in 1940 that he had a "progressive-democratic" outlook but had never belonged to any party or organisation. After Vipers's removal to Moscow, Švābe bitterly – but perhaps unfairly – described him as a "mercenary ready to serve any kind of power". See Lūsis, Kārlis (1990): "Roberts Vipers un 'Vēstures lielās problēmas' Latvijā", pp. 7–8.

[146] Belova, Marina (2000): "Per aspera ad astra", pp. 14–22. Despite Jenšs's decision, Uldis Ģērmanis's memoir still refers to him as a 'Baltic German' historian. Ģērmanis (1995), p. 243. Jenšs's background, as well as some of his historical writing in the 1930s, did not endear him to the Soviet authorities after 1945. He was dismissed from both the Historical Archive and the University, allegedly due to his 'insufficient' position on Marxism-Leninism, and had to work for some years as a carpenter. Only after losing his right forefinger in a workplace accident was he allowed to return to the Historical Archive.

suspected him of 'bourgeois nationalist tendencies'.[147] Many of his colleagues fled towards the end of the war: Ernests Blese, Anna Ābele, Pēteris Ķiķauka and Edīte Hauzenberga.[148] Juris Plāķis fared far worse. He was one of many Latvians who were arrested and deported by the Soviet authorities in June 1941 and he died in a Siberian labour camp the following year.[149] The young linguist Alvils Augstkalns also succumbed during the war; in a period of depression, no doubt partly occasioned by the situation in Latvia after the first Soviet occupation, he committed suicide in November 1940.[150]

Some of the faculty's academics left Latvia shortly after the Soviet occupation in the summer of 1940. Dag Trotzig, the Swedish ethnographer, pursued scholarly expeditions in 1939 and early 1940, but left for Sweden in August 1940.[151] Similarly, Francis Balodis, the figurehead of Latvian archaeology, fled to Stockholm in July 1940, officially to take part in some excavations in Sigtuna. Having escaped from the Soviet Union once before, he realistically assumed that he was not exceedingly popular with the Soviet authorities.[152] He was formally dismissed from his post at the by now Soviet-directed university for having "abandoned his country and his people".[153]

Balodis was obviously incensed by the Soviet-Russian presence in his native Latvia. His later writings are full of deprecations, not only of the Soviet system but also of the Russian people as such. The Russian peasants in eastern Latvia, for instance, are described as nefarious, slovenly, useless and unwanted elements, completely alien to Latvian language and culture.[154] Apart from these xenophobic writings, Balodis tried to continue his work on the settlements of Livonian and Latvian 'tribes' before the coming of the German crusaders.[155] However, he died in 1947.

---

[147] *Latvijas Universitātes Vēstures un filozofijas fakultātes vēsture padomju laikā. Personības, struktūras, idejas, 1944–1991* (2010), pp. 14, 107.

[148] About 65 per cent of the academics of Latvijas Universitāte fled the country in 1945. See Stradiņš, Jānis & Cēbere, Dzintra (2006): "Latvijas Zinātņu Akadēmijas veidošanās: zinātniskie un sabiedriski politiskie aspekti", p. 104.

[149] Kļaviņa, Sarma (2010): "LU profesora Jura Plāķa dzīves un ciešanu ceļi (1869–1942)", pp. 14–16. Altogether, around twenty academics from the university were deported in June 1940, among them church historian Ludvigs Adamovičs and former principal Jūlijs Auškāps. They were both later sentenced and shot. Stradiņš, Jānis (2004): "Totalitāro okupācijas režīmu represijas pret Latvijas zinātni un akadēmiskajām aprindām", p. 136.

[150] Kļaviņa (2008), p. 225.

[151] LVVA. Latvijas Universitātes fonds, 7427/13/1797. Staff records. Officially Trotzig went on a research trip, but never returned to Latvia.

[152] Balodis (1941), p. 182.

[153] LVVA. Latvijas Universitātes fonds, 7427/13/123. Staff records. Balodis made an attempt to retrieve his position at the university during the German occupation, but was not allowed to do so.

[154] Balodis (1941), p. 137.

[155] See, for instance, Balodis, Francis (1944): "Arkeologiska synpunkter på livisk bosättning i Lettland", pp. 146–157.

The turmoil of World War II naturally had major repercussions on the work of the Historical Institute. After the Soviet invasion in June 1940, Tentelis was dismissed as an alleged "representative of the old repressive regime" and narrowly escaped being deported to Siberia. After the German invasion, he resumed his position at the Institute but died shortly afterwards in 1942.[156] Švābe and Straubergs were also removed from their posts at the Institute,[157] but the Soviet regime allowed the former to continue as professor in the history department.[158] During the German occupation between 1941 and 1944 the Historical Institute was virtually closed, and teaching at the university was generally suspended. Tentelis's successor as director of the Institute during the Soviet occupation, Jānis Lieknis, was murdered by the Germans in 1941.[159]

The systematic murder of Latvia's Jewish inhabitants under the German occupation meant the virtual annihilation of the Jewish students at the university who remained in Riga. While Jewish youths had been an important part of the student body, in spite of various restrictions, their number in the Faculty of Philosophical and Philological in fact had always been relatively small.[160] Moreover, not a single Jewish academic was included in the faculty's teaching staff during the twenty years of the First Republic.[161] Covert discrimination and, during the Ulmanis period, a conscious policy of *latviskošana*, had made this virtually impossible. But there was always a risk that 'Jewishness' might be attributed somewhat arbitrarily and for more or less perfidious reasons. In 1942, Arveds Švābe actually had to defend himself against allegations of being Jewish, rumours he attributed to people who wanted to see him dismissed.[162] For this or

---

[156] LVVA. Latvijas Universitātes fonds, 7427/13/1760. Staff records. Principal's decision, 1940/10/24; Latvijas vēstures institūta fonds, 1865/1/41, Staff records; Šnē (2009), p. 23. The Minister of Education of the Soviet-Latvian puppet regime who signed the decision to dismiss Tentelis was in fact no other than Paulis Lejiņš, professor of agronomy at *LU*.
[157] LVVA. Latvijas vēstures institūta fonds, 1865/1/1. Director's book, 1940/06/10, 1941/07/07
[158] LVVA. Latvijas Universitātes fonds, 7427/13/1740. Staff records. Principal's decision, 1940/10/29.
[159] Ronis (1995), p. 25.
[160] In 1922, for instance, Jewish students constituted less than 2 per cent of the Faculty of Philology and Philosophy's student body, compared to almost 12 per cent in the university as a whole. See LVVA. LVVA. Latvijas Universitātes fonds, 7427/6/54, Gadu statistiskās ziņas par studentu un mācības spēku sastāvu.
[161] As shown in a previous chapter, the only Jewish academics who became full professors at *Latvijas Universitāte* during the First Republic were Mečislavs Centneršvērs in chemistry, Naum Lebedinski in zoology and Paul Mintz/Pauls Mincs in law. Mincs was later among those deported to the Soviet Union. See LVVA. Latvijas Universitātes fonds, 7427/13/1162. Staff records.
[162] LVVA. Latvijas vēstures institūta fonds, 1865/1/39. Arveds Švābe's personal file.

other reasons, Švābe lost his position at the university in 1943, but remained director of the Historical Archive until he finally went into exile.[163]

Švābe, Dunsdorfs, Ģērmanis, and Spekke all went into exile towards the end of the war, and later formed the nucleus of Latvian historians in exile. They continued to promote a 'national' Latvian type of history, publishing an extensive series of 'official' Latvian historical monographs in the 1950s and 60s. The project of writing a master national narrative was thus continued in exile, with Švābe as a central figure until his death in 1959. The archaeologists Valdis Ģinters and Eduards Šturms also managed to escape from Riga, and continued to contribute to Latvian academia in exile. Classicist and folklorist Kārlis Straubergs, who had served as vice-principal during the German occupation, fled to Sweden towards the end of the war. He later resumed his research on Latvian folklore and edited a new extensive collection of Latvian folksongs together with Švābe and the linguist Hauzenberga-Šturma.[164] The codification of Latvian culture and history continued in exile, now with the express aim of preserving its purity from Soviet adulteration.

Some historians at the Institute remained in Riga. Alfrēds Altements stayed on but died shortly after the war, just after he had resumed his teaching at the university.[165] Marģers Stepermanis and Teodors Zeids continued as historians at the university and the Academy of Science under Soviet rule – and supervision.[166] This meant they had to adapt Latvian historiography to the paradigm of Soviet academia. Their colleague Georgs Jenšs, as we have seen previously, had to abandon *Latvijas Universitāte* due to his 'unsatisfactory understanding' of Marxism-Leninism.[167]

Elvīra Šnore and her family also planned to go into exile, but narrowly missed the very last boat to Sweden. She nevertheless remained at the university and eventually became one of the most prominent Latvian archaeologists in the Soviet period.[168] Her archaeologist husband Rauls, however, was arrested in

---

[163] LVVA. Latvijas vēstures institūta fonds. 1865/1/39. Arveds Švābe's personal file. However, with teaching suspended at the University during the German occupation, the post at the Historical Archive was probably Švābe's last resort.

[164] *Latviešu tautas dziesmas* (1952–1956), 11 Vols.

[165] LVVA. Latvijas vēstures institūta fonds. 1865/1/26. Altements's personal file See also Caune (1997), p. 166.

[166] Auns, Muntis (1997): "Dr. habil. hist., Dr. hist. h.c. prof. Teodora Zeida (1912–1994) dzīve un veiktais darbs", pp. 9–15; Ronis (1995), pp. 26–35. The Soviet Latvian Jānis Zutis very soon became the dominant academic in the history department. See *Latvijas Universitātes Vēstures un filozofijas fakultātes vēsture padomju laikā. Personības, struktūras, idejas, 1944–1991* (2010), pp. 89–91.

[167] Belova (2000), p. 21.

[168] Guščika, Elīna (2010): "Elvīra Šnore un Latvijas agrā dzelzs laikmeta pētniecība", pp. 113–129.

January 1946 after a brief spell at the university as a lecturer in archaeology. He was imprisoned in a labour camp for nine years and never regained his health.[169]

Some of the earlier themes developed at the Historical Institute proved acceptable even in this new context, for instance the 'feudal' struggle between Latvian peasants and Baltic German noblemen. Similarly, some of the work of the Folklore Archive could continue under Soviet rule, and for a few years the Archive's founder, Anna Bērzkalne, held a position at both the archive and the university which had not possible during the First Republic. Already in 1950, however, she was dismissed on political grounds.[170] The national master narratives, on the other hand, had to bow to the official Soviet version of 'historical materialism'. From then on, Latvian scholarship in the 'national' disciplines became strictly divided between the exile Latvian and the Soviet Latvian academics. But that is another story.

Conclusions

When Latvia was subjected to authoritarian rule in 1934, the 'national' turn of academic scholarship became even more pronounced. Research in areas deemed of great 'national' importance, such as folklore, archaeology, and history, received the new Ulmanis regime's whole-hearted support; the further development of these scholarly fields was obviously regarded as a vital process in the desired 'Latvianization' of Latvia.

As shown in the previous chapter, a 'national' turn is actually discernible in folklore and archaeology as early as the 1920s. Initiated by the eminent scholars Pēteris Šmits and Francis Balodis and encountering no resistance from a previous generation of academics, Latvian folklore and archaeology focusing on peasant folklore and the culture of pre-German times could easily fit into a budding 'national' project. For these disciplines, the transition to authoritarian rule seems to have meant increased official recognition and more secure funding, but no dramatic change in scholarly directions. Balodis, however, was far more able than Šmits to form a circle of disciples and convey to the general

---

[169] LVVA. LVVA. Latvijas Universitātes fonds 7427/13/1705. Staff records; Šnore, Rauls (1997): "Raula Šnores dzīves un zinātniskās darbības apraksts (autobiogrāfija)", pp 45–46; Cimermane, Ieva (1997): "Par maniem vecākiem", pp. 80–83. Rauls Šnore was sentenced to 10 years' forced labour for his attempt to flee the country and his alleged 'anti-Soviet' and 'nationalist' inclinations. See Vīksne, Rudīte (1997): "Krimināllieta Nr. 15463", pp. 86–87, 95. Rauls Šnore died prematurely in 1962.

[170] Treija, Rita (forthcoming, 2011): "Anna Bērzkalne (1991–1956)". She was forced to leave the university in 1948 and the Folklore Archive in 1950, apparently because her writings were too influenced by the Finnish school of folkloristics and not sufficiently Marxist. See also *Latvijas Valsts Universitātes vēsture 1940–1990* (1999), p. 165.

public the new national narrative on prehistoric times, most specifically in his own journal *Senatne un Māksla*.

Changes were considerably more dramatic in the discipline of history. During the First Republic's first decade, academic history had far too few trained scholars to develop a more consistently 'national' Latvian history. Under the Ulmanis regime, tensions among historians at *Latvijas Universitāte* appear to have increased. In 1935 one of the main scholars, the Baltic German professor Leonid Arbusow, was forced to resign, which removed an important obstacle to the development of a more 'national' Latvian history project. His successor, Arveds Švābe, became the most forceful and creative promoter of the 'national' turn in history. This new direction was given strong political support in 1936 with the founding of the Historical Institute, which became the scholarly base for writing a new 'national' history.

A new generation of Latvian historians and archaeologists emerged at the Historical Institute in the late 1930s, led by professors Tentelis and Balodis, and with substantial personal political support from the dictator Kārlis Ulmanis; the concept of 'national history' became paramount in a general project to rewrite Latvian history from a national perspective. Ulmanis clearly saw the creation of 'national history' as a main way of promoting an increased national consciousness among the Latvian people; a vital part of the more general project of *latviskošana*, Latvianization.

The institutional setting, political ties and considerable resources for research seem to have made the academic Latvian historians into solid supporters of the official version of the 'national turn', forming what could be called a homogeneous epistemic community. In a comparative context, this tendency was somewhat less clear-cut in Estonia. At Tartu University, a form of scholarly compromise on the nationalist issue had already been achieved in the early 1920s, instigated by the Finnish professor Cederberg. When Estonia turned to authoritarian rule in 1934, some of the Estonian historians adopted a more 'patriotic' line, similar to their colleagues in Riga, while others stuck to the previously established scholarly position. Also, the political ties between Tartu historians and the Päts regime in Tallinn were probably less strong than those between the Latvian historians and Kārlis Ulmanis.

For the Latvian historians, folklorists, and archaeologists attached to the new Institute, one of the main aims of their scholarly endeavours was to question and complement the earlier Baltic German interpretations of history and culture. They should focus instead on the Latvian *tauta*, its achievements and destiny. In this way, interpreting history became contested terrain between Baltic German scholars and the Institute's Latvian historians and archaeologists. However, the insistence that only scholars belonging to the nation could correctly interpret its past amounted to a change in epistemological fundamentals, in obvious contrast to previous academic ideals of transnational scholarship and commensurability. The 'national turn' had clearly been taken to a new level.

During the four years of the Historical Institute's existence before the Soviet occupation in 1940, researchers there published a series of source collections and a historical journal, primarily devoted to the study of what they saw as previously neglected Latvian themes. The institute also constituted a formative academic environment for a new generation of young Latvian historians and archaeologists. However, compared to the other 'national' academic disciplines, this development, for many reasons, came rather late. Only during this later period, and in an authoritarian political context, did the 'national turn' in history predominate and reach a new and unprecedented level.

CHAPTER 9
Conclusions

Latvia emerged as an independent state in 1918–1919 after the collapse of the Romanov Empire. During 1919 and early 1920, its territorial integrity was threatened both by the Bolsheviks and by remnants of the German armed forces. After repelling these threats, Latvia swiftly developed as a 'nationalizing state' in Brubaker's sense, adopting the characteristics of a nation state model even though ethnic minority groups made up about 25 per cent of the population. In a process of 'ethnic reversal', the majority ethnic group, the Latvians, assumed political power at the expense of the previously hegemonic minority group, the Baltic Germans.

In 1919 the formation of a new Latvian university became a national project of great symbolic significance. For the first time, the previously subordinated Latvian population would have its own university, moreover an academic institution that would use Latvian, previously disparaged as a simple peasant vernacular, as the language of learning and instruction. For Latvian nationalist intellectuals, this was the fulfilment of a long-nurtured dream. In more theoretical terms, the formation of *Latvijas Universitāte* was clearly a material aspect of the ongoing process of 'ethnic reversal', the replacement of the previous Baltic German cultural hegemony with a solidly Latvian institution of higher education. The new university's organisation committee was therefore given a composition that would accord with these political and nationalist expectations: a majority of its members were initially representatives of ministries and members of Latvian cultural and professional societies.

However, the aspirations connected with this national agenda soon clashed with fundamental notions of academia. The professionalisation of European academia after 1850 had created a set of rules and practices concerning universities: the autonomy of science and scholarship, and the notion that all academic appointments should depend solely on merit and qualifications. This academic *habitus* was defended by most of the committee's faculty representatives.

How did the organisers of the new Latvian university manoeuvre between the imperatives of these two agendas? The critical issue in the formative years was the recruitment of qualified academic staff. For the organisers, the most serious problem was undoubtedly the scarcity of academically trained ethnic Latvians. Traditionally a nation of farmers, relatively few Latvians had previously been able to make careers in the Imperial Russian university system. Moreover, in

1919 most of the few Latvian academics were employed at universities in inner Russia and the exigencies of the Civil War and the restrictions imposed by the Soviet regime prevented them from moving to Riga. Not until the summer of 1920 had a number of more experienced ethnic Latvian academics reached Riga.

Even so, in the initial formative years there was a decided lack of qualified ethnic Latvians in several disciplines, especially in the technical faculties, natural science, law and medicine. In the technical faculties, the organisers could fall back on established academics from the previous Riga Polytechnical Institute (RPI). This Historical Institute, with its staff, library and moveable equipment, had been evacuated to Moscow during the war. In 1919, however, most of these academics, under the leadership of the ethnic Latvian chemistry professor Pauls Valdens, returned to Riga.

Probably due in large measure to Valdens's influential position and his strongly held notions of the weight of scientific merit, professors from the former RPI initially became deans in all the technical faculties at the newly created *augstskola*. However, practically all of these experienced professors, with the notable exception of Valdens himself, were Baltic Germans. This posed a problem for the 'national' wing of the organisation committee: for them it was absolutely essential to break with the previous tradition of Baltic German cultural hegemony. This problem for the 'national' wing was compounded by the fact that, as part of the original compromise in 1919, the appointed RPI professors were allowed to continue lecturing in Russian or German.

Early attempts to appoint poorly qualified ethnic Latvians instead of more merited Baltic German academics seem to have been rebutted. Paul von Denffer, dean of the Faculty of Mechanics, insisted that the organisation committee support faculty appointments based on scientific merit. The committee was forced to retreat: to openly advocate appointments based primarily on ethnicity rather than academic qualification was simply not possible. It would run counter to established notions in the academic field, and would certainly impair the new university's ability to gain an international reputation.

Instead of ethnicity, the organisation committee's 'national' wing chose to stress the need for proficiency in the Latvian language. This seems to have been a working compromise, allying those members who actually favoured an 'ethnic' selection of academics with those who saw the full introduction of Latvian as the language of instruction as the paramount issue. At the same time, a language criterion was naturally far more palatable for Baltic German academics than overt ethnic exclusion: a language can, after all, be learnt. Moreover, the language requirement did not run counter to fundamental notions of the academic field: the university systems in practically all European countries presupposed the monopoly of the state language in higher education.

9. CONCLUSIONS

Another compromise in the organisation committee during the formative years was that foreign academics from certain countries could be appointed if no reasonably qualified person could be found in Latvia. In such cases, foreigners would be granted a specified period of grace before being required to lecture in Latvian. This grace period was specified as five years for professors, but only three for the less qualified *docenti*. The obvious strategy here was to establish high academic standards by employing qualified foreigners for a specified time, while allowing a younger generation of Latvian academics to develop. This compromise also entailed strict enforcement of the language requirement for junior academic positions: these persons were meant to constitute the future staff of the university.

However, these compromises in the organisation committee were informal and their actual meaning was frequently contested. Proponents of the 'national' wing, for instance, often voted down the appointment of Baltic German or foreign academics, proposing instead that ethnic Latvians should be sent abroad for scholarly and scientific training. Deans of faculties in desperate need of qualified teaching staff generally did not find such solutions very helpful. The first two deans of the Faculty of Medicine, for instance, reacted angrily to the organisation committee's repeated refusals to appoint Baltic German specialists in medicine. Deans Eduards Zariņš and Roberts Krimbergs were both ethnic Latvians, and perhaps for this very reason more ready to question the committee's majority line than were the Baltic German deans in the technical faculties. For Zariņš and Krimbergs, the paramount issue seems to have been the very pressing pragmatic concern to recruit specialists in order to provide medical students with quality training.

The most eminent and prestigious Latvian academics who gathered in Riga in 1919–1920 were also the ones who most strenuously supported the established academic *habitus*. This group consisted primarily of Pauls Valdens in chemistry, economist Kārlis Balodis, Roberts Krimbergs in medicine, linguist Jānis Endzelīns and ethnographer Pēteris Šmits. Even though the influence of Valdens and Balodis was of very short duration, it had a decisive impact the strategic decisions during the *augstskola's* very first months of existence. These Latvian scholars and scientists in the organisation committee also strongly defended the tenets of the academic agenda, emphasising that appointments should be made entirely on the basis of verifiable merit and qualifications, and that foreign academics should be recruited for specified periods. Precisely by being Latvian, these prominent academics could question the nationalizing policies of the committee's non-academic members.

Latvian linguist Jānis Endzelīns was a particularly active and influential proponent of the academic agenda in the initial years. As dean of the Faculty of

Philology and Philosophy in this formative period, he was also an important driving force behind the relatively open recruitment policy that predominated in this faculty. Although the appointment of German citizens, Baltic Germans, Jews and Russians remained a controversial issue in the organisation committee, Endzelīns managed to gain support for the recruitment of philosopher Walter Frost and archaeologist Max Neubert from German universities. However, the faculty discussions on recruitment clearly show that it was deemed unwise to suggest the appointment of too many academics with German or Russian backgrounds. Sometimes not even Endzelīns, backed by a faculty majority, was able to persuade the committee to confirm the faculty candidates.

Many of the organisation committee's members were clearly unwilling to appoint German citizens, Baltic Germans and ethnic Russians, that is, academics with some ties to the previously hegemonic minority or the previous Imperial rule. Jewish academics were also clearly discriminated; just a few were appointed. Instead, when the recruitment of non-Latvians was considered necessary, candidates from smaller nations were preferred: above all Swedes, Finns, Austrians and Swiss. The Swedish anatomist Gaston Backman was appointed rather than some Baltic German specialist – even if Backman could only lecture in the German language. In the same manner, a Swiss professor of German literature, Max Nussberger, was preferred to a number of possible German or Baltic German candidates.

Clearly, this was not a matter of teaching language: academics from these targeted small countries could only lecture in German. Instead it was an academic version of the 'ethnic reversal' which characterized Latvia at the time: the Latvian majority had assumed political power, and the previously culturally and politically hegemonic Baltic Germans had been reduced to a disempowered minority. However, the number of academics from the targeted smaller nations was never substantial. At no time did the university have more than ten academics from these countries, constituting at the very most three per cent of the teaching staff.

In a general sense, the Latvian scholars and scientists who were most in favour of relatively open recruitment policies based on academic merit were those who had been firmly established at Tsarist universities, for instance Endzelīns and Pēteris Šmits, or those with ample experience from both Russian and German universities, like Krimbergs in medicine and the two economists, Kārlis Balodis and Ernests Birkhāns. They seem to have adhered more consistently to the transnational notions of the academic field. For them, the national meaning of the new university seems primarily have been the creation of an institution with high academic standards, providing high quality research and teaching.

The organisation committee's 'national' wing consisted primarily of younger, less established academics, such as psychologist Pauls Dāle and agronomist Paulis Lejiņš, and persons connected with Latvian associations and government ministries. The most active were Spricis Paegle, representing the Latvian Society, and Pauls Dāle in his role as chairman and representative of the Ministry of Education. Also, Latvian academics who had started their careers as elementary schoolteachers and only later received more advanced scholarly training often sided with the 'national' wing. This group included linguist Juris Plāķis, art historian and principal Ernsts Felsbergs, and a few years later, historian Augusts Tentelis.

The Faculty of Agronomy soon assumed a somewhat sharper national profile than the other faculties, and was represented in the organisation committee by Paulis Lejiņš, a strong proponent of a narrowly ethnic selection of academics. The explanation for this may have been that the discipline of agronomy lay very close to national Latvian issues: being primarily a nation of farmers, and having strong interests in educating agricultural specialists for various cooperative enterprises, this faculty obviously had direct political support for its markedly Latvian profile. Only a few Baltic German academics were ever appointed, and the Latvian language was used to a far greater extent for teaching.

When the *augstskola* was transformed into *Latvijas Universitāte* in 1922 and the elected university council replaced the previous government appointed organisation committee, some vital changes were implemented. Academic appointments no longer required a two-thirds majority – a simple majority sufficed. This meant that it was actually easier for the faculties to gain approval for their selected candidates. The appointment of the German archaeologist Max Ebert in 1922 and the ethnic Russian historian Robert Wipper/Roberts Vipers in 1924, for instance, would not have been possible under the previous voting rules. Also, the Council, unlike the committee, had no non-academic members from the Latvian associations and the government ministries. This meant that some of the 'national' wing's influential members, especially Spricis Paegle, could no longer influence recruitment. The university had gained a larger measure of autonomy, and this evidently strengthened the academic agenda.

Still, the Latvianization of the university continued. The academic power structure had already shifted decisively by 1923. The Baltic German deans of the technical faculties had been an influential group initially; by 1923 they had all been replaced as deans by younger Latvian colleagues. The Baltic German professors remained as active scientists in their respective faculties, but seem to have lost most of their influence on academic career paths for the younger generation, and on university politics in general. Using theoretical concepts developed by Pierre Bourdieu, the career patterns in the academic field had been firmly Latvianized.

However, the question of tuition language remained a thorny and contested issue. It was a national priority that Latvian should be the university's primary teaching language. This was clearly a vital part of the national agenda. At the same time, lecturers in many faculties had great difficulties in teaching in Latvian. This was especially the case in the technical faculties, the natural sciences and law, where many of the academics were Baltic Germans. Foreign specialists in certain disciplines were not expected to lecture in Latvian. Moreover, most textbooks of acceptable quality were printed in German or Russian.

This dilemma persisted for most of the 1920s. A series of compromises were worked out, defining which academics had the right to lecture indefinitely in German or Russian, and who had the right to do so for just a specified period. In general terms, professors from the former Riga Polytechnical Institute who had been appointed already in 1919 were granted unlimited rights. Academics recruited later who were not Latvian-speakers had no such rights; they had to shift immediately to the state language. Only specially recruited foreigners were given a specified grace period: five years for professors, three years for *docenti*. More crucially, all appointees to junior academic positions had to be fluent in Latvian. This meant that after a short transition, Latvian would become the predominant academic language.

But the language problem did not just concern the academic staff's abilities; the organisation committee soon learned that a substantial proportion of the students did not understand Latvian properly. This seems to have been a very unwelcome surprise. The admission rules stated that all men and women with a high school exam were eligible to enrol; unexpectedly, a substantial share of the first batch of students was not ethnic Latvian. In 1919 almost 22 per cent of those enrolled came from the Jewish minority. A sizeable proportion of them, especially those from the Eastern district of Latgale, were apparently not very proficient in Latvian: they were primarily speakers of Russian and Yiddish.

This was naturally a dilemma for the academic leadership: if teaching in Russian was allowed to dominate in some of the faculties, how could the national project be realised? On the other hand, if instruction was conducted in Latvian, a large part of the students would not be able to follow the lectures. Two lines of action developed: one more pragmatic, allowing teaching in Russian if many of the students could not manage Latvian, the other stricter, insisting on Latvian as the language of instruction. While the deans of the technical faculties generally advocated a pragmatic policy, linguist Jānis Endzelīns, who had favoured open recruitment of academic staff, was actually more uncompromising on this issue. For him, and probably also for the other Latvian linguists, the promotion of Latvian as an academic language was of paramount importance.

The language question was eventually used as a measure to curtail the enrolment of Jewish students. Following some violence perpetrated by Latvian nationalist students against Jews in the main university building, the academic leadership introduced more severe language tests in order to reduce the admission of Jews. Russian- and Yiddish-speaking Jews from the Eastern part of Latvia were obviously perceived as 'foreign elements' at the university, not as a fully legitimate part of the student body. Since it was politically impossible to introduce legislation that would exclude or limit the number of Jewish students on ethnic grounds, the university did this more informally, using written and oral language examinations. Discriminatory measures were masked as language tests. However, compared to the situation for Jewish students in Central European states such as Poland, Romania and Hungary, it has to be said that the level of violence and discriminatory practices was considerably lower in Latvia. Only after the Ulmanis coup in 1934 and the introduction of an authoritarian regime were discriminatory measures formalised.

On the matter of student enrolment from ethnic minorities, the academic agenda obviously clashed with national priorities. According to established notions of the academic field, applicants to universities should be selected on the basis of their formal record, not ethnic belonging. At the same time, implicit in the national agenda was clearly a strong conviction that the new university was primarily meant to serve as the educator of the *Latvian* youth, not the minorities. It is interesting, though, that this dilemma does not seem to have occasioned dissent among the members of the organisation committee or the university council. There seems to have been a general consensus in these ruling bodies that the "disproportional" number of Jewish students constituted a problem that had to be solved: the only question was how. Some leading academics, especially linguist Juris Plāķis, were clearly anti-Semitic but it is noteworthy that there was no one in the academic leadership who spoke out for the right of Latvian citizens from Jewish families to enrol and pursue their careers at the university. Supportive measures such as courses in Latvian as a second language were never discussed, probably because the language criteria remained the only feasible way of curtailing the admission of non-Latvian youth.

The recruitment of academic staff and the admission of students to the new national university in Riga highlight the democratic dilemmas of a nationalizing state. While functioning as a parliamentary democracy in other respects, in the field of higher education the national agenda entailed exclusionary and discriminatory measures directed at Latvian citizens belonging to the minorities. The interests of the politicians and academic establishment belonging to the 'core nation' gained predominance over the citizenship rights of the minorities. This democratic deficit has not been fully explored by previous research on nationalizing states, and definitely deserves more scholarly attention. Moreover, while the theoretical concept 'ethnic reversal' has proved very relevant for an understanding of the troubled relations between Latvians and Baltic Germans after 1919, it does not contribute much to an understanding of the discrimination of Jews. Here, it is probably more relevant to point to the legacy of ingrained anti-Semitism in Tsarist Russia, and the general compartmentalisation of society along ethnic lines during the last decades of the Empire. Using Brubaker's terminology, the official Latvian policy towards the minorities remained 'dissimilationist' rather than 'assimilationist'.

These findings also point to something of a blind spot in the dominant Latvian historical narratives. The discriminatory practices against academics and prospective students from the minorities have not received much acknowledgement from Latvian scholars. These practices have obviously not fitted the general picture provided by the official histories of the First Republic, stressing the fundamentally liberal character of the Latvian state, or the 'success narratives' of the history of the University of Latvia.

The fundamental tension between national and academic agendas is also evident in the production of the university's official journal, *Latvijas Universitātes Raksti (LUR)*. The main conflict here concerned publication in German. Members of the 'national' wing in the organisation committee severely criticised the first chief editor, Endzelīns, for allowing far too many articles in the journal's first issue to be printed in German. Since one of the main tenets of the new university was to promote Latvian as an academic language, and minimize the use of German in tuition, this was clearly not acceptable for the nationalists. Endzelīns was swiftly demoted as chief editor, and an official policy was formulated that articles in the *LUR* should primarily be printed in Latvian, English or French. Interestingly, Russian was never an acceptable language for *LUR* articles, even though a large majority of the academics at *Latvijas Universitāte* were quite proficient in Russian – to a far greater extent than in English or French.

Obviously, the *LUR*'s targeted readership included academics in Western Europe. Since relations with German academia remained problematic, the journal was to some extent directed at colleagues at Anglo-Saxon and French universities, displaying scientific and scholarly achievements at *Latvijas Universitāte*. However, even though Endzelīns's successors as editors were less prone to print articles in German, it was impossible to ignore the fact that German remained the dominant language for publications in medicine and the natural sciences. During its first four years, therefore, *LUR* printed almost twice as many articles in German as in English and French combined.

National topics were seldom discussed in the *LUR* – with the exception of a spate of articles on physical anthropology. This discipline, later dismissed as quasi-scientific, was introduced in Latvia by the Swedish anatomy professor Gaston Backman. Together with some Latvian disciples, he conducted investigations into Latvian and Livonian skull proportions, hair and eye colour, and brain weights. While momentarily attracting some attention, these attempts to explore anatomic differences between Latvian and Finno-Ugric populations in the Baltics eventually waned. The results of the quasi-scientific endeavours actually conflicted with strongly held notions among academics in the humanities researching the past and culture of the Latvian people.

In these humanistic disciplines, the university's national project materialized in the codification of the Latvian language, history and culture. However, this project proceeded at a very different pace in the various disciplines involved. The main reasons for the different trajectories seem to have been the availability of trained scholars who were also ethnic Latvians, and the ability of these established academics to form and inspire a younger generation of scholars who would continue to develop the national project. It also mattered to what extent these scholarly endeavours could utilise experience and research from the Tsarist universities.

Among the disciplines involved, it was in Latvian linguistics and literature that the national project was accomplished most swiftly and thoroughly. Here, an 'older' generation established at Imperial Russian universities – Jēkabs Lautenbahs and Jēkabs Velme – could work together with scholars of a 'middle' generation – Jānis Endzelīns and Juris Plāķis – while a 'younger' group of scholars emerged, among others Ernests Blese, Pēteris Ķiķauka and Anna Ābele. Together, this group of linguists and literary scholars standardised the Latvian language, developed a new orthography, expanded the range of Latvian by adding scholarly, scientific and technical terms, and produced new Latvian grammars and dictionaries. In literary studies, the work of Lautenbahs on Latvian folktales and folksongs, *dainas*, was continued by Ludvigs Bērziņš and ethnographer Pēteris Šmits.

The study of Latvian folklore had carried immense symbolic weight in the national movement in the late nineteenth century; in a way, the common folklore heritage was a major definer of the Latvian nation. A specialised folklore archive, *Latvijas Folkloras Krātuve*, was created in 1924 on the initiative of its first director, Anna Bērzkalne, with the mission to continue the collection and systematization of Latvian folklore. At the new university, however, the discipline of folklore and ethnography did not become one of the leading 'national' subjects. While its most prominent academic, Šmits, was clearly an eminent scholar and a highly respected figure in Latvian nationalist circles, he evidently did not manage to turn folklore and ethnography into a strong discipline within the faculty. A group of promising younger scholars never emerged, and ethnography hardly even figured in the faculty curriculum. The absence of a younger generation of scholars in this particular discipline is very conspicuous: after Šmits's death in 1938 the faculty chose to recruit a relatively inexperienced Swede, Dag Trotzig, to teach ethnography.

The reasons for this failure are probably manifold. The links with the previous generation of nationally minded folklorists were relatively weak: the national 'hero' Krišjānis Barons returned to Latvia after independence and assumed his position as honorary fellow of the university, but by that time he was too old to take an active part in academic work. Moreover, the collection and display of folklore material seems to have been more important than the 'academisation' of the discipline: instead, folklore was performed at song and dance festivals, displayed in museums, and collected and systematized in the Folklore Archive. It is also possible that Šmits's misogynist view of female academics may have played a part: the great majority of the students in the faculty were women, and Šmits did not encourage any of them to pursue an academic career.

In Latvian linguistics, literary studies and folklore, there were strong links to the previous endeavours of nationalist intellectuals. To some extent they could also develop within the framework of Imperial Russian academia. Moreover, in these disciplines there was no established Baltic German tradition, or for that matter any Baltic German academics, against whom the Latvian scholars would have had to position themselves. In the other two 'national' disciplines considered here, archaeology and history, the situation was materially different. These fields had previously been explored very little by nationalist intellectuals, and very few Latvians had opted for academic specialization in historical disciplines. In both these subjects, the existence of Baltic German master narratives of the past, and the recruitment of experienced ethnic German academics when these disciplines were first established at *Latvijas Universitāte*, meant that the development of nationally Latvian historical master narratives was considerably more complicated.

In archaeology, the lack of any scholarly trained Latvians meant that the initial work of developing the discipline was left to the Baltic German Karl Löwis of Menar and the German citizen Max Ebert. Löwis of Menar actually lacked proper scholarly competence, being an entirely self-taught archaeologist and cartographer. Ebert, on the other hand, was a thoroughly trained archaeologist with ample experience of excavations in the Baltic territories. However, the faculty clearly saw these appointments as temporary measures: the main aim was to develop the discipline and wait for a younger generation of Latvian archaeologists to gain the necessary expertise.

The situation changed dramatically in 1924 with the arrival of Francis Balodis, previously professor at Saratov University in Soviet Russia. Balodis started his academic career as an art historian and Egyptologist, but later developed an expertise on Mongol settlements on the lower Volga. While initially not perceived as an archaeologist by his faculty colleagues, Balodis swiftly reoriented and turned into a forceful promoter of a national brand of Latvian archaeology. Competing national narratives and interpretations soon lost their influence: Ebert soon chose to accept a professorship at the German Königsberg University, and Löwis of Menar's appointment was discontinued. Instead, the charismatic Balodis could assemble a group of younger scholars who then continued to develop a nationally inspired brand of archaeology in the 1930s.

In the discipline of history, matters were a little more complicated. Here, too, there was a decided lack of academically qualified Latvian scholars. The first historian appointed by the organisation committee in 1919 was a Baltic German, the medievalist Leonid Arbusow. Unlike Löwis of Menar and Ebert, however, Arbusow was immediately given tenure, and was promoted to professor in 1922. During the faculty's formative years, Arbusow was clearly its most qualified historian.

Two ethnic Latvians were eventually appointed on a permanent basis: Jānis Krīgers-Krodznieks and Augusts Tentelis. Krodznieks belonged to the 'older' generation of nationalist intellectuals, and actually made some attempts to formulate a national historical narrative. However, his academic record and responsibilities were rather slim: he was merely a *privātdocents* with very little teaching within the faculty. His main occupation, it seems, was as director of the State Historical Archive and editor of its historical journal. His death in 1924 also limited his influence on the discipline of history.

The other Latvian historian, Augusts Tentelis, had received his basic training at St Petersburg University. In spite of a very modest academic record – he had only written a *Magister* thesis – he was swiftly promoted to professor in 1921, probably as a counterweight to the Baltic German Arbusow. However, Tentelis clearly failed to meet expectations as a developer of a Latvian historical master narrative. There were probably three reasons for this: first, Tentelis had previously specialised in Italian medieval history, and was not very well acquainted with Latvian historical issues. Second, he was evidently not a productive writer. There are some suggestions that he suffered from writer's block, but he certainly never produced any major work of history.

Third, perhaps for this very reason, Tentelis soon chose to devote his time to administrative duties and politics. He was dean of faculty and principal of the university, as well as Minister of Education several times in the 1920s and 1930s. However, while failing to be the historiographer who codified a national master narrative, Tentelis played a very important role in academic leadership and politics, drawing up guidelines for a future national history and channelling resources to younger scholars. Although he was not clearly committed to the national agenda before the mid-1920s, Tentelis seems to have played a pivotal role in transforming the university in a more national-conservative direction.

Paradoxically, the historian in the faculty who emerged as the main promoter of a new national narrative was in fact an ethnic Russian, Roberts Vipers. Previously a professor at Odessa and Moscow Universities, he was a very experienced scholar – but hardly a specialist on Latvian or Baltic issues. Being initially appointed for a very short period, he soon redirected his scholarly interests and threw his weight behind the emerging Latvian historical narrative. Since it took a long time to develop a younger generation of historians – Vipers's own pupil Marģers Stepermanis did not become a *privātdocents* until 1936 – Vipers apparently managed to make himself indispensable, continuing to play an important role as a codifier of Latvian history all through the 1930s.

The lack of academically trained historians with an ethnic Latvian background is also the main reason why a national master narrative of the past was developed relatively late. Compared to archaeology, where the energetic and charismatic Francis Balodis had already managed to formulate and spread a new national narrative on Latvian prehistoric times in the late 1920s, similar tendencies in the discipline of history were weaker and developed considerably later. The main change occurred only after the implementation of an authoritarian regime under Kārlis Ulmanis: obviously under some pressure, the Baltic German historian Arbusow resigned from the university and was quickly replaced by the Latvian legal historian Arveds Švābe.

During the Ulmanis regime, the disciplines of history and archaeology were given clear priority. Ulmanis took a strong personal interest in the development of a national master narrative: a Latvian history produced by Latvian historians and archaeologists for the Latvian nation and providing solid support for his regime. Material means were supplied with the creation of the Historical Institute in 1936, an institution entirely in line with Ulmanis's general policy of *latviskošana*, a more thorough Latvianization of society. The Historical Institute, led by Tentelis, Švābe, and Balodis, was given resources for the publication of extensive source collections, the production of a new historical journal, and material support for a younger generation of historians researching national Latvian topics. At the same time, the Institute gave ample space to Ulmanis's personal reflections on history. The 'national turn' was taken to a new level: it was now not merely a matter of researching Latvian topics or developing a Latvian perspective on history. The doctrine that only Latvians could write their own history meant that academics at the Institute embraced what I have called a nation-grounded epistemology.

Balodis was also the main driving force behind the journal *Senatne un Māksla*. This publication was used as an important vehicle whereby accessible and condensed versions of the emerging master narratives on prehistoric and historic times were conveyed to the general Latvian public. It also served to inform and familiarise the Latvian public with the work and collections of the national museums, and to communicate the images of academic and artistic 'heroes' of the nation.

This part of the university's national agenda, the establishment of academic 'heroes' of the nation, was not a straightforward process. Rather, it contains some paradoxical twists. Jānis Endzelīns was clearly seen as the most prominent Latvian linguist but he adhered to a clearly transnational view of academia, often supporting the recruitment of merited Baltic German scholars. He certainly ruffled some nationalist feathers as chief editor of the *LUR*, and also by publishing a major Latvian grammar in the German language. Another 'hero', Pēteris Šmits, devoted much of his time to the exploration of Latvian pagan mythology and the publishing of Latvian folklore literature; at the same time, his main scholarly competence was in the Chinese language and the ethnography of some Far Eastern ethnic groups. Somewhat similarly, the acclaimed Francis Balodis became the founding father of national Latvian archaeology, but was really an expert on ancient Egypt before radically changing his scholarly priorities. He eventually emerged as something of an academic 'hero' in the early 1930s, gaining wide national and international recognition.

It should not be forgotten, though, that the two most promising academic 'heroes' of the nation never filled their expected role. Professor of chemistry Pauls Valdens, undoubtedly the most internationally recognised Latvian scientist when the *augstskola* started in 1919, was immediately cast in the role of future principal and academic figurehead. Instead, he stuck to his strongly held notions of science as a transnational or a-national undertaking, and eventually left to pursue his research at a German university. The second contender for the role of academic national 'hero', the renowned economist Kārlis Balodis, soon disqualified himself for this position – and in fact for any leading academic position at the new university – by refusing to relinquish his German citizenship.

In a comparative perspective, there seem to have been some important differences between *Latvijas Universitāte*, the Estonian Tartu University, and the University of Lithuania in Kaunas. While all three belonged to nationalizing states in the interwar period and were certainly perceived as national projects primarily catering to the majority ethnic group, they differed in some respects in terms of recruitment policy and key national disciplines. While Baltic German academics after the 'ethnic reversal' were seen as negative internal 'others' in both Riga and Tartu, the Estonians' possibility of recruiting established Finnish scholars did not have a counterpart in Latvia. The presence of these positive external 'others' seems to have tempered the national agenda among Estonian academics, and strengthened notions of an established academic field.

At the Lithuanian university in Kaunas, on the other hand, the main difference from Riga seems to have been that another 'national' discipline had primary importance: history. While history at *Latvijas Universitāte* played third or even fourth fiddle within the faculty, and developed a national master narrative surprisingly late, historians at Kaunas appear to have been much more central to the Lithuanian national project. The history of the previous Grand Duchy of Lithuania had been primary concern among nationalist intellectuals, and this field of study remained central at the new university in Kaunas. History also developed into a field of academic contention with Polish scholars, a tendency that mirrored the political tensions between Lithuania and Poland in the interwar period. Developing a 'correct' national historical narrative therefore became a priority.

In general terms, the nationalisation of *Latvijas Universitāte* seems to have taken place in stages. As could perhaps be expected, the formative years were characterized by a series of conflicts and compromises between proponents of the academic and national agendas. Baltic German academics remained influential in some of the faculties for the first few years, but later clearly lost much of their say in recruitment and promotion. Among the Latvian academics, disagreement continued as to the meaning of a national university: should this be seen primarily as a matter of ethnicity, language, or academic excellence?

Eventually, after the first turbulent years, a certain *modus vivendi* appeared. Among the university leadership there was a tacit understanding that proficiency in Latvian was a precondition for appointments to junior academic positions, and that foreign academics would be recruited only if there were no reasonable 'native' candidates – and if so, Germans or Russians should preferably not be chosen. Moreover, there seems to have been a tacit understanding that the university was primarily meant for ethnic Latvian students, and that "disproportionate" numbers of Jewish applicants should be reduced by means of language tests.

A further turn in a national direction is perceptible after 1925. Previously, the university leadership had been much influenced by proponents of the academic agenda such as Jānis Endzelīns and Pēteris Šmits, and pragmatists such as the medical professors Roberts Krimbergs and Jānis Ruberts. By 1925, however, more 'national' academics appear to have seized the initiative. Historian Augusts Tentelis, archaeologist Francis Balodis and linguist Juris Plāķis all played important roles in politics and university leadership in the late 1920s, and they materially contributed to a general shift in a more nationalist direction. This tendency became even more pronounced after the implementation of authoritarian rule in 1934, when the national disciplines within the humanities became a vital part of the general programme of *latviskošana*. Here, a new consensus on what constituted national scholarship was developed into what must be seen as a paradigmatic shift, the creation of a new epistemic community or a new *epistèmè* in a Foucauldian sense. In a process over fifteen years, academia in Latvia had become nationalised.

This study has shown that nationalising academia in a post-imperial state is a very complex and sometimes even paradoxical process, especially if the state is dominated by a previously subordinated national group and at the same time adheres to the principles of democratic government. The Latvian case illustrates the tensions and paradoxes when vital tenets and objectives of the national agenda clash with established notions of the academic field. In a more general sense, this case illustrates the difficulties that ensue when a multi-ethnic state in a short and dramatic process tries to adopt the excessively tight costume of a nation-state.

Appendix
Academics at *Latvijas Universitāte* 1919–1940 (referred to in this book)

ĀBELE, ANNA, b. 1881. Latvian linguist, specialist in phonetics.

ALTEMENTS, ALFRĒDS, b. 1902. Latvian historian. Wrote primarily on the Latvian national movement in the nineteenth century.

ARABASJIN, KONSTANTIN, Soviet citizen, ethnic Russian. Professor of Slavic literature at *LU* 1920–1922. His appointment was not extended.

ARBUSOW, LEONID, b. 1882. Baltic German historian, medievalist. Appointed in 1919, resigned in 1936.

BACKMAN, GASTON, b. 1883. Swedish citizen. Professor of anatomy between 1920 and 1925. Introduced human anthropology in Latvia.

BALODIS, FRANCIS, b. 1882. Initially an Egyptologist, later a developer of Latvian archaeology. Dean of Faculty several times in the 1930s.

BALODIS, KĀRLIS, b. 1864. Economist. Professor at Berlin University in 1905, and at *LU* in 1919. Died in 1931.

BARONS, KRIŠJĀNIS, b. 1835. Folklorist, Honorary Fellow.

BĒRZIŅŠ, JĀNIS, b. 1883. Latvian historian, primarily engaged in the teachers' training seminar.

BĒRZIŅŠ, LUDVIGS, b. 1870. Historian of Latvian literature. At *LU* from 1922. Member of the Steering Committee of the Folklore Archive.

BĒRZKALNE, ANNA, b. 1891. Folklorist. Founder and first Director of the Folklore Archive

BIRKHĀNS, ERNESTS, b. 1872. Professor of business studies. Dean of the Faculty of Law and Economics, 1920–1922. Previously on the academic staff of the Riga Polytechnical Institute.

BLESE, ERNSTS, b. 1892. Latvian linguist. Member of several government commissions on the standardisation of the Latvian language.

BRÜCH, JOSEF, Austrian citizen. Professor of German linguistics at *LU* between 1923 and 1926.

CELMS, TEODORS, b. 1893. Philosopher. Educated at German universities. At *LU* from 1927.

CENTNERŠVĒRS, MEČISLAVS, b. 1874. Polish citizen, Mosaic religion. Professor of chemistry at RPI, and at *LU* from 1919 to 1929. Honorary doctor in 1929.

DĀLE, PAULS, b. 1889. Psychologist. Chairman of the organisation committee, 1920–1922.

DAUGE, ALEKSANDRS, b. 1868. Pedagogue. Education Minister in the early 1920s.

VON DENFFER, PAUL, b. 1871. Baltic German. Professor of mechanics at RPI, and at *LU* from 1919. Dean of Faculty 1919–1923.

DIEHL, ERICH, b. 1890. Baltic German classical philologist. Evacuated in 1939.

DIŠLERS, KĀRLIS, b. 1878. Jurist, specialist in administrative law. At *LU* from 1920. Dean of Faculty several times between 1922 and 1939.

DREIMANIS, PĒTERIS, Latvian historian. Teacher at a Riga gymnasium. At *LU* during 1921 only.

DUNSDORFS, EDGARS, b. 1904. Latvian economic historian. Pupil of Švābe and Heckscher.

EBERT, MAX, German citizen. Archaeologist. At *LU* 1922–1925. Laid the scholarly foundations for the discipline of archaeology at *LU*.

ENDZELĪNS, JĀNIS, b. 1873. Prominent Latvian linguist. Dean of Faculty 1920–1922. Chairman of the Steering Committee of the Folklore Archive.

FELSBERGS, ERNSTS, b.1866. Art historian, classicist. Principal 1920–1923. Died in 1928.

FĒRMANIS, ERNSTS, b. 1872. Professor of medicine. Advocated 'racial hygiene' during the Ulmanis regime.

FROST, WALTER, b. 1869. German citizen, philosopher. Appointed at *LU* in 1920, died in 1936.

ĢINTERS, VALDIS, b. 1899. Latvian archaeologist. Director of the State Historical Museum.

GLASENAPP, MAXIMILIAN, b. 1845. Baltic German professor of chemistry at RPI, at *LU* from 1919. Died in 1923.

HAUZENBERGA, EDĪTE, Baltic German family background. Latvian linguist. Assistant to Jānis Endzelīns.

JANSONS, JĀNIS, b. 1892. Latvian linguist, specialist in Latvian literature.

KĀRKLIŅŠ, JĀNIS, b. 1877. Economist. Dean of Faculty several times between 1922 and 1939.

KARLSONE, ALĪSE, b. 1881. Lecturer, later *privātdocente* in German.

KAULIŅŠ, JĀNIS, b. 1863. Latvian linguist. Member of the Steering Committee of the Folklore Archive.

KJELLIN, TOR HELGE, b. 1885. Swedish citizen. Art historian.

KOLBUŠEVSKIS, STANISLAVS, b. 1901. Polish citizen. Professor of Slavic literature.

KRĪGERS-KRODZNIEKS, JĀNIS, b 1851. Latvian historian and Director of the State Historical Archive. Honorary doctor in 1924.

KRIMBERGS, ROBERTS, b. 1874. Professor of medical chemistry at *LU* in 1920. Dean of Faculty 1920–1922.

KŠIŽANOVSKIS, JULIANS, b. 1892. Polish citizen. Professor of Slavic literature.

ĶIĶAUKA, PĒTERIS, b. 1886. Latvian linguist.

LAUTENBAHS, JĒKABS, b. 1847. Historian of literature. Previously professor at Dorpat/Jur'ev University. Honorary doctor in 1924.

LEBEDINSKI, NAUM, b. 1888. Swiss citizen, Jewish/Lutheran religion. Professor of zoology. Recruited to *LU* in 1920.

LEJIŅŠ, PAULIS, b.1883 Latvian agronomist. Vice-Principal between October 1919 and September 1920. Very active member of the 'national wing' of the organisation committee 1919–1922. Later a *Saeima* delegate for the Social Democrats.

LIEPIŅA, MILDA, b. 1889. Psychologist. Senior assistant in 1939.

LUKSTIŅŠ, GUSTAVS, b. 1894. *Privātdocents* in ancient Roman history.

MAZING, OSKAR, b. 1874. Baltic German. Lecturer in German at RPI, and later at *LU* between 1919 and 1922. After that employed at the Herder Institute.

MINCS, PAULS, b. 1868. Jewish Latvian citizen. Professor of law. At *LU* from 1919. Deported to the Soviet Union in 1941.

NUSSBERGER, MAX, b. 1879. Swiss citizen. Professor of German literature. Recruited to *LU* in 1922, remained during the entire First Republic.

PAUKULIS, ERNSTS, b. 1872. Professor of pathology. At *LU* from 1920.

PLĀĶIS, JURIS, b. 1869. Latvian linguist. Professor at Kazan University, Russia, at *LU* from 1920. Minister of Education between June 1920 and April 1921. Vice-Principal1922–1924 and 1925–1927.

PRĪMANIS, JĒKABS, b. 1892. Professor of anatomy. Together with Gaston Backman a developer of Latvian human anthropology.

REINHARDS, GUSTAVS, *Privātdocents* in medicine. Proponent of 'racial hygiene'. Died in 1937.

RUBERTS, JĀNIS, Professor of ophthalmology. Principal 1922–?

RUDOVSKA, OLGA, *Privātdocente*, art history.

SCHNEIDER, ERNEST, Swiss citizen, child psychologist. Promoter of psychoanalysis.

SCHWEINFURTH, PHILIPP, b. 1887. Baltic German. Art historian, at *LU* between 1919 and 1926.

SPEKKE, ARNOLDS, b. 1887. Romanist philologist, later also historian. From 1933 part of the diplomatic service as Latvian ambassador to Italy. Remained affiliated to *LU*.

STEPERMANIS, MARĢERS, b. 1898. Latvian modern historian, pupil of Roberts Vipers.

STRAUBERGS, KĀRLIS, b. 1890. Professor of classical literature. From 1929 Director of the Folklore Archive. Minister of Education between January and December 1924.

ŠMITS, PĒTERIS, b. 1869. Sinologist, ethnographer and folklorist. Professor at *LU* in 1920. Academic director of the State Historical Museum. Member of the Steering Committee of the Folklore Archive. Died in 1938.

ŠNORE, ELVĪRA, b. 1905. Latvian archaeologist.

ŠNORE, RAULS, b. 1901. Latvian archaeologist.

ŠTURMS, EDUARDS, b. 1895. Latvian archaeologist.

ŠVĀBE, ARVEDS, b. 1888. Legal historian. From 1936 professor of Latvian history. Vice- Director of the Historical Institute.

TENTELIS, AUGUSTS, b. 1876. Professor of history in 1921. Vice-Principal 1924–1925, Principal 1925–1927, 1929–1932, Dean of Faculty 1927–1928, 1931–1933. Minister of Education in 1928 and 1935–1938.

TIANDER, KARL, Finnish citizen. Professor in German linguistics 1921–22, but actually an expert on Slavic languages. His appointment was not extended, primarily for political reasons.

TROTZIG, DAG, b. 1914. Swedish citizen. Ethnographer, at *LU* between 1938 and 1940.

VALDENS, PAULS, First Chairman of the organisation committee. Latvian professor of chemistry at RPI and at *LU* from 1919, but left the same year for a similar position at Rostock University, Germany.

WALLIN, HARRY, Swedish citizen. Lecturer in the Swedish language and Swedish history.

VELME, JĒKABS, b. 1855. Lecturer in German. Honorary doctor in 1924.

VĪGRABS, JURIS, b. 1881. Latvian historian and diplomat.

VIPERS, BORISS, Soviet citizen, ethnic Russian. Art historian, son of Roberts Vipers.

VIPERS, ROBERTS, b. 1859. Soviet citizen, ethnic Russian. Professor of history in Odessa and Moscow 1894–1923. At *LU* from September 1924.

ZĀLĪTE, PĒTERIS, b 1864. Philosopher. Joined *LU* in 1920, appointed professor in 1921. Before that primarily the editor of the important Latvian newspaper *Mājas viesis*.

ZĀLĪTIS, FRĪDIS, b. 1887. Latvian historian, primarily a teacher at a gymnasium in Rīga. At *LU* 1919–22.

ZĪLE, MĀRTIŅŠ, Professor of medicine. Principal in the early 1920s.

References

Manuscript sources
Latvijas Nacionālais arhīvs
Latvijas Valsts vēstures arhīvs (LVVA) Rīga
Izglītības ministrijas fonds (Ministry of Education archive)
Latvijas Universitātes fonds (the University of Latvia archive)
Latvijas vēstures institūta fonds (Historical Institute archive)

Printed sources
Latvijas Universitāte divdesmit gados 1919–1939 *(1939), Vol. I–II. [the University of Latvia during Twenty Years] Rīga.*

Latviešu konversācijas vārdnīca (1927–1928) [Latvian Conversation Dictionary] Rīga.

Latvijas Universitāte. Lekciju un praktisko darbu saraksts 1939/40 mācības gadam (1939) [Record of the teaching assignments for the academic year 1939–1940] Rīga.

Latvijas Universitātes Filoloģijas un filosofijas fakultātes Bibliografisks pārskats, 1919–1925 *(1926) [Bibliographic overview] Rīga.*

Latvijas Universitātes Filoloģijas un filosofijas fakultātes Bibliografisks pārskats, II, 1925–1930 (1930) [Bibliographic overview] Rīga

Latvijas Universitātes piecgadu darbības pārskats 1919–1924 (1925) [Overview of the first five years of academic work at *LU*] Rīga.

Latvijas Universitātes Satversme. [Constitution of the University of Latvia, 1922] *Izglītības Ministr. Mēnešraksts*, 1922:2.

Latvijas Universitātes Satversme. Projekts. [Suggestion for the Constitution of the University of Latvia, 1922] Rīga 1922.

Valsts statistikas gada grāmata, 1920–1934. [Government's Yearly Book of Statistics] Rīga.

Periodicals
Baltische Monatsschrift
Brīvā Zeme
Latvijas Sargs
Rigasche Rundschau
Sējējs
Students

Universitas

Memoirs

Arājs, Kārlis (2005): *Latviešu kauli ... Atmiņas par anatomikumu un antropoloģijas ziedu laikiem Latvijā.* Rīgas Stradiņa Universitāte, Rīga.

Balodis, Francis (1941): *Våld och frihet. En lettisk universitetsprofessors minnen.* Gebers, Stockholm.

Bērziņš, Ludvigs (1935): *Mūža rīts un darba diena. Atmiņu grāmata.* Gulbis, Rīga.

Ģērmanis, Uldis (1995): *Zili stikli, zaļi ledi.* Memento/Zinātne, Stokholma/Rīga.

Spekke, Arnolds (2000): *Atmiņu brīži.* Jumava, Rīga.

Šnore, Rauls (1997): "Raula Šnores dzīves un zinātniskās darbības apraksts (autobiogrāfija)", In *Arheologi Elvīra Šnore (1905–1996) un Rauls Šnore (1901–1962). Biobibliogrāfija, vēstules, laikabiedru atmiņas.* Latvijas vēstures institūta apgāds, Rīga 1997.

Contemporary publications

Adamovičs, Ludvigs (1937): "Senlatviešu reliģija", In Balodis, Francis (ed.): *Vēstures atziņas un tēlojumi. Vēstures skolotājiem 1936 gadā lasīto lekciju sakopojums.* Izglītības ministrijas izdevums. Rīga 1937.

Adamovičs, Ludvigs (1938a): "Latviešu tautības veidošanās un tautas izglītība latviešu un vācu apgaismojumā", *Latvijas Vēstures Institūta Žurnāls*, 1938:2.

Adamovičs, Ludvigs (1938b): "Latviešu tautības veidošanās un tautas izglītība latviešu un vācu apgaismojumā. (Beigas).", *Latvijas Vēstures Institūta Žurnāls*, 1938:3.

Altements, Alfrēds (1938): "Vidzemes zemnieku reformas jautājums 1795.–97. g.", *Latvijas Vēstures Institūta Žurnāls*, 1938:1

Altements, Alfrēds (1939a): "Studijas nacionālās atmodas vēsturē", *Latvijas Vēstures Institūta Žurnāls*, 1939:1.

Altements, Alfrēds (1939b): "Studijas nacionālās atmodas vēsturē II", *Latvijas Vēstures Institūta Žurnāls*, 1939:3.

Arbuzovs, Leonīds (1920a): "Peezīmes par XVI. g.s.vecakajeem latveešu literaturas peeminekļeem. Visagrakee rokraksti latveešu valodā kopš 1558. g.", *Izglītības Ministrijas Mēnešraksts*, 1920:1.

Arbuzovs, Leonīds (1920b): "Latveešu tēvreize senos textos", *Izglītības Ministrijas Mēnešraksts*, 1920:2.

Arbuzovs, Leonīds (1920c): "Atbilde uz R. Klaustiņa kga recenziju", *Izglītības Ministrijas Mēnešraksts*, 1920:2.

Arbuzovs, Leonīds (1921a): "Reformācijas kustība latviešu starpā", *Izglītības Ministrijas Mēnešraksts*, 1921:2.

REFERENCES

Arbusow, Leonid (1921b): "Studien zur Geschichte der lettischen Befölkerung Rīgas im Mittelalter und 16. Jahrhundert", *Latvijas Augstskolas Raksti* I.

Arbusow, Leonid (1923): "Kirchliches Leben der Rīgaschen Losträger im 15. Jahrhundert", *Latvijas Universitātes Raksti* VI.

Arbusow, Leonid (1924): "Ein Verzeichnis der bäurlichen Apgaben im Stift Kurland (1582/83)", *Latvijas Universitātes Raksti* X.

Arbusovs, Leonīds (1926): "Die handschriftliche Überlieferung des 'Cronicon Livoniae' Heinrichs von Lettland", *Latvijas Universitātes Raksti* XV.

Arbusovs, Leonīds (1929): "II. Römischer Arbeitsbericht", *Latvijas Universitātes Raksti* XX.

Augstkalns, A (1938): "Politiski dzejoļi 1863. gadā un Dinsberģa trimda", *Latvijas Vēstures Institūta Žurnāls*, 1938:3.

Auškāps, Jūlijs (1936): "Latviešu nākotnes ceļi", *Sējējs*, 1936:1.

Backman, Gaston (1925): "Antropologische Beiträge zur Kenntnis der Bevölkerung Lettlands", *Latvijas Universitātes Raksti* XII.

Ballod, C [Balodis, Kārlis] (1922): "La Latvie", *Latvijas Augstskolas Raksti*, III.

Balodis, Francis (1924a): "Otrā Tebu laikmeta Ēģiptes garīgā kultūra", *Izglītības Ministrijas Mēnešraksts*, 1924:2.

Balodis, Francis (1924b): "Mākslas reforma Echnatona laikā", *Latvijas Universitātes Raksti* XI.

Balodis, Francis (1926): "Alt-Sarai und Neu-Sarai, die Hauptstädte der Goldenen Horde", *Latvijas Universitātes Raksti* XIII.

Balodis, Francis (1930): "Latviešu aizvēsture", In Balodis, Francis un Šmits, Pēteris (ed.) *Latvieši. Rakstu krājums.* Vol. I. Rīga 1930.

Balodis, Francis (1937): "Senās latviešu zemes", In Balodis, Francis (ed.): *Vēstures atziņas un tēlojumi. Vēstures skolotājiem 1936. gadā lasīto lekciju sakopojums.* Izglītības ministrijas izdevums. Rīga 1937.

Balodis (1938): "Vēsture un vēstures palīgdisciplīnas", In *Zinātne tēvzemei divdesmit gados 1918–1938.* Latvijas Universitāte, Rīga

Balodis, Francis (1940): *Jersika un tai 1939. gadā izdarītie izrakumi.* Rīga.

Balodis, Francis (1944): "Arkeologiska synpunkter på livisk bosättning i Lettland", *Fornvännen*, 1944:3.

Balodis, Francis (1947): "Latvia and the Latvians", *Journal of Central European Affairs*, 1947:3.

Die Baltischen Provinzen am Rubicon. Ein Sendschreiben an die Deutschen der Ostseeländer. Von einem Patrioten (1869), Berlin.

Baumanis, Arturs (1938): "Kronvalda Ata un Krišjāņa Valdemāra senči", *Latvijas Vēstures Institūta Žurnāls*, 1938:2.

Beiträge zur Statistik der Stadt Rīga und ihrer Verwaltung (1909), I. von Schrenck, B (ed.) Rīga.

Bērziņš, Alfreds (1937): "Latvijas konservatorija ir mūsu universitātes akadēmiskā māsa.", *Universitas*, 1937:2

Bērziņš, Jānis (1937a): "Livonija un Lietuva 16. gadsimteņa sešdesmitajos gados", In Balodis, Francis (ed.): *Vēstures atziņas un tēlojumi. Vēstures skolotājiem 1936. gadā lasīto lekciju sakopojums*. Izglītības ministrijas izdevums. Rīga 1937.

Bērziņš, Jānis (1937b): "Kurzemes hercogiste XVI. un XVII. gs.", In Balodis, Francis (ed.): *Vēstures atziņas un tēlojumi. Vēstures skolotājiem 1936. gadā lasīto lekciju sakopojums*. Izglītības ministrijas izdevums. Rīga 1937.

Bērziņš, Ludvigs (1930a): "Tautas dzejas nozīme latviešu tautas dzīvē", In Balodis, Francis un Šmits, Pēteris (ed.) *Latvieši. Rakstu krājums*. Vol. I. Rīga 1930.

Bērziņš, Ludvigs (1930b): "Latviešu rakstniecība svešu tautu aizbildniecībā", In Balodis, Francis un Šmits, Pēteris (ed.) *Latvieši. Rakstu krājums*. Vol. I. Rīga 1930.

Biezbardis, Kaspars (1865a): *Der Sprach- und Bildungskampf in der Baltischen Provinzen Russlands*. Bautzen.

Biezbardis, Kaspars (1865b): *Zustände und Eigenthümlichkeiten in den baltischen Provinzen Russlands*. Bautzen.

Biļķins, V (1938): "Rimberta dati par kuršiem", *Latvijas Vēstures Institūta Žurnāls*, 1938:2.

Blanks, Ernests (1926): *Nācija un valsts*. Jelgava.

Blese, Ernsts (1930): "Latviešu valodas attīstības posmi", In Balodis, Francis un Šmits, Pēteris (ed.) *Latvieši. Rakstu krājums*. Vol. I. Rīga 1930.

Blese, Ernsts (1937): "Seno kuršu etniskā piederība", *Senatne un Māksla*, Nr. II, 1937.

Brežgo, B (1939): "Latgales zemnieku pretošanās dzimtbūšanai krievu laikos", *Latvijas Vēstures Institūta Žurnāls*, 1939:2.

Dāle, Pauls (1921): *Vēsturisks pārskats par Latvijas Augstskolas nodibināšanu un viņas darbību pirmā (1919/20.) mācības gadā*. Rīga.

Dokumenti par "Pēterburgas Avīzēm", Tentelis, Augusts un Altements, Alfrēds (ed.) Rīga.

Dokumenti par tautas atmodas laikmetu 1856.-1867.g., Tentelis, Augusts un Altements, Alfrēds (ed.) Rīga.

Dunsdorfs, Edgars (1937a): "Muižu redukcija Zviedrijā", *Latvijas Vēstures Institūta Žurnāls*, 1937:1

Dunsdorfs, Edgars (1937b): "Latvju zemnieka brīvības izredzes Kārļa XI laikā", *Latvijas Vēstures Institūta Žurnāls*, 1937:2.

REFERENCES

Dunsdorfs, Edgars (1938): "Klaušu beigu cēliens Kurzemē", *Latvijas Vēstures Institūta Žurnāls*, 1938:1.

Dunsdorfs, Edgars (1939): Review of Rudolf Schulze's *Der Deutsche Bauer im Baltikum*, *Latvijas Vēstures Institūta Žurnāls*, 1939:2.

Endzelīns, Jānis (1922): *Lettische Grammatik*. Rīga.

Endzelīns, Jānis (1928): "Ievads", In *Latvju tautas daiņas* Endzelīns, J & Klaustiņš, R (ed.) Vol. I. Literatūra, Rīga.

Endzelīns, Jānis (1930): "Latvieši un viņu valoda", In Balodis, Francis un Šmits, Pēteris (ed.) *Latvieši. Rakstu krājums*. Vol. I. Rīga 1930.

Felsbergs, Ernsts (1921a): "Dažas ziņas par Latvijas Augstskolu", *Izglītības Ministrijas Mēnešraksts*, 1921:1.

Felsbergs, Ernsts (1921b): "A Hieron Kylix", *Latvijas Augstskolas Raksti* I.

Goba, Alfrēds (1929): *Pirmās "Pēterburgas Avīzes" un viņu nozīme tautas atmodas gaitā*. Rīga.

Jerums, N & Vītols, T M (1928): "Beiträge zur Anthropologie der Letten", *Latvijas Universitātes Raksti* XVII.

Kjellins, T H (1932): "Latviešu māksla", In Balodis, F, Šmits, P un Tentelis, A (1932): *Latvieši. Rakstu krājums* Vol. II, Rīga 1932.

Klaustiņš, Roberts (1920a): "Die Einführung der Reformation in Liv-, Est- und Kurland. Bearbeitet von Dr. L Arbusow", *Izglītības Ministrijas Mēnešraksts*, 1920:2.

Klaustiņš, Roberts (1920b): "Peezimes pee Arbuzova kunga atbildes", *Izglītības Ministrijas Mēnešraksts*, 1920:2.

Krodznieks, Jānis (1920): "Kā zaudēta zeme" *Izglītības Ministrijas Mēnešraksts*, 1920:1.

Krodznieks, Jānis (1921a): "Līgumi ar kuršiem 1230. gadā", *Izglītības Ministrijas Mēnešraksts*, 1921:1.

Krodznieks, Jānis (1921b): "Paskaidrojumi", *Izglītības Ministrijas Mēnešraksts*, 1921:1

Krodznieks, Jānis (1921c): "Iz nesen pagājušiem laikiem", *Izglītības Ministrijas Mēnešraksts*, 1921:2.

Krodznieks, Jānis (1924): "Vidzemes muižnieku un zemnieku adreses ķeizaram Aleksandram II". *Valsts Arhīva Raksti*, II.

Kronwald, Otto [Kronvalds, Atis] (1872): *Nationale Bestrebungen*. Dorpat.

Kruus, Hans (1938): "Der Kampf um die Ostsee als Aufgabe der Geschichtsforschung", In *Pirmā Baltijas vēsturnieku konference Rīgā 16. – 20. VIII. 1937* (1938), Latvijas Vēstures institūta izdevums, Rīga.

Kurmis, Ansis (1940): "Baltijas skolotāju semināra nozīme latviešu garīgās kultūras celšanā un suverēnas Latvijas tapšanā", In Tomāss, E (ed.): *Baltijas skolotāju seminārs 1870–1919*. Rīga 1940.

Lapiņš, Jānis (1936): "Brīvība un vienības valsts", In *Brīvības piemiņekļa gada grāmata 1936*. Rīga.

Latvieši. Rakstu krājums. 2 Vol. Balodis, Francis un Šmits, Pēteris (ed.) Rīga 1930–1932.

Latviešu konversācijas vārdnīca (1927–1928), Vol. 1.

Latviešu kultūra X–XII gadsimtenī (1938), Rīga.

Latviešu pasakas un teikas, Šmits, Pēteris (ed.): 15 Vols. Rīga.

Latviešu tautas dziesmas (1952–1956), 11 Vols. Švābe, A, Straubergs, K & Hauzenberga-Šturma, E (ed.) Imanta, Copenhagen.

Latvijas Universitāte 1919–1929 (1929),Rīga.

Latvijas Universitāte divdesmit gados 1919–1939 (1939) Vol. I–II. Rīga.

Latvijas Universitātes piecgadu darbības pārskats 1919–1924 (1925), Rīga.

Latvju tautas daiņas (ed. Endzelīns, J & Klaustiņš, R) 9 Vols. Literatūra, Rīga, 1928–1931.

Lukstiņš, Gustavs (1936): "Rōmula un Rema problēma un tas atrisinājuma mēģinājumi", In *Veltījums Izglītības ministram un profesoram Dr. h.c. Augustam Tentelim.* Zeids, T (ed.) Ramave, Rīga 1936.

Merkel, Garlieb (1924) [1797]: *Die Letten vorzüglich in Liefland am Ende des philosophisches Jahrhunderts. Ein Beytrag zur Völker- und Menschenkund*. Rīga.

Mīlenbahs, Fricis (1908): *Latvieši un latvietes Krievijas augstskolās*. Jelgava.

Pirmā Baltijas vēsturnieku konference Rīgā 16.–20. VIII. 1937 (1938), Latvijas Vēstures institūta izdevums, Rīga.

Plāķis, Juris (1930): "Baltu tautas un ciltis", In Balodis, Francis un Šmits, Pēteris (ed.) *Latvieši. Rakstu krājums*. Vol. I. Rīga 1930.

Prīmanis, Jēkabs (1925): "Pāles galvas kausi", *Latvijas Universitātes Raksti* XII.

Prīmanis, Jēkabs (1929): "Latviešu ķermeņa uzbūve latvju daiņās", In *Latvju tautas daiņas* Endzelīns, J & Klaustiņš, R (ed.) Vol. IV, 1929. Literatūra, Rīga.

Rupjais, Jūlijs (1924): "Dziesmas un dziedāšana Latgalē", *Izglītības Ministrijas Mēnešraksts*, 1924:1.

von Schrenk, Erich (1933): *Baltische Kirchengeschichte der Neuzeit, Rīga*.

Siliņš, Jānis (1936): "Latviešu jaunā tēlniecība", *Senatne un Māksla*, II, 1936.

Siliņš, Jānis (1937): "Brāļu kapi Rīgā", *Senatne un Māksla*, I, 1937.

Skujenieks, M (1925): "Rīgas iedzīvotāju tautība", *Izglītības Ministrijas Mēnešraksts*, 1925:1.

REFERENCES

Sloka, Lauma (1923): "Kāda raganu prāva Latvijā 19. gadu simtenī", *Izglītības Ministrijas Mēnešraksts*, 1923:2.

Smilga, V (1936): "Cīņa ap Brīvības pieminekli. Īss vēsturisks atskats", In *Brīvības piemiņekļa gada grāmata 1936*. Rīga.

Spekke, Arnolds (1937): "Brēmenes Ādamu lasot ar latviešu tautas vēsturnieka acīm", *Latvijas Vēstures Institūta Žurnāls*, 1937:1.

Stepermanis, Marģers (1937a): "Kurzemes starptautiskais stāvoklis hercoga Jēkaba laikā", In *Balodis, Francis (ed.): Vēstures atziņas un tēlojumi. Vēstures skolotājiem 1936 gadā lasīto lekciju sakopojums*. Izglītības ministrijas izdevums. Rīga 1937.

Stepermanis, Marģers (1937b): "Latviešu apgaismotāji XVIII gadsimtenī", In Balodis, Francis (ed.): *Vēstures atziņas un tēlojumi. Vēstures skolotājiem 1936. gadā lasīto lekciju sakopojums*. Izglītības ministrijas izdevums. Rīga 1937.

Stepermanis, Marģers (1937c): "Piezīmes par kādu Kurzemes zemnieka pravietojumu hercogam Jēkabam", *Latvijas Vēstures Institūta Žurnāls*, 1937:3.

Stepermanis, Marģers (1939a): "Garlība Merķela uzskati zemnieku brīvlaišanas jautājumā", *Latvijas Vēstures Institūta Žurnāls*, 1939:3.

Stepermanis, Marģers (1939b): "Prof. Dr. hist. Roberts Vipers dzīve un darbos" In Stepermanis, M, Švābe, A Zeids, T (ed.): *Latviešu vēsturnieku veltījums profesoram Dr. hist. Robertam Viperam* Gulbis, Rīga.

Straubergs, Kārlis (1921): "Izrakumi Dienvid-Krievijā" *Izglītības Ministrijas Mēnešraksts*, 1921:2.

Straubergs, Kārlis (1923): "Piezīmes pie dažām latviešu burvju grāmatām", *Izglītības Ministrijas Mēnešraksts*, 1923:2.

Straubergs, Kārlis (1926): "Burvju grāmatas", *Latvijas Universitātes Raksti* XIII.

Straubergs, Kārlis (1930): "Latviešu tērps un viņa raksta ornamentika", In Balodis, Francis un Šmits, Pēteris (ed.) *Latvieši. Rakstu krājums*. Vol. I. Rīga 1930.

Straubergs, Kārlis (1939–1941): *Latviešu buŗamie vārdi*, Vols I & II. Rīga.

Straubergs, Kārlis (1939b): "Vilkaču ideoloģija Latvijā", In Stepermanis, M Švābe, A Zeids, T (ed.): *Latviešu vēsturnieku veltījums profesoram Dr. hist. Robertam Viperam* Gulbis, Rīga.

Šmits, Pēteris (1921): "Piezīmes pie J. Krodznieka kunga paskaidrojumiem", *Izglītības Ministrijas Mēnešraksts*, 1921:1.

Šmits, Pēteris (1923a): "The Language of the Negidals", *Latvijas Universitātes Raksti* V.

Šmits, Pēteris (1923b): "The Language of the Olchas", *Latvijas Universitātes Raksti* VIII.

Šmits, Pēteris (1923c): "Krišjāņa Barona Latvju Dainas", *Latvijas Universitātes Raksti* V.

Šmits, Pēteris (1923d): "Programma tautas garu mantu krājējiem", *Izglītības Ministrijas Mēnešraksts*, 1923:1.

Šmits, Pēteris (1923e): "Par mūsu tautas dziesmu vecumu", *Izglītības Ministrijas Mēnešraksts*, 1923:2.

Šmits, Pēteris (1928): "The Language of the Oroches", *Latvijas Universitātes Raksti* XVII.

Šmits, Pēteris (1930a), "Priekšvārdi", In Balodis, Francis un Šmits, Pēteris (ed.) *Latvieši. Rakstu krājums*. Vol. I. Rīga 1930.

Šmits, Pēteris (1930b): "Valodas liecības par senajiem baltiem", In Balodis, Francis un Šmits, Pēteris (ed.) *Latvieši. Rakstu krājums*. Vol. I. Rīga 1930.

Šmits, Pēteris (1930c): "Latviešu mitoloģija", In Balodis, Francis un Šmits, Pēteris (ed.) *Latvieši. Rakstu krājums*. Vol. I. Rīga 1930.

Šmits, Pēteris (1930d): "Tautas tradīcijas", In Balodis, Francis un Šmits, Pēteris (ed.) *Latvieši. Rakstu krājums*. Vol. I. Rīga 1930.

Šmits, Pēteris (1932): "Dažādi laikmeti tautas dziesmās" In Balodis, F, Šmits, P un Tentelis, A (1932): *Latvieši. Rakstu krājums* Vol. II Rīga 1932.

Šmits, Pēteris (1936): "Latvijā atrastas ķīniešu lietas", *Senatne un Māksla*, Nr. IV, 1936.

Šmits, Pēteris (1937): "Ai, kundziņ bajāriņ", *Senatne un Māksla*, Nr. IV, 1937.

Šneiders, Ernsts (1923); "Kas ir psichanalīze", *Izglītības Ministrijas Mēnešraksts*, 1923:1.

Švābe, Arveds (1920): "Ozols un liepa latveešu reliģijā", *Izglītības Ministrijas Mēnešraksts*, 1920:2.

Švābe, Arveds (1928): *Grundriss der Agrargeschichte Lettlands*, Rīga.

Švābe, Arveds (1932): "Latviešu tautas tiesiskie uzskati", In Balodis, F, Šmits, P un Tentelis, A (1932): *Latvieši. Rakstu krājums* Vol. II, Rīga 1932.

Švābe, Arveds (1937a): "Sigismunda Augusta Livonijas politika" *Latvijas Vēstures Institūta Žurnāls*, 1937:1.

Švābe, Arveds (1937b): "Sigismunda Augusta Livonijas politika. Viļņas sarunas", *Latvijas Vēstures Institūta Žurnāls*, 1937:4.

Tautas vēsturei. Veltījums profesoram Arvedam Švābem (1938), Abers, B, Zeids, T & Zemzaris, T (ed.) Rīga.

Tentelis, Augusts (1924): "Curlandiae quaedam notabilia" *Latvijas Universitātes Raksti* XI.

Tentelis, Augusts (1926): "Latvijas vēsturnieku tuvākie uzdevumi", In *Rīgas Latviešu biedrības zinību komisijas rakstu krājums*. Rīga.

Tentelis, Augusts (1930): "Latvieši Ordeņa laikā", In Balodis, Francis un Šmits, Pēteris (ed.) *Latvieši. Rakstu krājums*. Vol. I. Rīga 1930.

Tentelis, Augusts (1932): "Latviešu brīvības tieksmes", In Balodis, F, Šmits, P un Tentelis, A (1932): *Latvieši. Rakstu krājums* Vol. II, Rīga 1932.

Tentelis, Augusts (1936a): "Ievadam", *Senatne un Māksla*, I, 1936.

Tentelis Augusts (1936b): "Latviešu cīņa par izglītību", *Sējējs*, 1936:1.

Tentelis, Augusts (1937a): "Ievadam. Patiesība un nacionālisms vēstures zinātnē un mācīšanā." In Balodis, Francis (ed.): *Vēstures atziņas un tēlojumi. Vēstures skolotājiem 1936. gadā lasīto lekciju sakopojums*. Izglītības ministrijas izdevums. Rīga 1937.

Tentelis, Augusts (1937b): Lielo pārvērtību un ideālisma ceļš. Aicinājums akademiskai jaunatnei", *Universitas*. 1937:8.

Tentelis, Augusts (1937c): "Lasītājiem", *Latvijas Vēstures Institūta Žurnāls*, 1937:1.

Tentelis, Augusts (1937d): "Tautas Vadoņa dzīve un personība", *Latvijas Vēstures Institūta Žurnāls*, 1937:3.

Tentelis, Augusts (1938): "Arveds Švābe – vēsturnieks", In *Tautas vēsturei. Veltījums profesoram Arvedam Švābem* (1938), Rīga.

Tentelis, Augusts (1939): "Pieci gadi", *Latvijas Vēstures Institūta Žurnāls*, 1939:2.

Tomāss, E (1940): "Semināra vēsture. Semināra dibināšana, darbība, likvidācija", Tomāss, E (ed.): *Baltijas skolotāju seminārs 1870–1919*. Rīga 1940.

Tunberg, Sven (1937): "Gustavs Ādolfs", *Senatne un Māksla*, I, 1937.

Ulmanis, Kārlis (1936a): "Tauta un vēsture", *Latvijas Vēstures Institūta Žurnāls*, 1936:1.

Ulmanis, Kārlis (1936b): "Tautas brīvība un gods", In *Brīvības pieminekļa gada grāmata 1936*. Rīga.

Ulmanis, Kārlis (1937): "Klausaities vēstures soļos!", *Latvijas Vēstures Institūta Žurnāls*, 1937:2.

Ulmanis, Kārlis (1938a): "Valsts un Ministru prezidenta atgādinājums 1938. gadu sākot", *Latvijas Vēstures Institūta Žurnāls*, 1938:1.

Ulmanis, Kārlis (1938b): "Valsts prezidenta Dr. K. Ulmaņa uzruna 6. Rīgas pulka pieminekļa atklāšanā 1937. g. 31. oktobrī", *Latvijas Vēstures Institūta Žurnāls*, 1938:1.

"Vācu izglītība Latvijā" (1930), *Izglītības Ministrijas Mēnešraksts*, 1930:1.

Velme, Jēkabs (1922): "Atmiņas no manas Maskavas dzīves", *Izglītības Ministrijas Mēnešraksts*, 1922:2.

Veltījums izglītības ministram un profesoram Dr. h.c. Augustam Tentelim, (ed. Zeids, T), Ramave, Rīga 1936.

Vīgrabs, Juris (1927): "Vidzemes zemnieku tiesiskais stāvoklis XVIII gadusimteņa pirmajā pusē. I daļa.", *Valsts Arhīvu Raksti*, VI.

Vīgrabs, Juris (1930): "Vidzemes zemnieku tiesiskais stāvoklis XVIII gadusimteņa pirmajā pusē. II daļa.", *Valsts Arhīvu Raksti*, VIII.

Vīgrabs, Juris (1937): "Vidzemes bruņniecības uzstāšanās pret rakstnieku F. B. Albersu 1805. un 1806. gadā par bruņniecības apvainošanu rakstos", *Latvijas Vēstures Institūta Žurnāls*, 1937:2.

Vilde, Jānis (1924): "Materiāli par lībiešu antropoloģiju", *Latvijas Universitātes Raksti* XI.

Vilde, Jānis (1926): "Materiāli par latviešu smadzeņu svaru", *Latvijas Universitātes Raksti* XIV.

Vipers, Roberts (1927): "Piezīme prof. L. Arbuzova rakstam", *Izglītības Ministrijas Mēnešraksts*, 1927:2.

Vipers, Roberts (1930): "No XV. līdz XVIII. g. simtenim", In Balodis, Francis un Šmits, Pēteris (ed.) *Latvieši. Rakstu krājums.* Vol. I. Rīga 1930.

Vipers, Roberts (1932): "Vidzemes apgaismotāji XVIII gadsimtenī", In Balodis, F, Šmits, P un Tentelis, A (1932): *Latvieši. Rakstu krājums* Vol. II, Rīga 1932.

Vipers, Roberts (1937a): "Latviešu zemniecības tiesības un stāvoklis pirms dzimtbūšanas ievešanas", In Balodis, Francis (ed.): *Vēstures atziņas un tēlojumi. Vēstures skolotājiem 1936. gadā lasīto lekciju sakopojums.* Izglītības ministrijas izdevums. Rīga 1937.

Vipers, Roberts (1937b): "Pāreja no zviedru valdišanas uz krievu laikmetu", In Balodis, Francis (ed.): *Vēstures atziņas un tēlojumi. Vēstures skolotājiem 1936. gadā lasīto lekciju sakopojums.* Izglītības ministrijas izdevums. Rīga 1937.

Zālīte, Pēteris (1923) "Latviešu tautas dvēsele ar iepriekšēju dvēseles jēdziena un tautu dvēseles apskatu", *Latvijas Universitātes Raksti.*

Zinātne tēvzemei divdesmit gados 1918–938. (1938), Latvijas Universitāte, Rīga.

Literature

Aleksandravičius, Egidijus (2000): *Praeitis, istorija ir istorikai.* Vilnius 2000.

Alver, Brynjulf (1980): "Nasjonalisme og identitet. Folklore og nasjonal udvikling", In Honko, Lauri (ed.): *Folklore och nationsbyggande i Norden.* Nordiska Institutet för Folkdiktning, Åbo.

Amburger, Erik (1987): "Die Bedeutung der Universität Dorpat für Osteuropa. Untersucht an der Zusammensetzung des Lehrkörpers und der Studentenschaft in den Jahren 1802–1889", In von Pistohlkors, Gert, Raun, Toivo U., and Kaegbein, Paul (eds.): *Die Universitäten Dorpat/Tartu, Rīga und Wilna/Vilnius 1579–1979.* Quellen und Studien zur baltischen Geschichte, 9. Köln.

Anderson, Benedict (1991): *Imagined Communities. Reflections on the Origins and Spread of Nationalism.* Verso, London.

Apals, Gints (2008): "Izvēles iespējas Latviešu kultūrpolitiskajai orientācijai 19.gadsimta kontekstā", *Latvijas Arhīvi,* 2008:4.

Apsītis, Romāns (1998): "Kārlis Ulmanis un Satversme", In Caune, Andris et al. (ed.): *Kārlim Ulmanim 120.* Latvijas Vēstures institūta apgāds, Rīga.

Atamukas, Solomonas (2001): *Lietuvos žydu kelias. Nuo XIV amžiaus iki XX a. pabaigos,* Vilnius.

Auns, Muntis (1997): "Dr. habil. hist., Dr. hist. h.c. prof. Teodora Zeida (1912–1994) dzīve un veiktais darbs", In *Latvijas Vēsturnieki. Dr. habil. hist., Dr. hist. h.c. prof. Teodors Zeids (1912–1994),* Caune, Andris (ed.) Latvijas vēstures institūta apgāds, Rīga.

Auns, Muntis (2009): "Augusts Tentelis – vēsturnieks", In *Profesors Dr. honoris causa Augusts Tentelis. Dzīve un darbs.* LU Akadēmiskais apgāds. Rīga.

Arheologi Elvīra Šnore (1905–1996) un Rauls Šnore (1901–1962). Biobibliogrāfija vēstules laikabiedru atmiņas (1997), Latvijas vēstures institūta apgāds, Rīga.

Baár, Monika (2010): "Heretics into National Heroes: Jules Michelet's Joan of Arc and František Palacký's John Hus", In Berger, Stefan & Lorenz, Chris (ed.), *Nationalizing the Past. Historians as Nation Builders in Modern Europe.* Palgrave & Macmillan, Basingstoke.

Balabkins, Nikolajs & Šneps, Manfrēds (1993): *Kad Latvijā būs labklājības valsts. Tautsaimnieks Kārlis Balodis.* Zinātne, Rīga.

Belova, Marina (2000): "Per aspera ad astra", *Latvijas Arhīvi,* 2000:4.

Bērzkalns, Valentīns (1965): *Latviešu dziesmu svētku vēsture, 1864–1940,* Grāmatu draugs, USA.

Björklund, Fredrika (2003): "The Rhetoric of the Nation. Baltic Germans in the First Latvian Democracy", In Lindqvist, Mats (ed.) *Reinventing the Nation. Multidisciplinary Perspectives on the Construction of Latvian National Identity.* Mångkulturellt Centrum, Botkyrka.

Bolin Hort, Per (2003a): "Zeme un tauta: Conceptions of the Latvian Territory and the Latvian Nation", In Lindqvist, Mats (ed.) *Reinventing the Nation. Multidisciplinary Perspectives on the Construction of Latvian National Identity*. Mångkulturellt Centrum, Botkyrka.

Bolin Hort, Per (2003b): "The Latvian Nation and the Intellectuals. The Forming of Latvia's University during the First Republic", In Lindqvist, Mats (ed.) *Reinventing the Nation. Multidisciplinary Perspectives on the Construction of Latvian National Identity*. Mångkulturellt Centrum, Botkyrka.

Bolin Hort, Per (2004): "'Svešie elementi'. Latvijas Universitātes latviešu un ebreju studentu demarkācija un konflikts (1919–1940)", *Latvijas Arhīvi* 2004:4.

Bourdieu, Pierre (1996): *Homo academicus*. Brutus Östlings Bokförlag Symposion, Stockholm/Stehag.

Brading, D A (2001): "Monuments and nationalism in modern Mexico", *Nations and Nationalism*, Vol. 7, 2001:4.

Breidaks, Antons (1999): "Latviešu valodas dialektu un izlokšņu grupu cilme un teritoriālā izplatība", In Caune, Andris (ed.): *Latvijas zemju robežas 1000 gados*. Latvijas vēstures institūta apgāds, Rīga

Brenner, Michael (1996): *The Renaissance of Jewish Culture in Weimar Germany*. Yale University Press, New Haven and London.

Brubaker, Rogers (1996a): "Nationalising states in the old 'New Europe' and the new", *Ethnic and Racial Studies*, Vol. 19, 1996:2.

Brubaker, Rogers (1996b): *Nationalism reframed. Nationhood and the national question in the New Europe*. Cambridge University Press.

Bukšs, Miķelis (1957): *Latgaļu literatūras vēsture*, Latgaļu izdevnīceiba.

Bula, Dace (1996): "The Singing Nation: The Tradition of Latvian Folk Songs in the Self-Image of the Nation", *Humanities and Social Sciences, Latvia*, 1996:2.

Bula, Dace (2000): *Dziedātājtauta. Folklora un nacionālā ideoloģija*. Zinātne, Rīga.

Buldakov, Vladimir P (2011): "Freedom, Shortages, Violence: The Origins of the 'Revolutionary Anti-Jewish Pogrom' in Russia, 1917–1918", In Dekel-Chen, J, Gaunt, D, Meir, N M Bartal, I (ed.): *Anti-Jewish Violence. Rethinking the Pogrom in East European History*. Indiana University Press, Bloomington and Indianapolis.

Byford, Andy (2007): *Literary Scholarship in Late Imperial Russia. Rituals of Academic Institutionalisation*. Legenda, Maney Publishing.

Caball, Marc (2010): "History and Politics: Interpretations of Early Modern Conquest and Reformation in Victorian Ireland", In Berger, Stefan & Lorenz, Chris (ed.). *Nationalizing the Past. Historians as Nation Builders in Modern Europe*. Palgrave & Macmillan, Basingstoke.

von Campenhausen, Axel (2006): "Orellen und die Familie von Campenhausen. Aus der Geschichte einer livländische Familie", *Jahrbuch des baltischen Deutschtums*, 2006.

Carls, Lina (2004): *Våp eller nucka? Kvinnors högre studier och genusdiskursen 1930–1970*. Nordic Academic Press, Lund.

Cattaruzza, Marina (2010): "'Last stop expulsion' –The minority question and forced migration in East-Central Europe: 1918–49, *Nations and Nationalism*, Vol. 16, 2010:1.

Caune, Andris (1997): "Vēsturniekam Alfrēdam Altementam – 95", *Latvijas Vēstures Institūta Žurnāls*, 1997:2.

Cerūzis, Raimonds (2002): "Vācu minoritāšu faktors Vidus- un Austrumeiropā starpkaru periodā: vispārējais un īpašais", *Latvijas Vēstures Institūta Žurnāls*, 2002:3.

Cerūzis, Raimonds (2004): *Vācu faktors Latvijā (1918–1939). Politiskie un starpnacionālie aspekti*. LU Akadēmiskais apgāds, Rīga.

Cimermane, Ieva (1997): "Par maniem vecākiem", In *Arheologi Elvīra Šnore (1905–1996) un Rauls Šnore (1901–1962). Biobibliogrāfija,vēstules, laikabiedru atmiņas* (1997), Latvijas vēstures institūta apgāds, Rīga.

Colley, Linda (1994): *Britons. Forging the Nation 1707–1837*. Pimlico, London.

Connelly, John (2000): *Captive University. The Sovietization of East German, Czech, and Polish Higher Education, 1945–1956*. University of North Carolina Press, Chapel Hill & London.

David-Fox, Michael (1997): *Revolution of the Mind. Higher Learning among the Bolsheviks, 1918–1929*. Cornell University Press.

Delanty, Gerard (2001): *Challenging Knowledge. The University in the Knowledge Society*, The Society for Research into Higher Education & Open University, Buckingham and Philadelphia.

Dēliņš, Emīls (1998): "Prezidents Kārlis Ulmanis un Latvijas trīsdesmito gadu jaunatne", In Caune, Andris et al. (ed.): *Kārlim Ulmanim 120*. Latvijas vēstures institūta apgāds, Rīga.

Denisova, Raisa (1999): "Latviešu antropoloģija kultūrvēsturisko teritoriju atspulgā", In Caune, Andris (ed.): *Latvijas zemju robežas 1000 gados*. Latvijas vēstures institūta apgāds, Rīga 1999.

Díaz-Andreu, Margarita (2001): "Guest editor's introduction: Nationalism and archaeology", *Nations and Nationalism*, Vol. 7, 2001:4.

Donskis, Leonidas (1999): "Between Identity and Freedom: Mapping Nationalism in Twentieth-Century Lithuania", *East European Politics and Societies*, Vol. 13, 1999:3.

Dribins, Leo (2001a): *Antisemītisms un tā izpausmes Latvijā. Vēstures atskats*. Latvijas Vēsturnieku komisijas raksti, 4. sējums. Latvijas vēstures institūta apgāds, Rīga.

Dribins, Leo (2001b): "The History of the Jewish Community in Latvia. A Brief Chronological Survey", In Dribins, Leo, Gūtmanis, Armands and Vestermanis, Marģers (ed.): *Latvia's Jewish Community. History, Tragedy, Revival*. Latvijas vēstures institūta apgāds, Rīga.

Dunsdorfs, Edgars (1992): *Kārla Ulmaņa dzīve. Ceļinieks, politiķis, diktators, moceklis*. Zinātne, Rīga.

Eckel, Jan (2010): "Narrativizations of the Past: The Theoretical Debate and the Example of the Weimar Republic", In Berger, Stefan & Lorenz, Chris (ed.), *Nationalizing the Past. Historians as Nation Builders in Modern Europe*. Palgrave & Macmillan, Basingstoke.

Eellend, Johan (2007): *Cultivating the rural citizen. Modernity, agrarianism and citizenship in late Tsarist Estonia*. Studia Baltica II:1, Stockholm University/Södertörn University, Sweden.

Engel, David (2011): "What's in a Pogrom? European Jews in the Age of Violence", In Dekel-Chen, J, Gaunt, D, Meir, N M Bartal, I (ed.): *Anti-Jewish Violence. Rethinking the Pogrom in East European History*. Indiana University Press, Bloomington and Indianapolis.

Engman, Max (1994): "National Conceptions of History in Finland", In Lönnroth, E, Molin K and Björk, R (ed.): *Conceptions of National History*. Berlin/New York.

Engman, Max (2000): *Lejonet och dubbelörnen. Finlands imperiella decennier 1830-1890*. Atlantis, Stockholm.

Eriksen, Thomas Hylland (1998): *Etnicitet och nationalism*. Nya Doxa, Nora.

Ezergailis, Andrievs (1999): *Holokausts vācu okupētajā Latvijā 1941-1944*. Latvijas vēstures institūta apgāds, Rīga.

Ezergailis, Andrievs (2001): "Folklore versus History: A Problem in Holocaust Studies", In *The Issues of the Holocaust Research in Latvia*. Latvijas Vēsturnieku komisijas raksti, 2. sējums. Latvijas vēstures institūta apgāds, Rīga.

Ezergailis, Andrievs (2008): "Štālekera ziņojumi: holokausta vēstures pirmavots un atslēga", In *Holokausta pētniecības problēmas Latvijā*. Latvijas Vēsturnieku komisijas raksti, 23. sējums. Latvijas vēstures institūta apgāds, Rīga.

Feigmane, Tatjana (2000): *Russkie v dovoennoj Latvii*. Baltijas krievu institūts, Rīga.

Feldmanis, Inesis (1998): "15. maija Latvija un autoritārie režīmi Austrumeiropā (1926-1940): salīdzinošs raksturojums", In Caune, Andris et al. (ed.): *Kārlim Ulmanim 120*. Latvijas vēstures institūta apgāds, Rīga.

Folklore och nationsbyggande i Norden, (1980) Lauri Honko (ed.), Nordiska institutet för folkdiktning, Åbo.

Foucault, Michel (1972): *Vetandets arkeologi*. Bo Cavefors Bokförlag, Köthen.

20. gadsimta Latvijas vēsture I. Latvija no gadsimta sākuma līdz neatkarības pasludināšanai 1900-1918 (2000), Latvijas vēstures institūta apgāds, Rīga.

20. gadsimta Latvijas vēsture II. Neatkarīgā valsts 1918-1940 (2003), Latvijas Vēstures institūta apgāds, Rīga.

Garleff, Michael (1987): "Die Universität Dorpat im 19. Jahrhundert", In von Pistohlkors, Gert, Raun, Toivo U., and Kaegbein, Paul (eds.): *Die Universitäten Dorpat/Tartu, Rīga und Wilna/Vilnius 1579-1979*. Quellen und Studien zur baltischen Geschichte, 9. Köln 1987.

Garleff, Michael (2005): "Die baltischen Staaten und die Juden 1918-1940", *Jahrbuch des baltischen Deutschtums*, 2005.

Gellner, Ernest (1983): *Nations and Nationalism*. Cornell University Press.

Gellner, Ernest (1998): *Language and Solitude. Wittgenstein, Malinowski and the Habsburg Dilemma*. Cambridge University Press.

Gitelman, Zvi (2001): *A Century of Ambivalence. The Jews of Russia and the Soviet Union, 1881 to the Present*. Indiana University Press, Bloomington.

Gordon, Frank (1990): *Latvians and Jews between Germany and Russia*. Memento, Stockholm.

Graudonis, Jānis (1995): "Latvijas vēstures institūts Latvijas Republikas laikā", *Latvijas Vēstures Institūta Žurnāls*, 1995:1.

Grāvere, Rita (2006): "Lībiešu problēmas risinājuma aizsākumi Latvijas antropoloģijā (19. gs. beigas – 20. gs. pirmā puse", *Latvijas Vēstures Institūta Žurnāls*, 2006:1.

Grāvere, Rita (2008): "Latgales antropoloģija reģionālā griezumā", *Latvijas Vēstures Institūta Žurnāls*, 2008:3.

Greenfeld, Liah (1992): *Nationalism. Five Roads to Modernity*. Harvard University Press.

Grüttner, Michael, Hachtmann, Rüdiger, Jarausch, Konrad H, John, Jürgen, & Middel, Matthias (2010): "Wissenschaftskulturen zwischen Diktatur und Demokratie. Vorüberlegungen zu einer kritischen Universitätsgeschichte des 20. Jahrhunderts", In Grüttner, Michael, Hachtmann, Rüdiger, Jarausch, Konrad H, John, Jürgen, & Middel, Matthias (eds.): *Gebrochene Wissenschaftskulturen. Universität und Politik im 20. Jahrhundert*. Vandenhoeck & Ruprecht, Göttingen.

Guibernau, Montserrat & Hutchinson, John (2004): "History and National Destiny", *Nations and Nationalism*, Vol. 10, 2004:1/2.

Guščika, Elīna (2010): "Elvīra Šnore un Latvijas agrā dzelzs laikmeta pētniecība", *Latvijas Vēstures Institūta Žurnāls*, 2010:1

Haas, Peter M (1992): "Introduction: epistemic communities and international policy coordination", *International Organisation*, Vol. 46, 1992:1.

Hackmann, Jörg (2010): "Narrating the Building of a Small Nation: Divergence and Convergence in the Historiography of Estonian 'National Awakening', 1868–2005", In Berger, Stefan & Lorenz, Chris (ed.). *Nationalizing the Past. Historians as Nation Builders in Modern Europe*. Palgrave & Macmillan, Basingstoke.

Hagen, Manfred (1987): "Hochschulunruhen und Regierungspolitik im russischen Reich vor 1914", In von Pistohlkors, Gert, Raun, Toivo U., and Kaegbein, Paul (eds.): *Die Universitäten Dorpat/Tartu, Rīga und Wilna/Vilnius 1579–1979*. Quellen und Studien zur baltischen Geschichte, 9. Köln.

Hausmanis, Viktors (1998): "Literatūra un teātris trīsdesmit gados" In Caune, Andris et al. (ed.): *Kārlim Ulmanim 120*. Latvijas vēstures institūta apgāds, Rīga.

Havránek, Jan (1996): "The Czech, Slovak and Polish Intellectuals in the Habsburg Monarchy between the State and the Nations", In Norrback, Märtha & Ranki, Kristina (ed.): *University and Nation. The University and the Making of the Nation in Northern Europe in the 19th and 20th Centuries*. Studia Historica 53, Helsinki.

von Hehn, Jürgen (1987): "Deutsche Hochschulaktivitäten in Rīga und Dorpat zwischen den beiden Weltkriegen", In von Pistohlkors, Gert, Raun, Toivo U., and Kaegbein, Paul (eds): *Die Universitäten Dorpat/Tartu, Rīga und Wilna/Vilnius 1579–1979*. Quellen und Studien zur baltischen Geschichte, 9. Köln.

Henriksson, Anders (1983): *The Tsar's Loyal Germans. The Rīga German Community: Social Change and the Nationality Question*. Boulder, Colorado.

Hiden, John (2004): "Paul Schiemann on Reconciling 'Nation' and 'State'", In Metuzāle-Kangere, Baiba (ed.): *The Ethnic Dimension in Politics and Culture in the Baltic Countries 1920–1945*. Södertörn university, Södertörn Academic Studies, 18. Stockholm.

Hillerdal, Charlotta (2010): *People in Between. Ethnicity and Material Identity – a New Approach to Deconstructed Concepts*. Diss. Uppsala University Occasional Papers in Archaeology, 50.

Himka, John-Paul (1999): "The Construction of Nationality in Galician Rus': Icarian Flights in Almost All Directions", In Suny, Ronald Grigor and Kennedy, Michael D. (ed.): *Intellectuals and the Articulation of the Nation*. University of Michigan Press, Ann Arbor.

History of Tartu University, 1632–1982. Siilivask, Karl (ed.), Tallinn Perioodika 1985.

Hobsbawm, Eric J (1992): *Nations and Nationalism*, 2nd ed. Cambridge University Press.

Holokausta izpētes problēmas Latvijā, Latvijas Vēsturnieku Komisijas Raksti, 2. sējums. Latvijas vēstures institūta apgāds, Rīga.

Holquist, Peter (2011): "The Role of Personality in the First (1914–1915) Russian Occupation of Galicia and Bukovina", In Dekel-Chen, J, Gaunt, D, Meir, N M Bartal, I (ed.): *Anti-Jewish Violence. Rethinking the Pogrom in East European History*. Indiana University Press, Bloomington and Indianapolis.

Hroch, Miroslav (1985): *Social Preconditions of National Revival in Europe. A Comparative Analysis of the Social Composition of Patriotic Groups among the Smaller European Nations*. Cambridge University Press.

Hroch, Miroslav (2004): "From ethnic group toward the modern nation: the Czech case" *Nations and Nationalism*, Vol. 10, 2001:1/2.

Hutchinson, John (2001): "Archaeology and the Irish rediscovery of the Celtic past", *Nations and Nationalism*, Vol. 7, 2001:4.

Hutchinson, John (2004): "Myth against myth: the nation as ethnic overlay" *Nations and Nationalism*, Vol. 10, 2004:1/2.

Intellectuals and the articulation of the nation (2001), Suny, Grigor R & Kennedy, Michael D (ed.), University of Michigan Press, Ann Arbor.

Janužytė, Audronė (2005): *Historians as nation state-builders: The Formation of the Lithuanian University 1904–1922*. Diss. University of Tampere.

Jēkabsons, Ēriks (2005): "Poļu studenti Rīgas Politehniskajā institūtā (19.gs. II puse – 1915. gads", *Latvijas Vēstures Institūta Žurnāls*, 2005:3

Johansons, Andrejs (1987): "Die Lettländische Universität in Rīga 1919–1940", In von Pistohlkors, Gert, Raun, Toivo U., and Kaegbein, Paul (eds): *Die Universitäten Dorpat/Tartu, Rīga und Wilna/Vilnius 1579–1979*. Quellen und Studien zur baltischen Geschichte, 9. Köln.

Joonson, Arnold & Ney, Gottlieb (1968): "Die estnischen Korporationen", In von Rimsch, Hans (ed.) *Baltisches Burschentum. Die studentischen Korporationen der Deutschbalten, Esten und Letten einst und jetzts*. Der Baltischen Gesellschaft in Deutschland, Heidelberg.

Kamusella, Tomasz (2001): "Language as an instrument of nationalism in Central Europe", *Nations and Nationalism*, Vol. 7, 2001:2.

Kamusella, Tomasz (2009): *The Politics of Language and Nationalism in Modern Central Europe*. Palgrave, Macmillan.

Karady, Victor (2004): "Student Mobility and Western Universities: Patterns of Unequal Exchange in the European Academic Market, 1880–1939", In Charle, Christophe, Schriever, Jürgen & Wagner, Peter (eds.) *Transnational Intellectual Networks. Forms of Academic Knowledge and the Search for Cultural Identities*. Campus Verlag, Frankfurt & New York.

Kārlim Ulmanim 120 (1998) Caune, Andris et al. (ed.) Latvijas vēstures institūta apgāds, Rīga.

Kennedy, Michael D & Suny, Ronald Grigor (2001): "Introduction", In *Intellectuals and the articulation of the nation*. Suny, Grigor R & Kennedy, Michael D (ed.), University of Michigan Press, Ann Arbor.

Kivimäe, Sirjie & Kivimäe Jüri (1987): "Estnische Geschichtsforschung an der Universität Tartu 1920–1940. Ziele und Ergebnisse", In von Pistohlkors, Gert, Raun, Toivo U., and Kaegbein, Paul (eds.): *Die Universitäten Dorpat/Tartu, Rīga und Wilna/Vilnius 1579–1979*. Quellen und Studien zur baltischen Geschichte, 9. Köln.

Kļaviņa, Sarma (2008): *Latviešu valodas pētnieki. No klaušu laikiem līdz savai valstij*, Latvijas Universitāte. Latviešu valodas institūts.

Kļaviņa, Sarma (2010): "LU profesora Jura Plāķa dzīves un ciešanu ceļi (1869–1942)", *Laikmets un personība. Rakstu krājums* Nr. 12.

Kolbe, Laura (1996): "Rural or urban", In Norrback, Märtha & Ranki, Kristina (ed.): *University and Nation. The University and the Making of the Nation in Northern Europe in the 19th and 20th Centuries*. Studia Historica 53, Helsinki.

Komsars, Andrijs (1968), "Die lettische Korporationen", In von Rimsch, Hans (ed.) *Baltisches Burschentum. Die studentischen Korporationen der Deutschbalten, Esten und Letten einst und jetzts*. Der Baltischen Gesellschaft in Deutschland, Heidelberg.

Koreinik, Kadri (2011): "Public Discourse of (De)legitimation: The Case of South Estonian Language", *Journal of Baltic Studies*, 42, 2011:2.

Kornprobst, Markus (2005): "Episteme, nation-builders and national identity: the re-construction of Irishness", *Nations and Nationalism*, Vol. 11, 2005:3.

Kott, Matthew (2009): "Antropologen Gaston Backman och den uppsaliensiska rasbiologins spridning i tid och rum", In Müssener H and Jegebäck P (ed.) *Rasen och vetenskapen*. Centrum för multietnisk forskning, Uppsala Universitet.

Krapauskas, Virgil (2000): *Nationalism and Historiography: The Case of Nineteenth-Century Lithuanian Historicism*, East European Monographs, Boulder, USA.

Krēsliņš, Uldis (2005): *Aktīvais nacionālisms Latvijā, 1922–1934*, Latvijas vēstures institūta apgāds, Rīga.

Krūze, Aīda (2009): "Augusts Tentelis – izglītības ministrs", In *Profesors Dr. honoris causa Augusts Tentelis. Dzīve un darbs*. LU Akadēmiskais apgāds. Rīga.

Ķencis, Toms (forthcoming 2011a): "Kārlis Straubergs".

Ķencis, Toms (forthcoming 2011b): "Kārlis Arveds Švābe".

Langholm, Sivert (1996): "The New Nationalism and the New Universities – The Case of Norway in the Early 19th Century", In Norrback, Märtha & Ranki, Kristina (ed.): *University and Nation. The University and the Making of the Nation in Northern Europe in the 19th and 20th Centuries*. Studia Historica 53, Helsinki.

Latviešu literatūras vēsture. 1. sējums. No rakstītā vārda sākumiem līdz 1918. gadam (1998), Zvaigzne ABC, Rīga.

Latvija 19. gadsimtā. Vēstures apceres (2000), Latvijas vēstures institūta apgāds, Rīga.

Latvijas Universitāte 75 (1994), Rīga.

Latvijas Universitāte 90 gados. Dzīve. (2009), Rīga.

Latvijas Valsts universitātes vēsture 1940–1990 (1999), Rīga.

Latvijas Universitātes Vēstures un filozofijas fakultātes vēsture padomju laikā. Personības, struktūras, idejas, 1944–1991 (2010), Keruss, Jānis, Lipša, Ineta, Runce, Inese & Zellis, Kaspars (ed.) LU akadēmiskais apgāds, Rīga.

Leerssen, Joep (2006): "Nationalism and the cultivation of culture", *Nations and Nationalism*, Vol. 12, 2006:4.

Leerssen, Joep (2010): "Setting the Scene for National History", In Berger, Stefan & Lorenz, Chris (ed.) *Nationalizing the Past. Historians as Nation Builders in Modern Europe.* Palgrave & Macmillan, Basingstoke.

Leikola, Anto (1996): "In Service of the Truth or of the Emperor. Some reflections on the loyalties of the University of Finland", In Norrback, Märtha & Ranki, Kristina (ed.): *University and Nation. The University and the Making of the Nation in Northern Europe in the 19th and 20th Centuries.* Studia Historica 53, Helsinki.

Levin, Dov (2001): "Some Basic Facts on Latvian Jewry – Before, During and After World War II", In *The Issues of the Holocaust Research in Latvia.* Latvijas Vēsturnieku Komisijas Raksti, 2. sējums, Rīga.

Levinger, Matthew & Lytle, Paula Franklin (2001): "Myth and mobilisation: the triadic structure of nationalist rhetoric", *Nations and Nationalism*, Vol. 7, 2001:2.

Lindqvist, Mats (2003): "Giving Voice to the Nation. The Folklorist Movement and the Restoration of Latvian Identity", In Lindqvist, Mats (ed.) *Reinventing the Nation. Multidisciplinary Perspectives on the Construction of Latvian National Identity.* Mångkulturellt Centrum, Botkyrka.

Lohr, Eric (2011): "1915 and the War Pogrom Paradigm in the Russian Empire", In Dekel-Chen, J, Gaunt, D, Meir, N M Bartal, I (ed.): *Anti-Jewish Violence. Rethinking the Pogrom in East European History.* Indiana University Press, Bloomington and Indianapolis.

Lūsis, Kārlis (1990): "Roberts Vipers un 'Vēstures lielās problēmas' Latvijā", In Vipers, Roberts (1992) *Vēstures lielās problēmas* Zvaigzne, Rīga.

Löfgren, Orvar (1989): "The Nationalization of Culture", *Ethnologica Europea*, no 19, 1989.

Martinson, Karl (1990): "1900–1914: A Turning-Point in Estonian Science" In Loit, Aleksander (ed.): *The Baltic Countries 1900–1914.* Studia Baltica Stockholmensia 5:1, Stockholm.

Martis, Ela (1985): "The Role of Tartu University in the National Movement", In Loit, Aleksander (ed.): *National Movements in the Baltic Countries during the 19th Century.* Studia Baltica Stockholmensia 2, Stockholm.

McMahon, Richard (2009): "Anthropological race psychology 1820–1945: a common European system of ethnic identity narratives", *Nations and Nationalism*, Vol. 15, 2009:4.

Mendelsohn, Ezra (1987): *The Jews of East Central Europe between the World Wars.* Indiana University Press, Bloomington.

Metzler, Gabriele (2010): "Deutschland in den internationalen Wissenschaftsbeziehungen, 1900–1930", In Grüttner, Michael, Hachtmann, Rüdiger, Jarausch, Konrad H, John,

Jürgen, & Middel, Matthias (eds.): *Gebrochene Wissenschaftskulturen. Universität und Politik im 20. Jahrhundert.* Vandenhoeck & Ruprecht, Göttingen.

Meyer, Klaus (1987): "Die Universität im Russischen Reich in der ersten Hälfte des 19. Jahrhundert", In von Pistohlkors, Gert, Raun, Toivo U., and Kaegbein, Paul (eds): *Die Universitäten Dorpat/Tartu, Rīga und Wilna/Vilnius 1579-1979.* Quellen und Studien zur baltischen Geschichte, 9. Köln.

Morjānova, Irīna (2004): "Materiāli Rīgas politehniskā institūta vēsturē (1901-1907)", *Latvijas Vēstures Institūta Žurnāls*, 2004:3.

Mugurēvičs, Ēvalds (1997a): "Arheologam Dr. phil. Dr. hist profesoram Francim Aleksandram Balodim 125", In Caune, Andris (ed.): *Arheologs Dr. phil Dr. hist profesors Francis Balodis (1882-1947).* Latvijas vēstures institūta apgāds, Rīga.

Mugurēvičs, Ēvalds (1997b): "Elvīras Šnores dzīves un zinātniskās darbības apraksts", In Caune, Andris (ed.): *Arheologi Elvīra Šnore (1905-1996) un Rauls Šnore (1901-1962). Biobibliogrāfija, vēstules, laikabiedru atmiņas.* Latvijas vēstures institūta apgāds, Rīga.

von zur Mühlen, Heinz (1987): "Kontinuität und neue Anstösse der deutschbaltischen Geschichtsforschung in Estland nach dem ersten Weltkrieg", In von Pistohlkors, Gert, Raun, Toivo U., and Kaegbein, Paul (eds): *Die Universitäten Dorpat/Tartu, Rīga und Wilna/Vilnius 1579-1979.* Quellen und Studien zur baltischen Geschichte, 9. Köln.

Mycock, Andrew & Loskoutova, Marina (2010): "Nation, State and Empire: The Historiography of 'High Imperialism' in the British and Russian Empires", In Berger, Stefan & Lorenz, Chris (ed.). *Nationalizing the Past. Historians as Nation Builders in Modern Europe.* Palgrave & Macmillan, Basingstoke.

Naglinska, Evita (2007): "Mīts par Kārli Ulmani latviešu presē, 1989-2004", *Agora*, No. 6, 2007.

Nase, Marco (2009): *Johannes Paul und das Schwedische Institut der Universität Greifswald.* Master thesis, Erst-Moritz-Arndt-Universität, Greifswald.

Nationalizing the Past. Historians as Nation Builders in Modern Europe. (2010), Berger, Stefan & Lorenz, Chris (ed.). Palgrave & Macmillan, Basingstoke.

Nordin, Jonas (2000): *Ett fattigt men fritt folk. Nationell och politisk självbild i Sverige från sen stormaktstid till slutet av frihetstiden.* Symposion, Stockholm/Stehag.

Onken, Eva-Clarita (1998): *Revisionismus schon vor der Gewschichte. Aktuelle Kontroversen in Lettland um die Judenvernichtung und die lettische Kolloboration während der nationalsocialsitischen Besatzung.* Wissenschaft und Politik, Köln.

Pakalns, Guntis (2011, forthcoming): "Pēteris Šmits".

Paletschek, Sylvia (2010): "Was heist 'Weltgeltung deutscher Wissenschaft?' Modernisierungsleistungen und -defizite der Universitäten im Kaiserreich", In Grüttner, Michael, Hachtmann, Rüdiger, Jarausch, Konrad H, John, Jürgen, & Middel, Matthias (eds.): *Gebrochene Wissenschaftskulturen. Universität und Politik im 20. Jahrhundert* Vandenhoeck & Ruprecht, Göttingen.

Pálfy, Zoltán (2003): *National Controversy in the Transylvanian Academe: The Cluj/Kolozsvar University, 1900-1950.* Unpublished doctoral thesis, Central European University, Budapest.

Pearson, Raymond (1999): "History and historians in the service of nation-building", In Branch, Michael (ed.): *National History and Identity. Approaches to the Writing of*

National History in the North-East Baltic Region Ninteenth and Twentieth Centuries. Studia Fennica Ethnologica 6, Helsinki.

Penrose, Jan (2002): "Nations, states and homelands: territory and territoriality in nationalist thought", *Nations and Nationalism*, Vol. 8, 2002:3.

Pētera Stučkas Latvijas Valsts universitātei 50 gadi. (1969), Rīga.

Petersoo, Pille (2007): "Reconsidering otherness: constructing Estonian identity", *Nations and Nationalism*, Vol. 13, 2007:1.

Petronis, Vytautas (2007): *Constructing Lithuania. Ethnic Mapping in Tsarist Russia, ca. 1800–1914.* Diss. Södertörn University/Stockholm University.

Philipson, Joakim (2008): *The Purpose of Evolution. The 'struggle for existence' in the Russian-Jewish press 1860–1900.* Diss. Södertörn University/Stockholm University.

Plakans, Andrejs (1995): *The Latvians. A Short History.* Hoover Institution Press, Stanford.

Plakans, Andrejs (1999): "Looking Backward: The Eighteenth and Nineteenth Centuries in Inter-War Latvian Historiography", *Journal of Baltic Studies*, 1999:4.

Plakans, Andrejs (2010): "Celebrating Origins: Reflections on Latvia's Ninetieth Birthday", In Smith, David J, Galbreath David J Swain, Geoffrey (ed.) *From Recognition to Restoration. Latvia's History as a Nation-State.* Rodopi, Amsterdam & New York.

Plath, Tilman (2009): "Juden unter Ulmanis", *Jahrbuch des baltischen Deutschtums*, 2009.

Porter, Brian (2000): *When Nationalism Began to Hate. Imagining Modern Politics in Nineteenth-Century Poland.* Oxford University Press

Profesors Dr. honoris causa Augusts Tentelis. Dzīve un darbs. LU Akadēmiskais apgāds. Rīga.

Raun, Toivu U (1991): *Estonia and the Estonians.* Stanford 1991.

Raun, Toivo U (2003): "Nineteenth and early twentieth-century Estonian nationalism revisited", *Nations and Nationalism*, Vol. 9, 2003:1.

Redlich, Clara (1987): "Das Rīgaer Polytechnikum 1862–1918." In von Pistohlkors, Gert, Raun, Toivo U., and Kaegbein, Paul (eds): *Die Universitäten Dorpat/Tartu, Rīga und Wilna/Vilnius 1579–1979.* Quellen und Studien zur baltischen Geschichte, 9. Köln.

Reklaitis, Povilas (1987): "Die Vierhundert-Jahr-Feier der Universität Wilna/Vilnius in den Jahren 1978 und 1979", In von Pistohlkors, Gert, Raun, Toivo U., and Kaegbein, Paul (eds.): *Die Universitäten Dorpat/Tartu, Rīga und Wilna/Vilnius 1579–1979.* Quellen und Studien zur baltischen Geschichte, 9. Köln.

Remy, Johannes (2000): *Higher Education and National Identity. Polish Student Activism in Russia 1832–1863.* Bibliotheca Historica 57, Helsinki.

Rīga, Liliana & Kennedy, James (2009): "Tolerant majorities, loyal minorities and 'ethnic reversals': constructing minority rights at Versailles 1919", *Nations and Nationalism*, Vol. 15, 2009:3.

Rindzevičiūtė, Eglė (2010): "Imagining the Grand Duchy of Lithuania: The Politics and Economics of Rebuilding of Trakai Castle and the 'Palace of Sovereigns' in Vilnius", *Central Europe*, 8, 2010:2.

Robinson-Hammerstein, Helga (1996): "The Irish Nation and University Education in the Nineteenth Century", In Norrback, Märtha & Ranki, Kristina (ed.): *University and*

Nation. The University and the Making of the Nation in Northern Europe in the 19th and 20th Centuries. Studia Historica 53, Helsinki.

Ronis, Indulis (1995): "Latvijas vēstures institūts laikmeta kontekstā", *Latvijas Vēstures Institūta Žurnāls*, 1995:3.

Rothmets, Helen (2011): "The repatriation of Estonians from Soviet Russia in 1920–1923: a test of Estonian citizenship and immigration policy", *Journal of Baltic Studies*, 42, 2011:2.

Russification in the Baltic Provinces and Finland, 1855–1914 (1981), Thaden, Edward C (ed.) Princeton University Press.

Schöttler, Peter (2004): "French and German Historians' Networks: The Case of the Early Annales", In Charle, Christophe, Schriever, Jürgen & Wagner, Peter (eds.) *Transnational Intellectual Networks. Forms of Academic Knowledge and the Search for Cultural Identities*. Campus Verlag, Frankfurt & New York.

Seesemann, Heinrich (1987): "350 Jahre Universität Dorpat", In von Pistohlkors, Gert, Raun, Toivo U., and Kaegbein, Paul (eds): *Die Universitäten Dorpat/Tartu, Rīga und Wilna/Vilnius 1579–1979*. Quellen und Studien zur baltischen Geschichte, 9. Köln.

Senn, Alfred Erich (1985): "The Lithuanian Intelligentia in the Nineteenth Century", In Loit, Aleksander (ed.): *National Movements in the Baltic Countries during the 19th Century*. Studia Baltica Stockholmensia 2, Stockholm.

Siilivask, Karl (1987): "Über die Rolle der Universität Tartu bei der Entwicklung der inländschen und internationalen Wissenschaft" In von Pistohlkors, Gert, Raun, Toivo U., and Kaegbein, Paul (eds.): *Die Universitäten Dorpat/Tartu, Rīga und Wilna/Vilnius 1579–1979*. Quellen und Studien zur baltischen Geschichte, 9. Köln.

Sirutavičius, Vladas (2000): "Vincas Kudirka's Programme for Modernizing Society", *Lithuanian Historical Studies*, 2000:5.

Sirutavičius, Vladas & Staliūnas, Darius (2011): "Was Lithuania a Pogrom-Free Zone? (1881–1940)", In Dekel-Chen, J, Gaunt, D, Meir, N M Bartal, I (ed.): *Anti-Jewish Violence. Rethinking the Pogrom in East European History*. Indiana University Press, Bloomington and Indianapolis.

Smith, Anthony D (1986): *The Ethnic Origin of Nations*. Blackwells, Oxford.

Smith, Anthony D (1989): "The origins of nations", *Ethnic and Racial Studies*, Vol. 12, No. 3.

Smith, Anthony D (1991): *National Identity*. Penguin Books, St Ives.

Smith, Anthony D (1995): *Nations and Nationalism in a Global Era*. Polity Press, Padstow.

Smith, Anthony D (1999): *Myths and Memories of the Nation*. Oxford University Press.

Smith, Anthony D. (2001): "Authenticity, antiquity and archaeology", *Nations and Nationalism*, Vol. 7, 2001:4.

Smith, David J (2004): "The 'Russian Question' Yesterday and Today. Mikhail Kurchinskii and the Lessons of the Inter-War Period", In Metuzāle-Kangere, Baiba (ed.): *The Ethnic Dimension in Politics and Culture in the Baltic Countries 1920–1945*. Södertörn Academic Studies, 18. Stockholm.

Smith, David J (2010): "Inter-war Multiculturalism Revisited: Cultural Autonomy in 1920s Latvia", In Smith, David J, Galbreath David J Swain, Geoffrey (ed.) *From Recognition to Restoration. Latvia's History as a Nation-State.* Rodopi, Amsterdam & New York.

Smooha, Sammy (2002): "Types of democracy and modes of conflict management in ethnically divided societies", *Nations and Nationalism,* Vol. 8, 2002:4

Snyder, Timothy (2003): *The Reconstruction of Nations. Poland, Ukraine, Lithuania, Belarus, 1569-1999.* Yale University Press, New Haven & London.

Spires, Scott (1999): "Lithuanian linguistic nationalism and the cult of antiquity", *Nations and Nationalism,* Vol. 5, 1999:4

Staliūnas, Darius (2000a): *Visuomenė be universiteto?* Lietuvių Atgimimo istorijos studijos 16. Vilnius.

Staliūnas, Darius (2000b): "'The Pole' in the Policy of the Russian Government: Semantics and Praxis in the Mid-Nineteenth Century" *Lithuanian Historical Studies,* 2000:5.

Staliūnas, Darius (2002): "Aukštosios mokyklos sukūrimo (atkūrimo) sumanymai Lietuvoje XXa. pradžioje", In *Vytauto Didžiojo Universitetas. Mokslas ir visuomene 1922-2002.* Kaunas.

Stichweh, Rudolf (2004): "From the *Peregrinatio Academica* to Contemporary International Student Flows: National Culture and Functional Differentiation as Emergent Causes", In Charle, Christophe, Schriever, Jürgen & Wagner, Peter (eds.) *Transnational Intellectual Networks. Forms of Academic Knowledge and the Search for Cultural Identities.* Campus Verlag, Frankfurt & New York.

Stradiņš, Jānis (1982): *Etīdes par Latvijas zinātņu pagātni.* Zinātne, Rīga.

Stradiņš, Jānis (1994): "Akadēmiskā izglītība Baltijā un Latvijas Universitātes priekšvēsture", In *Latvijas Universitāte 75,* Rīga.

Stradiņš, Jānis (1998): *Latvijas Zinātņu akadēmija: izcelsme, vēsture, pārvērtības.* Zinātne, Rīga.

Stradiņš, Jānis (1999): "Jānis Čakste un demokrātijas ideju iedibināšana Latvijā", In Čakste, Jānis (1999): *Taisnība vienmēr uzvarēs. Atziņas, runas, dokumenti, raksti, vēstules.* Jumava, Rīga.

Stradiņš, Jānis (2004): "Totalitāro okupācijas režīmu represijas pret Latvijas zinātni un akadēmiskajām aprindām", In *Totalitārie okupācijas režīmi Latvijā 1940.-1964. gadā.* Latvijas vēstures institūta apgāds. Rīga.

Stradiņš, Jānis & Cēbere, Dzintra (2006): "Latvijas Zinātņu Akadēmijas veidošanās: zinātniskie un sabiedriski politiskie aspekti", *Latvijas Vēstures Institūta Žurnāls,* 2006:3.

Stranga, Aivars (1997): *Ebreji un diktatūras Baltijā (1926.-1940. gads.),* Rīga.

Stranga, Aivars (1998a): "Liberālisms, demokrātija un autoritārisms Eiropā un Latvijā (20.-30. gadi)", In Caune, Andris et al. (ed.): *Kārlim Ulmanim 120.* Latvijas vēstures institūta apgāds, Rīga.

Stranga, Aivars (1998b): *LSDSP un 1934. gada 15. maija valsts apvērsums. Demokrātijas likteņi Latvijā,* Rīga.

Stranga, Aivars (2001): "Ebreju bēgļi Latvijā. 1933–1940", In *The Issues of the Holocaust Research in Latvia*. Latvijas Vēsturnieku komisijas raksti, 2. sējums. Latvijas vēstures institūta apgāds, Rīga.

Stranga, Aivars (2008): "Holokausts vācu okupētajā Latvijā: 1941–1945", In *Holokausta pētniecības problēmas Latvijā*. Latvijas Vēsturnieku komisijas raksti, 23. sējums. Latvijas vēstures institūta apgāds, Rīga.

Strods, Heinrihs (1990): "Die Erforschung der traditionellen Kultur des lettischen Volkes in der zweiten Hälfte des XIX. und den Beginn des XX. Jahrhunderts" In Loit, Aleksander (ed.): *The Baltic Countries 1900–1914*. Studia Baltica Stockholmensia 5:1, Stockholm.

Strods, Heinrihs (1994): "Latvijas Universitāte (1919–1940)", In *Latvijas Universitāte 75*. Rīga.

Sugar, Peter (1994): "Nationalism in Eastern Europe", In Hutchinson, John & Anthony D Smith (ed.): *Nationalism*. Oxford University Press.

Sörlin, Sverker (1996): "Science and National Mobilisation in Sweden", In Norrback, Märtha & Ranki, Kristina (ed.): *University and Nation. The University and the Making of the Nation in Northern Europe in the 19th and 20th Centuries*. Studia Historica 53, Helsinki.

Šalda, Vitālijs (2000): "Jaunlatvieši Maskavā", *Latvijas Vēstures Institūta Žurnāls*, 2000:2.

Šenavičiene, Ieva & Šenavičiene, Antanas (2002a): "Universiteto organizavimo pradžia: Aukštieji (vakariniai) kursai", In *Vytauto Didžiojo Universitetas. Mokslas ir visuomene 1922–2002*. Kaunas.

Šenavičiene, Ieva & Šenavičiene, Antanas (2002b): "Vytauto Didžiojo universiteto struktūra 1922–1950 metais: genezė, raidos metmenys", In *Vytauto Didžiojo Universitetas. Mokslas ir visuomene 1922–2002*. Kaunas.

Šilde, Ādolfs (1976): *Latvijas vēsture, 1914–1940*. Daugava, Stockholm.

Šnē, Andris (2009): "Latvijas Universitātes rektors profesors Augusts Tentelis". In *Profesors Dr. honoris causa Augusts Tentelis. Dzīve un darbs*. LU Akadēmiskais apgāds. Rīga.

Šterns, Indriķis (1998): "Vēsturnieks profesors dr. iur. Arveds Švābe (1888–1959)", In Caune, Andris (ed.) *Latvijas vēsturnieki. Vēsturnieks profesors Dr. iur. Arveds Švābe (1888–1959)*. Latvijas vēstures institūta apgāds, Rīga.

Taagepera, Rein (2011): "Albert, Martin, and Peter Too: Their Roles in Creating the Estonian and Latvian Nations", *Journal of Baltic Studies*, 42, 2011:2.

Tankler, Hain (1996): "Dorpat, a German-speaking International University in the Russian Empire", In Norrback, Märtha & Ranki, Kristina (ed.): *University and Nation. The University and the Making of the Nation in Northern Europe in the 19th and 20th Centuries*. Studia Historica 53, Helsinki.

Tankler, Hain & Rämmer, Algo (2004): *Tartu University and Latvia, with an Emphasis on Relations in the 1920s and 1930s*. Tartu.

von Taube, Arved & von Rimscha, Hans (1968): "Die deutschbaltischen Korporationen", In von Rimsch, Hans (ed.) *Baltisches Burschentum. Die studentischen Korporationen der Deutschbalten, Esten und Letten einst und jetzts*, Der Baltischen Gesellschaft in Deutschland, Heidelberg.

Thaden, Edward C (1981): "The Russian Government" in Thaden, Edward C (ed.): *Russification in the Baltic Provinces and Finland, 1855–1914*. Princeton University Press.

Timšāns, Sigismunds (1998): "Kārlis Ulmanis un tautas izglītība Latvijā", In Caune, Andris et al. (ed.): *Kārlim Ulmanim 120*. Latvijas vēstures institūta apgāds, Rīga.

Torstendahl, Rolf (1996): "The transformation of professional education in the nineteenth century", In Rothblatt, Sheldon & Wittrock, Björn (ed.): *The European and American university since 1800. Historical and sociological essays*. Cambridge University Press.

Treija, Rita (forthcoming, 2011): "Anna Bērzkalne (1991–1956)".

Trigger, Bruce G (1993): *Arkeologins idéhistoria*. Symposion, Stockholm/Stehag.

Valantiejus, Algis (2002): "Early Lithuanian nationalism: sources of legitimate meanings in an environment of shifting boundaries", *Nations and Nationalism*, Vol. 8, 2002:3.

Valenius, Johanna (2004): *Undressing the Maid. Gender, Sexuality and the Body in the Construction of the Finnish Nation*. Bibliotheca Historica 85, Helsingfors.

Vanaga, Lilita (2009): "Eduards Volters (1856–1941) Latvijas etnoloģijas kopainā 19 gs. 80.–90. gados", *Latvijas Vēstures Institūta Žurnāls*, 2009:2.

Vanags, Pēteris (2004): "Language Policy and Linguistics under Ulmanis", In Metuzāle-Kangere, Baiba (ed.): *The Ethnic Dimension in Politics and Culture in the Baltic Countries 1920–1945*. Södertörn Academic Studies, 18. Stockholm.

Vasks, Andrejs (2005): "Latvijas pilskalnu izpētes gaita", *Latvijas Vēstures Institūta Žurnāls*, 2005:4.

Vēsturnieks profesors Dr. iur. Arveds Švābe (1888–1959) (1998). Latvijas vēstures institūta apgāds, Rīga.

Vīksna, Arnis (2011): *Latvijas Universitātes Medicīnas fakultāte 1919–1950*. LU Akadēmiskais apgāds, Rīga.

Vīksna, Māra (1996): "The History of the Collection of Folklore in Latvia" *Humanities and Social Sciences, Latvia*, 1996:2.

Vīksne, Rudīte (1997): "Krimināllieta Nr. 15463", In Caune, Andris (ed.): *Arheologi Elvīra Šnore (1905–1996) un Rauls Šnore (1901–1962). Biobibliogrāfija, vēstules, laikabiedru atmiņas*. Latvijas vēstures institūta apgāds, Rīga.

Wagner, Peter (2004): "Varieties of Interpretations of Modernity: On National Traditions in Sociology and the Other Social Sciences", In Charle, Christophe, Schriever, Jürgen & Wagner, Peter (eds) *Transnational Intellectual Networks. Forms of Academic Knowledge and the Search for Cultural Identities*. Campus Verlag, Frankfurt & New York.

Walicki, Andrezej (1999): "Intellectual Elites and the Vicissitudes of 'Imagined Nation' in Poland", In Suny, Ronald Grigor and Kennedy, Michael D. (ed.): *Intellectuals and the Articulation of the Nation*. University of Michigan Press, Ann Arbor.

Weeks, Theodore R (1996): *Nation and State in Late Imperial Russia. Nationalism and Russification on the Western Frontier, 1863–1914*. Northern Illinois University Press, DeKalb.

Weeks, Theodore R (2000): "Official Russia and the Lithuanians, 1863–1905". *Lithuanian Historical Studies*, 2000:5.

Weeks, Theodore R (2006): *From Assimilation to Antisemitism. The 'Jewish Question' in Poland, 1850–1914*. Northern Illinois University Press, DeKalb.

Weisz, George (1983): *The Emergence of Modern Universities in France, 1863–1914*. Princeton University Press, Princeton, New Jersey.

Whelan, Heide W (1999), *Adapting to Modernity. Family, Caste and Capitalism among the Baltic German Nobility*. Böhlau Verlag, Köln.

Wörster, Peter (2007): "Vor 60 Jahren. Nachruf Reinhard Wittrams auf den 1947 verstorbenen Germanisten Oskar Masing", *Jahrbuch des baltischen Deutschtums*, 2007.

Zeids, Teodors (1990a): Foreword to Švābe, Arveds [1925]: *Latvijas vēsture. 1. daļa*, Rīga 1990.

Zeids, Teodors (1990b) "Latvijas Vēstures Institūta nozīme Latvijas vēstures zinātnes attīstībā", *Latvijas Zinātņu Akadēmijas Vēstis*, 1990:8.

Zeids, Teodors (1992): *Senākie rakstītie Latvijas vēstures avoti līdz 1800. gadam*. Zvaigzne, Rīga.

Zelče, Vita (2000): "Jaunstrāvnieki", *Latvijas Vēstures Institūta Žurnāls*, 2000:4.

Zelče, Vita (2001): "Jānis Krodznieks – Latvijas Republikas pirmā arhīva direktors", *Latvijas Arhīvi*, 2001:2.

Zelče, Vita (2002): *Nezināmā. Latvijas sievietes 19. gadsimta otrajā pusē*. Latvijas arhīvistu biedrība, Rīga.

Zelče, Vita (2006): "Vara, zinātne, veselība un cilvēki: Eigēnika Latvijā 20. gs. 30. gados", *Latvijas Arhīvi*, 2006:3.

Zelče, Vita (2007a): "Ievads. Reiz dzīvoja/reiz bija…", *Agora*, Nr. 6, 2007.

Zelče, Vita (2007b): "'Bēgšana no brīvības': Kārļa Ulmaņa režīma ideoloģija un rituāli", *Agora*, Nr. 6, 2007.

Zelče, Vita (2007c): "The Establishment and Early Activities of the Weekly '*Mājas viesis*' in the Second Half of the 1850s. A Declaration of Latvian Nationalism", *Latvijas Arhīvi*, 2007:1.

Zelče, Vita (2008a): "Latvijas Satversmes sapulces vēlēšanu kampaņa. 1920. gada marts– aprīlis", *Latvijas Arhīvi*, 2008:1.

Zelče, Vita (2008b): "XI Latviešu dziesmu svētki – Kārļa Ulmaņa Latvijas mūžības zvērests", *Latvijas Arhīvi*, 2008:2.

Zelče, Vita (2008c): "Svinēšana. Ieskats Latvijas valsts dibināšanas 10. un 20. gadadienas svētkos", *Latvijas Arhīvi*, 2008:3.

Zelče, Vita (2009): *Latviešu avīžniecība. Laikraksti savā laikmetā un sabiedrībā, 1822–1865*. Zinātne, Rīga.

Zeps, Valdis J (1995): "Latgalian Literature in Exile", *Journal of Baltic Studies*, XXVI, 1995:4.

Zvirgzdiņš, Kārlis (2009): "Vācbaltiešu arhīvu pārņemšana valsts glabāšanā (1935. gada rudens)", *Latvijas Arhīvi*, 2009:3.

Özkirimli, Umut (2003): "The nation as an artichoke? A critique of ethnosymbolist interpretations of nationalism", *Nations and Nationalism*, Vol. 9, 2003:3.

Södertörn Studies in History

1. Madeleine Hurd, Tom Olsson, Lisa Öberg (red.), *Iklädd identitet: historiska studier av kropp och kläder*, 2005
2. Kekke Stadin (red.), *I all anspråkslöshet: en vänbok till Lars Björlin*, 2005.
3. Andrej Kotljarchuk, *In the shadows of Poland and Russia: the Grand Duchy of Lithuania and Sweden in the European crisis of the mid-17th century*, 2006.
4. Monica Einarsson, Robert Sandberg, Kekke Stadin & Martin Wottle (red.), *Blad till Bladh: en vänbok till Christine våren 2006*, 2006.
5. Tom Olsson, *Rätten att tala politik: medieintellektuella och manlig medielogik under 1900-talet*, 2006.
6. Yulia Gradskova, *Soviet People with Female Bodies: performing beauty and maternity in Soviet Russia in the mid 1930–1960s*, 2007.
7. Kekke Stadin, *Maktens män bär rött: Historiska studier om manlighet, manligt framträdande och kläder*, 2010.
8. Git Claesson Pipping & Tom Olsson, *Dyrkan och spektakel: Selma Lagerlöfs framträdanden i offentligheten i Sverige 1909 och Finland 1912*, 2010.
9. Heiko Droste (ed.), *Connecting the Baltic Area: The Swedish Postal System in the Seventeenth Century*, 2011.
10. Susanna Sjödin Lindenskoug, *Manlighetens bortre gräns: tidelagsrättegångar i Livland åren 1685–1709*, 2011.
11. Anna Rosengren, *Åldrandet och språket: En språkhistorisk analys av hög ålder och åldrande i Sverige cirka 1875–1975*, 2011.
12. Steffen Werther, *SS-Vision und Grenzland-Realität: Vom Umgang dänischer und „volksdeutscher" Nationalsozialisten in Sønderjylland mit der „großgermanischen" Ideologie der SS*, 2012.
13. Per Bolin, *Between National and Academic Agendas: Ethnic Policies and 'National Disciplines' at the University of Latvia, 1919–1940*, 2012.

Södertörn Academic Studies

1. Helmut Müssener & Frank-Michael Kirsch (Hrsg.), *Nachbarn im Ostseeraum unter sich. Vorurteile, Klischees und Stereotypen in Texten*, 2000.
2. Jan Ekecrantz & Kerstin Olofsson (eds), *Russian Reports: Studies in Post-Communist Transformation of Media and Journalism*, 2000.
3. Kekke Stadin (ed.), *Society, Towns and Masculinity: Aspects on Early Modern Society in the Baltic Area*, 2000.
4. Bernd Henningsen et al. (eds), *Die Inszenierte Stadt. Zur Praxis und Theorie kultureller Konstruktionen*, 2001.
5. Michal Bron (ed.), *Jews and Christians in Dialogue II: Identity, Tolerance, Understanding*, 2001.
6. Frank-Michael Kirsch et al. (Hrsg.), *Nachbarn im Ostseeraum über einander. Wandel der Bilder, Vorurteile und Stereotypen?*, 2001.
7. Birgitta Almgren, *Illusion und Wirklichkeit. Individuelle und kollektive Denkmusterin nationalsozialistischer Kulturpolitik und Germanistik in Schweden 1928–1945*, 2001.
8. Denny Vågerö (ed.), *The Unknown Sorokin: His Life in Russia and the Essay on Suicide*, 2002.
9. Kerstin W. Shands (ed.), *Collusion and Resistance: Women Writing in English*, 2002.
10. Elfar Loftsson & Yonhyok Choe (eds), *Political Representation and Participation in Transitional Democracies: Estonia, Latvia and Lithuania*, 2003.
11. Birgitta Almgren (Hrsg.), *Bilder des Nordens in der Germanistik 1929–1945: Wissenschaftliche Integrität oder politische Anpassung?*, 2002.
12. Christine Frisch, *Von Powerfrauen und Superweibern: Frauenpopulärliteratur der 90er Jahre in Deutschland und Schweden*, 2003.
13. Hans Ruin & Nicholas Smith (red.), *Hermeneutik och tradition. Gadamer och den grekiska filosofin*, 2003.
14. Mikael Lönnborg et al. (eds.), *Money and Finance in Transition: Research in Contemporary and Historical Finance*, 2003.
15. Kerstin Shands et al. (eds.), *Notions of America: Swedish Perspectives*, 2004.
16. Karl-Olov Arnstberg & Thomas Borén (eds), *Everyday Economy in Russia, Poland and Latvia*, 2003.
17. Johan Rönnby (ed.), *By the Water. Archeological Perspectives on Human Strategies around the Baltic Sea*, 2003.
18. Baiba Metuzale-Kangere (ed.), *The Ethnic Dimension in Politics and Culture in the Baltic Countries 1920–1945*, 2004.
19. Ulla Birgegård & Irina Sandomirskaja (eds), *In Search of an Order: Mutual Representations in Sweden and Russia during the Early Age of Reason*, 2004.

20. Ebba Witt-Brattström (ed.), *The New Woman and the Aesthetic Opening: Unlocking Gender in Twentieth-Century Texts*, 2004.
21. Michael Karlsson, *Transnational Relations in the Baltic Sea Region*, 2004.
22. Ali Hajighasemi, *The Transformation of the Swedish Welfare System: Fact or Fiction?: Globalisation, Institutions and Welfare State Change in a Social Democratic Regime*, 2004.
23. Erik A. Borg (ed.), *Globalization, Nations and Markets: Challenging Issues in Current Research on Globalization*, 2005.
24. Stina Bengtsson & Lars Lundgren, *The Don Quixote of Youth Culture: Media Use and Cultural Preferences Among Students in Estonia and Sweden*, 2005.
25. Hans Ruin, *Kommentar till Heideggers Varat och tiden*, 2005.
26. Людмила Ферм, *Вариативное беспредложное глагольное управление в русском языке XVIII века*, 2005.
27. Christine Frisch, *Modernes Aschenputtel und Anti-James-Bond: Gender-Konzepte in deutschsprachigen Rezeptionstexten zu Liza Marklund und Henning Mankell*, 2005.
28. Ursula Naeve-Bucher, *Die Neue Frau tanzt: Die Rolle der tanzenden Frau in deutschen und schwedischen literarischen Texten aus der ersten Hälfte des 20. Jahrhunderts*, 2005.
29. Göran Bolin et al. (eds.), *The Challenge of the Baltic Sea Region: Culture, Ecosystems, Democracy*, 2005.
30. Marcia Sá Cavalcante Schuback & Hans Ruin (eds), *The Past's Presence: Essays on the Historicity of Philosophical Thought*, 2006.
31. María Borgström och Katrin Goldstein-Kyaga (red.), *Gränsöverskridande identiteter i globaliseringens tid: Ungdomar, migration och kampen för fred*, 2006.
32. Janusz Korek (ed.), *From Sovietology to Postcoloniality: Poland and Ukraine from a Postcolonial Perspective*, 2007.
33. Jonna Bornemark (red.), *Det främmande i det egna: filosofiska essäer om bildning och person*, 2007.
34. Sofia Johansson, *Reading Tabloids: Tabloid Newspapers and Their Readers*, 2007.
35. Patrik Åker, *Symboliska platser i kunskapssamhället: Internet, högre lärosäten och den gynnade geografin*, 2008.
36. Kerstin W. Shands (ed.), *Neither East Nor West: Postcolonial Essays on Literature, Culture and Religion*, 2008.
37. Rebecka Lettevall and My Klockar Linder (eds), *The Idea of Kosmopolis: History, philosophy and politics of world citizenship*, 2008.
38. Karl Gratzer and Dieter Stiefel (eds), *History of Insolvency and Bankruptcy from an International Perspective*, 2008.
39. Katrin Goldstein-Kyaga och María Borgström, *Den tredje identiteten: Ungdomar och deras familjer i det mångkulturella, globala rummet*, 2009.
40. Christine Farhan, *Frühling für Mütter in der Literatur?: Mutterschaftskonzepte in deutschsprachiger und schwedischer Gegenwartsliteratur*, 2009.

41. Marcia Sá Cavalcante Schuback (ed.), *Att tänka smärtan*, 2009.
42. Heiko Droste (ed.), *Connecting the Baltic Area: The Swedish Postal System in the Seventeenth Century*, 2011.
43. Aleksandr Nemtsov, *A Contemporary History of Alcohol in Russia*, 2011.
44. Cecilia von Feilitzen and Peter Petrov (eds), *Use and Views of Media in Russia and Sweden: A Comparative Study of Media in St Petersburg and Stockholm*, 2011.
45. Sven Lilja (red.), *Fiske, jordbruk och klimat i Östersjöregionen under förmodern tid*, 2012.
46. Leif Dahlberg och Hans Ruin (red.), *Fenomenologi, teknik och medialitet*, 2012.
47. Samuel Edquist, *I Ruriks fotspår: Om forntida svenska österledsfärder i modern historieskrivning*, 2012.
48. Jonna Bornemark (ed.), *Phenomenology of Eros*, 2012.
49. Jonna Bornemark and Hans Ruin (eds), *Ambiguity of the Sacred*, forthcoming.
50. Håkan Nilsson, *Placing Art in the Public Realm*, 2012.
51. Per Bolin, *Between National and Academic Agendas: Ethnic Policies and 'National Disciplines' at the University of Latvia, 1919–1940*, 2012.
52. Lars Kleberg and Aleksei Semenenko (eds), *Aksenov and the Environs/Aksenov i okrestnosti*, 2012.

www.ingramcontent.com/pod-product-compliance
Lightning Source LLC
Chambersburg PA
CBHW080406230426
43662CB00016B/2337